The Literature of the Piano

THE LITERATURE OF THE

PIANO

A Guide for Amateur and Student

ERNEST HUTCHESON

Second Edition, Revised by

RUDOLPH GANZ

HUTCHINSON OF LONDON

HUTCHINSON & CO (*Publishers*) LTD
3 Fitzroy Square, London W1

London Melbourne Sydney Auckland
Wellington Johannesburg Cape Town
and agencies throughout the world

First published in Great Britain 1950
Second impression 1958
Second edition, revised, 1969
Third edition, revised, 1974
Second impression 1975

Printed in Great Britain by litho by The Anchor Press Ltd
and bound by Wm Brendon & Son Ltd
both of Tiptree, Essex

ISBN 0 09 119120 3

THE TITLE

Dr. Hutcheson's subtitle, "A Guide for Amateur and Student," does unusual honor to the "amateur." The author might have dedicated his wonderfully informative volume to the student of the piano, to young and older pianists, to teachers of piano-playing, and to the ambitious amateur. One dictionary defines the amateur as "one who engages in art or sport on a non-professional basis" and "one who practices a sport, profession or art for the love of it, or for mere enjoyment, not for money." I have known dilettantes of music whose understanding and appreciation of the art were very good and whose warmth in performance was more in evidence than that of some professionals in their public appearances. And yet, I object to the frequent statement that an amateur plays only for his *pleasure*. I beg to correct this with a shift of emphasis: an amateur more likely plays only for *his* pleasure. It is true that members of this non-professional guild often express opinions about music and artists which are based on emotion rather than on knowledge. But amateurs are always welcome as lovers of music, and we, the artists, need thousands of them to fill our halls.

RUDOLPH GANZ

Publisher's Note

It was with great regret that lovers of music learned of the death in 1972 of Rudolph Ganz. The time has not yet come for the complete updating of his revision of Ernest Hutcheson's original work which he foresaw that subsequent research would eventually make necessary, but some additions have been made to the bibliography so that the reader may trace for himself the more recent developments in research. In respect of the modern period generally there can be no finer guide than his own book, *Rudolph Ganz Evaluates Modern Piano Music*, the outgrowth of his revision of the Hutcheson text, which was published in 1968 by the Instrumentalist Co., Evanston, Illinois.

Preface

It was a challenging though not an easy task to add important data
and general information to a book that has enjoyed great popularity
in the United States and in England. Ernest Hutcheson's *The Literature
of the Piano* is an excellent inspirational document of brilliant personal
comments upon the music of the last few hundred years. Dr. Hutcheson
and I were close friends for many years. I always admired him for his
keen judgment based upon a wide knowledge of the music of all
eras, and I held him in high esteem for his uncompromising integrity
and frankness of opinion. His book, a real handbook of music for the
piano, is still widely used all over the land, as I can attest from my
continual visits to universities and colleges, as well as to meetings of
musical organizations. However, the book, its 1949 revision by the
author himself, and the last printing of the year 1952 have been
unobtainable since 1961. Updating it has been a large undertaking, and
I feel privileged and honored to have been invited by the publisher
to accomplish this ambitious and interesting project.

The two special articles that I am contributing to the revision:
"Technique" and "Fingerings," should be of much interest to teachers
and awakened students. The first contains a number of contemporary
finger exercises (long overdue); the second is a protest against some
illogical—may I say irresponsible and misleading—fingerings, in well-
known and popular editions making piano playing more complicated
than necessary.

Great changes of style, of expression, and of attitude have occurred
during the past twenty-five years, not only in the creating of music, but
also in its performance. We Americans have risen rapidly in the ranks
of those who contribute important new works to the world literature of
music. We now vie successfully with the composers of Europe and
those of South America. We have come to the fore in the production of
works in the large symphonic and concerted forms as well as in

instrumental music in general. Sonatas for piano and all branches of chamber music by American men and women are being published by alert heads of music-publishing houses, with foresight and confidence, and—last but not least—with considerable national pride. Real, powerful American opera is in the making, and recognition of the first works of this greatly delayed form of good entertainment is in evidence here and in Europe, where the history of opera is more than 350 years old. American opera is alive, and the country at large is taking notice.

Our present era of speed and always more speed, of bold experimentation and accelerated wide research, has produced a daring disregard for all that formerly had been accepted as standards. Yet, that little three syllable word, DISSONANCE, is still a most controversial attribute in evaluation of style and character, as it has been at all times during music history. Beauty is a relative expression, especially NEW BEAUTY. It is everywhere if you look with open eyes and listen with open ears, and with a heart that can separate itself from the usual, the conventional, and the accepted.

Rossini, the one-sided sparkler of gay but repetitious *stretta*-opera, was certainly wrong when he stated: "What is beautiful is not new, and what is new is not beautiful." All the masters of music, or of any of the other arts, have been temporarily humiliated at some time, by lack of understanding on the part of contemporary colleagues and audiences, in particular those who sit in judgment professionally or supposedly so. Any "new art" does not replace anything that preceded it: it simply creates new values and continues the inevitable evolution. Today's "new art" and the youth proclaiming it represent our time. Not all that is created today can possibly be lasting. Only works that emanate from the heart and are controlled by the head—in other words, result from inspiration plus craftsmanship—are bound to survive. After all, we know there is no progress in music itself. Progress, if any, occurs only in the means of expressing it as a communication to listeners. Did not Ernest Renan, the French philosopher, state: "He is not progressive who does not respect the past"? And may I at this moment quote Voltaire, whose famous remark about beauty is, in my humble view, final: *"Pour le crapaud, la crapaude est belle* [To the he-toad, the she-toad is beautiful]."

It is rather curious that the lesson of "not understanding" or of "misunderstanding" the approach and presence of a new era is never learned. The word "modern" is hundreds of years old. So is "dissonance." Johann Sebastian Bach's colleague, Johann Adolph Scheibe, attacked Bach in his journal *Der critische Musicus* for "forgetting that music is supposed to be beautiful." The Italian critic and music scholar Giovanni Maria Artusi ridiculed and belittled the music and orchestration of Claudio Monteverdi's epoch-making and tradition-breaking opera *Orfeo,* which stands as a monument of a new art in music history. This "learned" writer insisted that the addition of pizzicati and tremolos of the strings and the presence of kettle drums were "tricks to cover up the absence of ideas, especially melody." And our great onetime ambassador to France, Benjamin Franklin, himself a virtuoso on the glass harmonica and a self-appointed music critic, reported from Paris that Gluck's *Orphée et Eurydice* was a complete failure and loss of art, not having any ideas of musical value. And how could Richard Wagner find "weakness" in Beethoven's Ninth Symphony? And was not Chopin accused of writing music devoid of melody, harmony, and form, by one of Berlin's very influential and well-regarded music reviewers, Heinrich Friedrich Ludwig Rellstab? This incomprehensible misunderstanding took place after Franz Liszt's first all-Chopin recital.

And so it has been through the centuries up to today. Having been an alert listener for sixty-five years, an ambitious performer for at least sixty, and having been present at many important events and historically tumultuous concert hall demonstrations—as, for example, the Salzburg festival of 1922 during which local police quelled an anti-Webern riot—I should be permitted to speak both of the peculiar general hesitation to accept the "New Art" produced during the last three generations and of its final triumph. Having been an unsolicited pioneer of the masters of impressionism and of later movements, and having happily survived many unfavorable criticisms of my propagandistic programs from well-known, mature, and otherwise highly esteemed music reviewers, I face—with appropriate curiosity and impartial willingness to become convinced—the most recent efforts and newest elements of creative music: the prepared piano, magnetic tape, *musique concrète*, the electronic approach to sound through generators, and, finally, the performances improvised by the participants. The existence of many electronic laboratories in Europe and America is bound to make us aware that still newer ways of producing sound are in store for us. The young musicians of America and some of us "elastic" oldsters are ready to meet whatever develops. Some efforts of the new approach are naturally still in the experimental stage, but they are bound to become forceful influences upon the future pages of music history. My added last Chapter (XV), "Recent Composers," provides more detailed information about the present state of music.

Brahms used to say that the piano was a harplike instrument, an opinion that accounts for the presence in his works for the piano of so many arpeggioed chords in both hands and broken octaves in the bass. Stravinsky declared the piano to be a percussion instrument. I still think that a beautifully voiced and immaculately tuned concert grand is and for a long time to come will be the king of all instruments. The indestructible masterworks of the baroque, classical, romantic, impressionistic, and expressionistic eras are there to safeguard the self-expression that is a pianist's privilege and honor. Whoever will be asked to up-date the Rudolph Ganz revision of the Ernest Hutcheson book will be expected to have evaluated and fully digested all the present varied, bold, and daring offerings of the forerunners and masters-on-the-way of an electronic age that is bound to follow, but will not replace, the music of the past which appeals to the heart.

I wish at this time to express my deep gratitude to my dear wife, Esther La Berge Ganz, who has been of inestimable help in compiling this book; to my nephew, Dr. Felix Ganz; to my friends Dr. Hans Moldenhauer and George Anson for their welcome comments. I have deeply appreciated the many courtesies accorded me by music publishers here and abroad.

RUDOLPH GANZ

Acknowledgements

I acknowledge with much gratitude my indebtedness to Mr. James Friskin, to M. Isidor Philipp, and to my son, Harold Hutcheson for their kindness in reading the book with minute care and pointing out many mistakes that might otherwise have escaped attention.

E. H.

Contents

Chapter

The Literature of the Piano

PUBLISHER'S NOTE

Material printed within brackets has been added by Rudolph Ganz.

Introduction

SINCE the beginning of the eighteenth century the piano has been the friend and confidant of the great composers. Scarlatti, Handel, Bach, Haydn, Mozart, Beethoven, Schubert, Mendelssohn, Schumann, Chopin, Brahms, Liszt, Debussy, to mention only the most eminent of a long lineage,[1] wrote voluminously for it or its predecessors the spinet, harpsichord, and clavichord, and lavished on it much of their finest thought and inspiration. A majority of them not only were great composers for the instrument but also rank among its most famous performers.

Some interesting exceptions to this general statement may be noted. Many composers of opera have kept exclusively to their own special field, contributing practically nothing in the purely instrumental forms. One may spend a lifetime in the enjoyment of music without encountering a single original piano piece by Gluck, Rossini, Bizet, Gounod, Verdi, Wagner, or Puccini. Almost all the Italian and most of the French opera-writers might be added to this group. The talented English contemporaries Elgar, Delius, Holst, and Vaughan Williams and a few of the leading exponents of ultra-modern music, notably Schönberg and Stravinsky, have also written comparatively little for the piano.

[As to pianistic ambitions of composers of opera, Gioacchino

---

[1] [The names of Couperin, Rameau, Franck, and Ravel should appear in the list of "great composers." They all wrote important works for the keyboard which will last.]

Rossini wrote some 190 pieces, many of them for piano, during the last ten or twelve years of his life, when his muse was reluctant to inspire him to create new operas. He called them *Quelques Riens* (Some Nothings) or *Péchés de vieillesse* (Sins of Old Age), and many of them are known to be very entertaining. Ottorino Respighi arranged some of them for a brilliant ballet, *La Boutique fantasque*. Benjamin Britten too has written an orchestral suite of five movements, *Soirées musicales*, based upon these "nothings." Five of Rossini's "nothings" become "somethings" in the 1962 publication by Peters. Soulima Stravinsky edited and fingered them excellently for students who enjoy a somewhat lighter fare and for teachers who refuse to stay in a rut. Verdi is said to have written six piano concertos, probably in his early life. Did he have pianistic ambitions at first? Young Wagner composed three Piano Sonatas of somewhat Mendelssohnian character, a Fantasy, and three Album Leaves. His very brilliant and pompous Polonaise in D major for four hands at one piano has been republished by Kalmus and should be taken notice of by duettists for home use. Jules Massenet composed an elegant and easy-to-listen-to Piano Concerto in E flat major in three movements which I performed in Chicago in 1902 to please the French *Maître* and his friend, Florenz Ziegfeld, founder of Chicago Musical College (who, incidentally, was instrumental in bringing me to the United States). Did not Umberto Giordano in his *Fedora* add a piano cadenza for the young Polish pianist who accompanies the heroine in one of her arias? Both Schönberg and Stravinsky have written considerably and very importantly for the piano. Schönberg's powerful but extremely difficult Piano Concerto and his epoch-making piano pieces, op. 11, 19, 23, 25, and the single piece op. 33a, and Stravinsky's Piano Concerto, Sonata and Concerto for two pianos, Capriccio for piano with orchestra, Sonata, four Etudes, Serenade in A, unusual and amusing piano duets, and Piano Rag Music are challenging works. Lasting? I think so. Time, the only dependable critic, will tell.]

It remains true that the piano is the favored daily companion of the musician, and it is scarcely surprising that its literature is one of amazing wealth, surpassed in music only by that of the orchestra. Most complete of instruments with the exception of the grand, unwieldy organ, the piano may justly be accounted a miniature orchestra within itself. The most intricate scores are susceptible of adaptation to its keyboard for use in the rehearsal and illustration, sometimes in the actual performance of operas and other large works when the full orchestra is not available. Commanding an immense range of pitch, dynamics, and polyphony, the ten fingers of the pianist can execute almost anything that is capable of expression in tone.

The piano is the friendliest of all musical instruments. Though entirely independent of others, it by no means wraps itself in haughty isolation. It willingly and effectively co-operates with strings or wind instruments in any conceivable combination for the performance of chamber music, and it obligingly offers its services to the soloist who may need a harmonic background to his melody. It thus becomes the most universal and indispensable medium of music. It is a familiar sight and sound in every cultured home, and in these days of transmission by air no radio station could operate without it for twenty-four hours.

As an essential feature of its friendliness the piano is the most merciful of instruments to the beginner. If you take up the violin, assiduous effort is required before you can play even a simple piece in tune and with attractive tone, whereas on the piano a very novice can produce agreeable sounds, and though you may hit wrong notes, you cannot play too flat or too sharp.[2] With a tone and a pitch ready-made, so to speak, and with the advantage of sitting in a natural and comfortable position, the player with but a moderate facility can almost from the start make real music, creating beauty for himself and others.

It would be as foolish as it is unnecessary to make extravagant claims where so many are valid. Admittedly the piano cannot sing like the violin or the human voice, for the simple reason that it cannot sustain an undiminishing tone, let alone swell on a note. But it has its own idiom, and within that idiom it attains a melos perfectly satisfactory to the ear. In fact, the singing quality of the piano is constantly emphasized by musicians, teachers, and the public, doubtless partly because, being difficult of acquirement, it is held a special merit alike of a good instrument or a good player. Long ago, in his preface to the *Inventions,* Bach desired the student "above all to obtain a cantabile style of playing." When Mendelssohn wrote his *Songs without Words* for piano, the implicit assumption went uncontested by the world. Later we find Thalberg entitling a series of transcriptions *L'Art du chant appliqué au piano,* and still later Anton Rubinstein[3] confesses that he modeled his noble tone in emulation of the rich voice of the famous tenor Rubini. [The printing in the Transcriptions of Sigismond Thalberg is indeed unusual, original, and "telling": all

---

[2] If the piano itself has gone off pitch, you have only to telephone for a tuner; in two hours the trouble is remedied.

[3] See *Free Artist,* by Catherine Drinker Bowen, and Rubinstein's *Autobiography.*

cantilena or melodic notes appear in larger type than the notes of the accompaniment. And, no doubt, Liszt took note of this device when the two rivals "sang" against each other in the salons of Paris.]

No one would wish to deny that the action of the piano is naturally percussive: the strings are struck by hammers of felt. Instead of being ashamed of the fact, it should be one of our aims to take the greatest possible advantage of it whenever proper occasion presents itself. It is precisely the extraordinary variety of effect possible between extremes of tone and quality that gives the piano its peculiar character and value.

From what has been said it should be clear that the piano is an ideal vehicle for the art of the amateur. The wonders of its literature are easily accessible to him; a very great proportion of the material is well within the reach of a moderate technique, and the most difficult masterpieces are at least readable for better acquaintance. I think of the amateur in a very wide sense, from the lover of music who slowly and painstakingly masters a few pieces, each one a small triumph of pleasurable labor, to the more accomplished player who reads with facility, associates himself with others, sometimes professionals, in chamber music, and acquires a fairly large repertory that he performs well and musically. I have known amateurs who had no reason to quail before the *Sonata Appassionata* of Beethoven or some of the standard concertos; nor would their performance excuse a merely indulgent nod of recognition from the listening artist.

In some respects the amateur is at a distinct advantage over the professional. His activity is devoted entirely to music of his own choice; he is under no obligation to a ticket-buying audience, and therefore need not hesitate to play although his program is not quite "up to concert pitch"; and he has the leisure to browse in the lush pastures of the literature often denied to the traveling artist busied with a limited yearly concert repertory. The concert player is made sadly aware that the best of everything is not good enough for the critical fraternity, but no one reproaches the sincere amateur for failure to achieve impossible perfection, maintain breakneck speeds, or fathom all the depths of Beethoven's soul. Finally, the amateur enjoys an enviable freedom in forming and expressing personal opinions without the responsibility to the public and the restraint of courtesy toward colleagues to which the expert is rightly subject.

It is to the amateur and the student that this survey of the literature of the piano is addressed. [As a compliment of esteem to Ernest Hutcheson, I should like to change the wording of these two lines as follows: It is to the serious amateur, to the anxious student, to the responsible teacher and the exploring young artist that this survey of the literature is addressed. There is a bridge between the big "Island of Conscious and Unconscious Solo Playing" and the "Continent of Symphonic Discipline." It is called "Chamber Music," and your first step upon it, coming from the Island, is bound to acquaint you with the happy State of Perfect Musicianship.]

I suggest that the reader equip himself with volumes of *The Well-Tempered Clavier* of Bach, the sonatas of Mozart and Beethoven, the best-known works of Schubert, Mendelssohn, Chopin, Schumann, and Brahms, and with whatever music of other composers his taste may lead him to acquire. It is difficult to speak intelligibly about certain aspects of music unless one can rely on ready comparison with the text itself.

CHAPTER ONE

The Instrument

THE MODERN grand piano is the outcome of a long series of experiments in making keyboard instruments. Its immediate predecessors were the harpsichord and clavichord, the harpsichord in turn being preceded by the spinet or virginal. If we wish to trace the ancestry farther back, it is fairly true to say that the clavichord was a direct descendant of the monochord, the spinet and harpsichord of the psaltery, and the piano, less directly, of the dulcimer.

In the Germany of the seventeenth and eighteenth centuries, the word *Klavier* was applied indifferently to the clavichord, harpsichord, and pianoforte—in short, to any keyboard instrument, or for that matter to the keyboard itself, though the latter was more generally known as a *Klaviatur*. The modern pianoforte, or, for short, piano, so called in almost all languages, is still optionally and indeed preferably a *Klavier* in German, the grand piano being differentiated as a *Flügel* ("wing," from its shape) and the upright piano as a *Pianino*. At first the Italian name was *fortepiano*, a form still preserved in Russian usage. The change of emphasis in *pianoforte* is apparent only, and indeed seems to carry a trace of irony, the actual development having tended to ever greater sonority.

The broad use of the word *Klavier* gave rise to endless confusion, for in French and English *clavier* means simply a keyboard, not an instrument. In English it sometimes designates a practice keyboard entirely destitute of tone. Champions of the harpsichord and clavichord respectively grow heated in their claims that *Klavier* always means the one or always means the other. *Das Wohltemperirte Klavier* is to these enthusiasts a special bone of contention, and clarity is hardly promoted by mistranslations like *The Well-Tempered Clavichord* and *Le Clavecin bien tempéré.* The plain fact remains that music written for *Klavier* was intended to be played on any available keyboard instrument. Many of the preludes and fugues from Bach's masterpiece would sound much better on the clavichord than on the harpsichord, and *vice versa*, and it would not be difficult to divide them into two groups accordingly. For instance, the first and fourth Preludes and Fugues of *The Well-Tempered Clavier* obviously need the truer legato of the clavichord, while the second and third seem to call for the brighter harpsichord. But as we now play them all on the piano, endeavoring to give appropriate tone color to each one, the question is of more academic than practical interest except to harpsichordists.

Here are the correct names in English, French, and German for the three types of instrument:

ENGLISH	FRENCH	GERMAN
Harpsichord	Clavecin[1]	Clavicembalo
Clavichord	Clavichorde	Klavichord
Piano	Piano	Klavier *or* Piano

[1] N.B. *Clavecin* does *not* mean clavichord.

The favorite instrument in early times was the spinet, in England called the virginal or virginals because it was considered particularly suitable for young ladies. The name may have been retained in compliment to Queen Elizabeth. Later the harpsichord, much more adequate in every way than the spinet, became popular in England, France, and Italy. Scarlatti, Handel, Couperin, and a host of others wrote specifically for it. In Germany, on the contrary, a long-lasting preference was given to the clavichord. It was the favorite instrument of Bach, and it held the affection of German musicians long after the piano had displaced it elsewhere.

[As to Bach, the teacher, admonishing his pupils to play *cantabile*, he no doubt was thinking of the warmth produced by string and wind instruments or was he hearing his beloved clavichord, on which he could interpret certain Preludes and Fugues with greater personal sensitivity than the more brilliant but dynamically colder harpsichord would permit? What of the E-flat minor Prelude in the first book of *The Well-Tempered Clavier*, which I would like to call "two pages waiting for a concert grand"? It cries for the same deep feeling as does a beautiful nocturne of Chopin or an intimate intermezzo of Brahms. See

Busoni's (Schirmer) interpretation of this precious early gem, which calls upon human emotions and all of them expressed within the narrow range of four octaves: from *misterioso* to *drammatico,* from *dolcissimo armonioso* to *deciso* and *appassionato.* I well recall a discussion with an eminent musicologist before a large class of piano students. The subject of the encounter was the following: "Should we try to imitate the special character and the limited dynamic possibilities of expression of the harpsichord or play Bach with the evident warmth which is in his music, and which we are able to express so much better on the piano"? I answered my partner's final question: "Was not this very Prelude composed for the harpsichord, the one and most popular instrument he had at his command?" "No," I said emphatically, "this Prelude was not written for any special instrument. It was meant for posterity." When Bach visited Frederick the Great, at Potsdam, the royal flutist and composer made the master sit down at a recently arrived Cristofori type of *fortepiano,* the direct forerunner of our pianoforte, and play on it. Bach adhered to the King's wish, but, seemingly, thought the instrument "very loud." No wonder! His beloved clavichord was a more intimate music-maker for him. Its intimacy is such that, at a recent recital by an eminent baroque performer in a rather large hall, it took this listener several minutes to catch the sound, get used to it, and enjoy it.]

The chief difference between the three instruments lies in their action, or method of tone-production. This is quite easy to explain:

1. In the clavichord, the strings are pressed by a tangent (a small blade of brass).

2. In the harpsichord, the strings are plucked by a plectrum operated by a "jack." The plectra used to be made of crow or raven quills or leather.

3. In the piano, the strings are struck by a felt-covered hammer.

The earliest spinets and clavichords were often small enough to be carried by a lady from room to room as needed; their compass might be no more than two octaves. Their bigger brother the harpsichord acquired by successive improvements the wing shape of the modern grand piano and a normal compass of four octaves, from C to c''':

Most of Bach's clavier works, including *The Well-Tempered Clavier,* were written for keyboards of this range, though sometimes he had three lower notes, down to the A at the lower end of the scale, at

his command. The better harpsichords were made with two keyboards, permitting contrasts of tone by the use of different plectra and
the bringing out of a melody over its accompaniment. So-called
"pedals," quite unlike the pedals of the piano but resembling the
couplers of an organ in their effect, enabled the player to double
everything in the octave and to throw the two keyboards together.
After Bach's time the compass was extended to five octaves. In its
full maturity the harpsichord was a justly honored instrument of many
possibilities, tempting and rewarding the utmost skill of contemporary
players. Its tone was powerful enough to blend effectively with the
small orchestras of the period before Beethoven and to be heard to advantage in fairly large halls. To the eye it was a thing of beauty; its
shape was slim and graceful, the best cunning of the cabinetmaker went
into its manufacture, and its woodwork was tastefully ornamented,
possibly with a painting of merit on the lid. But it necessarily remained
a somewhat unemotional instrument, for inflection by varying pressure
of the artist's finger was not possible, and the plucked string[1] (profanely
likened to "a scratch with a sound at the end of it") had little poetry to
it.

Happily, although its literature lies in the past and composers now
seldom write for it, the harpsichord has been cultivated as a solo instrument by artists like Wanda Landowska, Ralph Kirkpatrick, and many
others. These players treat it with admirable mastery of its individual
touch and style, with consummate taste, and with degrees of expression
and climax almost unbelievable. They are heard, too, by delighted
audiences, and indeed every pianist should make it his business to hear
them. Much old music, notably that of Handel, is incomparably more
effective on the harpsichord than on the piano. I do not care if I never
again play or hear *The Harmonious Blacksmith* on the piano, but it is a
first-rate piece in its native form. In conclusion, it is only fair to
mention that its tone, unlike that of the piano, is intrinsically suitable
to radio performance. The harpsichord seems to take to the air like a
bird.

[The harpsichord has indeed come to the fore once more. Ralph
Kirkpatrick has become its outstanding performer, and the fine new
instruments, both American and European, are heard frequently in
our concert halls. Much is written for the instrument by contemporary
composers, and American universities and colleges have successfully

---

[1] Strings are best plucked by hand, as in the harp, lute, and guitar. Even so,
the tone is better when the tension of the string is not too high. The pizzicato of
the violin and the cello is not in itself beautiful, though capable of striking effects
when massed in the orchestra.

established harpsichord departments. However, the advent of a wonderfully gifted Bach pianist and Bach scholar, Rosalyn Tureck, has greatly helped those in our profession who believe the piano of today to be the instrument that can most fully express the beauty and the range of emotions hidden in the master's works. Our piano blends victoriously with the strong orchestra in the D minor Concerto, a forceful, healthy display of manly music. And as to the fifth "Brandenburg" Concerto? Am I not a more equally equipped partner to vie with the warmly expressive flute playing, the sensitive vibrato of the violinist, or the body of orchestral string players if I have at my command an instrument that permits me to respond to all dynamic demands of the general performance? As to Bachian warmth and Bachian emotions, I am thinking of the brilliant suites for orchestra, the expressive cantatas, the dramatic recitatives and choral singing in the Passions.]

The clavichord retained throughout its history a pristine simplicity and beauty. Its tone was soft and rather dull, of too little penetration to be heard without effort except in rooms of moderate size. But it was more truly a singing instrument than any of its competitors. Within its tiny range of amplitude the player had complete control of dynamic inflection. He not only could produce crescendo and diminuendo, but by continued or increased finger pressure could prolong a tone with undiminished volume or even cause it to swell. The modern concert grand in all its glory cannot emulate this soulful distinction of the clavichord. No wonder that Bach, always annoyed by any suspicion of showing off, dearly loved this modest, sensitive confidant of the intimate mood. Because of its small tone it could hardly be used as a concert instrument. This mattered little in an age when concerts in the modern sense were unknown, but it is probably the chief reason that opportunities to hear it are now regrettably rare.

It would be pointless and tiresome to offer a lengthy description of the piano. Like Aaron's rod turned serpent, it swallowed all its rivals. Suffice it to say that the modern piano has a compass of seven octaves and a quarter, exceeding the shrill heights of the orchestra's piccolo and the lowest rumble of the double bass. Through most of this compass three strings are furnished to each note; the lower notes require only two strings and a few of the lowest only one. The hammers are cleverly disposed to strike at a point on the strings' length calculated to eliminate the harsher harmonics. The repetition action of the French maker Érard enables it to speak with extraordinary precision and rapidity. Its tone is so enduring that dampers are needed to check overlong vibration of the strings; the dampers, however, can be lifted when desired by means of the damper pedal to allow unrestricted resonance. A "soft" pedal shifts the action to the right side;[2] when it is used, the hammers contact two strings only instead of three. The unstruck third string, set into sympathetic vibration, imparts a peculiarly ethereal quality to the tone. The "sostenuto" pedal is a device by which the dampers may be kept lifted from any note or combination of notes selected, thus permitting their sound to be sustained indefinitely without holding other, undesired tones. Only American makes of piano are equipped with a "sostenuto" pedal.

[The advent of the third pedal, the *"sostenuto"* pedal, produced a famous letter by Franz Liszt in answer to one sent him by the Steinway firm. He was glad, he wrote, to hear about this new invention, but he regretted having to admit his lack of knowledge of "what was going on inside of the instrument." This American invention has served well in special works written with the purpose of making use of it, as for instance in some of the Bach organ transcriptions of Liszt and Busoni. It is not generally known that neither Debussy nor Ravel composed with a *sostenuto* pedal in mind. The instruments in their homes were of French make and had no third pedal, a fact that seems to escape some performers, teachers, and editors of impressionistic music. Contemporary composers (Elliott Carter in his Sonata, for example) use the *sostenuto* pedal to create combinations of new sounds.]

The piano is not a perfect instrument like the violin. In granting it ascendancy over all its forerunners we have incurred certain penalties, losing in particular the charming doublings of the harpsichord and that invaluable property of the clavichord, its power to swell on a single tone.

What, we may inquire, is the future destiny of the piano? Is it reasonable to expect further improvement, or should we rather accept our present blessing gratefully and ask no more?

The answer must be a mixed one. Hundreds of patents have been taken out by piano manufacturers in the past fifty years. Many of these have effected minor improvements in the mechanism of the instrument. Few, it must be confessed, have attempted to better the quality of its tone. Neither the "resonator" of the London branch of the Érard firm nor the Mason & Hamlin "spider" gave the added amplification they aspired to. The "Aliquot Grand" of Blüthner make promised well; the idea was to tune an unstruck fourth string to the octave of each note to fortify the consonant harmonics, but for some reason the result was

---

[2] On upright pianos the soft pedal usually shifts the hammers nearer to the strings, thus reducing their stroke and limiting the tone.

negligible. Interesting experiments were made by Charles Mehlin and John Hays Hammond, still without convincing effect.

Many proposals have been put forward for the improvement of the keyboard. By far the most valuable of these was that of Paul von Janko, in which the digitals were arranged in six tiers, each spaced in whole tones, giving the entire scale in triplicate. Each key could be played in one of three positions. The most important consequence of the construction was that all fingering, whether of scales, chords, arpeggios, or any passages whatever, was identical for all keys. Try, reader, to realize what a beneficent revolution this would bring about in piano technique. Then, all wide stretches were reduced, tenths becoming as easy to stretch as are octaves on the ordinary keyboard. Glissandos were easy in chromatics of single-note scales and in thirds and sixths, though not feasible on white notes. In short, the technical advantages were highly remarkable, and any good pianist could convert his skill to the novelty with about three months' practice. It is true that some difficulty was encountered in adjusting the leverage to equalize the touch of the six banks of keys, though this problem would doubtless have been solved in the workshop. I believe that the piano lost a historic chance of progress by our failure to adopt Janko's invention. For a time it flourished and was introduced in some conservatories of music. Today it is a forgotten name. The most valid reasons for its ultimate rejection were three: (1) Janko lacked funds to exploit his keyboard by offering financial inducement to pianists and makers. (2) No special literature existed for it beyond the arrangements of Janko himself, and to the best of my knowledge no composer of standing came to the rescue by writing for it. (3) Although the keyboard could readily be set up on any grand piano, manufacturers were fearful of a threatened competition. They pointed out, too, that the extra digitals called for more ivory and increased to some extent the cost of production.

[To all the efforts of the piano makers to improve the instrument during the past one hundred years, a most interesting and constructive invention one must comment upon is the Clutsam Curved Keyboard. In 1908, when I had my headquarters in Berlin, the German piano house of Ibach had built an instrument with a new keyboard according to the plans of George H. Clutsam, a curious Australian inventor who was not a musician. Many pianists were invited to come, look, play, and remark upon it. I seem to have made the most plausible statement on the new shape of this keyboard, for I was immediately asked to demonstrate before a large professional audience what the advantages of its revolutionary adjustment of keys were and would be. To me the invention was perfect, final. I well remember how my initial offering, the first Chopin Étude, was received. Into the applause a voice roared: "Ganz, you could not play this Étude that well and that fast on the old keyboard!" It was the voice of my friend Ernst von Dohnányi, and it was the first spontaneous tribute to the new keyboard.

Sometime later I performed the Tchaikovsky Concerto at an evening Festival concert on the Clutsam Keyboard (how agreeable and easy it was), and then played a recital the next afternoon on the old keyboard. I was confused, and decided not to mix shapes any more despite the fact that Ibach offered me the Clutsam piano "for as many as possible" of my European concerts. Piano manufacturers, especially the Americans, offered very large amounts in return for the sole rights for up to five years, to produce the novelty. The deals became so intricately commercial that the whole thing had to be dropped, which was, I feel today, a great misfortune. The Clutsam Keyboard was played in public by Dohnányi for about one season. It is a great pity that this brilliantly conceived new approach to greater comfort in playing the piano was completely given up. Around 1870 Bechstein, had produced what they called a *Strahlenklavier* (beamlike piano), a delightful miscalculation (Diagram A). Because both shoulders were centers (x) of arm activities, to play on its keyboard was well-nigh impossible, both arms having to be pressed against the player's torso. Clutsam also took both shoulders as individual centers, but overlapped their curves, thus creating the curve C (Diagram B). This enabled the performer to play the Tchaikovsky chords over the entire keyboard without changing hand positions.]

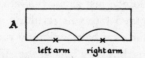

The Bechstein *Strahlenklavier*

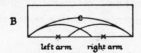

The Clutsam Piano Keyboard

A more recent innovation is the auxiliary Duplex Coupler keyboard of Emanuel Moor. It is placed below the main manual, has a smaller compass, and is applicable both to grands and uprights. Its chief merit rests in a partial restoration of the octave doublings of the harpsichord. Wide stretches, too, are greatly reduced. The Moor piano has been ably brought to public notice by Winifred Christie, wife of the inventor.

The upright piano has also been furnished with a footboard, if I may coin the word, like that of the organ. Probably its modest intention was rather to provide a convenient practice instrument for organists than to create an improved piano. The pedal piano aroused the interest of Schumann, always ready to break a lance for a new departure. He wrote some studies for it. Its value, however, was dubious and its vogue extremely restricted. The pianist had to sacrifice the damper and soft pedals to make place for the footboard, and the organist could derive little benefit from a one-manual instrument.

Attempts have been made at various times to construct a manual capable of producing quarter-tones, or to use two pianos differently tuned to obtain the same result. The Mexican musician Julián Carillo succeeded in making a keyboard divided into sixteenth-tones. The effect of a polychromatic scale rapidly played on this instrument, embracing as it does ninety-six intervals to the octave, is indescribably charming. Advocates of a quarter-tone or more minutely divided system, however, whether in piano construction or in composition, are always foiled by the natural resistance of the human ear to intervals not readily perceptible. Apparently we hear enough unpremeditated quarter-tones and smaller steps from singers and violinists of poor intonation, not to speak of ill-tempered pianos. And even when string players make artistic and legitimate use of enharmonic differences, we prefer to accept them on the fringe of our aural consciousness, not scrutinizing them too closely, just as we tolerate the slight discrepancy between true and tempered intervals resulting when violin and piano are played together. Our ears have willingly recognized first diatonic and then chromatic steps, but they balk at the effort of finer discrimination. Imagine a lesson in ear-training for a class learning sixteenth-tone scales and the harmonies based on them! As in other cases, history applies its acid test; composers experiment tentatively with quarter-tones but do not write them.[3]

[Alois Hába's quarter-tone string quartet induced a manufacturer of pianos to build a two-keyboard piano with the strings of the upper keyboard tuned one quarter of a tone higher than those of the lower

---

[3] Ernest Bloch's *Piano Quintet* is a shining exception. In this piece quarter-tones are necessarily allotted exclusively to the strings, risking a pardonable jealousy of the participating pianist.

one. Although a quarter-tone music department was established at the Prague Conservatory and still is active, I never have heard of further evolution of the piano designed to take part in this delicate differentiation of tones. I used to perform the Bloch Quintet with a very friendly foursome, imitating their quarter-tone effects by playing an upper acciaccatura on every important note—but only at rehearsals.

For me, the piano was, is, and always will be the King of Instruments. A concert grand in perfect tune is bound to be an inspiration to the performer, be he performing at his own recital or surrounded by a symphony orchestra.]

The possible development of an electrotonal piano has attracted a good deal of modern research, so far without very satisfactory results. The scientist can admittedly combine electrotonally the overtones peculiar to any given instrument in their exact balance. Theoretically, then, we should be able to produce substitute pianos, violins, and so on, at will. The difficulties involved might seem to be merely technical, but apart from these one curious factor enters, perhaps unexpectedly, into the problem. Electrotonal sounds are acoustically pure, whereas the musical tone of all instruments contains a certain admixture of baser noise, and this alloy or impurity contributes more than might be supposed to their individual characters. The buzz of the oboe may be cited as definitely idiosyncratic; not lovely in itself, it lends the oboe a timbre all its own. By entirely eliminating the percussive effect of the piano due to the impact of the hammer on the strings we might rob the instrument of its essential personality. Even the tone of the violin is influenced by the drawing of the bow across the strings, the noise element becoming more noticeable in the détaché and martelé strokes. To many ears at least, there is a fatal monotony in the cold purity of electrotonal sound. At its best it is emasculated, hardly human. At its worst, crude blending of overtones produces sounds rivaling in atrocity the movie-house organ.

The frequency generating keyboard instruments are represented by the Hammond family—the Hammond organ, the Novachord, and the Solovox. A basically different kind of instrument simply amplifies electrically a small tone originated by a skeleton violin, piano, and so forth. None of either group except the Hammond organ has proved useful to serious music.

To sum up: it would appear that since the introduction of the Erard repetition mechanism and the steel frame supporting the sounding board, the one as beneficial to the action as the other to the tone, no really basic improvement has added substantially to the potentialities of the piano. But it would be presumptuous to set limits to human research and ingenuity. Radical change may be unlikely but need not be excluded from speculation. I permit myself to offer a few suggestions that I hope are not too trivial:

1. The action of the keys themselves and of the sostenuto pedal is still somewhat clumsy. Greater sensitiveness of the key would facilitate greater delicacies of touch and inflection. The accelerated action of Frederick Vietor is a step in the right direction.

2. The shape of the pedals is faulty, too easily allowing the foot to slip off. In this respect Charles Mehlin, already commended as a pioneer, has devised a form offering a much securer hold, but it has not been adopted.

3. A fourth pedal of unknown properties may conceivably give valuable new effects.

4. Further exploration of plastics may bring about economies of manufacture, for instance in an adequate substitute for ivory.

5. One can imagine a successful device enabling the piano to stay longer in tune.

6. Means will doubtless be found to improve the reception of the piano on recording instruments and in radio technique. Hitherto this has remained a baffling problem.

7. Once, on the clavichord, we could swell a tone. Why not again, by some new method?

Perhaps it is ungracious to warn against possible deterioration of the piano. Yet we face certain dangers. The prevailing insistence on smaller and ever smaller grands to accommodate themselves to small apartments is one threat. Too much of the makers' effort is now concentrated on meeting this desire of the buying public, and it is idle to flatter ourselves that instruments made with such an end in view can be as good as when excellence is the sole purpose. A second threat lies in the increasing difficulty of finding skilled labor and the decline of pride in workmanship. A fine piano is not merely assembled from perfect materials; an element of love must go into its making. Last, the manufacture of pianos has for many years past been increasingly unprofitable in spite of steeply rising sales prices, especially the manufacture of the larger models. It would be lamentable indeed should the best makers be driven out of business by economic discouragement. We must have faith that cultural values will still prevail over the pressure of the material.

CHAPTER TWO

The Literature Before Bach

EVERY age has its favorite forms of art. Epic, drama, lyrics, history, and fiction alternate in popularity; so do religious painting, mythological subjects, landscapes, and portraiture. Primitive periods yield to classical, and they in turn to the romantic and modern. Music has undergone a similar experience. With its most primitive history we need not concern ourselves, as it was not reflected in piano literature. We can safely begin with the music written for the spinet or virginal in the sixteenth and seventeenth centuries. Here we find at once a surprising wealth of material, the best of which has happily been preserved, engaging a continuing interest far from merely academic.

It is natural enough that in letters the larger forms were among the first to be cultivated. In the civilized ancient world, language was already capable of expressing the most profound thought of man, and until the invention of printing there existed among all peoples a veritable passion for story-telling. Hence the Homeric poems and the histories of Herodotus, Thucydides, and Tacitus; the Icelandic sagas, the *Arabian Nights*, the French romances, and the *Morte d'Arthur*— long immortal flights of fact and fancy. Music, on the contrary, was much later in finding its medium of ordered tone and was dependent, except for the human voice, on instruments of limited range, power, and technical resource. The smaller forms of composition, therefore, were the first to be explored, and the epical sonata and symphony had to await the advent of the modern piano and orchestra. It must be remembered, too, that instrumental music originated as an accompaniment to song or dance. Only gradually did it emancipate itself from this service to assume full independence. Following the folk song, and contemporaneously with the madrigal and glee, instrumental music became a prime and finally an honored vehicle of secular expression.

The favorite forms of composition for the early keyboard instruments were dance forms (sometimes grouped into suites), the rondo, the various types of variations, and the canon (or round) and fugue. There were naturally countless numbers of less easily classifiable short pieces, but those I have mentioned were the principal ones.

Not only did the period show strong preferences, but to a lesser degree each nation favored certain dances and other compositions above others. In England the grave pavin (pavane) and the merrier galliard and hornpipe were popular; in France and Germany the sarabande, minuet, gavotte, and bourrée were more in vogue. The gigue was liked everywhere. These partialities are indicated in such titles as Anglaise, Française, Allemande, Ecossaise, Polonaise. The family of variation forms—divisions on a ground, air with variations, chaconne, and passacaglia—were all well known in England; the early French composers contributed the first program music for harpsichord; and German writers, elaborating canon and fugue, paved the way for Bach.

The amateur, unless he be an ardent enthusiast for the older music, will scarcely delve very deeply into the literature before Bach. Nor shall I attempt to treat of it exhaustively. Most of it is contained in famous collections. Two of these, the *Fitzwilliam Virginal Book* and the *Alte Meister* of the Breitkopf & Härtel edition, are especially valuable. Schirmer's *Golden Treasury* also deserves honorable mention for the judicious selection of its numbers. None of these has been available during the second World War except in libraries, though the Breitkopf & Härtel firm had brought out a complete standard edition of the *Fitzwilliam Virginal Book* by Fuller Maitland and Barclay Squire in the years 1894-9. The Universal Edition now prints a good selection from the *Virginal Book* in two volumes. The *Golden Treasury* is out of print, but is partially replaced by two volumes of *Early Key-Board Music* in the Schirmer Library, the first volume inclusive from Byrde to Scarlatti and the second from Couperin to Rameau. There are many smaller albums devoted to individual composers or national schools.

Here is a list of some of the outstanding clavier writers of the period:

1. ITALIAN

Baldassare Galuppi	1706–1785
Leonardo Leo	1694–1744
Benedetto Marcello	1686–1739
Giovanni Battista Martini	1706–1784
Pietro Domenico Paradies	1710–1792
(Padre) Michel-Angelo Rossi	Early 17th century
Giuseppe Domenico Scarlatti	1685–1757
Francesco Turini	1595–1656

2. FRENCH

François Couperin (le Grand)	1668–1733
Louis Claude Daquin	1684–1755
Jean Baptiste Lœillet	? –1728
Jean Philippe Rameau	1683–1764

3. ENGLISH

John Blow	1648–1708
Dr. John Bull	1562–1628
William Byrde	1538–1623
Giles Farnabie(y)	Flourished *c.* 1600–1620
Orlando Gibbons	1583–1625
Thomas Morley	1557(?)–1603
John Munday	? –1630
Henry Purcell	1658–1695

4. GERMAN

Dietrich Buxtehude	1637–1707
Johann Jacob Fro(h)berger	? –1667
Karl Heinrich Graun	1701–1759
George Frideric Handel	1685–1759
Johann Kuhnau	1660–1722
Johann Mattheson	1681–1764
Johann Pachelbel	1653–1706
Georg Philipp Telemann	1681–1767

A few of these at least deserve more than passing notice.

DOMENICO SCARLATTI wrote upwards of five hundred pieces for harpsichord, now incorrectly called sonatas, but originally going under the modest title of *Esercisi.* The complete set is published by Ricordi.

Less formidable selections may be found in the Twenty-five Sonatas edited by Emil Sauer in the Peters Edition, the Eighteen Pieces (arranged rather arbitrarily in suites) edited by Hans von Bülow in the same edition, the Twenty-two Pieces edited by Buonamici in the Schirmer Edition, and the Twenty Sonatas, laudably unedited, of the Breitkopf & Härtel Edition. An excellent selection of Sixty Sonatas, unedited, was formerly published by Breitkopf & Härtel but is no longer in print.

Scarlatti was a brilliant player of the harpsichord, equalling even Handel, and he wrote with complete understanding of its idiom. Many of the "sonatas" find merited place on modern programs, and enterprising pianists frequently introduce attractive specimens still unfamiliar to the public. Their style is bold and effective, with a pronounced preference for fast tempi; it abounds in tricky finger technique and perilous leaps of crossed hands. Scarlatti occasionally indulged in amazingly modern combinations of tones, anticipating in fact the much later "note clusters" of Henry Cowell. Too often his startling dissonances have been bowdlerized by timid editors.

[There are now several editions of the works of this great master, who is beginning to emerge from a state of neglect and lack of artistic recognition. Colombo, formerly American Ricordi, publishes the only complete edition (ten volumes) of the five hundred or more sonatas (*sonata* simply means "a thing sounded," *i.e.*, "played," as distinct from *cantata*, "a thing sung"). It is edited by Alessandro Longo, splendidly, but too romantically, and therefore is an over-edited publication. You can use it to good advantage, however, if you have an Urtext edition to compare it with, and thus can approve or disapprove of what Longo added in phrasings, dynamics, and expression marks! I cannot recommend the wilfully interpreted Sauer and Bülow editions. But I strongly endorse the sixty unedited sonatas published by Kalmus. In the one hundred and fifty sonatas brought out by Peters in three volumes (fifty Sonatas in each of the three books), the text is untouched, but tactfully, in small type, the editors, Keller and Weismann, have added tempo and metronome marks, some fingerings, and expression suggestions. The outstanding contribution to the Scarlatti literature is the first complete biography by Ralph Kirkpatrick. This book is of the utmost importance and a real inspiration (Princeton University Press). Mr. Kirkpatrick published sixty sonatas (Schirmer) in two volumes, chronologically arranged. He also recorded them. Students and teachers as well as some of the public performers of Scarlatti should take advantage of the most informative and excellently written text preceding the music. Unfortunately, Mr. Kirkpatrick does not intend to continue to publish additional sonatas. Two books of Scarlatti sonatas edited by James Friskin (J. Fischer and Brothers) are warmly recommended for Urtext comparison.]

COUPERIN and RAMEAU are the high lights of the old French school. The first wrote prolifically for the harpsichord, both as a solo instrument and as a participant in chamber music. He was a pioneer of keyboard program music, some of his fanciful titles being well justified by the musical mood. Rameau, celebrated for his operas and his treatise on harmony, wrote comparatively little for harpsichord, but the quality of his work is high.

[I have in my library the two precious, because out-of-print, volumes of Rameau's music in the Durand luxury edition of 1896. The first volume contains the fifty-three clavecin pieces, which are unedited. The Preface is by Camille Saint-Saëns, and the Bibliography and all the comments, including Rameau's description of his own method of playing the clavecin, were supplied by the distinguished Charles Malherbe. The second volume includes the keyboard pieces in trio arrangements and orchestrations of string sextets, all in transcriptions by the composer himself. It is charming to notice on one of the original title-page engravings that all this printed music can be bought *"chez M. Bordet, à la Musique moderne, rue Saint-Honoré, vis-à-vis le Palais-Royal."* This in 1752.

It is a great satisfaction and a happy piece of news to mention the recently issued complete edition of all the clavecin music of Rameau by the German music publisher Bärenreiter of Kassel. It has an excellent preface in three languages by Erwin R. Jacobi, with tables of ornaments and comments about style and technique. Another new, equally excellent edition is also patterned after the early Durand-Saint-Saëns volumes. It is published by the International Music Company, New York, and should find immediate favor with teachers and students. A third, entirely different reprint of the original Rameau clavecin pieces can be had in miniature format and should be welcomed by concertgoers. This is my opportunity to pay my respects to the publishers of Lea Pocket Scores, New York, for their ingenious gift to the music world and to musicians of all ages in particular: their catalogue includes the Urtexts of a large number of classical and romantic composers, to be had at small cost.]

The efflorescence of English music in the period centering in the reign of Queen Elizabeth is a marvel of cultural history. In no other society, at any time or in any land, did the art so enter into the daily life of court, gentry, and the lower classes. Playing and singing were an essential part of the education of every lady and gentleman, and the folk songs of the day still echo through the remote mountains of Kentucky. We are sometimes told that the barrenness of the two centuries following was due to the overwhelming popularity of Handel and foreign music in general. This is hard to believe, for genius does not kill genius. Instead of reproaching dear old Handel for a baneful influence, it were fairer to admit that English talent ran its course, exhausted its vitality, and perforce awaited rejuvenescence by the much later group of composers that began with Edward Elgar. Strangely enough, no piano-writer has arisen in modern England to rival the authors of the *Fitzwilliam Virginal Book,* just as Italy still seeks a worthy successor to Scarlatti.

Pre-eminent among the writers of their time are ORLANDO GIBBONS and HENRY PURCELL. Their works for spinet and harpsichord were but a small fraction of a large productivity. Those of Purcell have been collected and published by Novello in a handsome volume too little known.

The critical reader will have observed that not a few of the composers included in my list were partly contemporaneous with Bach. HANDEL, born in the same year and outliving the greater master by nine years, is a case in point. An accomplished harpsichordist, equaled only by Scarlatti, he wrote much and well for the instrument. If pianists have unduly neglected his *Leçons, Pièces et Fugues* and the sixteen suites, they may plead that his idiom is not easily translatable to modern keyboards. But harpsichord-players of today would acquire merit by specializing in his works. The suites, planned without particular attention to dance forms, are quite dissimilar to those of Bach except for their restriction of the component numbers to a single tonality. Handel writes in a more serious vein than Scarlatti, who composed few good slow movements.

It is easy enough to advise the amateur to browse in the various collections of old music and old composers. He will find pleasure and profit in them, and he will meet nothing that is immoderately hard to read or play. But the wealth of the material makes it difficult to single out particular numbers recommendable for more sustained study. Not to fail the student completely, I attempt a very short list of representative pieces:

Couperin   Les Cloches de Cythère (*or* Le Carillon de Cythère)
            Les Petits Moulins à vent

Daquin	Le Coucou
Gibbons	The Lord of Salisbury his Pavin
Handel	Variations in E (*Harmonious Blacksmith*)
	Suite No. I in D minor
Leo	Arietta in G minor
Lœillet	Gigue in G minor (MacDowell edition recommended)
Mattheson	Gigue in D minor (MacDowell edition recommended)
Paradies	Toccata (or the whole Sonata) in A
Purcell	Ground in C minor
Rameau	Gavotte with Variations
	Le Tambourin
Scarlatti	Cat's Fugue
	Pastorale and Capriccio (original or in Tausig's well-known arrangement)[1]
	Selected sonatas

The interpretation of the early music as played on the modern piano calls mainly for delicacy, grace, tasteful style, and agile finger technique. The utmost clarity should always be preserved. There is ample scope for expressiveness, but one must realize that the deeper feelings, passion, and grandeur find no place. Sudden contrasts of touch and tone are more appropriate than elaborate shading. The imagination will find congenial exercise in contriving piano equivalents for the varied effects of the two-manual harpsichord. The use of the wrist for staccato should be discreet, and heavy arm action is entirely unsuitable. One need not refrain altogether from the pedals. Rubinstein played most of this music with the soft pedal, and the damper pedal, if sparingly employed, will often beautify legato passages and arpeggios. The range of dynamics, starting from a light pianissimo, had best not exceed a moderate forte even in the strongest climaxes.

So much of the old music seemed to transcend the limits of clavichord and harpsichord that we can hardly wonder if modern pianists have been tempted to revise it for their own instrument. This has been

---

[1] [The Tausig "arrangement" of two Scarlatti sonatas—E minor (original in D minor) and E major—now is decidedly obsolete. We live in an era of greater respect for the Urtext and first editions and for the masters themselves. Self-respecting American piano teachers, and they are legion, should have in their studios both the Urtext, if available, and at least one well-edited publication of all the classical literature, for information, comparison, and comprehension. The result is certain to be assurance of attitude and authority.]

done with good taste and commendable restraint by Tausig, Mac-Dowell, Respighi, and others. Unfortunately, once we embark on the process of arranging, it is all too easy to go too far. With profoundest respect for that super-pianist Leopold Godowsky and unbounded admiration of the skill and musicianship of his transcriptions, I cannot help feeling that the old literature loses its native flavor and becomes quite transmogrified in the versions offered in his *Renaissance*. I can forebodingly imagine a pianist of the distant future elaborating the pieces of Godowsky's own *Triakontameron* to the destruction of their simple charm.

CHAPTER THREE

Johann Sebastian Bach
(1685–1750)

JOHANN SEBASTIAN BACH was in the opinion of many the greatest of all composers. There is solid ground for this belief. In any case, few musicians would dispute that he, Beethoven, and Mozart, a trinity of genius, reached heights of creation unattained before or since their time. [I belong among the many who believe that Bach's genius was such that everything before and after him can be measured and adjudged by his profound greatness. With him, form and content are always balanced, the sign of the supreme architect. However, in my picture, Mozart and Beethoven are his close neighbors in this trinity of genius.]

Bach was not a pioneer, for Palestrina had already brought vocal counterpoint to rare perfection, Schütz had written Passion music according to the four Evangelists, and Bernhard Christian Weber had anticipated *The Well-Tempered Clavier* by a work of the same intent and title. [It is interesting that Jan Pieterszoon Sweelinck, the Dutch master, wrote a Chromatic Fantasy and Fugue in D minor for organ about one hundred years before Bach's unique romantic masterpiece was created.]

Rather, he represented the summation of two centuries of polyphony, carrying everything that had gone before him to completion and to heights of beauty and grandeur yet undreamed. He was to be the inspiration of all future composers, the pure well of music undefiled from which they drank with eager gratitude.

Bach's command of tonal expression was almost inconceivably profound and universal; he was equally at home in a purely musical idiom, in interpreting the multifarious moods of human experience, and in the utterance of religious fervor, penitence, or praise of God. His output was prodigious and its quality so uniform in value that there is hardly anything in it that we could now lose without regret. Too much, alas, was irretrievably lost in the scattering of his belongings after his death. Had Bach written only the B minor Mass, or only the *St. Matthew Passion*, or only the church cantatas, or only the works for organ and clavier, or among these last only *The Well-Tempered Clavier*, we should still be compelled to rank him among the greatest masters. There are devotees today who study and perform all his compositions for organ or clavier, orchestras that from time to time play all his concertos in series, festivals devoted solely to his choral works, and one might venture to predict that some day a musical society will undertake the magnificent task of presenting, over a suitable period of time, the 199 church cantatas that have been preserved.

What facilities did Bach have for the performance of these mighty works? They were lamentably meager. The modern orchestra was not yet born, and the only instruments that had been perfected in his day were the strings. The harpsichord and clavichord (the latter was generally preferred by Bach) were well developed, but it was long before his fingers touched the first crude pianos. The organ lacked all the modern improvements that have so materially lightened the labor of playing it. Even at the St. Thomasschule in Leipzig, a special school for choristers, it was difficult to assemble more than a small chorus of good voices. The *St. Matthew Passion*, calling for double chorus, ripieno soprano, four vocal soloists, and double orchestra, was first given on Good Friday 1729, by sixteen singers, two orchestras numbering eighteen players, and two organs, one of which was an old discarded instrument not yet dismantled. The grand work had to wait a hundred years for a second performance, under Mendelssohn. The first hearing made no impression at all; the second revolutionized musical history.

Probably, however, Bach could rely on his performers for good executive ability. There were fine organists, harpsichordists, flute-players in plenty. Voices were doubtless as good then as now, and Bach had the advantage of training them himself to meet the demands of his intricate polyphony. Proud of his talented family, he boasted: "All my children are born musicians, and I can assure you that I can already form an ensemble both *vocaliter* and *instrumentaliter* within my family, particularly since my present wife sings a good, clear soprano, and my eldest daughter, too, joins in not badly."

The ceaseless activity of Bach was by no means limited to composition. The most famous organist in history, a master of the harpsichord and clavichord, he also played well the violin, viola, and lute. His improvisations were wonderful, and his sight reading so ready that he fearlessly undertook to read anything set before him in print or manuscript. Much of his time, especially in the later years at Leipzig, was spent in teaching. Printed music being scarce, he did a vast amount of copying, thereby impairing his eyesight and eventually bringing on blindness. He personally engraved a good deal of the small portion of his works published during his life. He kept his own instruments in tune and repair—no small job, as the old keyed instruments held their pitch but briefly and the quills of the harpsichord needed constant trimming. Finally, he devoted considerable time and thought to the improvement of existing instruments and the invention of new ones.

We are inevitably so impressed by the colossal industry of the musician and by the intense natural piety of the servant of the Church that Bach the man is often overlooked. Yet he was a very human person, and this should never be forgotten in playing his music. His extraordinarily vital personality was not free from foibles; we hear, for instance, of many acrimonious and prolonged disputes in his professional contacts, often over trivial matters, indicating a readiness to quarrel in defense of his rights and privileges. But he was warmhearted, fundamentally genial, hospitable, generous in admiration of other noted musicians, and blessed with an abiding sense of humor. Busy as he was, he found ample time for his family and friends. He lavished care on the education of his children, with the happy result that several of his sons became musicians of eminence. His two marriages were happy and fruitful. The second, to Anna Magdalena Wülcken, was ideal. The story of their wedded life reads like a tender romance; the record of her subsequent lapse into poverty, of her lonely years in an almshouse, neglected and forgotten by the world, is a saddening testimony to the lack of appreciation accorded to Bach the composer by his contemporaries.

Bach consciously dedicated his gifts to the service of the Lutheran Church, and his sacred compositions outnumber the secular by far. Only a few of the choral works, such as the *Coffee Cantata* and *Phœbus and Pan,* are secular. These cantatas, ebullitions of Bach's humor, hint that lack of inclination, not of ability, deterred him from producing operas.[1] On the other hand, at least one of the instrumental works, a little-known musical commentary on the Lutheran catechism, is of avowedly religious intention.

The Inventions, Preludes, and Fugues

So many of Bach's clavier works are written in the strictly contrapuntal forms (invention, fugue, and canon) that it is impossible to speak of them without using a few technical terms. With apologies to the well-informed reader, who will not need them, I shall try to give simple definitions of these terms:

VOICE. Any melodic part, whether vocal or instrumental.

COUNTERPOINT. The weaving together of melodic parts or voices, as distinguished from the setting of a melody to a harmonic accompaniment.

IMITATION. The device of repeating a melodic phrase or figure in different parts, at different intervals, etc.

INVERSION. This term has three distinct meanings in music:

1. Harmonic inversion occurs when any tone of a chord other than the root is in the bass.

2. Contrapuntal inversion occurs when lower and upper voices exchange position by transposition in the octave,[2] a soprano part, for example, changing places with the bass.

3. Thematic or melodic inversion occurs when the steps by which a part moves are reversed in direction, upward becoming downward steps of the same extent (interval) and vice versa.

DOUBLE COUNTERPOINT. Counterpoint so written that the parts can be inverted without loss of correctness. The two- and three-part Inventions of Bach are studies in double counterpoint. Fugues, when strict, are necessarily written in double counterpoint, for all the parts must be invertible.

CANON. A piece in which two or more parts imitate each other strictly and continuously. The shorter the interval at which the imitations occur, the "closer" the canon is said to be. *Three Blind Mice*

---

[1] *Phœbus and Pan* has occasionally been presented on the operatic stage, most recently by the Metropolitan Opera Association of New York.

[2] Transposition in the tenth or twelfth is also possible, though more rare.

and the French folk song *Frère Jacques,* popular tunes that may be sung as canons in the unison or octave, are good popular illustrations of the form. Interspersed among Bach's "Goldberg" Variations are examples of canons at all intervals, from the unison through the second, third, etc., to the ninth. It is possible to write madly intricate varieties of canon; most of these—e.g., "table," "mirror," and "riddle" canons—easily degenerate into mere curiosities, musical futilities. We may safely ignore them in our study of the piano literature.

AUGMENTATION. Presentation of a motive in notes of double value, halves instead of quarter-notes, quarters instead of eighths, etc.

DIMINUTION. Reduction of a motive to notes of half the original value.

FUGUE cannot be explained in a bare definition. I must therefore ask the reader's patience for a succinct description of this noblest of all contrapuntal forms. For simplicity I shall in future use the abbreviation *W.T.C.* for *The Well-Tempered Clavier,* adding the book and number of any fugue referred to—e.g., *W.T.C.* II, 17. A fugue, then, is based on a theme or subject, usually short (from a few notes to a few measures), and first announced by a stipulated number of voices entering successively in what is called the "exposition." Any voice may be the first to enter, and the others may follow in any order. The second entering voice is said to give the "answer," which consists of the subject transposed a fifth higher or a fourth lower. Voices entering later continue to alternate between subject and answer. An answer is "real" if all its notes are exactly a fifth higher (or a fourth lower) than those of the subject; it is "tonal" if modified in relation to the dominant of the key. The principle of a tonal answer is that any important dominant note occurring near the entrance of the subject is "answered" by the tonic, not by its fifth above. Sometimes the change spreads over more notes than one. Here are a few typical examples of tonal answers:

Ex. 1

The second note of Ex. 1 and the first note of Ex. 2 are dominants, so the answer is tonal. In Ex. 3 the tonal change involves three notes. Another possible change in the subject occurs when its first or last note is lengthened or shortened for convenience; the last note, too, may be altered diatonically or chromatically to ensure smooth progression or promote a modulation. As each voice makes way for the next to enter, it adds a new counterpoint or melodic part, which if sufficiently important will be called a "countersubject."

It is evident that the exposition of a fugue is quite a complicated piece of workmanship. Small wonder that frivolous minds sometimes regard a fugue as a composition in which the voices come in one by one and the audience leaves in a similar manner.

One good example is worth pages of explanation, and if the reader will take the trouble to analyze the first twelve measures of the Fugue in B flat, *W.T.C.* I, 21, he will at once get a perfectly clear idea of the exposition of a three-part fugue. It might be represented in the following diagram:

	Measures 1–4	Measures 5–8	Measures 9–12
Soprano	Subject	1st Counterpoint	2nd Counterpoint
Alto	——	Answer (tonal)	1st Counterpoint
Bass	——	——	Subject

Not all expositions, however, are quite so simple and straightforward as that above. Here is a diagram for the exposition of the four-part Fugue in F minor, *W.T.C.* I, 12.

	Measures 1–3	4–6	7–9	10–12 (codetta)	13–15
Tenor	Subject	1st Cpt.	2nd Cpt.	(1st Cpt.)	3rd Cpt.
Alto	——	Answer (tonal)	1st Cpt.	(1st Cpt.)	2nd Cpt.
Bass	——	——	Subject	——	1st Cpt.
Soprano	——	——	——	(1st Cpt.)	Answer

Cpt. = Counterpoint.

It will be observed that there is here an interruption to the orderly introduction of the voices before the last entry of the answer in the soprano. Measures 10–12 constitute a short free interlude, in this case based on the first counterpoint, and designed to obviate any possible rigidity of effect. A link of this kind is commonly, though not very appropriately, termed a "codetta"; it is often only a few beats of a measure in length, and may just as well be placed before the entrance of the third voice, as for example in the A minor Fugue, *W.T.C.* I, 20.

The strictness of construction characterizing the exposition is amply offset by the extreme freedom indulged in by all good writers in the further development of the fugue. Roughly speaking, the continuation consists of "episodes," designed to afford relief from the more formal part of the structure, and re-entrances of the subject or answer whenever, however, in any key, and for as long as the composer chooses. Toward the end there will usually be a more or less well defined return of the subject in the tonic by way of climax and a recognizable coda to mark the close. Yet in the main the writer, once he has stated his subject in the accepted form, is free to expatiate on it as his fancy suggests.

It is true that respectable theorists have made many attempts to lay down rules for the development (or middle section) and climax of the fugue, but to little avail. Efforts were made, for instance, to regulate the modulations permissible. On this point Vaughan Williams, writing in *Grove's Dictionary*,[3] remarks that "not a single one of the fugues, either in the *Wohltemperirtes Clavier* or in the *Kunst der Fuge,* follows the scheme of modulation which was afterwards prescribed by Cherubini." Note that "afterwards" as a peak of *post eventum* folly! Again, the textbooks would have us believe that the exposition is com-

---

[3] Under the excellent article "Fugue," fourth edition.

monly followed by what they call a counter-exposition; but as a matter of cold fact, anything resembling this counter-exposition as described is fairly rare. Nowhere, indeed, is it wiser to seek information from music itself instead of from books on music than in this matter of fugue. I personally knew and understood a great many fugues before ever reading an article or a book about them. To this day I find the fugues themselves beautifully clear and most of the books dreadfully confusing. A. Madeley Richardson's lucid volume *Fugue Writing* is a laudable exception.

To return to the development of the fugue: while there is practically nothing that the composer *must* do, there are a number of appropriate and interesting devices that he *may* employ. To begin with, the episodes, though their main function is to lighten the severity of the style, offer great scope for ingenuity. They are usually built up from fragments of the subject or the counterpoints or countersubjects, though it is allowable to use new motives (see *W.T.C.* I, 13, in F sharp). Episodes of exceptional workmanship and symmetry adorn the Fugue in F minor, *W.T.C.* I, 12. It may happen, on the other hand, that a fugue such as that in C, *W.T.C.* I, 1, will be so closely compacted of the essential subject matter that all episodic material is crowded out.

Next, in the course of the fugue the subject may be introduced in thematic inversion, in augmentation, and in diminution. These terms have already been explained, but it might here be added that the word *direct* is sometimes applied to the original subject in distinction to the term *inverted*. Good examples of inversion occur in *W.T.C.* I, 6, 15, 20, 23 and II, 3, 4, 22. Augmentation of a theme can hardly fail to have a stately, imposing effect. Bach uses it to great advantage in *W.T.C.* I, 8 and II, 2 and 3. Diminution, on the contrary, may easily sound frivolous, and is best employed with humorous purpose. See *W.T.C.* II, 3, near the beginning, and the Fugue in A minor, II, 20, in which the theme obviously contains its own diminution. An outstanding and rare example of dignified diminution is seen in the most melodious of all fugues, that in E major, *W.T.C.* II, 9. Here the tempo is so slow that the doubling of the rate of movement incurs no suspicion of levity. In the final section of his Sonata in A flat, Opus 110, Beethoven uses first a diminution and then a *double* diminution without impairing the lyric serenity of the fugue.

I pass over the *cancrizans* or "crab," meaning a theme (originally a canon) in retrogression, because it would be hard to find more than one familiar example (Beethoven, finale of Sonata Opus 106) in the entire classical piano literature. But I must add a warning to students of Schönberg and his disciples that they will find it absolutely necessary to inform themselves on this matter.

The most typical device of all, the most suitable and effective in fugal style, is that of the stretto. The word, Italian for "close" or "narrow," hardly explains itself, especially as it often is used in a lighter sense to denote a hastened tempo. The German *Engführung,* literally "narrow leading," is more expressive. A stretto, in the fugal sense, is a means of bringing subject and answer closer together than normally. The voices are telescoped, as it were, response beginning before statement is finished. The nearer response to statement, the "closer" the stretto is said to be (as in a canon). If the compression involves all the voices and is exact, we have what the learned call a *stretto maestrale,* or masterly stretto.

Probably all this can only be made clear by examples. In those below, Ex. 4 is a simple stretto in two parts, Ex. 5 a *stretto maestrale* for four voices, and Ex. 6 a three-part stretto, the parts respectively in direct, augmented, and inverted motion:

Ex. 4

Ex. 5

Ex. 6

Before the climax of a fugue or at the coda the writer may effectively introduce an organ point, for which if necessary he is allowed an extra voice. The organ point is most advantageously employed in choral and organ fugues.

Let me repeat that none of these devices is obligatory. Some of the finest fugues, including many of the grand works for chorus and organ and the mighty Chromatic Fugue of Bach, are entirely innocent of contrapuntal complexities.

Premature exaltation at our ease in comprehending these simpler structures receives something of a check when we learn that we still have to deal with "double" and "triple" fugues. Without attempting to exhaust all the possible intricacies of these formidable creations we can fairly easily get a good working understanding of them. A double fugue is one written on two subjects; a triple fugue has three. There are different ways of stating and developing the subjects, and the authorities sometimes disagree as to whether a piece is a real triple fugue or merely a fugue with two prominent countersubjects. Argument has arisen, for instance, over the five-voiced Fugue in C-sharp minor, W.T.C. I, 4. If you examine this you will see that new subjects (or countersubjects) enter respectively at the thirty-fifth measure in the soprano and at the forty-ninth measure in the first tenor. They are interwoven for some time with the main subject and at the climax the second of them continues with the main subject in a wonderful, close double stretto. At no time, however, are these new subjects or countersubjects introduced in a regular exposition. The Fugue in F-sharp minor, W.T.C. II, 14, is of closely similar type. In both cases the music itself is transparent enough and the only question possible is one of nomenclature. Somewhat different is the Fugue in G-sharp minor, W.T.C. II, 18. Here the first subject is regularly introduced and developed for sixty measures. At the sixty-first measure it drops out and a new subject appears in a distinct, only slightly irregular exposition followed by an independent development until at the ninety-seventh measure the two subjects enter together, are regularly "answered," and remain combined to the end. This must be considered an unquestionable double fugue. The celebrated *St. Anne's Fugue*, written for organ but available to pianists of sufficient daring in the transcription of Busoni, is an equally unmistakable instance of a triple fugue.

Fortunately no confusion of nomenclature surrounds the words *fughetta* and *fugato*. A fughetta is universally understood to be a small fugue. A fugato is a passage in fugal style, but not a complete fugue.

The fugato is often introduced with telling effect in the development sections of sonatas and symphonies, especially in the finales of these compositions. Many examples will be found in Beethoven's sonatas.

We may now turn with relief from these necessary but unavoidably rather tedious explanations to the enjoyment of the works that gave occasion to them.

Among the minor works of Bach are two sets (one of twelve, one of six) of Little Preludes for Beginners and a number of Little Fugues. In some editions these are published together under the collective title of *Little Preludes and Fugues*. They merit notice as sterling study material. Some such selection as the following:

12 Little Preludes, Nos. 1, 3, 8, 10

6 Little Preludes, Nos. 1, 4, 5

Little Fugues in C minor (two-voiced) and C major (three-voiced)

would furnish adequate preparation for the study of the Inventions and *The Well-Tempered Clavier*.

THE INVENTIONS

In a rather elaborate title too often omitted from reprints or overlooked by students, Bach explained the purpose of these pieces. They were to be "a guide to clean performance in two, later in three, independent parts and to the conception and development of good ideas (inventions), with special emphasis on cultivation of a cantabile style of playing and acquirement of a strong foretaste of composition." They were to be models, then, for player and composer alike.

The three-part Inventions were alternatively called Symphonies; we may mention and at once conveniently forget the fact. It is much more important and interesting to realize that we possess in the Inventions two sets of pieces written in the fifteen major and minor keys available on keyed instruments before the introduction of equal temperament. Under the old system of tuning by a circle of true fifths, some keys were necessarily too out of tune to be pleasant. The musicians of the period, forced to a choice, naturally elected to be able to use the commonest keys, excluding only those with many sharps and flats. This left as good keys the majors and minors of C, D, E, F, G, and A, as well as E-flat major, B-flat major, and B minor. E major and F minor were the only usable keys with as many as four sharps or flats, while F-sharp minor, though with only three sharps, stayed in the banned group. Under the circumstances, of course, a wise composer not only did not write in the out-of-tune tonalities; he did not even modulate into them except passingly.

It is profitable to heed Bach's intention and invest a little time in examining the structure of the Inventions. Starting with those in two parts, we quickly become aware of a considerable variety of form. In some (see Nos. 1, 7, 10, 13) a short motive is developed by imitation, often in inversion. In others (3, 4, 14, 15) the theme is longer, extending perhaps to two measures, and many of the imitations repeat only one half of the complete theme. Or there may be a long subject with a well-marked countersubject, four measures long (5, 6, 9, 11), again with many fragmentary entrances in the style of episodes. No. 12 belongs in this group except that the length of the subject is two measures of compound time instead of four measures. The second Invention presents a series of two-measure phrases or counterpoints entering imitatively and eventually reappearing in contrapuntal inversion. The eighth is freely canonic in style.

It is quite a simple exercise to transpose the parts of any two-part invention, putting the upper part an octave or two lower in the left hand and the lower part two octaves higher for the right hand. When this is done, the nature of double counterpoint is immediately seen, for the euphony of the piece will nowise be injured by the change.

Many of the three-part Inventions might be regarded as small fugues except that the first announcement of the theme is accompanied by a counterpoint or countersubject and the responses do not follow strictly the rules of fugal exposition. For good examples of this, consult Nos. 7, 8, 10, and 13. No. 5, in E flat, is a curious little piece, stiff and formal because of its many embellishments, and composed of two melodic parts and a bass that is really only an accompaniment. No. 7, in E minor, is beautiful, the gem of the set, full of poignant melody. And the ninth, in F minor, is probably the best extant exercise in three-part double counterpoint, exhibiting all the six different combinations of which the skillfully contrasted voices are capable by contrapuntal inversion.

Pianists rightly regard the Inventions as the best possible preparation for the larger works of Bach, especially the preludes and fugues, but it would be wrong to underestimate their intrinsic value. They belong to that fine, wholesome mass of musical literature which outlasts passing tastes and never palls. Since few are fortunate enough to be able to study them all, the amateur may be willing to accept the following selection as representative:

Two-part Inventions—Nos. 1, 5, 6, 8, 12
Three-part Inventions—Nos. 2, 6, 7, 9, 13.

[In his analysis of the two-part and three-part Inventions, *The Well-Tempered Clavier*, the Chromatic Fantasy and Fugue, the suites, partitas, and toccatas, the Italian Concerto, the "Goldberg" Variations, the Capriccio in B flat, and the C minor Fantasy, Dr. Hutcheson has indeed made a noble contribution to the understanding of Bach and the performance of his music.]

THE WELL-TEMPERED CLAVIER

At Cöthen, on January 22, 1720, Bach began to keep a musical note-book for his oldest son, Wilhelm Friedemann, then in his tenth year. He called it a Klavierbüchlein, meaning "a little book for clavier." After an explanation of notation, clefs, and keys comes a series of short exercises in all the twenty-four keys, major and minor. He did not omit the pious invocation "In Jesus' Name" which heads so many of his manuscripts.

The booklet was destined to grow into *The Well-Tempered Clavier*. In the first prints of the more famous work its origin is trace-able in the shortness and simplicity of some of the preludes. Later Bach expanded these preludes to their final and now familiar state.

We may note with special interest that as early as this Bach had committed himself to the new equal temperament, abandoning the old tuning of the clavier that restricted the composer to the use of fifteen keys. *Well-Tempered* means simply "well-tuned."

It was the first set of twenty-four preludes and fugues, completed in 1722, that Bach himself called *The Well-Tempered Clavier*. For convenience of reference we customarily extend the title to the second set also, which was not finished until twenty years later.

It is possible to view this monumental work from several different standpoints. First, it is a conspicuous example of the best kind of propaganda, for unquestionably Bach's sponsorship was decisive in the adoption of a twelve-tone chromatic system on which the future of modern music hinged. Again, it is a treasury of musical scholarship, giving final definition to instrumental counterpoint and fugue. It needed Bach himself to amplify it by his ultimate masterpiece, *The Art of Fugue*. Last, we have come to prize it as a library of human emotion recorded in moods ranging from the lightest and gayest to the most sublime and tragic.

I hope to escape the charge of impertinence if I suggest a division of the preludes and fugues into two categories, a greater and a lighter. The "lighter" list would comprise the following:

Nos. 2, 3, 5, 6, 9, 11, 13, 19, 21, 23 of Part I
Nos. 6, 12, 13, 15, 19, 21, 24 of Part II.

It is marked by the comparative simplicity of the fugal structure, which makes almost no use of the devices of inversion, augmentation and diminution, or stretto. Need I add that many of this group are no less beautiful than the more complex pieces?

The "greater" preludes and fugues are:

Nos. 1, 4, 8, 12, 14, 15, 16, 17, 18, 20, 22, 24 of Part I

Nos. 2, 3, 4, 5, 7, 8, 9, 10, 11, 14, 16, 17, 18, 20, 22, 23 of Part II.

There remain a few examples hard to group because in them the preludes are of far greater consequence than the fugues; these are Nos. 7 and 10 in Part I, and No. 1 in Part II.

A detailed description of each one of the forty-eight preludes and fugues would require a book to itself. I must be content to give a condensed tabulation of their chief points of interest.

PART I

1, *C major.*   Bach starts off with his best foot foremost. The prelude an unassuming succession of arpeggiated harmonies, simple enough to have been one of the first pieces studied by Wilhelm Friedemann. The fugue, a 4,[4] impressive in its masterly polyphony, abounding in highly ingenious strettos of remarkably smooth, easy effect.

2, *C minor.*   The prelude one of several in toccata style, sturdy, a good finger exercise for both hands. The fugue, a 3, light, piquant, inviting a staccato touch; a favorite of teachers and students.

3, *C-sharp major.*   Here and in the corresponding number of Part II Bach prefers the seven sharps to the five flats of D-flat major. The prelude flowing, spontaneous; the fugue gracefully sportive. Bach's free use of the thumb on black keys is very evident. Extremely popular, though the slippery technique of the fugue makes it the *pons asinorum* of the W.T.C.

4, *C-sharp minor.*   A magnificent composition, justifying the comparison often made with the architecture of a Gothic cathedral. The prelude a dirge, tragically lyrical. The fugue, one of only two five-voiced examples in the W.T.C., may be regarded either as a triple fugue or as a fugue with two countersubjects. It is extremely grave in mood, rising to a poignant climax combining two subjects in double stretto. Shortest fugue theme (four notes only) of the W.T.C.

5, *D major.*   The prelude, again in toccata style, bubbles along like a cheerful brook. The fugue, a 4, inspiritingly martial, not

---

[4] "A 3," "a 4," etc., in speaking of a fugue, indicate the number of parts or voices used. In the W.T.C. Bach gives a statement of this kind at the beginning of each fugue.

essentially contrapuntal in texture but a fine piano piece, said to have been a favorite of Rubinstein. A young pianist once aptly said to me that she could march right up to the cannon's mouth if this fugue were played to her. The rhythm ♩. 𝅘𝅥𝅯𝅘𝅥𝅯𝅘𝅥𝅯 at the third measure and later should be interpreted ♩𝅘𝅥𝅯𝅘𝅥𝅯𝅘𝅥𝅯𝅘𝅥𝅯, not ♩. 𝅘𝅥𝅯𝅘𝅥𝅯𝅘𝅥𝅯, the value of the dot being variable in the old notation.

6, *D minor.*   A simple, unpretentious piece, not highly important. The end of the prelude must necessarily read:

Ex. 7

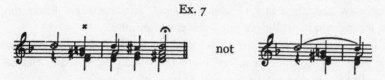

in the right hand, to avoid parallel octaves with the bass; see Bischoff's accurate note in the Steingräber edition. Alternatively, one might venture to omit the B natural marked *x* in my quotation to make the voice-leading sound correct to the ear. Fugue a 3.

7, *E-flat major.*   The prelude a masterpiece, immeasurably greater than the fugue (a 3); in fact, from the tenth measure on, it actually becomes a fugue (a 4), employing the motive of the first measures as a countersubject. The disparity led Busoni to suggest coupling the prelude with the E-flat major fugue of Part II—a doubly thoughtful proposal, since the serious subject of that fugue shows marked resemblance to the main theme of this prelude.

8, *E-flat minor.*   Prelude and fugue rival each other in dignity and beauty. The prelude a penitential psalm charged with intensest feeling. The fugue, though in only three parts, a monument of scholarship, packed with inversions of the subject, strettos of every imaginable kind, and toward the end an imposing series of augmentations. So natural are all the progressions, however, that the formidable learning is almost concealed.

9, *E major.*   A good concert piece; the prelude a charming pastorale; the fugue, a 3, quite short, joyous, very brilliant.

10, *E minor.*   The prelude passionately lyrical; an ideal clavichord piece, far exceeding the companion fugue in beauty and value. The fugue, the only two-voiced specimen in the *W.T.C.*, is in my opinion of doubtful authenticity;[5] if Bach really wrote the parallel

---

[5] It was far from unusual for composers of Bach's day to include in their larger works or collections an occasional movement written by a friend or pupil. No acknowledgment was deemed necessary.

octaves in measures 18–19, it was his sole offense against the nature of fugal polyphony. The fugue is often recommended by teachers as an octave study.

11, *F major.*   The piece as a whole happy and debonair. Prelude of the Invention type; should be played rather showily, not heavily. Fugue, a 3, simple, though containing a few strettos in two parts; rather more sedate than the prelude.

12, *F minor.*   Another number in the grand manner. Both prelude and fugue grave and lovely. The prelude, in dispersed four-part counterpoint, gives special opportunity for a singing legato. The fugue, a 4, with a fine chromatic theme, is particularly interesting in its ingenious, well-developed series of episodes.

13, *F-sharp major.*   The prelude a gently flowing two-part Invention. The fugue, a 3, continues the placid mood. Note the belated entry of a countersubject at the twelfth measure.

14, *F-sharp minor.*   An energetic, incisive prelude. The fugue, a 4, severer, more melodious. The theme should be played strictly legato, the countersubject with a more detached touch.

15, *G major.*   An effective, brilliant concert piece of irrepressible gaiety. The bright prelude is based mainly on arpeggio figures. The fugue, a 3, very pianistic, in fast $\frac{6}{8}$ tempo; deserves inclusion in the "greater" group because of the captivating inversions of the theme. Some incomplete strettos. (Observe that when Bach desires the effect of a stretto he is not always solicitous that it should be either strict or complete.)

16, *G minor.*   As mournful as the preceding piece is gay. Beautiful dispersed counterpoint in the prelude. The fugue, a 4, has a theme composed of two motives, the second of which is also used throughout as countersubject. Voice-leading not easy to keep distinct because of the frequent crossing of theme and countersubject.

17, *A-flat major.*   A genial, serene piece, at the end of the fugue (a 4) reaching a climax of comparative grandeur.[6]

18, *G-sharp minor.*   One of the clavichord pieces, without doubt. Tuneful, tinged with melancholy. The pensive fugue, a 4, is not complicated.

19, *A major.*   A sprightly number. In the fugue, a 3, a rapid countersubject begins in the middle part and continues, with one

---

[6] This is a passage where it is permissible, if unpedantic, to double the bass in octaves. Similar places occur at the end of the fugues in C minor, I, 2, and D major, I, 5.

short interruption, to the end. Though exhilaratingly pianistic, the fugal workmanship is not of Bach's best. The clamorous *sforzando* prescribed by Czerny for the first note of the theme is in questionable taste.

20, *A minor.* The prelude virile, fiery. The fugue, a 4, an astounding display of contrapuntal skill, tossed off with such consummate ease as to seem deliberately humorous. One of the few fugues in which one can point to a complete counter-exposition (here in inversion). After this comes a long series of the closest possible strettos written with meticulous care to treat all the voices with equal fairness; if one stretto uses soprano and tenor, the next will be allotted to alto and bass, and so on. In the last measure the four voices, reinforced by a double organ point above and below, join in a triumphant proclamation of the "motto," as one might call the initial motive. The construction is a marvel of symmetry.

This is one of the most difficult fugues. Play it lightly wherever possible and "let in the air," as Tausig used to say.

21, *B-flat major.* The prelude a sparkling toccata, well illustrating Bach's dexterity in dividing rapid passages between the two hands. The fugue, a 3, has a subject of exactly four measures in length, and runs almost continuously in four-bar phrases.[7] The counterpoints are strictly adhered to in every repetition of the theme.

22, *B-flat minor.* The prelude religious, supplicating. The fugue, a masterpiece of polyphony, one of the two in the *W.T.C.* written in five voices. Note the striking leap of a minor ninth in the short theme of only six notes, and the abandonment of the effect in favor of the tonal answer. The *stretto maestrale* at the climax, for all its wonder, looks better on paper than it actually sounds on the piano. It is a sheer impossibility to make the succession of half-notes:

Ex. 8

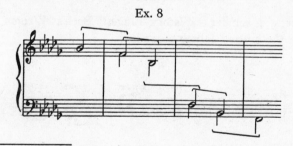

---

[7] This is unusual in fugue, where the rhythmic regularity of the four-bar period is generally avoided, and even the difference in stress between the first and third beats of common time is often disregarded. Fugue subjects of a measure and a half are quite common.

intelligible as five distinct voices. One does the best one can, and relies on the succeeding quarter-notes to establish the imitations.

23, *B major.*   A gracious piece, prelude and fugue well paired. The prelude is another three-part Invention. In the fugue, a 4, note the tonal answer affecting four notes of the subject. Except for a single inversion the construction is quite simple.

24, *B minor.*   Prelude and fugue, though entirely different in character, combine admirably in an imposing whole. The prelude is written in continuous though not canonic imitation of two upper voices accompanied by a freely moving bass. The repeats of the two sections may be omitted with good conscience. Hunters of plagiarisms, fond of deriving the

Ex. 9

of César Franck's D minor Symphony from the

Ex. 10

of Liszt's *Les Préludes,* may find the origin of both near the end of this prelude:

Ex. 11

The fugue, a 4, somber, expiatory, suggests Bach's *"Weinen, Klagen"* motive in the slurred falling seconds:

Ex. 12

PART II

1. *C major.*   The prelude is a beautiful example of dispersed counterpoint in four parts, a continuous melody threading its way

effortlessly from voice to voice. More serious and important than the gay, fluent fugue, a 3.

2. *C minor.* The prelude is of the invention type. The short but fine fugue, a 4, is remarkable for the much belated entrance of the tenor, which, when it does come in, appears in augmentation as part of a stretto, the other voices giving the theme directly and in inversion (see Ex. 4).

3. *C-sharp major.* But for the allegro coda in $\frac{3}{8}$ time (a later addition) this prelude resembles I, 1 in mood and style. In the three-part fugue we find a little model of easy scholarship. Note especially that the exposition is written in stretto—a quite unusual procedure—with the third voice entering in inversion.

Ex. 13

4. *C-sharp minor.* The prelude requires careful management of the numerous ornaments, which otherwise sound stilted. Here it is advisable not to adopt any one strict rule for performing the appoggiaturas but to play them with the value of eighth-notes or sixteenths as the ear suggests. The fugue, a 3, in rapid $\frac{12}{16}$ time, has a distinct virtuoso quality; it is difficult but effective. Notice the easy flow of the inversions.

5. *D major.* The prelude should be played heroically, with a thought of Bach's "festival" trumpets. Here the dotted notes must be accommodated to the prevailing $\frac{12}{8}$ rhythm in sextuplet sixteenths. Most of the dotted notes should be performed as triplet eighths. Some may be given the value of a sextuplet sixteenth. The fugue, a 4, is a dignified piece of architecture in which almost every note is thematic, the episodes being formed from a fragment of the theme in close imitation. Example 1 gives one of the simplest of its many strettos; the most complicated occurs near the end and is hard to make clear because of the crossing of voices.

6. *D minor.* The spirited prelude lies particularly well under the fingers and is delightful to play. The theme of the three-voiced

fugue combines diatonic and chromatic passages, the effect of the piece as a whole being decidedly chromatic. Otherwise the fugue is simple.

7. *E-flat major.*   One of the most melodious of the preludes, singularly natural and unaffected and a highly appropriate introduction to the fugue. The latter, a 4, is noble and almost as tuneful as the prelude. The resemblance of the theme to the prelude of the first part in the same key was pointed out above. No augmentations, diminutions, or inversions are used and the strettos are not complicated, yet the fugue could only have been written by a learned master.

8. *D-sharp minor.*   The prelude again takes the form of a two-part Invention. It has something of the character of an allemande shorn of the distinguishing rhythm of beginning and end. The four-part fugue is grave, well wrought, but not so striking as many others.

9. *E major.*   The crowning glory of the forty-eight, breathing an ineffable serenity. Every note of the prelude and fugue is permeated with noble lyricism. It is this fugue, not the C major prelude of Part I, that might without irreverence have been set as an *Ave Maria*—but for *a cappella* chorus, not for a solo voice. The scholarly perfection of the four-part fugue (see Ex. 5 for one of its many strettos) may pass almost unnoticed if we give ourselves up to the exalted spirituality of the mood. Notice, however, the modification of the theme from

Ex. 14

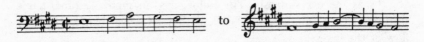

10. *E minor.*   Yet another prelude of the invention type, smooth and flowing. The energetic fugue, a 3, has the longest theme of any in the *W.T.C.* The characteristic rhythms of the subject should be well marked; here the dotted notes should receive their strict value in the exposition, though in the episodes they may be accommodated to the triplet eighth-notes of the other parts. An exceptionally effective piano piece.

11. *F major.*   One of the most interesting preludes, well formed in lyrical dispersed counterpoint of four parts. The lightsome, brilliant fugue, a 3, offers an agreeable contrast. Bach shows his contrapuntal daring in the clash of D flat and D natural near the climax:

Ex. 15

and his humor by the change to D flat in the theme, emphasized by full harmonies, immediately after:

Ex. 16

N. B.

12. *F minor.*   A slight piece, but rightly a great favorite of students. The pleading character of the prelude is heightened near the beginning of the second section by the poignant "false relations" A flat—A natural and G natural—G flat:

Ex. 17

On no account accept the "correction" of the alto G natural to G flat, as some editions print. A trace of melancholy lingers in the three-part fugue.

13. *F-sharp major.*   A longer prelude than usual, in two parts, very melodious. The rhythm in the first measure and elsewhere should be read ♩ ♪♪♪♪ as in the fifth fugue of Part I. The theme of the simple fugue, a 3, appears to depart from Bach's

custom by starting on the leading note instead of on the tonic or dominant:

Ex. 18

but if we remember that trills of this kind begin on the note above (in this case F sharp) we realize that there is no true exception.

14. *F-sharp minor.*   A very fine piece, the prelude highly expressive, calling for a well-inflected touch, the fugue, a 3, elaborately developed, easy as it looks. Here we have a free triple fugue, the subjects taken up one by one and finally combined at the climax.

15. *G major.*   Both prelude and fugue light, gay, quite easy. The prelude may be played fairly fast, the three-part fugue in moderate time and staccato, giving to the whole the character of the spinet. Busoni has enlarged the fugue into an arrangement for two pianos without destroying its dainty fragility.

16. *G minor.*   Very different from No. 15, both prelude and fugue are grave, almost stern. The prelude suggests a Handelian overture. The fugue, a 4, has a distinct countersubject. The theme does not lend itself to treatment in stretto, but occurs several times in two voices simultaneously, in either thirds, sixths, or tenths.

17. *A-flat major.*   The theme of the long prelude moves through a cycle of keys in definite sections. The fugue, a 4, begins tranquilly, gradually working up to an imposing end. The entrance of the fourth voice is delayed until the twenty-second measure.

18. *G-sharp minor.*   Two motives are announced in the theme of the prelude. The second of these:

Ex. 19

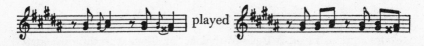

reminds us of the beseeching prelude in F minor of the same book. The double fugue, a 3, has been described on a former page.

19. *A major.*   One of the less important pieces of Part II, agreeable in mood but seldom played.

20. *A minor.*   The prelude finds Bach in one of his chromatic moods; the second section is a free contrapuntal and thematic inver-

sion of the first. (Compare it with the Gigue of the D minor English Suite.) The three-part fugue revels in a trenchant kind of humor and may be played very boldly, without finesse. Observe that the theme contains within itself a diminution of the first four notes:

Ex. 20

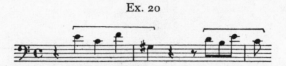

21. *B-flat major.* Another case in which the prelude is longer and more significant than the fugue. The whole piece is extremely amiable and fluid. The fugue is unique in that the theme begins on the supertonic, quite contrary to Bach's almost invariable practice.

22. *B-flat minor.* One of the greatest preludes and fugues, very severe in tone and of monumental scholarship. The elegiac prelude is developed fugally. The great four-part fugue abounds in inversions and strettos, culminating in the marvelous stretto of the coda, an example of counterpoint in the tenth and twelfth.

Ex. 21

The staccato marks in the first measure of the fugue are authentic.

23. *B major.* The prelude, serene and beautiful, is followed by one of Bach's most genial four-part fugues. There is no resort to inversion or stretto, but after the exposition a countersubject is woven in and thenceforth accompanies the theme to the end in happy union.

24. B minor.   Bach concludes his colossal work simply, al-most naïvely. The prelude is a charming little piece that I have loved since childhood. Nothing remarkable distinguishes the fugue, but I quote its last measures in illustration of Bach's ingenuity in hinting at a stretto even when it was impossible to form one literally:

Ex. 22

The Well-Tempered Clavier does not exhaust Bach's fugal writ-ings for piano. Magnificent fugues are to be found sprinkled through the toccatas; there are eighteen smaller fugues or preludes and fugues (three of them on themes by Albinoni) among the miscellaneous works; the Capriccio in B flat ends with a fugue, and there is yet another in the Prelude, Fugue, and Allegro in E flat. I may pass over the smaller fugues without special comment. The toccatas, the Capriccio, and the Prelude, Fugue, and Allegro will be dealt with a little later.

The Art of Fugue was not written for clavier, though it may profitably be studied in the piano version. It was submitted as abstract counterpoint, independent of any particular instrumental setting. There is an admirable orchestral version by Wolfgang Gräser, first introduced to American music-lovers at Mrs. Coolidge's Chamber Music Festival in the small hall of the Library of Congress, Wash-ington, Leopold Stokowski conducting, and twice presented to New York audiences by the Juilliard Graduate School under the leadership of Albert Stoessel in 1930 and 1931. These performances went far to dispel the illusion that the work was a mere academic exercise not fit for concert use.

There remain three pieces that should be considered in this place. All three are printed in the first volume of the Steingräber edition of Bach's piano works.

1. The Prelude and Fugue in A minor, a noble piece with an organ-like prelude, remarkable for its use of five to six voices, and a highly interesting double fugue in four parts.

2. The Fugue in A minor, in three voices, resembles a rushing wind; distinctly a virtuoso concert number, it needs the deftest fingers. It should go fast, but it is not easy to control the speed and keep it steady enough. This fugue is preceded by a few chords, not amounting to a prelude, to be arpeggiated by the player.

3. The Chromatic Fantasia and Fugue, undoubtedly the most famous single piece of Bach, is a Himalayan peak of musical literature. The three-part Fugue, simple enough in its polyphonic texture, is a masterpiece of cumulative effect, gradually mounting in excitement from a very quiet beginning to a powerful, extraordinarily telling climax. Grand as the Fugue is, however, it is in the Fantasia that Bach's genius flowers to perfection. Here we have one of his inspired improvisations, as if he sat at the harpsichord today giving full rein to his fancy. Here, if ever in music, is melody of freest line; rhythm absolved from the time-beat; modulation pure, bold, imaginative; and form completely its own master. No words can describe creation of such rounded liberty. The discipline of the succeeding Fugue offers the strongest of contrasts, yet the Fantasia foretells the Fugue and the Fugue is born from the Fantasia as an inevitable complement.

Wilhelm Friedemann Bach sent a copy of the Chromatic Fantasia (without the fugue) to Johann Forkel, who was so enraptured that he wrote on an inserted leaf a doggerel verse that has become famous for the prophecy contained in its last line:

> *Anbey kommt an*
> *Etwas Musik von Sebastian,*
> *Sonst genannt:* Fantasia chromatica;
> *Bleibt schön in alle Saecula*[8]

One cannot fail to notice that the key of D minor frequently aroused the spirit of chromaticism in Bach Look through the fourth three-part Invention, the sixth prelude and fugue of *W.T.C.* II, and the Gigue from the sixth English Suite, and my point will quickly be evident.

---

[8] Literally:

> Herewith arrives
> Some music by Sebastian,
> Otherwise called: *Fantasia chromatica;*
> 'Twill stay beautiful in all generations.

The Performance of Polyphony

The leading principle for a correct and beautiful performance of polyphony is to give each part its own individual touch, phrasing, and shading. Often the differentiation of rhythm is almost enough in itself. There are countless pages in Bach consisting of two voices, one in notes of double the value of the other—quarters and eighth-notes, or eighths and sixteenths. The difference helps to keep the parts distinct; an added difference in touch, usually staccato for the notes of longer value and legato for the others, makes the effect doubly clear. See, for example, the two-part Invention in F major or the Gigue from the French Suite in E. It will be found, indeed, that in all good counterpoint, and especially in Bach's music, the parts, whether two, three, or four, are carefully varied in their rhythmic movement and in the placing of accents and climax points. This care on the part of the composer makes it possible for the ear to distinguish the progression of voices even on uninflected instruments like the organ.[9]

It takes some skill and independence of the fingers to phrase and inflect each part individually. Still, if you have a feeling for polyphony, the technique of playing it will to a large extent find itself. It is one of the many things that are always far better done by instinct than by labored calculation. Judicious practice, of course, does wonders. Try the E minor three-part Invention, playing each part separately as expressively as you can; then put the voices together and notice how naturally they will seem to swell and recede in turn as their momentary importance becomes greater or less. Here is another excellent exercise: take any short fugue (that in C minor, W.T.C. I, 2, or the one in B flat, W.T.C. I, 21, would serve well) and first play the subject wherever you can find it in its complete form, regardless of what voice it is placed in. Watch for possible inversions, and so forth, and use two hands if you come to a stretto. If you like, repeat the exercise, this time picking traceable fragments of the subject wherever you find them, or adding any important recurring counterpoint or countersubject. Next play each single voice through from beginning to end, noting as you go whether it plays the subject, a counterpoint, a short figure developed in episode, or merely adds a

---

[9] It is interesting to know that in Bach's time it was customary to play organ fugues without any attempt at "registration" of the different parts.

free part. Now play your fugue, and it is quite possible that if you are new to the game you will be amazed by your enriched understanding.

It is always a virtue to hold notes to their full time value and no longer. In polyphony it is a prime necessity, for the very existence of the parts depends on it. A faulty execution in this respect may either reduce two voices to one or add unwelcome extra parts, as in Ex. 23, where the result of releasing the notes of the two-voiced phrase (a) too soon is shown at (b) and the effect of prolonging them unduly at (c):

Ex. 23

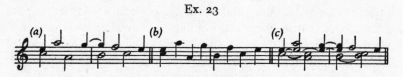

Pianists should always try to imagine passages resembling Ex. 23(a) as sung, not played on a keyboard.

In ordinary playing the correct procedure is usually to give prominence to the melody and subdue the accompaniment. In strict counterpoint there is no such thing as accompaniment, yet the voices are by no means at all times equally important. Generally one voice will claim first place if only for a very short time, for it will carry some melodic figure, motive, or subject until it yields supremacy to another part. Imitation is the presiding genius of counterpoint, canon, and fugue. Hence good performance of polyphony calls for a clear marking of the entrances of subjects. This does not mean that we should mercilessly pound out the theme of a fugue at its every appearance. Why do violence to the composer and at the same time insult the intelligence of the audience? It is extraordinarily helpful, in fact, to remember that the softer the general level of tone the easier it is to make any one voice stand forth. In playing an exceptionally complicated fugue, say the one in E-flat minor, *W.T.C.* I, 8, it is wise to start pianissimo and stay soft whenever possible, reserving marked increases of tone for climactic spots. Of course in any such interpretation the character of the piece would have a strong modifying influence. We should bear in mind, too, that when a theme or motive has been heard often, it becomes familiar and expected. A mere hint, a slight stress on the first note or two, is then enough to indicate its return. There may even be a danger of satiety, in which case a normally subordinate counterpoint may be brought to special notice for the sake of relief. In a close stretto, where it is clearly impossible to play each of two or more parts stronger than all the others, be satisfied to mark the *entering* voices distinctly, trusting the ear to carry on for itself, and in any case at least to get the essential effect of the stretto— namely, a crowding of voices.

In any contrapuntal composition, take advantage of the episodes to lighten up the touch. The function of episodes is to give release from tension and over-seriousness.

Some strait-laced pedagogues have objected to the use of the pedal in the old music on the specious ground that the old instruments had no such thing as a damper pedal. Surely they forget that these in- struments also had no dampers! While the resonance was far less than on the modern piano, there was nothing to stop what there was of it. Everybody has seen a harpist "damp" the strings with his hands to shorten the tone. The harpsichordist could not even do this, so that there was at times considerable blurring of harmonies due to the un- checked resonance. On the piano, of course, tone ends the moment a finger releases the key unless we use the pedal. Whenever you play a piece of the old literature on the piano you are making a transcrip- tion, whether you like it or not. Can anyone imagine old Bach himself, ardent lover of the keyboard, playing on any instrument whatever without availing himself to the utmost of its natural resources?

Another misconception is that we should altogether avoid rubato in playing old music. This is as erroneous historically as it is ugly musically. All emotional music requires the rhythmical freedom that we call rubato, with the possible exception of the exalted passion of religious moods. I think it safe to assert that no music more inevitably rubato than the Chromatic Fantasia has ever been penned. Talking once with Arnold Dolmetsch, an acknowledged authority, after listen- ing to one of his memorable concerts, I expressed my pleasure in the freedom of his performance. "Why, of course," he said, "the old fel- lows played much more rubato than we do." Bear in mind that the metronome (incidentally, the most abjectly unmusical of instruments) did not exist in those days. Its invention has conceivably had much to do with the fact that we have made something of a fetish of strict time.

The old writers gave almost no directions for tempo, phrasing, or inflection to the player, because music was at first taught almost en- tirely by oral tradition. To the real musician this is more of a help than a hindrance, for the internal evidence of a piece is the best possi- ble guide to its interpretation. The student, however, will usually welcome help in making decisions where he feels a modest distrust of his own judgment. For information on the various editions of Bach see the section at the end of this chapter.

No Bach enthusiast need be dismayed by the abundant ornaments in his piano works or by the confusion that has always existed, from his day to ours, as to their correct rendering. I was once a great stickler for the strict tradition as I understood it. As I grow older I am less positive of my infallibility, and in this spirit of humility I offer the following comforting suggestions to the earnest but maybe puzzled student:

1. The very essence of an ornament is that it is something *inessential*. Hence it is no fatal disaster even if you get a few of them wrong.

2. Most ornaments have lost much of the importance they originally possessed. The harpsichord was incapable of accents, and their place was quite customarily taken by a mordent or pralltriller; this gave a sort of fillip to the note. Again, it was impossible to sustain a tone on the harpsichord for even a moderate time, and accordingly most long notes were embellished by trills to keep them going. When we transfer this music to the piano we can give accents at will and prolong the tone very considerably, so the *raison d'être* of the ornaments tends to vanish. It is not surprising that all good harpsichordists are painstaking in the execution of details so appropriate to their instrument. But as for the pianist, one of the best rules for playing ornaments is "When in doubt, leave 'em out." This applies with special force to graces of doubtful authenticity and to cases where *two* ornaments are placed over a single note. One may add another valuable rule: of two optional versions, choose the simpler and less embellished. This is wise, for example, in the Prelude in C-sharp minor, *W.T.C.* I, 4, and in the Chromatic Fantasia.

3. Most modern pianists, editors, and dictionaries have agreed (or might we say conspired?) to construe the pralltriller as what is called in English an "inverted mordent." It commonly goes by that name and is practically universally so played—namely, as a single shake with the auxiliary note above instead of with the note below as in the mordent. Bach's own idea of the pralltriller, however, was that it should begin on the note above, thus:

Ex. 24

Pralltriller   Inverted Mordent (or Schneller)   Mordent

For the sake of completeness I have given in Ex. 24 the execution of pralltriller, inverted mordent, and mordent. The notation is based on performance in a moderate tempo.

Taking a broad view of history, it is a fair question whether either the world of music or Bach's reputation as a composer has suffered appreciably from our misreading of the pralltriller.

4. Let me translate freely a passage from the preface to the *Urtext* of the French and English Suites, written for the Breitkopf edition by Ernst Neumann:

"Correct musical instinct and sound judgment must always decide the interpretation of the various ornaments, for Bach evidently moved with considerable freedom in this field, which in his time [*sic*] was in no small confusion. Strict application of the rules later[1] formulated by Philipp E. Bach, Marpurg, and Türk would therefore be out of place. To avoid lack of taste in playing Bach, the time values of the appoggiaturas, the length of the trills, and the rhythmical division of all graces must be governed by fine musical intuition, not by rule of thumb."

5. Please do not think that I would encourage carelessness or mere caprice. Bach's ornaments are a part of Bach's style, and a completely inappropriate rendering of them offends as Moorish arabesque would offend Norman architecture. There is one detail, for instance, in which the amateur may with a minimum of effort establish a cardinal point of accuracy, one on which, moreover, scholars are in absolute agreement: the first note of all ornaments, appoggiaturas, shakes, or trills, invariably falls on (not before) the beat. Consistent observance of this rule goes a long way toward an intelligent idiom.

6. It is often difficult to determine the value that should be given to an appoggiatura. The so-called *short appoggiatura,* properly an *acciaccatura* (crushed note), is simple enough; it should be played as short as possible, without any time value whatever and therefore preferably together with its main note. It is written as a small-type eighth-note intersected by a stroke, ♪. The appoggiatura proper, or *long appoggiatura,* may be written in almost any time value, ♩, ♪, ♪, or ♪, and the best rule for performance is to play it *exactly as long as written,* on the beat, however, and deduct the value from the principal note. The rule ordinarily given—namely, that the appoggiatura re-

---

[1] I hope the reader will relish with me this "later."

ceives half the value of the principal note—is very unreliable and subject to innumerable exceptions hard to remember.

7. Observe particularly that in the old notation the value of the dot was variable; it might be more or less than half the value of the preceding note. For instance, ♩♪ must often be read ♩ ♪ or ♩.. ♪ , and ♩. ♫♫ becomes ♩ ♫♫♫ . See *W.T.C.* I, 5 and many examples in the suites and partitas. It was only later that the dot acquired a theoretically strict value of exactly half of the preceding note.

Finally, it is well to remember that on the harpsichord it was customary to arpeggiate all full chords to avoid the unpleasant clang of many strings plucked simultaneously.

The Suites and Partitas

BACH had a curious fondness for writing pieces in sets of six and multiples of six. Among the well-known collections of this kind are six French Suites, six English Suites, six partitas, six concertos, and of course the celebrated Forty-eight Preludes and Fugues for clavier, six sonatas or suites for violin alone, six suites for cello alone, six sonatas for clavier and violin, six sonatas for clavier and flute, six sonatas and eighteen preludes and fugues for organ, eighteen chorales, and the six Brandenburg Concertos.

It is still more curious that for some of these hexads Bach adopted a style and form peculiar to the group and possibly never used elsewhere. The Brandenburg Concertos, the sonatas for violin and flute with clavier, and the three groups of clavier suites and partitas, all have marked individual characteristics distinguishing them from each other and from the rest of Bach's works. It is hardly strenuous and extraordinarily rewarding to make a comparative examination of the French and English Suites and the partitas in illustration of this point. Taking first the most constant features, we find that Bach's general conception of the suite or partita was that of a series of pieces in dance form and in the same key. This was not invariable. In the larger suites the dances were preceded by a prelude, usually in brilliant pianistic style, and for melodic relief an "air" was sometimes inserted. As to key, the only departure from uniformity was in the alternative movements of dances accompanied by what we now call a "trio," such as gavottes, bourrées, and minuets; here minor might be changed to major or vice versa. Bach also followed a fairly regular order in the sequence of the dances: first came an allemande, next a corrente (or courante), then a sarabande, and at the end a gigue. Between the sarabande and the gigue he always placed at least one other movement, sometimes more; in this optional position came such favorites as the gavotte, bourrée, and minuet, or less common dances like the passepied and polonaise.

Turning now to the points of dissimilarity, we have at once a hint of intimacy in the title *French or Smaller Suites* and a claim to greater importance for the *English or Larger Suites*. In the former set the movements are shorter but often more numerous; though there is no opening prelude, there may be as many as four movements between sarabande and gigue. The French Suite in E, for instance, contains in this optional space a Gavotte, a Polonaise, a Bourrée, and a Minuet. The six English Suites, on the other hand, all begin with a Prelude written (except for the first, in A major) in a distinctive form with identical opening and closing sections and a digressive middle part. There is never more than one piece between the Sarabande and the Gigue, and all the movements are cast in a larger mold than that of the French Suites.

While the French and English Suites closely follow patterns of their own, the partitas are remarkable rather for their *irregularity*. Each has an introductory movement, but no two of them are named alike; in the first Partita it is a Præludium, in the next a Sinfonia, in the third a Fantasia; then come an Overture, a Preambulum, and finally a Toccata. Not only the names, but the forms too vary greatly. I must leave it to the interested reader to discover other divergences from Bach's normal procedure, such as the use of a Capriccio instead of a gigue as the last number of the second Partita and the placing of an Aria between the Corrente and the Sarabande in the fourth. Everywhere there is a greater freedom and expansion of form than in the suites, and the rhythmical treatment, especially in the allemandes and correntes, is far more elaborate. From internal evidence alone we could with full assurance assign the partitas to a late period of Bach's activity, and in fact they were written at Leipzig, the suites dating from his residence at Cöthen. This is the more striking because it is seldom possible from internal evidence to determine even approximate dates for Bach's compositions. Few indeed show signs on the one hand of immaturity or on the other of the abstruseness of a "third period" of genius.

For a proper understanding of the suites and partitas, the student should acquaint himself with the characteristic features of the various dances. Here is a minimum summary of information:

1. Dance form in general: a piece in two sections, each repeated; the first ending on the dominant, the second on the tonic; the second part often longer than the first.

2. *Allemande.* A somewhat stately movement, usually in moderately flowing sixteenth-notes, each section beginning with either one or three upbeat sixteenths. $\frac{4}{4}$ time.

3. *Corrente* or *Courante.* A "running" piece, as the name implies. There are two distinct forms of it. The first is nearly always[2] in $\frac{3}{2}$ time with many dotted rhythms and with the peculiarity that the last measure of each section denies the signature by changing to $\frac{6}{4}$ time. The upbeat is a single note. In the other and freer form the time may be $\frac{3}{8}$, $\frac{3}{4}$, or $\frac{9}{8}$; the typical motion is in rapid sixteenths or triplet eighths, with an upbeat of one or three notes. In rare cases a courante is followed by a "double" (variation). The A major English Suite quite exceptionally has *two* Courantes, to the second of which are appended two Doubles.

4. *Sarabande.* The slow movement of the suite, in $\frac{3}{4}$ time, beginning without upbeat and with a tendency to pause on the second beat. Supposedly of Spanish origin. The "agréments" following the sarabandes of some suites are highly ornamented repetitions; often they are omitted in performance, or the ornamented version is alternated in both sections with the plainer statement.

5. *Gavotte. Grove's Dictionary*[3] states erroneously that the gavotte and the bourrée may be distinguished from each other by the $\frac{4}{4}$ time of the former and the *alla breve* of the latter. *All* of the gavottes in these suites and partitas, however, are in *alla* breve time. Nevertheless it is true that the gavotte was orginally a sedate, courtly dance.

---

[2] Two pieces of Bach necessitate the "nearly": the Courante of the B minor French Suite is written in $\frac{6}{4}$ time, and the Corrente of the Partita in D, though bearing a $\frac{3}{2}$ signature, actually scans as $\frac{6}{4}$. [Few people seem to realize that Bach in some of the Courantes juxtaposes $\frac{6}{4}$ and $\frac{3}{2}$ times in the same measure (French Suite in B minor, measures 11 and 12; also in the D major Partita). This mixing of $\frac{6}{4}$ and $\frac{3}{2}$ meters is supposed to be derived from an old Spanish dance form, and is beautifully illustrated in Debussy's *"Masques"* (two measures of $\frac{6}{8}$ followed by two in $\frac{3}{4}$).]

[3] Under the article "Bourrée," fourth edition.

It always begins on the third quarter-note of a measure. Often there is an alternative movement marked Gavotte II or Musette, and this may be in contrasting mode.

6. *Bourrée. Alla breve* time, livelier and more rustic than the gavotte and beginning on the fourth quarter-note of the measure instead of the third. It often has an alternative movement marked Bourrée II.

7. *Minuet (Menuet).* $\frac{3}{4}$ time. Originally a graceful, courtly dance, but in the suite usually of faster tempo. Another of the dances often accompanied by a second minuet or trio. Bach begins his minuets on the first beat of the measure. Later, in Beethoven, we shall find a preference for starting on the third beat.

Here it may be well to explain that the word *trio* has two meanings in music. In the original and more restricted sense it was a movement written for three instruments or in three parts. Later, and more freely, the name was applied to any alternative movement to a dance, so that we speak currently of the trio of a minuet, scherzo, or march. It has always been the custom to repeat the main movement after the trio, and the pianist should observe this *da capo* even when it is not specifically directed.

8. *Gigue.* A fast finale to the suite or partita written in one of many possible time signatures, $\frac{3}{8}$, $\frac{6}{8}$, $\frac{9}{16}$, $\frac{12}{8}$, $\frac{12}{16}$, and even common time and $\frac{2}{1}$. There is usually but not always a single note of upbeat. An outstanding peculiarity of Bach's gigues is that he often wrote them in fugal form, in which case it was his habit to use the inversion of the subject for the second half. In the Gigue of the G major Partita a new theme begins the second section and the two subjects are finally combined as in a double fugue. The Gigue of the English Suite in D minor is an extraordinary contrapuntal stunt in which the second part presents a free *thematic and contrapuntal* inversion of the first.

Being founded on dance tunes, the suites and partitas abound in lighter, gayer moods than the majority of the more strictly contrapuntal writings of Bach. They offer an ideal field for keyboard browsing, since the amateur is under no obligation to perform them in their entirety but may pick out any single gavotte or gigue that strikes his fancy and without reproach play it as an excerpt. In the hope, however, that every pianist will wish to study at least one complete suite, let me recommend the charming example in G major, No. 5 of the French series. This is said to have been a favorite with Chopin, who liked to practice Bach rather than his chosen program immediately before playing in public.

FRENCH SUITE IN G

Play the Allemande in moderate time, say *andante con moto*, legato, melodiously and expressively. Be careful to give full time value (in this and all allemandes) to the long concluding note of each section. The Courante may go as fast and brilliantly as you please. It is appropriate to play the sixteenth-notes legato and almost all the eighth-notes staccato for contrast. In the Sarabande, reflect that Bach had a big heart as well as a great mind. This is romantic music, so give it all the feeling you have. Do not hesitate to use the pedal for enhancement of singing effect. A child can play the Gavotte well; all it needs is naturalness and a spirit of enjoyment. The Bourrée is tricky and takes practice, though simple enough to the eye. In the Loure we meet a rare and obscurely named dance. There was a kind of bagpipe called a loure, and some authorities describe the dance as a kind of gigue, but these facts offer no suggestion even remotely fitting the style of this piece, which is formally sedate, as if the author had donned court dress and periwig. The flowing bass definitely precludes the idea of a bagpipe drone. It seems much more probable that the title is associated with the French word *louré*, meaning slurred, legato. The final Gigue bubbles with gaiety; the fugal style cannot o'er-crow its merry spirit. Movements of this type should be played with resilient fingers, *quasi staccato* in spite of the speed.

For the execution of the ornaments in the Allemande, Sarabande, and so on, consult the table of graces in the prefatory note of the Steingräber edition, which is exceptionally simple and accurate as far as it goes.

The six French Suites (in D minor, C minor, B minor, E flat, G, and E) are all charming and all only moderately difficult. In a well-rounded course of study they may be placed between the *Three-part Inventions* and *The Well-Tempered Clavier* or interspersed between the easier and harder preludes and fugues. Most popular of the English Suites are Nos. 2 and 3, in A minor and G minor; those in F and E minor, however, are equally good and effective. The last, in D minor, is the longest, finest, and most difficult of the set. Two *Suites pour le clavecin*, not included in either series of six, are usually printed after the French Suites; they are very seldom played.

The partitas are extraordinarily fine in invention and workman-

ship. They call for the expert performance of a trained pianist and
Bach-player. The First and Second Partitas, in B flat and C minor,
are best known to students and public. Mature artists prefer the
magnificent Partitas in D and E minor. Appended to the series is a
less familiar *Ouverture nach französischer Art* or Partita in B minor.

The Toccatas and Miscellaneous Works

A TOCCATA (the word is derived from the Italian *toccare,* to touch)
is usually defined as a piece calculated to display the touch and execution of the performer. It is distinguished by the maintenance of a
rapid, undeviating motion in sixteenth-notes, and partakes of the
character of an extended étude. Fine specimens of the genre have
been provided by Paradies, Schumann, Debussy, Ravel, and Prokofiev; a more mechanical example by Czerny held a long sway as a
nut for students to crack. In this sense several of the preludes from
the *W.T.C.* have been described above as of the toccata type. The
pieces for clavier and organ entitled Toccatas by Bach deviate widely
from this conception. They are more in the nature of fantasias in
several movements or connected sections, largely improvisational,
and they almost invariably contain at least one slow movement and
one fugue. The internal evidence proves incontestably that they
were intended for performance on the harpsichord. We find in them
the utmost diversity of rhythm instead of the persistent movement
of the toccata as generally understood. Their fugues are far more
extemporaneous in quality, far less strict in workmanship, than those
of *The Well-Tempered Clavier.* They may digress into purely harmonic
episodes, and they quite commonly end with a few measures of free
fantasia by way of coda. The answers to the subjects are often so
irregular in comparison with Bach's normal practice as to seem eccentric. A few conspicuous instances are quoted below:

Ex. 25

Both fugue themes from the D minor Toccata are answered in the octave instead of the dominant. Note the relationship of the subjects at (a).

Ex. 26

Here there is no attempt at a tonal answer, although the beginning of the subject would ordinarily call for it.

Ex. 27

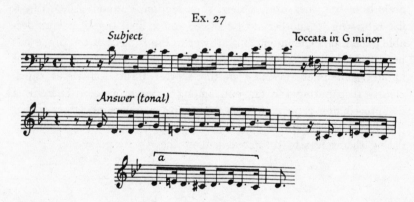

Example 27 is a unique instance of the prolongation of a fugue theme in the answer; see the measure marked (a). The longer form is adhered to in most of the subsequent entrances.

The best of the toccatas, in my judgment, are those in C minor, D major, and G minor. I shall therefore describe them in some detail.

Toccata in C minor. A free introduction of eleven measures precedes an expressive Adagio, which should be played with grave decorum. There follows a long fugue, aptly characterized by Busoni as "somewhat loquacious." Just when a brief cadenza leads us to expect the end, the fugue takes on a new lease of life, introduces a new counterpoint and more complicated rhythms, and continues at greater length than before, ending with a few more measures of fantasia. It needs crisp playing with all possible variety of tone; otherwise it will sound monotonous. The performer need not hesitate to slow down imperceptibly when the thirty-second notes threaten a hurried effect.

Toccata in D major. This is one of Bach's happiest moods. Ten measures of fantasia lead to an Allegro of great decision, giving opportunity for grateful contrasts of forte and piano. The next movement is an Adagio of more serious tone, followed by a longish movement in informal fugal style and ending in another passage of pure fantasia. In this place Bach's direction *con discrezione* should probably be interpreted "discretely" rather than "discreetly"; that is, well separated in the phrasing, as indicated in the original. Needless to say, all the obviously extemporaneous portions of the toccata should be played in very free time; the Chromatic Fantasia will serve excellently as a model for the style. The final fugue may be dashed off with bacchanalian jollity, though a measured tempo is in order.

Toccata in G minor. The form may be analyzed thus: a flourishing prelude of four measures, a short slow section, a quaint Allegro in B flat returning to another slow section, and a final fugue of considerable expansion. The anomalous answer to the subject of the fugue has been remarked on above (see Ex. 27). Bach makes it a source of humor, sometimes reverting to the shorter form, sometimes capriciously distributing the tag end among different voices. There is a definite counter-exposition with the theme in inversion. Observe that the dotted rhythms must be played throughout as triplets, accommodating themselves to the movement of the counterpoints:

Ex. 28

It is essential for the interpreter to participate whole-heartedly in Bach's sense of fun.

Coming now to the miscellaneous pieces of Bach, it will be sufficient to comment on five.

The Italian Concerto, or, to give it its full title, the *Concerto in the Italian Style, for Clavicembalo* (i.e., for harpsichord), is a solo piece written on the plan of the concertos with accompaniment of string orchestra. It has, like them, three movements, marked in this case Allegro, Andante, Presto. The concerto form of the period appears in the *tutti*-like[4] recurring themes of the first and last movements and in the *ostinato* bass of the Andante. In recommending this delightful piece to the special attention of amateurs, I may point out that they will for once have the advantage of explicit guidance to its interpretation from Bach himself. It is seldom indeed that the great master favors us by so much as a general tempo mark. Here he not only gives distinctive headings to the three movements but frequently writes *forte* and *piano* to indicate contrasts between loud and soft sections, and balance of tone between melody and accompaniment. Originally, of course, these fortes and pianos referred to the two-manualed harpsichord, so that the pianist must apply some discretion in the degree of prominence he gives to the melody. Little need be added to Bach's own instructions. The first movement is virile and cheerful. The opening theme may be variously phrased:

Ex. 29

and

are both good; personally I prefer the first. Bischoff's note that the soulful Andante should be played in the manner of a violin solo, availing oneself of all gradations of tone, may well be laid to heart. Observe the exceeding beauty of the coda (the last five measures), which may be played a little slower than the rest. The eighth-notes of the Presto should be faster than the sixteenths of the Allegro; ¢ would be a better signature than C.[5] Beware throughout of redundant

----

[4] In the concerto, a *tutti* is a passage played by the orchestra, in contradistinction to the solo parts. In symphonic parlance, a *tutti* is a passage in which the full orchestra is employed.

[5] C, *tempo ordinario*, equals $\frac{4}{4}$, the player or conductor to count or beat four quarter-notes to the measure. ¢, *alla breve*, equals, $\frac{2}{2}$, meaning to count or beat two half-notes. ¢ therefore denotes a faster tempo than C.

rallentandos at the many cadences; the slightest broadening is sufficient to sign off the sections and clarify the form to the listener.

Fantasia in C minor. A recital program might fitly open with this manly, energetic piece. It is not a fantasia of the improvisatory type, but has the general fixed form of Bach's dance movements, two repeating sections closing respectively on dominant and tonic. There is, however, a more than rudimentary second subject. A sturdy touch, not too legato, is appropriate, with a more clinging effect and more pedal in the second subject (where the crossing of the hands begins). The mordent of the first measure should be taken with F natural, not F sharp, the old rule for all ornaments being to use the diatonic second below or above unless otherwise marked by an accidental. Short trills like the one for the right hand at the end of the first measure sound best when played with an exact number of notes, in this case twelve, beginning with the auxiliary note above. Long trills, on the contrary, are best executed with an indefinite number of notes, quite independently of the movement of other parts. An unusual ornament, , occurs at the beginning of the eighth measure. The correct performance is to lengthen the first auxiliary note, F natural, before starting the trill, regardless of the clashing dissonance with the F sharp of the bass.

The "Goldberg" Variations, properly, *Aria with Thirty Transformations* (*Veränderungen*). The common title is based on an amusing story. A certain Freiherr von Kayserling suffered badly from chronic insomnia and retained Johann Gottlieb Goldberg, a pupil of Bach, to solace his uneasy nights with music. Goldberg was a distinguished player of clavier and organ, blessed with a phenomenal virtuosity; Bach thought highly of his talent and diligence. Count Kayserling conceived the happy idea of commissioning Bach to write a piece of "soothing music for the clavier," and the composer filled the order by turning out a masterpiece. The Count must have been a dilettante of rare taste, for he took great delight in the work, affectionately called it "his" variations, and often asked Goldberg to play it. To his credit be it further recorded that he repaid Bach with a very handsome fee, giving him a golden goblet and one hundred louis d'or. Later he rendered the master a signal service by recommending him for a position at the court of Saxony.

This titanic piece, requiring nearly an hour for a complete performance, presents enormous difficulties to the player. Indeed, I have heard more than one competent artist flatly assert that it is impossible on the piano, this in face of the fact that at least James Friskin and Rosalyn Tureck play it without the omission or alteration of a single note. In any case, it is no morsel for the amateur, or even for any professional not a devotee. A poor rendition would go far toward inducing the slumber so elusive to the suffering patron.

Bach has intimated in a number of the variations whether they were intended for one manual or two of the harpsichord. In others he offers a choice or says nothing. Nine of them, as already noted, are strict canons at various intervals from the unison to the ninth. Many are astonishingly modern in their bravura technique; others, including some of the canons, are of touching beauty. The piece ends with a *quodlibet* preserving the general form and harmonization of the original Aria while interweaving two folk songs.

Capriccio in B flat (On the departure of his beloved brother). Bach was a confirmed writer of program music. The church cantatas and the sacred music in general are full of symbolic figures representing variously grief, joy, peace, and the like. There are many "step"-motives illustrating ascent, descent, confidence, weariness, or hesitation, and so on. Specific words often receive definite treatment wherever they occur. In the *St. Matthew Passion,* every word uttered by Jesus is accompanied by sustained chords on the strings, contrasting vividly with the drier harpsichord chords allotted to the recitatives of the Evangelist. If all this is not program music in the ordinary sense, it is a method of characterizing moods and emphasizing the text comparable in every way with the use of the leitmotiv. The Capriccio in B flat goes farther; it is a frank story-telling in music with a fairly elaborate "program" or explanation furnished by the composer. The movements are headed as follows:

a) His friends coax him[6] to desist from the journey.
b) They represent to him the dangers of traveling. (In those days it was a formidable undertaking.)
c) A general lament of the friends.
d) Seeing that he is immovable, they assemble to bid him farewell.
e) Air of the postilion (who has come for his passenger).
f) Fugue in imitation of the postilion's bugle.

The musical value of this *jeu d'esprit* is far higher than might be

---

[6] The brother, Johann Jakob, was setting out to enlist as an oboe-player in the Swedish army of Charles XII.

expected from the description, and as program music it stands head and shoulders above any previous work of the kind for piano. It is easily within the powers of a good amateur.

Prelude, Fugue, and Allegro in E flat. A charming piece, designated for performance on lute or clavier. Note the compass, from BB flat to e" flat, adapted to the lute. Observe too the happy surprise of the modulation from the chord of F-flat major to

Ex. 30

nine measures from the end of the Prelude.

The Chamber Music and Concertos

BESIDES the works for clavier alone, attention should be directed to Bach's chamber music and concertos. The six sonatas for violin and piano, apart from their great intrinsic beauty, shed light on Bach's conception of the sonata form. They all follow the pattern of four movements, alternately slow, fast, slow, fast. The sonatas for flute and clavier as well as the trios for flute, violin, and clavier are hardly practical for the amateur, since the clavier parts are only written as figured basses, and in no edition that I know have the figured basses been constructed with taste.

The concertos constitute a small literature in themselves. Here is a list of them:

1. *Concerto in D minor for harpsichord and string orchestra,* an important work.

2. *Six concertos for harpsichord and string orchestra,* rather slight in structure, but charming. Those in E, F minor, and A are particularly good. These concertos are seldom played with orchestra and sound rather ineffective in two-piano arrangements.

3. *Two concertos for two harpsichords and string orchestra, in C and C minor,* both very fine. The C major Concerto has a slow move-

ment for the harpsichords alone, and in the splendid final fugue the entrance of the orchestra is delayed for some time. The piece sounds well for two pianos unaccompanied.

4. *Two Concertos for three harpsichords and string orchestra, in D minor and C.* That in D minor is the only one of the multiple concertos giving the most important role to the first piano. For this reason it is especially suitable for performance by amateurs or by a master and two good students. The other three-piano concerto is one of Bach's best works and is often heard from distinguished artists.

5. *Concerto in A minor for four harpsichords and string orchestra,* transcribed by Bach from a concerto by Vivaldi for four violins.

6. The fifth *Brandenburg Concerto,* in D, has *concertante* parts for harpsichord, flute, and violin. This magnificent work is conspicuous for the great interest and difficulty of the piano solo.

7. The *Concerto in A minor for harpsichord, flute, and violin concertante with string orchestra* is similar in every respect to the fifth Brandenburg Concerto.

8. A *Concerto in F for harpsichord and two flutes concertante with string orchestra.* This piece is little known.

9. The *Sixteen Concertos after Vivaldi,* arranged for clavier alone by Bach for his own study, may be ignored except possibly as reading material.

Transcriptions of Bach

[WE HAVE somewhat outlived programming Bach transcriptions in recitals, and yet pianists have been able through them to get acquainted with much organ and violin music of great beauty, strength, and grandeur. It would be unwise to eliminate this part of our literature. But in the interest of musicology and music itself, I suggest that performers lay aside the once popular but now dated and partly incorrect Tausig transcription of the Organ Toccata and Fugue in D minor and, in its place, do honor to the one that Busoni created with a much finer ear for organ sonorities.

The three series of Bach "Adaptations" by the late gifted American pianist Walter Rummel are extremely rich, nearly symphonic in sound. Most of these transcriptions are from cantatas, and they were heard a great deal in Europe, especially in England. A very good transcription of the other organ (Dorian) Toccata and Fugue in D minor by Joseph Prostakoff (Schirmer, 1961) should interest advanced students. A major work. Another very effective transcription of the Vivaldi-Friedemann Bach Concerto Grosso in D minor by Ray Lev (Carl Fischer) is also recommended for performance. It will let us forget the monstrous version of Stradal.

Carl Fischer has discovered a new transcriber from the organ to the piano, Dr. Arthur Briskier, an eminent organist whose informative booklet, *New Approach to Piano Transcriptions and Interpretation of Johann Sebastian Bach's Music* (Carl Fischer) is sincerely recommended. Dr. Briskier has offered the Fantasy and Fugue in G minor, the Prelude and Fugue in B minor (known as "The Great"), the Passacaglia and Fugue in C minor, and the Fugue in G minor (known as "The Little"). These new transcriptions are made with much care. They hold close to the manuscript, which, in the case of the Passacaglia and Fugue, is reproduced completely in facsimile. In the B minor Prelude and Fugue the facsimile of Bach's manuscript is printed right next to the transcription, page by page. There is only one facsimile page of the G minor Fugue, and it is not in Bach's handwriting, though very imitative of it, seemingly from the hands of a pupil. It takes an accomplished performer to do justice to this new way of transcribing. He must be endowed with a bright mind, a large hand, and a good ear for held notes and must be a virtuoso in the simultaneous use of the sustaining and damper pedals. Fingerings are decidedly derived from organ-playing. As to octave-playing in the left hand, I myself am more interested in the legato of the thumb than in the silent changing of fingers on the low notes of the octave. Is not the thumb the melodic line? After all there is such a thing as pedal legato in modern piano-playing. I feel that the Briskier version of the Chromatic Fantasy and Fugue is overedited. There are too many slurs where the word legato would be sufficient and some unnecessary continuity-breaking phrasings (page 9, second line, and page 13, fifth line). And why all the solid, un-arpeggioed chords in the Fantasy? I have concluded after many years of research and study that performers in the baroque era hardly ever played a solid chord. The purpose of the arpeggio was to enable the listener to hear all the notes of the chord. Consult the E-flat minor Prelude or the last measure of the E minor Fugue in Book I of *The Well-Tempered Clavier*. I may as well make another very personal statement about performance. I believe that all pianists (perhaps with rare exceptions) from Beethoven up to the time of Busoni's appearance—including Clara Schumann (Sigismund Stojowski and Isidor Philipp heard her),

Paderewski, Harold Bauer, Ossip Gabrilowitch, and even Franz
Liszt and such of his disciples as Emil von Sauer, Moriz Rosenthal,
Eugène d'Albert, just to mention those whom I heard often—always
played the left hand ahead of the right.]

Countless transcriptions of Bach exist. I shall list only a few of
the best.

D'ALBERT.	Passacaglia in C minor (originally for organ)
	Prelude and Fugue in D (organ)
BAUER.	Partita in B flat
	Concertos for two and three pianos, arranged with incorporation of the orchestral accompaniment in the solo parts
BUSONI.	Chaconne (violin)
	Toccata in C (organ)
	Toccata and Fugue in D minor (organ)
	Prelude and Fugue in D (organ)
	Ten Choral Preludes (organ)
GODOWSKY.	Three Sonatas (violin) and three Suites (cello)
MYRA HESS.	*Jesu, Joy of Man's Desiring* (organ choral prelude)
VAN KATWIJK.	Prelude in E (violin)
LISZT.	Fantasia and Fugue in G minor (organ)
	Six Preludes and Fugues (organ)
REGER.	Choral Preludes (organ)
OLGA SAMAROFF-STOKOWSKI.	Fugue in G minor, the "Lesser" (organ)
SAINT-SAËNS.	Twelve Pieces (violin, church cantatas, etc.)
SILOTI.	Prelude in G minor (organ)
TAUSIG.	Toccata and Fugue in D minor (organ)

Add to these a number of arrangements for two pianos by Bauer,
Guy Maier, Philipp, Rheinberger, Siloti, etc.

Editions

The volumes of the Bach-Gesellschaft, published by Breitkopf &
Härtel, are the standard authority for all Bach's works. These, however, are accessible only in well-stocked libraries, where they should
be consulted on doubtful points.

The most practical edition of the piano works that can be wholly trusted by the student is that of Hans Bischoff, published by Stein-gräber. A unique feature of this scholarly edition is that it furnishes in footnotes a harmony of important variations in the various manu-scripts and other sources. The Steingräber edition is now unprocur-able, but it is effectively replaced by the reprints of Edwin Kalmus, in which the footnotes are conveniently translated into English.

Kroll's edition (Peters) of the *W.T.C.* presents an uncorrupted text without any additions whatever of dynamics, phrasing, or com-mentary.

The French and English Suites were reprinted in an *Urtext* by Breitkopf & Härtel.

The edition of the *W.T.C.* by Harold Samuel and Donald Francis Tovey prints an authentic, unadorned text in two volumes, and the illuminating comments of Tovey in two separate volumes.

Busoni has edited for Schirmer the Inventions and the first part of the *W.T.C.* with elaborate notes and directions for interpretation, inter-esting to all musicians and useful to teachers and students needing a guide. Busoni[7] completed this edition by adding the second part of the *W.T.C.* and the toccatas, suites, and partitas. Though Busoni's instruc-tions may be over-analytical, dogmatic, and occasionally arbitrary, they are offered by a deeply thoughtful artist and scholar, and the student may safely and willingly follow them. Other works of Bach edited by Busoni, such as the "Goldberg" Variations, the Capriccio in B flat, etc., partake more of the nature of transcriptions than editions of the originals.

The editions of Mugellini (Colombo, formerly Ricordi) are like-wise scholarly, but so overloaded with analytical notes that the com-ment almost buries the text.

The Czerny edition of the piano works (Peters) was the first to

---

[7] [I well remember my beloved and revered friend and teacher, the late Ferruccio Busoni, saying how well he realized that his editions of Bach's two-voice and three-voice Inventions (Schirmer) as well as of the first volume of *The Well-Tempered Clavier* (Schirmer) were overedited as to phrasings, finger-ings, dynamics, and pedals, results of overanxious youthful enthusiasm. But we also know that the footnotes in these three publications, and especially the Appendix to Volume I of the Preludes and Fugues, hold rare values and inspiring information for the Bach student and Bach scholar. He then added: "Wait until you see my edition of the second volume of *The Well-Tempered Clavier*, in which the Bach text has been left alone and where I, Busoni, have added ever so little." I own this out-of-print Breitkopf & Härtel edition, which has been replaced by a Carl Fischer publication as "revised by Busoni and Egon Petri," his late eminent disciple. However, this later edition is strangely overphrased and over-fingered, and is a long, long way from the Urtext as published by Kalmus and by Peters (Landshoff for the Inventions, Kroll for the two volumes of the forty-eight Preludes and Fugues).]

become widely known and did a great service in making Bach familiar to the musical world. Czerny claimed that his dynamics and phrasing of the *W.T.C.* were based on Beethoven's interpretations. Though the inaccurate text has been superseded by later research and access to sources unknown to Czerny, his edition has historical importance and is still widely used by the older generation of teachers.

Bülow's editions of the Chromatic Fantasy and Fugue, Italian Concertos, etc., cannot be recommended for either accuracy or style.

The edition of the *W.T.C.* by Casella is well worth consulting.

[The first step leading to our Declaration of Musical Independence from European Publishers took place when the University of Michigan reprinted the more than forty volumes containing the complete works of Bach as published by the Bach Gesellschaft through Breitkopf & Härtel. This great German undertaking had begun in 1850, some twenty years after Bach had been rediscovered by Mendelssohn. The new and immensely active German publishing house of Bärenreiter, mentioned previously, is eminently interested in the publication of Urtexts of baroque and classical works, and is in the process of re-publishing the complete works of Bach in an ultimate, final edition. Some ten volumes have already appeared, one sixth or one seventh of the entire project.

Urtext editions of the piano works of Bach are available from several American publishers. Kalmus reprinted the out-of-print Steingräber edition, the editor of which was the eminent German Bach scholar, Hans Bischoff. The unique feature of this publication is that it furnishes in footnotes the important variants in the manuscripts and other sources. The Peters edition of *The Well-Tempered Clavier*, both volumes, edited by Franz Kroll, is highly recommended. Kroll, another German Bach authority, presents the text uncorrupted, without any additions of dynamics, phrasing, or commentary except a few good fingerings. Peters has published the Urtext of the French and English suites and partitas as well as the clavier concertos in E major and A major, the F-minor Concerto being badly overedited by Robert Teichmüller. Schirmer is offering the Urtext of *The Well-Tempered Clavier* according to the Bischoff edition. An outstanding contribution of distinct authority to popularize the Bach Urtext is the volume of the two-part Inventions and Sinfonias by Ludwig Landshoff (Peters), with a very important and informative supplement. An interesting and authoritative edition of the "Goldberg" Variations by Ralph Kirkpatrick can be considered the ultimate advice for the understanding and performance of this gigantic work.

The House of Durand in Paris has the Urtext of the complete works of Bach's keyboard music, absolutely untouched. My urgent recommendation that Carl Czerny's editions be retired is meant in the interest of music in general. This early edition has served well for more than a hundred years, which is a long time. The fact that Czerny studied with Beethoven (1800-1803) and was justifiably impressed by the master's warm and passionate playing of the preludes and fugues and some of the suites accounts for the romantic spirit and overpresence of dynamics that permeate every measure of his editions. The German publisher Henle of Munich issues Urtext editions of the Inventions and of the (three-voice) Sinfonias, the six Partitas, and *The Well-Tempered Clavier*.

Very welcome is the new and excellent Bach edition by the late Swiss pianist and master teacher, Edwin Fischer (1955, Hansen through Schirmer), of the Chromatic Fantasy and Fugue, the Italian Concerto, the French and English suites, the two- and three-voice Inventions and the four piano concertos (A and E major, F and D minor). There are interesting prefaces.

A very important and most valuable contribution to the study of Bach is the 1960 publication by the Oxford University Press of three books by Rosalyn Tureck, *An Introduction to the Performance of Bach*, subtitle: *A Progressive Anthology of Keyboard Music Edited, with Introductory Essays by Rosalyn Tureck*. The essays about "Fingering, Phrasing, Dynamics, Touch, the Function and Use of the Pedals, Ornamentation, Harpsichord, Clavichord and Piano," and finally "Bach's attitude to music and instruments—and ours" are invaluable. What more could an eager Bach-lover or a curious Bach scholar ask for? The musical examples are excellently chosen, knowingly phrased, and wisely fingered (except, it may be, the unnecessary changing of fingers on slowly repeated notes). The first and second pieces are given in the original and then in a realized version. What a valuable lesson for teachers! Books II and III continue the illumination of this perfect approach to Bach playing. With a table of ornaments and direction for the use of the sustaining pedal added, the illustration of the Invention in C major—first the original and then with inverted hands—becomes a telling demonstration in contrapuntal thinking. The rise of Chicago-born Rosalyn Tureck to international fame and recognition is a boon to all those who believe in Bach and to those among them who believe in playing his music on the piano.

And please remember the clarifying saying by Bach's son, Carl

Philipp Emanuel, in his treasured book, *Essay on the True Art of Playing Keyboard Instruments:* "Methinks that music must principally stir the heart, and no true performance on the pianoforte will succeed merely by thumping and drumming, or by continual arpeggio-playing."]

CHAPTER FOUR

From Bach to Beethoven

THERE came a time in the history of music when a revulsion against polyphony set in. No composer arose of a stature to excel the counter-point of Palestrina and Bach. Less gifted writers made canon ridiculous by unmusical essays in eight and nine voices and barren ingenuities like "table" and "riddle" canons. The world yearned for a new, a simpler and more direct medium of tonal expression. Hence the rise and triumph of what we call homophony, in which preference is given to a single melodic line with harmonic accompaniment.

The period of transition is best exemplified in CARL PHILIPP EMANUEL BACH, best known of the Leipzig cantor's sons. Some of his smaller pieces are perennial classroom favorites; the Solfeggietto, the Allegro in F minor, and the Rondo in B minor may confidently be recommended. You must look farther, however, for a just estimate of his importance. Examine the six sonatas edited by Bülow in the Peters edition, or say the two in A minor and G minor, and you will realize that C. P. E. Bach was the pathfinder of the classic sonata form, blazing a trail that was broadened by Haydn to a thoroughfare and by Mozart and Beethoven to a highway. He wrote over two hundred solo pieces, fifty-two concertos, and many sonatas for piano. His *Essay on the True Art of Playing Keyboard Instruments*[1] is deservedly famous as the first orderly exposition of the art.

[Carl Philipp Emanuel Bach's famous book had to wait a long time for an Anglo-Saxon translator, but the delay was worthwhile. W. W. Norton and Co., New York, entrusted William J. Mitchell of Columbia

---

[1] *Ein Versuch über die wahre Art das Clavier zu spielen.*

University with the enormous task of transforming the somewhat old-style German into very distinguished English. The large volume is splendidly printed, with all the musical examples in clear type. English-speaking Bach scholars and lovers of his music should rejoice.]

The other sons of the great Bach, even WILHELM FRIEDEMANN, most talented of them all in the estimation of his father, but the prodigal and disgrace of the family, did little to further the course of piano history. Some of their works will always be found in collections of old music. Wilhelm Friedemann wrote one or two excellent concertos. He stole so unblushingly from Vivaldi that he incurred odium even in a day when liberal borrowing from other composers was generally condoned. The Organ Concerto in D minor that became popular in a piano arrangement by Stradal is now ascribed to Vivaldi. His sonatas and fugues offer little of interest to modern students, but the twelve polonaises contain beautiful numbers. JOHANN CHRISTIAN BACH deserves passing mention, if only for his finely developed Prelude and Fugue in C minor, contained in Isidor Philipp's *Clavecinistes allemands* (Durand edition).

Franz Joseph Haydn (1732–1809)

It was left for HAYDN to establish the sonata and symphony as unmistakable, universally recognized new forms of homophonic composition.

Many of us are still apt, perhaps, to think of Haydn principally as an amiable, rather unsophisticated forerunner of Mozart and Beethoven. This is a complete misconception of his genius, only to be accounted for by the fact that the effortlessness and spontaneity of his writing easily delude us into an impression of naïveté. In truth he was a greater originator than either Mozart or Beethoven: he created the sonata form, they adopted it, expanded it, and experimented with it. It may be thought extravagant to claim the creation of an art form for any one individual, yet in the case of Haydn the assertion seems irrefutable, for it is impossible to discover in earlier writers (including Carl Philipp Emanuel Bach) a true parallel to the structure of his symphonies, sonatas, and quartets. His grouping of measures into periodic units was freer than that of Mozart and Beethoven; they stabilized the eight-bar period, and in the end it threatened a rigidity from which modern composers were driven to rebel. The first section of the double theme of Haydn's F minor Variations, for instance, divides into five periods

of six, six, five, five, and seven measures respectively; while the
themes of Beethoven's variations from the sonatas Opus 26, Opus 109,
and Opus 111 are composed entirely of eight-bar periods, each sub-
divided into two four-bar phrases, excepting only the third period
of the theme in Opus 26, which is extended to ten measures. Again,
Haydn's range of keys was far wider than that of Mozart, whose
sonatas and concertos rarely venture as far as signatures of three
sharps or flats, whereas Haydn is undaunted by tonalities like A flat,
D flat, and C-sharp major and minor. He is equally bold in modulation
and in direct leaps from key to key by simply moving a semitone up or
down, as Beethoven afterwards loved to do. In sufficient proof of this
harmonic daring I need only refer to the first of the thirty-four sonatas,
with its three movements in E flat, E major (sic), and E flat. In the
first movement he introduces his second theme in the conventional
dominant, B flat, but in the development section he springs surprises
on us. Twice he comes to a pause on a G major triad, thence proceeding
to entrances of the second theme, first, with happy effect, in C major
and then, most astonishingly, in the utterly remote key of E major,
eventually stealing back to E flat for the recapitulation by gliding
chromatically from the dominant seventh of B minor to that of E-flat
major. The whole passage merits close study. The C major Fantasia,
too, furnishes several examples of abrupt and effective key transitions.
One may safely believe that Haydn took delight in unexpected effects
of every kind; not to speak of the *Surprise* Symphony with the jolt
of its famous forte chord, what is the finale of the *Farewell* Symphony
but one long-drawn-out mystification?

[I rally wholeheartedly to Dr. Hutcheson's opinion that Haydn
"was a greater originator than either Mozart or Beethoven," both of
whom studied with him at one time. Haydn and the temperamental
young Beethoven did not get along very well with each other. When
asked about the talent of his new pupil, Haydn is supposed to have
answered: "Yes, he has a distinct talent for the piano" (see footnote 2,
on page 80).]

The term "sonata form" may be somewhat misleading to the un-
initiated, for it is used both in reference to the sonata as a whole and,
more strictly, to describe the structure of what is usually the first
movement. In both senses sonata form is the basis of the sonata itself,
of the symphony and classical concerto, and of the trios, quartets,
and so on, of chamber music. The concert overture, in addition, is
written in the first-movement form, omitting the repetition of the
first section. In these pages I shall try to preserve a distinction by

writing *sonata form* in two words when the entire work is concerned and *sonata-form* (hyphenated) when the structure of the first movement only is referred to.

A general definition of the sonata cannot be given. It may have two, three, or four movements, very rarely one or five. Typically, however, it consists of three movements, the first (usually an allegro) in sonata-form, the second a slow movement, variable as to form, the last another fast movement, often in rondo or again in sonata-form. When a fourth movement is added, it will be a minuet or scherzo in dance form, following or occasionally preceding the slow movement. This arrangement is primarily due to Haydn, who gave the first-movement form its modern shape and selected from the known favorites of his time the rondo, the minuet, and the variation form as best suited for possible if not invariable use in the later movements. The rondo was found to be appropriate as a finale; the minuet acquired distinction as the only dance to survive, at least temporarily, in the symphony; and the errant theme with variations served equally well as slow movement or finale, at times even usurping the place of the regular first movement.

Haydn's immense service to music in molding its greatest instrumental form would have availed comparatively little had he not been able to endow the form with beauty, interest, and variety. One may expatiate on his achievement as a pioneer, then, without in any way slighting his creative genius. On both counts his title to fame rests secure.

Haydn wrote voluminously for orchestra, string quartet, and piano. Not all of his works have come down to us; for instance, of twenty concertos and divertimenti for piano and orchestra, only one is extant. [Another Concerto in G major has been published by the International Music Company in the Urtext, arranged for two pianos, while the edition by Nagel (through Bärenreiter) has the piano part in the Urtext and the orchestral score arranged for a second piano. Boosey & Hawkes has published a Concerto in C major. A Concertino in C major is now available in an edition for two pianos by George Anson.] Haydn's piano sonatas have met better fortune, most editions printing thirty-four, Breitkopf & Härtel forty-two. The piano trios have also fared well; of a total of thirty-five, thirty-one are published. A scant dozen of smaller piano solos have been preserved. From this considerable bulk of material most modern pianists, yielding to a natural preference for Mozart and Beethoven, select only a few for their permanent repertoire.

Two of the smaller pieces are noteworthy, the Variations in F minor and the Fantasia in C. The theme of the Variations is dual, having two sections in F minor and F major respectively. There are only two variations on the double theme; these are followed by a long coda beginning with a formal return to the minor theme and continuing with an inspired improvisation. The piece, which was a favorite of Rubinstein and Paderewski, is a model of classic style. The alternating themes with alternating variations foreshadow the slow movement of Beethoven's Ninth Symphony, and the extemporaneous character of the coda is prophetic of the Arietta in the same composer's Sonata Opus 111.[2] The Fantasia in C, a capriccio in extended rondo form, is full of witty quips and quirks. When played with carefree spirit and appreciation of its humor, it is a most effective concert number. [The Variations in F minor and the delightful, frolicking Fantasy in C major can be had in the Henle editions in the Urtext. What a relief from over-edited publications!]

The slim volume of the smaller pieces also includes other sets of variations, two Adagios, and a Capriccio.

Some of Haydn's sonatas are written in the grand manner. Among these are the one in E flat, Opus 78, usually printed as No. 1,[3] that in C minor, No. 10, last of the set published in 1780, and one in A flat, the only sonata in that key. Important, too, is the E-flat Sonata, No. 3, less heroic but beautifully balanced in its three movements. Several others start out with largely molded movements, but fail to sustain an epic quality throughout. Many of the shorter sonatas are held in affectionate regard by amateurs, for example the two in C and D, Nos. 1 and 3 of the 1780 series, and the one in E minor, No. 17. Not less interesting are the three of Opus 13, in C, E, and F respectively, and No. 27, again in E major.

Haydn's sonatas, his greatest contribution to the piano literature, offer an ideal pasture for browsing. It is by no means necessary always to play them complete; often one movement or another will strike us as particularly fascinating and entirely self-sufficient. The rondos are remarkable for their gaiety and esprit. Very seldom do we fail to find flashes of wit and musicianship that redeem the simplest of them from triviality. One can always depend on Haydn, too, for a graceful minuet,

---

[2] Beethoven studied with Haydn but denied that he learned much. His disparagement was unfair alike to pupil and teacher.

[3] I give the numbering of the *Édition classique*, as at the time of writing it is probably the most easily accessible complete edition. Not many of the sonatas bear opus numbers except the set of six, Opus 13, and another set of three, Opus 14. Six more are identifiable as a series "published in 1780."

which may often be placed at the end of a sonata. The sweetness of the man's nature is reflected in his lightest creations. When he adds depth of thought to charm he is truly great, and he was not unlike most later composers in customarily putting his weightier ideas into his first movements or into his Adagios and Andantes.

Haydn's chamber music with piano requires little remark. The trios are seldom played, probably because the cello parts are too uninteresting. Page after page the discouraged instrument does nothing but double the bass of the piano, so that there is little inducement for an accomplished cellist to join in a performance. Once, on a summer vacation, I played through the entire series with an amateur violinist and found very little trouble in supplying at the piano all that was of any significance in the cello part. The best known is the Trio in G major, concluding with the catchy *Gypsy Rondo*—sometimes heard by itself as a popular excerpt. Others have far greater merit; for instance, that in C major.

The sonatas for piano and violin are completely neglected, not without reason, as they are easily surpassed by those of Mozart and Beethoven. Haydn concentrated his genius for chamber music in the imperishable string quartets, the model for all future writers in that field and the essential basis of modern instrumentation.

The D major Concerto, sole survivor of the many composed by Haydn, is a rather lightweight work. Probably it is heard to best advantage on the harpsichord as performed by Mme Landowska. It was reserved for Mozart to bring the classical concerto form to its perfection. [Regarding the well-known D major Concerto which I do not consider a lightweight work, I beg to recommend the Schirmer-Ganz Urtext edition. I invested it with two ample cadenzas written in the spirit of the daring ways of modulations, key changes, and free voice-leading for which I admire Haydn so much. The Teichmüller edition by Peters is distorted by improper additions and doublings. To do justice to this concerto you do not need an imitation Stein piano or a harpsichord if you are well equipped pianistically to prove your good taste in performance.]

Haydn's style differs as strikingly as his form from that of Bach. It is homophonic instead of polyphonic; the interest centers in accompanied melody instead of in the interweaving of equally important parts. Needless to say, Bach sometimes writes homophonically, as for instance in the slow movement of the Italian Concerto, and Haydn makes free use of counterpoint when he sees fit. To anticipate the history of voice-leading, the tendency of modern composers has been

to combine harmonic and contrapuntal interest in more equal proportions. A perfect example of this blending is shown in Wagner's *Meister-
singer* Prelude.

The performance of homophonic music, while less complicated
than that of polyphony, makes its own special demands. A keen sense
of melodic line and inflection is called for and the subjugation of accompaniment, especially of repeated chords and the broken-chord
figures known as "Alberti basses," becomes increasingly important. The
technique of Haydn closely resembles that of Mozart and the early
Beethoven, abounding in scale and arpeggio passages, trills and ornamentation.

Wolfgang Amadeus Mozart (1756–91)

MOZART is the outstanding miracle of music. We can never explain
genius, and perhaps it is idle to try. We can only humbly recognize
its divine incarnations and seek to make ourselves worthy in appreciation. True, we may speak or write of it more or less intelligently; we
may study its creations and point to their special beauties; but the
innermost essence will eternally elude definition and defy analysis.
Much ink has been wasted in attempts to distinguish genius from talent,
but even this apparently simple difference baffles the ablest thinkers.

This is peculiarly true of Mozart. In him all the loveliness and
magic of music are comprehended. Never has melody gushed forth
from so exhaustless a spring. Never have form and style been so
supremely attained. Never has a composer lived of comparable reign in
the usually antagonistic domains of opera and symphonic music.

On a casual view, it might seem that Mozart wrote with complete
lack of effort. This is by no means the case, for nothing is more
remarkable in his life than the continuous growth of his art. From
childhood he was a tireless student, grasping every opportunity to
learn and improve from his teachers and from the works of other
composers. Far from tossing his pages off with unpremeditated ease,
he made many preliminary sketches and later corrections. If dissatisfied
with any piece already begun, he cheerfully cast it aside to begin afresh
rather than tinker with imperfection. We are told that his first acquaintance with Bach's *Well-Tempered Clavier* was a crisis in his artistic
development. He *thought* music, the native language of his ideas, incessantly, to the hour of his death. Frail in appearance, health, and
morals, in artistic virtue he was unassailable. He could and did satirize

bad writing, but except in parody he was incapable of it. Mozart's music is for the pure in heart.

It has been said above that Haydn was a bolder innovator than his immediate successors in the establishment of homophonic music. Mozart was content, with one striking exception, to accept forms already provided, to use the orchestra and the piano as he found them, and to write even his most elaborate arias for the voices of singers whom he knew personally. His piano works, accordingly, rarely transcend the limitations of the instrument as it existed in his day, when the harpsichord had not yet been definitely displaced for public performance. If you turn the pages of his piano sonatas in an authentic edition, you will see that they abound in the dynamic directions of forte, piano, *sforzando,* and crescendos of short duration. Fortissimo and pianissimo occur very seldom indeed, for the excellent reason that while it was easy to make clean distinctions between loud and soft and to inflect the tone at will within that range, it was still difficult to achieve gradations between forte and fortissimo, piano and pianissimo, or to sustain a crescendo for more than a measure or two. [It is interesting that in some of the piano concertos, and especially in the cadenzas, a certain boldness makes itself felt. See the wonderful cadenzas that Mozart wrote for the E-flat major Concerto (K. 271).]

Now, if you will, turn the pages once more and note the exactness of Mozart's markings of legato and staccato. In this respect he is often more accurate than Beethoven. If you wish to study touch in all its variety and modulation, go to Mozart and make him the model of your phrasing. You need take only one precaution: namely, to remember that the classics were accustomed to close their slurs at the end of the measure, or even at the end of the beat, without intending a break in the legato. They used the legato slur, in other words, much as they used it in writing for strings, where it merely indicates the notes to be played with a single bow,[4] not necessarily ending a phrase. Two examples will suffice as illustration.

Ex. 31

---

[4] One of the first things to learn in violin-playing is to take a new bow without interrupting the legato.

This is obviously a single phrase, and it is clear that the accompaniment must be continuously legato. The melody, however, might tastefully be played thus:

Ex. 32

because the F in the fourth measure is actually a free suspension within a dominant harmony over an organ point. This, I am afraid, sounds complicated, but the F really *is* a suspension and as such invites a slight separation and a slight accent.

In the next example (first measure, left hand, of the slow movement of the same sonata):

Ex. 33

the slurs close at the end of every beat, but there should be no break in the legato.

With this one exception, Mozart's phrasing may safely be read quite literally. Even where it seems unduly disconnected, as in many of the slow movements, it will almost always prove correct if played with discretion. Take the Adagio of this sonata as an instance. The legato slurs of the melody seldom cover more than four notes at a time, and if played gaspingly the piece will sound horrible. But once you look on the slurs as groupings *within the phrase*, everything becomes smooth. It may help to imagine it with a long slur added over the short ones, thus:

Ex. 34a

Ex. 34b

Adagio

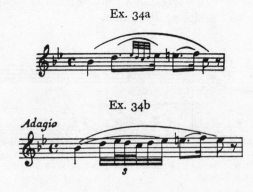

By the way, if you have ever been told that the last note of a slur should be played shorter than its written value, I implore you promptly to forget the mischievous advice.

When Mozart puts no marking whatever over a passage, he is usually paying you the compliment of not writing you down an ass. Again let me illustrate by the F major Sonata, this time from the opening measures of the last movement. You cannot play it otherwise than legato in the fast tempo however hard you try, and you will certainly recognize it as a brilliant passage requiring clear articulation rather than clinging melodic touch. So, if you can't go wrong, why trouble to instruct you? Modern editors bent on amplifying Mozart's phrasing only succeed in obscuring it.

THE MISCELLANEOUS PIECES AND VARIATIONS

Every pianist should own a copy of the miscellaneous pieces of Mozart, a volume small but worth its weight in gold. It contains three Fantasias, three Rondos, an *Overture in the Style of Handel*, an Adagio, a Minuet, and a Gigue. Commendable editions are those of Peters, Augener, and the Universal Edition. The three Fantasias are included in the Breitkopf & Härtel *Urtext* of the sonatas and the Kalmus reprint.

The three Fantasias differ widely from each other in form. In mood they are among Mozart's most serious compositions. The shortest, in D minor, deserves a better fate than to be used, as it mostly is, as a teaching piece. An artist can make much even of the unassuming slow arpeggios of the introductory Andante. The second, in C minor, must not be confused with the *Fantasia and Sonata* in the same key always printed in the collection of sonatas. This C minor Fantasia is an adagio written in regular sonata-form with an extended development section. The rather florid ornamentation does not detract from its grave majesty. The player's style and powers of expression are put to a severe test if he would do it justice. The third Fantasia, in C major, bears considerable resemblance in outline to the toccatas of Bach. A short Adagio leads to a rather long improvisational Andante ending on the dominant; the finale is a splendid fugue adorned with strettos, augmentation, and abbreviated diminutions. Though the influence of Bach is apparent, there is nothing imitative of his manner. In this respect the piece contrasts with the *Overture in the Style of Handel*, which is obviously an imitation and perhaps for that reason one of the least valued of Mozart's works.

The pleasant Rondo in D major is peculiar in that it goes through all the motions of the sonata-form while keeping throughout to one main theme. This form is rare. A distinct analogy may be traced in the first movement of Schumann's *Piano Concerto*. The second Rondo, in A minor, far the finest of the three, might be selected as truly representative of Mozart's piano idiom at its best, touchingly beautiful, perfect alike in form and content, and wonderfully rounded out by the deep emotion of the coda. As for the last Rondo, in F major, I must confess that to me its *galanterie* seems overdone.

Another lovely piece is the Adagio in B minor, too important to serve as the slow movement of a sonata and therefore rightly thought as an independent work. Two small pieces, a Menuetto in D and a Gigue in G, complete the list of miscellaneous compositions.[5] Both are gems, the Minuet unusually serious for its type, the Gigue sparkling and full of finesse.

No one who examines with care the three Fantasias, the Rondo in A minor, the B minor Adagio, and the Minuet will make the mistake of considering this piano music essentially light or shallow. Mozart was not a *Jupiter tonans,* and it would be vain to seek in him the heaven-storming tragedy of Beethoven, the impetuosity of Schumann, the turbulence of Chopin's scherzos, the orchestral sonorities of Liszt. Nevertheless he excels in accents of profound emotion and brings tears to the eye more often, perhaps, than they—the tears that well up in us when we are stirred by pure beauty, deep pathos, or superlative joy.

Mozart wrote many sets of variations for piano. Seventeen of them are authentic, and four more by other composers (one by E. A. Förster, two by Anton Eberl, one by an unknown writer) are commonly ascribed to him and included in his published works. Incidentally, at least three of the supposititious sets are remarkably good and might easily deceive an expert. On the other hand, the popular *Pastorale variée*, from the pen of Franz Bendel, is obviously spurious to any reader conversant with Mozart's style.

Speaking of the variations in general, it may be noted that, apart from the usual artifices of ringing changes on a theme by elaborations of melodic line or accompanying figuration, Mozart often resorts to more marked contrasts. Sometimes he will shift from tonic major to tonic minor or vice versa. He often introduces an adagio for relief, usually highly ornamented or expanded to greater length. Again, he may prolong the last variation to a coda or finale of larger proportion,

---

[5] Some editions add a March and a Waltz, assumedly genuine but hardly worthy of the master's genius.

perhaps altering the time signature for additional novelty. None of these devices is original with Mozart or peculiar to him; Haydn anticipated some and Beethoven adopted all of them. Still, they are characteristically Mozartean. The paradoxical difficulty in composing variations is to secure variety, and evidently Mozart was well aware of the danger of monotony inherent in the form.

The best sets of variations are the following:

1. *On the air "Je suis Lindor," E flat.* We have remarked on Mozart's small range of tonalities; here, quite exceptionally, he inserts a variation in E-flat minor.

2. *On the air "Ah! vous dirais-je, Maman," C major.* Simple but charming.

3. *On Paisiello's air "Salve tu, Domine," F major.* Rather less simple than the last and still more charming. Note the cadenzas in variations 5 and 6.

4. *On an (original?) Allegretto, F major.* A delight to the ear.

5. *From the Clarinet Quintet, A major.* Beautiful, but heard to more advantage in the original setting.

6. *On the air "Unser dummer Pöbel meint," G major.* The best of all, rich in humor and perfect in workmanship. Observe the long Adagio and the enlarged finale, the latter varying between $\frac{3}{8}$ and common time.

THE SONATAS

Coming now to the sonatas, we are confronted with an annoying difficulty in identifying them accurately. Mozart's works are not designated by opus numbers, and the sequence of the sonatas is different in the various editions. Add to this that there are four sonatas in C, four in F, three or four in B flat, and three in D, and we see that it is meaningless to speak of a Sonata in F, No. 12, unless we also refer to a particular edition probably not owned by the reader. The only means of positive identification is the invaluable *Thematic Catalogue* of Köchel, an expensive book hard to procure and confusing to any but an expert and a German scholar, since it, too, uses two different numberings and has not yet been translated into English. Köchel, be it noted, follows the chronological order of composition. The numbers in the Köchel catalogue are indicated by K, as K. 279. [An entirely new and corrected, but very expensive, edition has recently been published by Breitkopf & Härtel; it can be obtained through C. F. Peters, New York.

Kalmus's thirty-four sonatas in two volumes are in the Urtext. Peters's Urtext appears in four volumes containing forty-three sonatas

and is well edited by Carl Adolf Martienssen. The German G. Henle
Verlag of Munich is in process of publishing the complete works of
Haydn in the Urtext, and we have every right to look forward to the
first entirely unedited publication of the sonatas and all the smaller
pieces. These latter, six of them, and the six easy divertimenti are well
published by Peters. In addition to Kalmus, Durand, Universal, and
Peters editions we have a splendid, somewhat final one recently
revised by Nathan Broder (Presser). It is prepared from both autographs and the earliest printed sources and includes all the sonatas.
Mills Music, Inc., is the agent for the Associated Board Edition
(London) in two volumes. It is a very good publication, with analytical
notes, but, unfortunately, full of finger-changing on slow repeated notes,
not Mozart's fingerings. See Appendix B, "Fingerings," pages 421 ff.

Peters has an Urtext edition of eleven Mozart pieces, selected
and edited by Soldan. Each piece in this collection is a gem, and the
contrast between different moods is astounding. Who has written anything more delightful, gay, and chatty than the Gigue in G major?

The charming Viennese sonatas are published by Schirmer in a
new edition by Prostakoff.

Regarding Mozart's own pedaling in performance I came upon a
significant sentence penned by the eminent Czech composer and
theorist, Anton Reicha, who stated that "as to pedal, he took very little."
So he did take some pedal! Artur Schnabel often played Mozart with
Beethoven pedaling in contrast to Robert Casadesus's very economical
use of it. Short harmonic pedaling is sufficient.]

In commenting on the sonatas individually I shall follow the order
of the *Urtext.* To describe the form briefly, I shall call it regular whenever a sonata contains three movements, the first in sonata-form, the
second a slow movement, and the third in rondo or condensed sonata-
form.

No. 1, *K.* 279, *C major.* Form regular.   One of the larger sonatas,
though not very well known nor of remarkable importance; somewhat
formal, except for the expressive slow movement.

No. 2, *K.* 280, *F major.* Form regular.   A truly Mozartean piece,
possibly the best of the easier sonatas. The pathetic Adagio is rarely
touching.

No. 3, *K.* 281, *B-flat major.* Form regular.   The first movement
may be thought a trifle dry; the Andante and Rondo are musically
superior.

No. 4, *K.* 282, *E-flat major.*   This sonata opens with a slow movement, followed by a Minuet and Rondo. It is seldom played and cer-

tainly not one of Mozart's best works. The Cotta and the first Schirmer Edition omit it.

No. 5, K. 283, G major. Form regular. Despite its small proportions this graceful piece is one of the most attractive of the early sonatas. Myra Hess has meritoriously acquainted the concert-going public with its elegance.

No. 6, K. 284, D major. First movement in sonata-form; second movement entitled *Rondeau en Polonaise;* last movement a set of variations. Mozart makes a great stride forward in the first movement, rejecting the ornamental style for something far more meaningful and virile. The slow movement holds its own, if not conspicuously beautiful, but the variations, agreeable as is their theme, make a rather weak ending to a work that started out with high promise.

No. 7, K. 309, C major. Form regular. One of the greater sonatas, faultless in structure, well balanced in its moods, pianistically and musically effective.

No. 8, K. 310, A minor. Form regular. A work of genius in which every movement is masterly. Excepting the *Fantasia and Sonata* this is Mozart's only sonata in the minor mode. A gripping composition, dramatically conceived and calling for an impassioned interpretation. Even the final Rondo has a touch of *Weltschmerz* and must not be taken playfully.

No. 9, K. 311, D major. Form regular.

No. 10, K. 330, C major. Form regular. Mozart has now attained full control of the sonata form. These two works and all their successors are perfect alike in construction, content, and symmetrical alternation of mood.

No. 11, K. 331, A major. Form irregular. The first movement is a Theme with Variations, the second a Minuet, the last the famous *alla Turca* march. The Variations and Minuet are in Mozart's best style, and the Turkish March when played with the needed *élan* is irresistibly exciting. Mozart had a pronounced fondness for the Turkish idiom and the Janizary band; witness many of the numbers in *Die Entführung aus dem Serail,* where piccolo, triangle, cymbals, and bass drum lend Oriental color to the score. This piece should be played as if it were a piano transcription of Janizary music.

No. 12, K. 332, F major. Form regular. A work of outstanding beauty, peculiarly suitable for concert performance because of its grateful pianistic quality, culminating in an exceptionally brilliant finale. The slow movement wears its lavish ornamentation with grace, and the additional embellishments of early editions on the repetition of the themes, though not present in the autograph, have been adopted by pianists without hesitation.

No. 13, K. 333, B-flat major. Form regular. Another work of finished perfection. The Rondo is unusually important in thematic material and development.

No. 14ᵃ and 14ᵇ, Fantasia (K. 475) and Sonata (K. 457) in C minor. Though the sonata was composed two years before the fantasia, they were published together in the first authorized edition, and Mozart's own title proves that he regarded them as a single work. While it is permissible to play each separately, the spiritual affinity is obvious. Together they constitute Mozart's magnum opus for piano solo. The plan of the fantasia is singularly symmetrical. There are five sections: a tragic adagio, a dramatic interruption, a lyrical intermezzo (andantino), a second dramatic passage, and a return to the tragic opening. *De Profundis* would be a fitting name for this eloquent piece. The modulations are astonishingly rich and adventurous: after passing in the first ten measures from C minor through B-flat minor, D flat, and E-flat minor to B major, Mozart reaches a wonderful succession of harmonies which I may shortly indicate in their skeleton chords:

Ex. 35

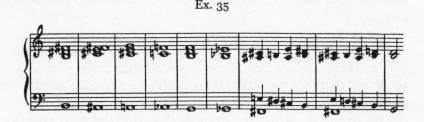

The sonata is regular in form. Less grave in feeling than the fantasia, it is intensely dramatic in the first and last movements; in the last (*Molto allegro* according to the autograph, *Allegro assai* in Artaria's early edition), the syncopations of the main theme create an impression of disquietude. The Adagio is pure song. In the middle section of this movement we discover an anticipation of the *Adagio cantabile* from Beethoven's *Sonate pathétique;* even the key and pitch are the same:

Ex. 36

No. 15, *K.* 545, *C major.* Form regular. Known the world over as the "Easy" Sonata in C, this little jewel is as perfect in its tiny form as any symphony in all its grandeur. I can think of few things more enchanting than to hear it well played by a talented child. A mature mind is apt either to "play down" to it or to load its fragile frame with greater pretension than it can bear; therefore, it should be learned in early youth.

No. 16, *K.* 570, *B-flat major.* Form regular. Here is a golden opportunity for the amateur to acquire merit by taking into his repertory a piece at once unhackneyed, charming, and not difficult. It appears only in the *Urtext,* the Universal and the Augener editions. There is an inferior version with an unauthentic violin part added.

No. 17, *K.* 576, *D major.* Form regular. Another valuable concert number, difficult but remunerating. As usual, it contains a lovely slow movement. The imitative treatment in the first movement is uncommon in the sonatas and doubly interesting on that account.

Sonata in F, K. 547 *and* 547ᵃ. This and two other sonatas still to be mentioned are not printed in the *Urtext.* It is an arrangement by Mozart himself of a sonata for piano and violin in the same key. K. 547 follows the reading of the violin sonata for the beginning of the first movement:

Ex. 37

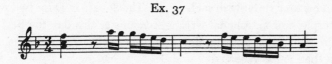

Only the Universal Edition reproduces this variant. Peters, Durand, and Schirmer give:

Ex. 38

as in K. 547ᵃ. There are only two movements (Allegro and Rondo) as always printed, but there is little doubt that Mozart intended the Variations on an Allegretto in F to add a third movement to the piece. The Allegro and the Variations appear also in the Sonatina for piano and violin, K. 547. The Rondo had already been used by Mozart as the finale of the "Easy" Sonata in C. An animated work, useful in the classroom but not of special importance.

Sonata in B flat, K. 498ᵃ. Printed only in the Cotta, Schirmer, and Augener editions. Four movements (Allegro, Andante, Minuet, Rondo).

Only the Allegro and the dainty Minuet are genuine. The Andante is a much abbreviated version by another hand of the slow movement of the Piano Concerto in B flat, K. 450. The Rondo, an unauthentic medley of themes from three different concertos in B flat, is not even clever patchwork.

Sonata in F, K. 533. The Allegro and Andante cited by Köchel were completed by the Rondo in F, K. 494. All movements are genuine. Though the form in general is regular, the Rondo departs from convention by presenting no fewer than four distinct themes, with four appearances of the main subject in addition to its re-entry in the coda. From its length and elaborate form we may well believe that the Rondo was originally written as an independent piece. The sonata is among Mozart's best and contains much interesting contrapuntal and imitative treatment. Yet I have never heard it played publicly.

Mozart's compositions for four hands and for two pianos are few but far from negligible. The four-hand sonatas equal the solo works in beauty and genius. They are not at all easy, partly because Mozart, like most composers and arrangers, at times forgets the difficulties caused by interference of the left hand of the *primo* part with the right hand of the *secondo*. Curiously enough, too, the scoring is occasionally heavy in the lower parts; the *secondo* player must therefore restrain his tone suitably in such places. The Sonata in D for two pianos, a masterpiece of antiphonal writing, remains to this day the best composition of its kind, and the fine Fugue in C minor deserves more attention than it has received.

The amateur will profit by devoting part of his leisure to Mozart's chamber music. I suggest as a minimum the Sonatas for piano and violin in E minor, K. 304, B flat, K. 378, and G, K. 379, and the Piano Quartet in G minor, all exquisite specimens of Mozart's style and of medium difficulty. There is plenty of room for choice, however, among the forty authentic violin sonatas, seven piano trios, and two piano quartets. The finest of the trios are those in B flat, K. 502, E major, K. 542, and C major, K. 548.

THE CONCERTOS

It would seem impossible to exceed the power and beauty of the works we have hitherto reviewed. Yet Mozart did surpass them all in his piano concertos, which reveal the amazing scope of his genius even more perhaps than his symphonies. Nothing short of the operas, the Twelfth Mass, and the Requiem can compare with them. It has already been

observed that Mozart was not the originator of the sonata, the
symphony, or the string quartet, nor, for that matter, of the Mass. But
he was the creator of the classical concerto, a very different thing
from the old *Concerto Grosso,* and of German opera. The form that he
devised for the concerto was something entirely new, although founded
on the sonata form. The most striking departures from that form were
made in the first movement. Here the thematic material was first presented in a long orchestral *tutti;* the piano then joined in, repeating the
subject matter more elaborately and often starting with a new auxiliary
theme of great importance. This replaced the repeated first section of
the sonata-form. The end of the section was proclaimed by a brilliant
tutti leading over to the development, where soloist and orchestra
again combined or alternated phrases. The development was as a rule
shorter, considering the length of the whole movement, than in the
sonata or symphony. The recapitulation was shared by soloist and
orchestra. At the end of the restatement the orchestra again played a
short, brilliant episode, this time ending in a pause on the $^6_4$ tonic chord,
and at this point the soloist was invited to improvise or perform a
cadenza. The formula would be as follows:

Ex. 39

or in $^3_4$ time:

Ex. 40

The trill for the soloist was an indication how to end the cadenza
and a warning to the conductor to bring the orchestra in for the coda.
   The classic concerto invariably had three movements, omitting
the minuet or scherzo of the symphony. In the slow movement and
finale the composer was free to distribute his material between solo
and orchestra as he saw fit. Often the last movement offered a second
opportunity for a cadenza, but this was not essential.

We shall see later that the cadenza at length became a nuisance. Many later composers followed the concerto form as shaped by Mozart, but either, like Mendelssohn and Chopin, did away with the cadenza altogether, or, like Schumann, Saint-Saëns, Brahms, Tchaikovsky and Rachmaninoff, varied their practice, sometimes omitting it entirely, at other times writing it in as an integral part of the composition.

Outside of their immense musical value the outstanding technical merit of Mozart's concertos rests in the happy partnership of a solo instrument and a co-operating orchestra to produce a completely natural effect. Never has this difficult problem been solved with such unfailing art. The scoring is uniformly beautiful, rising far above the level of mere accompaniment; on the other hand it never over-powers the soloist. The two elements are blended perfectly or alternate with each other in willing teamwork. If Mozart had not written a single symphony the concertos would prove him a past master of instrumentation. The handling of the woodwind and horns, in par-ticular, is the last word in delicate mastery of their potentialities and individual qualities. This group is usually quite small; a single flute, a pair of oboes or clarinets, two bassoons, and two horns normally com-plete the woodwind palette. Occasionally trumpets and kettledrums are added; in the great C minor Concerto, K. 491, both oboes and clarinets are used. Wise conductors, recognizing the hugeness of modern orchestras, cut down the number of strings in order to maintain the fine balance of such intimate scoring.

Mozart wrote concertos for piano, violin, flute, oboe, clarinet, bas-soon, and horn, besides a concerto for three pianos and several double concertos, one each for two pianos, two violins, violin and viola, and flute and harp. Of the twenty-three piano concertos only that in F major for three pianos (composed for three lady amateurs) is insig-nificant. The best-known are those in B flat, K. 450, G major, K. 453, D minor, K. 466, C major, K. 467, E flat, K. 482, A major, K. 488, C minor, K. 491, D major (the Second *Coronation* Concerto), K. 537, [and E flat, K. 271].

The limits of this book do not permit a full description of these works, extraordinary even for Mozart alike in invention and work-manship. For a detailed and sympathetic appraisal I refer the reader to Alfred Einstein's *Mozart, His Character, His Work*, chapter xvii. I add with pleasure that the musical world is indebted to this eminent musicologist for the authoritative revision of Köchel's catalogue.[6]

---

[6] Ludwig von Köchel: *Chronologisch-thematisches Verzeichniss der Werke W. A. Mozarts*, third edition (Leipzig: Breitkopf & Härtel; 1937).

The short lists below are recommended for study and reading. About ten pieces selected from these lists and learned over a period of years would constitute a good repertory for the amateur.

A. FOR YOUNG PLAYERS

"Easy" Sonata in C
Sonata in B flat, K. 570
Fantasia in D minor
Rondo in D
Single movements (minuets, etc.) from the sonatas

B. I. FOR MATURE PLAYERS

Rondo in A minor
Gigue in G (short but tricky)
Fantasia in C minor, K. 475
Sonata in A
Any sonata for piano and violin
Concerto in A

B. II. MORE DIFFICULT

Sonata in A minor, K. 310, or Sonata in D, K. 576
Adagio in B minor
Piano Quartet in G minor
Concerto in D minor, K. 466, or Concerto in D major,
    K. 537, or Concerto in G, K. 453.

Minute directions for the playing of each piece are unnecessary if the student will bear in mind the chief requirements for a correct performance, namely:

(a) Distinction of melody from accompaniment.
(b) Clean-cut difference between piano and forte.
(c) Exact observance of touch, phrasing, and inflection as marked.
(d) Beauty of tone and purity of style.

CHAPTER FIVE

Ludwig van Beethoven
(1770–1827)

BEETHOVEN'S pre-eminence among composers rests on the sublimity of his thought. His only peers in this respect are Bach and, in the domain of opera, Wagner. All great men reach moments of grandeur; of Beethoven we may say that grandeur was the habit of his mind. Not that he was austere; fine frenzy alternated with moods of serenity, tenderness, gaiety, and humor; he ran the whole gamut of musical expression; but above and beyond all else there remained an essential nobility of inspiration.

While still a youth, Beethoven impressed all who heard him by the eloquence of his improvisations. His gift for extempore playing was unique; he would hold an audience rapt for hours by its spell, reducing the listeners to tears, as Czerny relates, by the intensity of the emotions he evoked. This ease of ephemeral composition stands in sharp contrast with the painful labor of his pen in setting down permanent ideas. Hence he was slow in fulfilling the expectations of the musical world. At the age of twenty-two his finished works were few and unimportant compared with the early output of Mozart, Mendelssohn, and others. At this time, however, he was already well known as a pianist. This must have been due chiefly to his own efforts, for in the long list of his instructors no piano teacher of importance is mentioned. His father scented in the child prodigy a source of income, and drove a tearful infant to the practice of the clavier. Next, *mirabile dictu*, we hear of his taking piano lessons from a tenor singer of the opera company at Bonn. It is doubtful whether Van den Eeden and Neefe, both organists, taught him piano as well as organ. The young Beethoven became Neefe's assistant at the organ, at first without pay, but afterward receiving a small salary welcome enough to the needy family. In Vienna Beethoven had a few lessons in composition with Mozart and a good many in counterpoint with Haydn, but no piano teaching from either. It seems clear, then, that he never studied piano with a pianist. We can understand his complaint in later years that his musical education had been insufficient. Certainly his general education was disastrously scanty, putting him at a life-long disadvantage in the world of men. He learned at school no more than reading, writing, arithmetic, and a little Latin, and he stopped attending school when thirteen years old. Somehow, probably from the kind-hearted Zambona,[1] he also acquired some French and Italian. Of moral education he had none whatever.

The faults of his early training explain many of the difficulties of his life. Nothing came easily to him; not the creation of his masterpieces, nor success in his career, least of all happiness and peace in human contacts. By nature a rebel, socially ungifted, at times surly and suspicious, equally violent in his good and bad impulses, he was constantly embroiled with his fellows. The staunch friends who were drawn and held to him by his talents had much to put up with in their association with him. His manners, in short, were abominable, and it is not on record that anyone ever called him a gentleman. Fundamentally generous and full of deep inscrutable tenderness, he was awkward and tongue-tied when it came to revealing his better self in the amenities of daily intercourse. It is amazing that the cultured aristocracy of Vienna tolerated a disposition so uncontrolled. Tolerate it they did; his genius opened all doors to him. Stranger still, this ugly, uncouth little man exercised a singular fascination on the high-bred ladies of the court, who forgave his eccentricities for the force of his personality. Their intuition was sound, and it must have had some softening influence on his heart if not on the asperity of his conduct. Other influences too were at work for his good: self-improvement by reading, a steady growth of personal morality, his trust in God, his love of nature, and the discipline of his art—the one discipline to which he rigorously submitted himself. He wrestled mightily with the demons of misfortune, with the long agony of his deafness, to a musician the supreme affliction; but he also wrestled to his salvation with the angels of the Lord.

---

[1] See *Grove's Dictionary*, fourth edition, article "Beethoven," and Thayer's *Life of Beethoven*, translated by Henry E. Krehbiel, Vol. I, p. 65. Thayer throws doubt on the story.

The background of his personal life explains a persistent note of Beethoven's creative work, the strife of the soul against evil fate, its defiance of adversity and ultimate triumph through its own strength. Fate knocked at his door as a foe; he met it blow for blow and conquered.

The Sonatas

I have said that it is difficult to define a sonata. It would also be hard to formulate a definition that would include all and exclude none of the works so designated by Beethoven. His earlier sonatas contained either three or four movements and closely followed the classic tradition of Haydn and Mozart, though even here he added weightily to the length and importance of the development sections and codas (see the sonatas in C, Opus 2, No. 3, in E flat, Opus 7, and in B flat, Opus 22). In the C minor Sonata, Opus 13 (the *Pathétique*), we note the growing influence of an orchestral quality coloring his piano idiom. The Sonata in A flat, Opus 26, is the first to show distinct irregularity of form. The two sonatas of Opus 27 depart so widely from convention that the composer thought it wise to describe them as *Sonatas quasi Fantasias*. Other works of little conformity to accepted standards are Opus 54, Opus 109, and Opus 110. In Opus 106, Opus 110, and the Sonata for piano and cello in D we are startled to see the fugue invading the sonata form as an end movement.

Evidently Beethoven thought favorably of two movements as sufficient for a sonata. It is natural enough to find this minimum in the *Two Easy Sonatas* (properly sonatinas) of Opus 49, but more remarkable that it recurs in no fewer than five of the more mature works. The absence of a third movement in Opus 53,[2] Opus 90, and Opus 111 is thoroughly well-considered and characteristic.

Opus 90 (E minor) and Opus 57 (the *Appassionata*) afford further examples of Beethoven's emancipation from established usage. In both of these he omits the familiar repeat in the first movement, governed by a growing doubt of its value or logical necessity. Modern opinion has tended strongly to support the omission, yet with Beethoven himself the doubt never became a fixed conviction, for he reverts to the repeat in several of the late sonatas, including Opus

---

[2] The *Introduzione* to the rondo of the *Waldstein* Sonata is exactly what it purports to be, not a movement in itself.

106, the *Hammerklavier* (long enough in all conscience without it) and Opus 111. It is noteworthy that the master refused to be bound by his own innovations. He abandoned them on occasion as readily as he had introduced them, remaining to the end an experimenter and a student.

Superfluous as it may be, and regardless of Beethoven's pioneering, the repetition of the first section was retained by Schubert, Weber, Schumann, Chopin, and Brahms. It is usually omitted in performance, but there it stands in print. Habit dies hard. Indeed, it was not altogether easy to get rid of the antiquated and illogical repetition of the entire development section and recapitulation also. Haydn called for this second repeat in about half of his sonatas. Mozart apparently took it for granted, indicating it in all his sonatas except the one in D, Köchel 576. After following Mozart's custom in a few early works (Opus 2, Nos. 1 and 2, Opus 10, No. 2) Beethoven abandoned this second repeat, but once more he wavered, for in the last movement of the *Appassionata* and in the first movements of Opus 78 and Opus 79 he deliberately prescribes it. I say deliberately because in each case special provision had to be made for the return to the beginning of the development—a small effort of composition, but more than simply a matter of putting signifying dots before a double bar, as might be done thoughtlessly.

Until Beethoven's time the sonata form was still so new that composers made a point of defining it very clearly. Mozart's habit in preparing the entrance of his "second subject" was to aim at a cadence *above* the dominant or relative major—that is, on the dominant of the new key—so as to drop on it from above—an unmistakable proclamation. The reprises are usually equally obvious. Beethoven soon became more insidious in his approaches, seeking to avoid the finality of cadences except at the end of the first section of the sonata movement and so concealing rather than exposing the skeleton of the form. In the choice of key for the second subject, too, he frequently shunned the almost inevitable dominant in favor of a more refreshing tonality. Examples of his individual treatment of the second theme abound in the earliest sonatas; see all three numbers of Opus 2 and Opus 10, No. 1. Opus 10, No. 2, contains a charmingly elusive reprise of the main theme, starting in the unexpected key of D major and ending in the orthodox tonic of F.

Haydn had frequently preceded the opening allegros of his symphonies by a slow introduction, but he never incorporated this feature into the sonata. Mozart did so rarely: the Sonata in G for piano and violin, K. 454, has an introductory adagio. Beethoven was the first to do so, and we find such prefaces in five of the piano sonatas and several of the sonatas for piano with violin or cello. Still more often he writes slow introductions to his finales. These preludes vary in length from a measure or two (Opus 31, No. 2; Opus 78) to several pages (Cello Sonata in G minor). Long or short, they are invariably significant and beautiful, and must be counted among Beethoven's valuable additions to the form.

So much has been said of Beethoven's handling of the development section that I shall confine myself to two points of interest. The first is a small personal idiosyncrasy that often leads him to begin his development by an echo of the last notes of the first section. He does it in the F major Sonata just mentioned, and in this case it must for some reason have tickled his fancy, for he devotes the major part of the development to a pursuit of the idea. Who but Beethoven would even have descried a "motive" in the unpromising tag:

Ex. 41

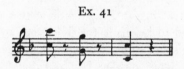

closing the previous section?

In any event, it must be admitted that this particular development section is a poor specimen of the master's craft. Better examples of the use of a concluding motive to introduce the development will be found in Opus 2, No. 2, the *Waldstein* Sonata, Opus 90, and the *Hammerklavier* Sonata.

An analogous though not strictly parallel instance in the rondo of the G major Piano Concerto shows very clearly Beethoven's enjoyment in elaborating a small detail. The main theme is stated in a ten-bar period ending with a humorous little twist of three notes:

Ex. 42

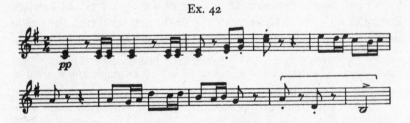

resembling the "tag" quoted in Ex. 41. Apparently the composer himself sees no special significance in them until he has nearly finished

the movement. Then he happens to use them, legato, on the violas
and in the key of B flat. Instantly they arrest his attention; has he
been missing a trick all this time? If so, watch him make up for it!
After repeating the notes meditatively thrice, he tries them out as an
independent motive on the woodwind, then comes to a bold decision
to use them as the *beginning* instead of the end of his theme:

Ex. 43

Compare Ex. 43 with the first four and the last two measures of the
original theme in Ex. 42 to appreciate the shift of position.

Now Beethoven's hand is in; henceforth he plays with the fragment
like a child with a new toy. A few pages later the French horn has the
motive under brilliant piano passage-work, closely followed by a
reduction to two notes instead of three in the basses, which proceed
to diminution and chromatic alteration:

Ex. 44

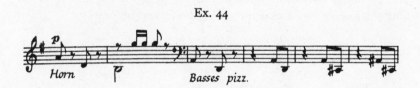

The horn entrance of Ex. 44 must have struck Beethoven as a particularly happy thought, for he returns to it, this time in an augmented
rhythm, as the piano trills its way out of the cadenza:

Ex. 45

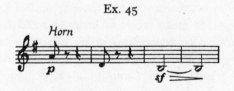

Even now the conjurer's bag is not empty; the main theme (simplified
in outline) emerges from it as a close canon! The passage begins as
follows, the first two measures of Ex. 42 being elided:

Ex. 46

It is again, however, the "tag" that chiefly concerns us. It appears thus:

Ex. 47

The two-note contraction jubilates in the presto coda, and as a last fling the motive steals an extra note of prefix and becomes:

Ex. 48

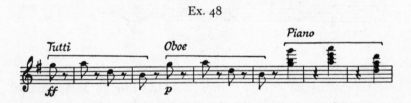

If I have dwelt at some length on a minor detail of Beethoven's workmanship, it is because nothing is more typical of his genius than this unique power to make much of little, to build from tiny units musical structures of immense proportions, coherence, and grandeur. The essential motive of the C minor Symphony may be likened to a small block of granite. From a multitude of such blocks, and from nothing else save four measures of relieving lyricism, he erects one of the most imposing monuments of orchestral architecture. Again, the entire thematic material of the first movement of the Ninth Symphony may easily be compressed into a very few measures of quotation. It is scarcely heresy to venture the opinion that other composers of inferior talent could have invented the themes, but it is sheerly unthinkable that any composer except Beethoven himself could have written the movements.

The other feature of Beethoven's method of development that I wish to enlarge on is the process of reducing a theme by successive curtailments to its smallest component parts and extracting the last drop of juice from every fragment. Others too avail themselves of this familiar procedure, but none uses it more characteristically, skillfully, and effectively than he. Let us take the development section of the first movement of the Sonata in D, Opus 28, known as the *Pastoral* Sonata. At the outset the main theme has been announced in a period of ten measures. Beethoven begins his development by a restatement of this period in G Major; on repeating it he shifts to G minor and introduces a new counterpoint to the last four measures:

Ex. 49   (a)

These four measures are repeated three times in double counterpoint, treble and bass alternating their parts. Next the four measures are reduced to two [(a) in Ex. 49]. There are four repetitions of the two measures, still inverting the parts. Now the two measures are compressed into one, thus:

Ex. 50

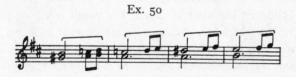

The single measure continues for twelve measures without further change, after which a new formula appears:

Ex. 51

Here the left hand presents the germ in inversion, while in the right hand it is further contracted from the space of a whole measure to two quarter-note beats. Finally the motive loses itself in downward-moving F-sharp major triads, through which we may still imagine faint echoes:

Ex. 52

If the reader will pardon a frivolous simile, it is something like the slow fading of the Cheshire cat to spare Alice's dazed eyes, until nothing was left but the grin.

The application of the method is seldom quite so clean-cut as in the example chosen as illustration. For a most remarkable development section constructed on the same plan I may refer to that in the first movement of the great B-flat Trio, Opus 97, for piano, violin, and cello.

We must not minsunderstand the nature of the device I have been trying to explain. It is not a trick of dissection, but on the contrary a fruitful process of formation. The object is not to chop a theme into little pieces, but to expand it by culture of its living germs; to make much of little, not little out of much. The result is a long passage of consecutive thought, not a display of mere *disjecta membra*. It would be an error, too, to suppose that Beethoven necessarily waits for a development section before beginning to develop his themes. Creation and development go hand in hand with him. Even a hasty glance at the opening measures of Opus 2, No. 1, Opus 53, Opus 57, and the Allegro of Opus 111, will prove conclusively that the working-out of his subjects frequently begins with their initial statement. Nor does evolution stop with him when he reaches the recapitulation; the themes are often considerably modified as they reappear and his more extended codas often amount to new development sections. What is musical development, indeed, if not the gradual evolution of an idea by varied repetition, by paraphrase and elaboration, by presentation from different angles and in fresh hues, by fulfillment of its subtler implications, until in the master's own words the idea attains *"il suo proprio proposto affetto,"* its own special and intended effect?

The unusual length of many of Beethoven's codas may be studied in the Rondo of Opus 2, No. 2, the first movement of Opus 2, No. 3 (beginning with the fortissimo A-flat chord and including a cadenza), the last movement of Opus 31, No. 2, the first and last movements of the *Waldstein* Sonata, Opus 53, the first movement of Opus 57 (the *Appassionata*), and the finale of Opus 101. Strikingly beautiful examples, which I reserve for later comment, occur in Opus 81^a, the *Sonate caractéristique.* The most magnificent coda ever written by mortal man is that of the first movement of the *Eroica* Symphony; it deserves the absorbed attention of every musician.

Beethoven was fond of interrupting himself near the home stretch by a fermata and a few measures of slower tempo—a pensive review of some former passage. Various phases of this habit may be examined in the first and last movements of the *Sonate pathétique,* the finales of Opus 27, No. 2, and Opus 31, No. 3, the first movement of the *Waldstein* Sonata, and the last movement of Opus 81^a.

Except in the Sonata *Appassionata,* Beethoven never resorted to a quickening of speed for the close of his first movements. He does so more frequently in his rondos and finales; for instance, in Opus 27, No. 1, Opus 28, Opus 31, No. 1, Opus 53, and Opus 57. It is reasonable to trace in this the influence of Mozart's concertos.

We may fairly conclude that while Beethoven in some respects experimented with the sonata form without ever arriving at a fixed conviction, he quite definitely and purposefully determined to raise the development section and the coda to a new level of importance.

One important change made by Beethoven in the symphony and sonata was the frequent replacement of the staid minuet by the swift-foot scherzo, or at least by a dance movement too fast rightly to be called a minuet. This was a complete innovation. Not that he definitely forsook the minuet, but almost from the first he used discretion in naming his dance movements according to their character. When he wants a minuet he marks it *Menuetto* or *Tempo di Menuetto* (see Opus 10, No. 3, Opus 22, Opus 31, No. 3, and Opus 49, No. 2). When the tempo or the mood is too fast for a minuet but not vivacious enough for scherzo, he is satisfied to write Allegro or Allegretto (see Opus 7, Opus 10, No. 2, Opus 14, No. 1, and Opus 27, Nos. 1 and 2).

Sixteen of the thirty-two sonatas contain no movement in dance form, though the first movement of Opus 54 has the flavor of a minuet and the *Presto alla tedesca* of Opus 79 that of a rustic dance. Two sonatas include marches, the funeral march of Opus 26 and the *Vivace alla marcia* of Opus 101. The Scherzo of Opus 31, No. 3, is written in condensed sonata-form and in $\frac{2}{4}$ time. Finally, the *Allegro molto* of Opus 110, also in $\frac{2}{4}$ time, slightly irregular in its dance form, might with propriety be called a scherzo.

It was only in the last period of his activity that Beethoven began to compose what may be called "multiple" finales. Opus 110, in A flat, is a solitary instance among the sonatas. For further examination of this novelty we must consult the later string quartets and above all, of course, the choral portion of the Ninth Symphony.

Beethoven was quick to avail himself of the enlarged resources of the piano introduced during his lifetime. It is remarkable that no fewer than twenty of the thirty-two sonatas were composed for an instrument no greater in compass than the later harpsichords and clavichords—namely, from FF to f³,

The same is true of the early concertos in C and B flat, except for one lonely inexplicable f³ sharp in the former. After this the upward compass rises rapidly, in the *Waldstein* Sonata to a³, in the *Appassionata* to c⁴, in Opus 81ᵃ to f⁴,

Not until very late, however, was one note added *below* the low F. Beethoven must have waited longingly for this deep tone, for in the finale of Opus 101 he builds up a climactic entrance for it and announces it triumphantly to the world by marking it "Contra E," boldly written in his autograph. The final compass is reached in Opus 106, where it is no less than six octaves and a fourth, CC to f⁴, another gain of a third for the low register.[3]

The enrichment of the piano's sonority kept pace with its growing compass, so that Beethoven had a far more sumptuous range of tone at his service than any of his predecessors. He used the larger palette with the utmost freedom, at times, no doubt (as is the prerogative of genius), straining its resources almost beyond their endurance in the passion of creation. It is still the despair of the pianist to match Beethoven's intentions of loudness and softness, though he may easily satisfy the tenuous brushwork of Debussy or the clamant idiom of Prokofiev. The protracted crescendo leading to the reprise in the first movement of the *Waldstein,* the towering heights of the *Appassionata,* the ineffably tender murmurs and ethereal lacery of the fourth variation in the Arietta of Opus 111: these were revelations that may indeed have struck contemporaries as extravagances of an inspired madman.

Beethoven was extraordinarily venturesome in his use of the pedals, notably of the damper pedal. Many passages in his works give evidence of his strong liking for clouded effects produced by holding the pedal through harmonic changes. It is startling to be told by Czerny that Beethoven, when playing the C minor Concerto at a concert in 1803, held the pedal throughout the entire theme of the slow movement. Czerny adds that this was not objectionable on the piano of the period, especially if the soft pedal was also used, but counsels greater restraint on more modern instruments. But Beethoven's own directions call for several changes of pedal, shifting from *senza sordini* (=with pedal) to *con sordini* (=without pedal) and back no fewer than eight times, so the story is at least partly discredited. Quite probably Beethoven, an accomplished pianist, had already acquired the modern refinement of shaking out dissonances by rapid imperceptible movement of the foot not amounting to a full release of the pedal; this might easily have escaped the eye and ear of an observer. More reliable examples of unusual pedaling are found in the sonatas Opus 31, No. 2 (first movement, in the two recitatives at the reprise), Opus 53 (theme of the Rondo), and Opus 57 (the six measures toward the end of the first movement, just before the *più allegro*). Commentators have attempted to explain these places by repeating, after Czerny, that the tone of the older instruments was less enduring, or by assuming that Beethoven's growing deafness made him less sensitive to blurred har-

---

[3] This is very near the compass of Liszt's earlier pianos, as is neatly proved in an *ossia* written into the *Waldesrauschen* to avoid the high a⁴, evidently not yet to be expected on all keyboards.

monies. There is of course a measure of reason in the first gloss, and it is up to the pianist to find means of reading Beethoven's meaning without undue offense to the ear. But I cannot believe that Beethoven's deafness had anything to do with the matter, else we should find these peculiarities in the later sonatas instead of in those written before 1807. There is convincing testimony that Beethoven knew perfectly well what he was about in his answer to a criticism of the reverberation in the recitatives of Opus 31, No. 2: "I wish it," he said, "to sound as if someone were speaking in a vault." Further, when Beethoven wished for clear distinction of harmonies, or when he wanted a change of pedal while the harmony remained unaltered, he indicated it with minute accuracy. He went so far as to prescribe the exact moment when the pedal was to be released, as in the following example from the *Waldstein* Sonata:

Ex. 53

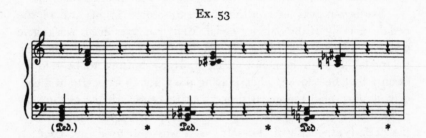

where the use of two quarter-note rests instead of the customary whole-note rests in the second, fourth, and sixth measures, combined with the release signs for the pedal, give exactest instruction to the performer. When it mattered to him, then, Beethoven gave exceptionally careful directions for pedaling. When it mattered little, or when the right pedaling was self-evident, he was willing to trust the intelligence of the player. Little did he foresee the mutilations of future editors!

[It is immensely interesting to note how Dr. Hutcheson is circumnavigating the use of Beethoven's (too long at times) pedal indications, especially in the slow movement of the C minor Concerto, the second theme in the third movement of the G major Concerto, the theme of the rondo in the Sonata op. 53, and the celebrated six measures before the *più allegro* (the coda) in the first movement of the Sonata op. 57. I too believe that Beethoven knew the secret of half- and quarter-pedals, perhaps subconsciously. In the two recitatives in the first movement of the Sonata op. 31, no. 2, I certainly hold my pedal throughout the first one and hold the C major chord of the left hand in the second one so as to be able to half-pedal on the C and the B flat in measure two. Beethoven wrote *"con espressione e semplice,"* which means that any sentimentality would be distasteful. One little suggestion regarding measure 381 in the third movement of the same sonata: take the 32nd note "d" with the left hand and play the two "f's" as a sharply marked right hand octave so as to get a real forte.

The most admirable, precise and delicate example of pedal notation anywhere occurs in measures eleven and ten from the end of the slow movement of the fourth, G major, Piano Concerto.

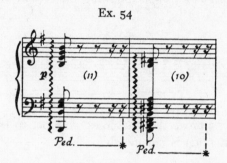

Ex. 54

The top notes of the two rather slow, thoughtful arpeggios are on the beat. Lift your hands on the second eighth rest as a harpist would, but hold the pedal faithfully until the second sixteenth rest, producing an effect similar to a short sigh of sadness.]

In the earlier works Beethoven indicates the use and release of the pedal by the expressions *senza sordino* (more correctly *senza sordini*) —that is, without the dampers and therefore with the pedal—and *con sordino,* of opposite meaning. Later he uses the familiar notation *Ped.* or *Pedale* and the release sign * as has since been the almost invariable custom.

There was a short time during the evolution of the piano when it was possible to use the soft pedal so that it would strike either one string or two instead of three. Beethoven tried to turn this possibility to account, and we find in the introduction to the finale of Opus 101 the curious prescriptions *"mit einer Saite,"*[4] *"Nach und nach mehrere Saiten," "Alle Saiten,"* together with the Italian equivalents of the first and last phrases, *"Sul una corda"* and *"Tutto il cembalo"* (the whole piano). In Opus 110, too, Beethoven writes *"poi a poi tutte le corde."* The slow movement of Opus 106, the *Hammerklavier,* is chock full of

---

[4] Archaic for *Seite* (= string).

markings for the soft pedal; ten times we find *"una corda,"* sometimes for long stretches (for example, at the beginning), ten times *"tutte le corde,"* and twice *"poco a poco due e allora tutte le corde"*—that is, "little by little two and then all the strings."

Another effect possible on the early pianos as well as on the clavichord was the *"Bebung,"* literally "trembling," by which fresh impetus could be given to a tone by finger pressure without striking the key anew. It is remotely akin to the vibrato of the violin and the tremolo of the voice, to both of which the term is occasionally applied. The best-known case of Beethoven's use of the device occurs in Opus 110, in the *Adagio, ma non troppo* following the second movement:

Ex. 55

The ties of Ex. 55 prove that the notes were not to be struck again, also that the intention is not merely:

Ex. 56

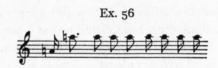

Other passages calling for the *Bebung* occur in the Scherzo of the A major Sonata for piano and cello (main theme), and in the second subject of the first movement of Opus 28:

Ex. 57

Skillful pianists of today simulate the effect by a combination of finger and pedal action, preferably with a change of finger, 43. Though tricky and rather uncertain, the equivalent is satisfactory when well executed, the result being best on syncopations like those of Ex. 57.

In general Beethoven's phrasing closely resembles that of Mozart. The following observations may be welcome to the student:

1. The legato slurs tend to become longer, less interrupted by the

bar lines (see the notation of the left hand in the second subject of the Sonata in F, Opus 10, No. 2, the Allegretto of the same sonata, and the finale of Opus 26).

2. In his autographs Beethoven never wrote dots for staccato, but always the wedge-shaped signs. It is a matter of regret that even in the *Urtext* of Breitkopf & Härtel, now most laudably reprinted by Edwin Kalmus in an American edition, this habit is ignored. Beethoven reserves dots exclusively for the portamento, where he invariably places them under a slur, thus: ⌒ . . . . He explains this with great care in a letter written to his publishers in reference to the slow movement of the A major Symphony. Note too that the staccato mark, in both Mozart and Beethoven, has the significance of detachment, not necessarily of an extreme shortening of the notes. It is important to remember that, just as a quarter-note is twice as long as an eighth-note, so a staccato quarter is twice as long as a staccato eighth.

Occasionally the staccato is used to draw attention to notes of special melodic value, and in such cases it implies a prolongation rather than a shortening of tone. The *Sonate pathétique* affords an excellent example:

Ex. 58

Beethoven was the first composer to use the portamento touch with clear design. The portamento, on the piano,[5] calls for the full value of the notes, yet with a detached, not a legato effect. Properly understood, it will always need the pedal to sustain the tone while the fingers take care of the detachment.

3. Beethoven's use of the *sforzando* (abbreviated indifferently *sf*, *sfz*, or *sforz.*) is extremely individual. At first he neglected the customary signs for accents, > or ∧, and marked every accent, however slight, with a *sforzando*. The word should therefore always be read in relation to its context. If the prevailing tone is piano, a *sforzando* will be a quite gentle stress, as in the fifth measure of the slow movement of the *Appassionata*. If the passage as a whole is fortissimo, a *sforzando* indicates a very strong emphasis. It is necessary to bear this in mind because the modern idea of *sforzando* is that of a powerful accent, weaker stresses being indicated by the mark > or the "stamp"-.

---

[5] The word has an entirely different meaning in singing.

In Mozart and Beethoven a *szforando* often affects more than a single note or chord; in these cases it has much the same meaning as the better term *rinforzando*. When Mozart and Beethoven wish an immediate return to normal tone, they prefer to write *fp*.

4. Let the amateur be warned against beginning Beethoven's crescendos prematurely; nothing is more repugnant to his style. Individual taste will often warrant inflections unmarked by the composer, but when a crescendo is prescribed, let it begin exactly where it stands in the score.

5. The student will be considerably bewildered by Beethoven's use of the *alla breve* (₵) time signature unless he compares it with the printed words above and also considers the unit of fastest motion called for. The appended table may throw helpful light on this point:

	Sonata and movement	Direction	Smallest unit of motion	Metronome speed
1.	Opus 27, No. 2, I	Adagio sostenuto	triplet eighths	♩ = 60
2.	Opus 27, No. 1, I	Andante	sixteenths	♩ = 76-84
3.	Opus 14, No. 2, II	Andante	sixteenths	♩ = 96
4.	Opus 31, No. 1, III	Allegretto	triplet eighths	𝅗𝅥 = 96
5.	Opus 13, III	Allegro	triplet eighths	𝅗𝅥 = 104
6.	Opus 81ᵃ, I	Allegro	eighths	𝅗𝅥 = 120
7.	Opus 13, I	Allegro di molto	eighths	𝅗𝅥 = 152
8.	Opus 27, No. 2, III	Presto agitato	sixteenths	𝅗𝅥 = 84
9.	Opus 10, No. 3, I	Presto	eighths	𝅗𝅥 = 138
10.	Opus 10, No. 1, III	Prestissimo	sixteenths	𝅗𝅥 = 120

Some items of the list above still seem baffling. Why should the *Allegro di molto* of No. 7 be faster than the prestos and prestissimo? We wonder why it should not be marked *prestissimo*, and why No. 8 should not be marked *allegro agitato* rather than *presto*. The character of the technique gives a partial explanation, accounting also for the slower tempo of movements involving the performance of sixteenth-notes. Nevertheless we must admit that Beethoven was a little capricious in his distinction between common time and *alla breve*.

Another source of trouble to the student lies in the essential difference between andante and adagio. Here, however, Beethoven himself is always perfectly consistent. *Andante* always means "going," *adagio* (literally *ad agio*, at ease) invariably means slow. Hence *più andante* means faster, *più adagio* means slower, *meno adagio* means faster, and andantino is slower than *andante*. In the classical period all composers studied Italian, the common language of music, as French was of diplomacy and Latin of scholarship. Only later writers began to confuse *andante* with the conception of slowness, and we find in them such solecisms as *molto andante* for very slow and *andantino* as an equivalent for *quasi allegretto*. It would seem that even in Beethoven's time this misunderstanding had become prevalent, for in the Sonata Opus 109 he gently corrects the ignorant by writing *"un poco meno andante, cio è un poco più adagio come il tema"* (a little less going; that is, a little more slow than the theme").

The Sonatas

Judged by their spiritual elevation, the grandest sonatas of Beethoven are Opus 13 (the *Sonate pathétique*), Opus 27, No. 2 (the misnamed "Moonlight"), Opus 31, No. 2 (D minor), Opus 57 (the *Appassionata*), Opus 81ª (*Sonate caractéristique*), Opus 90 (E minor), and the last five, with opus numbers 101, 106, 109, 110, and 111. In these the formal element is transcended; first and last they are dramas of the soul. Another group of sonatas, while containing single movements of equally deep feeling, may be considered primarily as ideal compositions for the piano. We may place here Opus 2, No. 2 (in A), Opus 2, No. 3 (in C), Opus 10, No. 3 (in D), Opus 26 (in A flat), Opus 27, No. 1 (in E flat), Opus 28 (the *Pastoral*), Opus 31, No. 3 (again in E flat), and foremost in this category Opus 53 (the *Waldstein*). Perfect in their smaller proportions are Opus 10, Nos. 1 and 2 (C minor and F major), Opus 14, No. 2 (G major), and Opus 78 (F-sharp major). I risk censure, and am truly humble, in thinking Opus 7 (E flat), Opus 22 (B flat), and Opus 31, No. 1 (G major) not quite so fine. All three are elaborately worked out and undeniably pianistic; all contain slow movements of great beauty; yet they seem to be not free from a certain formal dryness, and in the rondos with which they conclude a harsh critic might describe some passages as "padding." I beg the reader, here and elsewhere, to take my opinion with the proverbial grain of salt, to make his own examination and form his independent conclusions. I have less hesitation in suggesting that Beethoven's reputation would not suffer appreciably had he never written the remaining sonatas: Opus 2, No. 1 (admitting the Mozartean charm of its Adagio); Opus 14, No. 1, a slight work; the two Easy Sonatas, Opus 49, really sonatinas;[6] Opus 54, in F, a cryptic piece to which it is hard to find a musical clue; Opus 78, favorite of many artists and incontestably a minor work of the mature Beethoven, and the Sonatine, Opus 79.

In commenting serially on the sonatas I shall limit myself to those most representative of his genius.

Sonata No. 2, Opus 2, No. 2, A major.   An effective concert number. The first movement is brilliant and joyous. The *Largo appassionata* might fitly be scored for string quartet; the staccato basses have the effect of cello *pizzicati.* Note how soon Beethoven began to substitute the scherzo for the minuet, though here he does not reach the speed of the later scherzos. The main subject of the rondo is gracefully embellished at its recurrences, but there is a suspicion of padding in the A minor middle theme.

Sonata No. 3, Opus 2, No. 3, C major.   The marked pianistic idiom of this work led Eugen d'Albert to remark that it might be regarded as a preliminary study for the *Waldstein.* The first and last movements abound in varied technical passages grateful to the pianist's fingers. The Adagio is a good example of the comparative difficulty of memorizing slow movements. One can play it well after a few readings, but it takes much longer to learn it by heart. In rapid movements, on the other hand, we usually have to practice the technique so assiduously that they are memorized before we can perform them adequately. The Scherzo goes very fast, counting only one to each measure; the Trio may be a trifle steadier because of the triplet eighth-notes. In the last movement, be careful throughout to observe the difference between staccato quarters and eighths.

Ex. 59

Sonata No. 5, Opus 10, No. 1, C minor.   For the first time Beethoven writes in true dramatic style for the piano, though there are strong rumbles of premonition in Opus 2, No. 1. The lyrical *Adagio*

---

[6] In the second of the Easy Sonatas, Beethoven uses a theme for the Tempo di Menuetto identical with one in his Septet.

molto contrasts tellingly with the other movements. A short but fiery sonata, more important than it seems on casual acquaintance. Great intensity of expression is needed to bring out the full meaning.

Sonata No. 6, Opus 10, No. 2, F major. Another short sonata, very different from the last, light in character but convincing when well played. Mme Olga Samaroff-Stokowski acquired merit by featuring it on her programs, and it is said that the fugato finale was a favorite piece of Anton Rubinstein. The Allegretto takes the place of the customary slow movement and the tempo should be adjusted accordingly.

Sonata No. 7, Opus 10, No. 3, D major. Perhaps the most delightful of the early sonatas, prevailingly happy with an inspired slow movement, *Largo e mesto,* surcharged with passionate grief. In the first movement we need not hesitate to supply the high F sharp in the twenty-second measure, a note not yet in the compass of Beethoven's piano. The appoggiaturas of the second subject are long (see the *Urtext*) and should be played as regular eighth-notes:

Ex. 60

The fanciful starts, stops, and pauses of the rondo must be interpreted with light humor.

Sonata No. 8, Opus 13, C minor (Sonate pathétique). The title, for once, is original with Beethoven and therefore deserves serious attention. The pathos of the first movement is indeed unmistakable without the name, but one often hears the rondo played almost jauntily, quite out of line with the intention. The slow movement, as often in Beethoven's works of similar character (cf. Opus 10, No. 1, Opus 27, No. 2, and Opus 57) relieves the tension by an interval of peace.

This sonata would have fared well in an orchestral setting. The performer will find it extremely helpful in molding his tone to imagine the quality of the various string and woodwind instruments.

No better test of a student's sense of rhythm could be posed than the *Grave* introduction to the first movement, usually murdered by failure to measure the note and rest values with precision. The tremolo basses of the *Allegro di molto* are exact eighth-notes, not indeterminate repetitions of the broken octaves.

Sonata No. 10, Opus 14, No. 2, G major. A miniature sonata, simple, polished, and charming. I shall return to it in recommending a selection to students and amateurs.

Sonata No. 12, Opus 26, A flat. Beethoven's first important departure from the traditional sonata form, presenting some similarity to Mozart's Sonata in A major. The first movement is a set of variations. Two successive movements in dance form follow, the Scherzo and the funeral march (*Marcia funebre sulla morte d'un Eroe*). The concluding Allegro is in rondo form. The composer is said to have transcribed the funeral march for orchestra in the key of B minor;[7] this version, I believe, was never printed.

Though the structure is informal, the sonata hangs together perfectly. The movements are well contrasted, each contributing its share to the rounded whole. Again I reserve some detailed remarks for a later page.

Sonata No. 13, Opus 27, No. 1, E flat (Sonata quasi una Fantasia). The subtitle is amply justified. The beginning Andante, interrupted by an energetic Allegro section only to return in unruffled calm, is a true fantasia. The *Allegro molto e vivace,* in dance form, doubtless seemed too serious to be called a scherzo, though a more playful tone brightens its Trio. The first measure of this movement is a "weak" measure; play it like the upbeat of a $\frac{6}{4}$ rhythm:

Ex. 61

The *Adagio con espressione* must be taken as an introduction to the finale, not a separate movement. The finale itself, a rondo with a development section replacing the middle subject, breaks off near the end, just before the last measures of presto, to recall the melody of the slow introduction.

Sonata No. 14, Opus 27, No. 2, C-sharp minor. The unparalleled popularity of this sonata has been enormously aided by the ridiculous nicknames ("Arbor" and "Moonlight") and the aprocryphal love story tacked on to it by irresponsible romanticists. The nicknames are pure caprice. The tale of Beethoven's devotion to the Countess Giulietta Guicciardi, to whom the sonata is dedicated, and of her jilting him for Count Gallenberg, whom she married, may have some foundation in fact, but there is no evidence that the composer suffered the broken heart attributed to him in consequence. Many were the ladies of

---

[7] Thayer's *Life* translated by Krehbiel, Vol. II, pp. 298–9.

quality with whom Beethoven was at one time or other in love; once at least he seriously contemplated marriage; but none of these affairs of the heart ever went beyond a platonic stage. Attempts to link the Countess Guicciardi with the "immortal beloved" of Beethoven's famous letter (discovered in his desk after his death) have been as inconclusive as research into the identity of the dark lady of Shakespeare's sonnets. Why not permit the musician to dramatize his feelings in a sonata and the man to address his ideal woman in a letter without pinning him down to one emotion or a single object of worship?

Looking at the composition, then, in the light of its own merit, we are struck by the known fact that Beethoven himself was inclined to belittle it. In fact, he was actually vexed by its outstanding popularity. "Everybody is always talking about the C-sharp minor sonata!" he exclaimed to Czerny. "Surely I have written better things. There is the Sonata in F-sharp major—that is something very different." The master, however, was notoriously erratic in his estimation of his own works, and this is only one of numerous cases in which the world has respectfully declined to endorse his verdict. To us it remains, and bids fair long to remain, a masterpiece and an indispensable item of our literature.

The least-disciplined fingers can easily play the notes of the first movement, but only profoundest feeling can give expression to its yearning anguish. Sadder tones than these have never been penned:

Ex. 62

The throb of pain in the minor ninth, C natural, is indescribably affecting. The following Allegretto was beautifully described by Liszt as a "flower between two abysses." It is an intermezzo of utmost simplicity. The *Presto agitato* plunges us into a tornado of passion where the restraint of the first movement is thrown aside in open rebellion.

Sonata No. 15, *Opus* 28, *D major* (*Sonata Pastorale*). The designation "pastoral," though unauthorized by the composer, is (as Thayer remarks) not inept, certainly not a gross misnomer like that of its immediate predecessor. The untutored public is not always wrong. The idyllic character of the piece is best illustrated in the first and last movements. Carl Reinecke, a thorough-going adherent of "absolute" music, once confided to me that he heard in the opening bass notes of the rondo:

Ex. 63

the sound of Sunday evening village bells—a pretty fancy. Czerny, to whom we owe many interesting side lights on Beethoven's music, tells us that the Andante in D minor of this sonata was long a favorite of the composer, who played it often for his own pleasure.

Sonata No. 17, Opus 31, No. 2, D minor. This fine sonata belongs to the group that I have called dramas of the soul and is therefore spiritually related to the C-sharp minor Sonata, though outwardly the points of difference are many. Whereas the earlier sonata is extraordinarily free in structure, this is one of the most regular, compact, and balanced in form. Here the storm and stress center in the first movement, while the last is the more restrained. Again, the long rounded phrases of the lovely Adagio are quite unlike the studied unpretentiousness of the Allegretto of Opus 27, No. 2.

The boding slow arpeggio introducing the first movement is quickly succeeded by the panting eight-note figures of the Allegro, full of disquiet. At the twenty-first measure the slow opening arpeggio is transformed to furious clamor, and the two moods of the motive recur at intervals throughout. The second theme, in the dominant minor instead of the relative major, sustains the tragic tone of the movement. In speaking of Beethoven's unusual pedal effects I have already noticed the two ghostly recitatives occurring at the reprise; they come like a voice from the tomb. The last movement, in sonata-form, is for the most part melancholy and wistful, with occasional outbursts of agitation. It is remarkable for the persistent use of the four-note motive:

Ex. 64

and an unbroken series of four-bar phrases, both so skillfully managed as to avoid monotony.

Sonata No. 18, Opus 31, No. 3, E-flat major. A lyric of adorable serenity and happiness. The appealing motive of the first measure was once charmingly translated by Liszt into the question:

Ex. 65

for the benefit of a young lady in his class at Weimar who was playing the notes with wooden lack of sentiment. The falling interval, often dropping the unessential sixteenth-note and changing to the diminution:

Ex. 66

dominates the movement. The Scherzo, in $\frac{2}{4}$ time and written in sonata-form, has an almost Mendelssohnian lightness. The songful Menuetto contrasts admirably with the continuous staccato of the Scherzo. Saint-Saëns used the theme of its trio for his clever Variations and Fugue for two pianos. The gaiety of the final *Presto con fuoco* (once more in sonata-form) is inescapably contagious.

Sonata No. 21, Opus 53, C major (Waldstein Sonata). Like the *Kreutzer* Sonata for piano and violin and the three "Rasoumowsky" string quartets, this work is universally known by the name of the person to whom it was dedicated, Count Ferdinand Gabriel von Waldstein. Superbly scored for piano, it is inevitably a *pièce de résistance* of concert programs, yet performers and public are tireless in their devotion. As has already been pointed out, the piece is in two movements, the first in regular sonata-form, the other a very extended rondo prefaced by a short slow introduction. Beethoven had at first included a long slow movement, whereupon a friend ventured to say that the sonata was too lengthy. After berating the candid critic unmercifully, Beethoven profited by his advice and made a change of undoubted wisdom. (See, later, the Andante favori in F.) The form of the rondo is that variety in which the entries of the subject are interspersed with episodes; there is nothing that could be called a second theme. Both movements have elaborate codas. It takes a professional technique to , cope with the difficulties of the sonata. On modern pianos, very few players can execute the octaves of the concluding Prestissimo in the glissando called for. Various substitute renderings have been offered, that of Bülow being probably the most acceptable:

Ex. 67

though clever players might venture on the following variant of the third and fourth measures:

Ex. 68

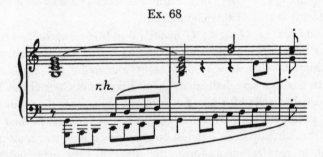

The tempo of the first movement may be as fast as clarity permits; in the rondo, on the other hand, the direction *Allegretto moderato*

should be faithfully observed, especially for the lyric main theme. The episodes may be somewhat faster, for though purely a rule of thumb, it is a good general principle that the difficult passages of any piece require the quickest tempi.

Sonata No. 23, Opus 57, F minor (Sonata Appassionata). The title does not appear in the autograph; it was added in an early edition and has rightly been retained ever since. It is in truth a nobly impassioned work, grandly conceived and grandly carried out. The almost unbearable fire of the first movement subsides to soothing repose in the short set of variations (*Andante con moto*), only to be fanned again to hottest flame in the tremendous sweep of the finale. Beethoven thought it his best sonata.

Fate's "knocking at the door" is traceable in the motive:

Ex. 69

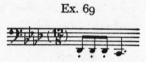

Compare this with the

Ex. 70

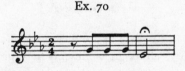

of the Fifth Symphony and the

Ex. 71

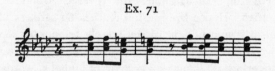

of the *Egmont Overture*, written at about the same period of Beethoven's activity. Observe, too, the similarity between the two chief themes of the first movement; the second is but a new phase of the first. Together they tend to confute the commonly accepted theory that the best themes move in diatonic progression.

I venture the opinion that an accomplished amateur will have better success in attempting the *Appassionata* than the *Waldstein*. Both are extremely difficult, but in the heat of passion it is a venial offense to strike a few wrong notes, whereas technical slips show up more glaringly when polished finger work is demanded.

Sonata No. 24, Opus 78, F-sharp major. This slight two-movement sonata hardly justifies the composer's high regard. Certainly few will agree with him in rating it above the C-sharp minor sonata, as we know he did. We may regard it as a minor product of Beethoven's maturity. Many of my colleagues admire it more than I am able to, and it is by no means a stranger to concert audiences. Indeed, it is easy enough to surrender oneself to the amiable melodic lines of the *Allegro ma non troppo,* or to the graceful caprice of the *Allegro vivace.* I defer respectfully, therefore, to more enthusiastic judgments than my own.

Sonata No. 26, Opus 81ᵃ, E-flat major (*Sonate caractéristique: Les Adieux, l'absence et le retour*). One of Beethoven's rare acknowledged essays in program music. He inscribed the motto of the first movement over the first three notes of the introductory Adagio:

Ex. 72

It goes just as well in English: "Fare thee well." But alas for romance! this is no love story, although commonly interpreted in that sense. The manuscript bears two inscriptions in Beethoven's own hand: "The Farewell, Vienna, May 4, 1809, on the departure of His Imperial Highness the revered Archduke Rudolph," and to the finale: "The Arrival of His Imperial Highness the revered Archduke Rudolph, January 30, 1810." Hence the music breathes no sadness of farewell; from the outset it is confident of the merely temporary separation of friends. Toward the end of the first movement, it is true, there is a beautiful lingering dialogue suggestive of Juliet's words: "I shall say good night till it be morrow."[8] This passage justifies the most tender treatment. The "Absence" movement is more pensive than

---

[8] Beethoven was well acquainted with Shakespeare's play. He even toyed with the idea of composing an opera on the subject. Once, after playing the Adagio from the F major Quartet, he asked a friend what impression it had made. To the answer: "It pictured for me the parting of two lovers," he rejoined: "Good! I thought of the scene in the burial vault in *Romeo and Juliet.*" This is one indication among many that Beethoven often indulged programmatic ideas not publicly divulged.

grieving; memory of the last presence mingles with anticipation of the next. Bülow thought he detected amid the impetuous introduction to the finale a motive

Ex. 73

reminding him of Isolde waving her welcoming scarf to the approaching Tristan in Wagner's opera. The "Return" comes suddenly: a forte chord startling us from reverie, a quick rush of meeting, and then a long pæan of joy. To match the confidence of the parting there is a ring of triumph as well as happiness in the reunion. The movement is pianistically brilliant and exciting.

Sonata No. 27, Opus 90, E minor. If disappointed in Opus 81ª, the sentimentally minded will find compensation in the story of the dedication of Opus 90 to Count Moritz Lichnowsky. The Count had contracted a second marriage, long opposed by his family, with a virtuous and talented opera singer. On receiving the sonata, he asked Beethoven if its two movements had any special meaning, and was told that they were a musical setting of his courtship and might be headed "Struggle between heart and head" and "Conversation with the loved one." Here, then, is a genuine romance. The music fully bears out its secret program, especially if we examine the endings of the movements. The last twenty-four measures of the Allegro subtly confirm a victory of the heart. The tender rondo, in fine harmony with Beethoven's suggested title, ends apparently very ineffectually in a sudden piano

Ex. 74

difficult to interpret. But imagine the conversation ending with a kiss, and light breaks on us at once. The sonata is a masterpiece of feeling.

Sonata No. 28, Opus 101, A major. We come now to the five magnificent sonatas of Beethoven's ripest genius. They form a special group within the longer series, and it used to be a favorite stunt of pianists to play them on a single program—a feat to be deprecated, since too much meat cannot be healthily digested at one feast. I have heard Eugen d'Albert, after a recital of this kind, throw in the *Appassionata* as an encore!

At this time Beethoven had made up his mind (erroneously, as it happens) that the piano was a German invention and should receive a German name. He gave directions that in future all his works should be for the *Hammerklavier*, not the Italian *pianoforte*. Opus 101, accordingly, was entitled a *Grand Sonata for the Hammerklavier*. Posterity has forgotten this, and the only sonata to which the name has stuck is Opus 106.

Returning to Opus 101 in particular, we may begin by admiring the emotional variety of its contents: the ineffable lyricism of the Allegretto; the heroism of the *Alla Marcia;* the yearning sadness of the Adagio (an introduction to the last movement); the splendid determination of the final Allegro ("*Mit Entschlossenheit*," is Beethoven's command), sustained with incomparable nerve. Perhaps the inward feeling (*Innigste Empfindung*) of the first movement clings longest to memory when the sonata is finished. The canon in the trio of the march is not wholly grateful to the ear, but the fugato in the development section of the last movement is masterly. The sonata-form of the Allegretto is condensed, that of the finale expansive. The march, naturally, is in dance form.

Sonata No. 29, Opus 106, B flat. Full title: *Grosse Sonate für das Hammer-Klavier.* The immensity of this composition cannot fail to strike us with awe. We gaze at its vast dome like pygmies from below, never feeling on an intellectual or moral level with it; its lonely grandeur inhibits it from inspiring love except in the wonderful Adagio sostenuto. The first movement cries aloud for the limitless resources of the orchestra; no hammers, strings, and sounding-board can convey its titanic force or the rich palette of its color scheme. The humor of the Scherzo, judiciously placed before the Adagio, is somewhat inscrutable. One notices in passing the harmonic simplicity of its trio (only two triads, B-flat minor and D-flat major, figure in it), and the easygoing canon of its second phrase, contrasting with the more labored canon in Opus 101. Words can no more than hint at the dolor, the resignation, the heavenly aspiration of the Adagio. One must play or hear it to win any perception of its beauty. The first measure was a genial afterthought, added when the sonata was already in print.

Can the colossal fugue be enjoyed as music? Great artists strain at it, oppressed by its bristling difficulties and fearful of slips of memory.

Yet I have heard a mere conservatory student, a young girl blessed with infallible fingers and memory and sublimely unconscious of Herculean effort, toss it off with resistless aplomb and intelligent grasp of its complicated structure, bringing positive chuckles of glee from Harold Bauer and Ossip Gabrilowitsch, who attended the recital. The moral, I suppose, is that the nettle should be grasped firmly, not approached in fear and trembling. Ease of performance, however, must be preceded by painstaking study. The most expert Bach-player may find himself at fault in this stupendous piece unless he is willing to revise and enlarge his knowledge of fugue. The intricate polyphony, employing every device of inversion, augmentation, stretto, and even the rare *cancrizans* ("crab," or playing of the theme backwards, note for note, preserving the original intervals and rhythm); the treatment of the shorter motives and countersubjects; the independent episodes; the restful new theme of the D major section and its later combination with the main subject; the cycle of remote keys through which the piece moves; the freedom of the coda; each detail of the architecture claims thoughtful examination before it can be placed in proper relation to the whole. At the very beginning, ask yourself where the principal theme ends; your impulse will be to say offhand that its length is ten measures, up to the entrance of the tonal answer. Wrong! Look well ahead and you will discover the actual length to be only six measures; the other four are a long "tag" or extension, never adhered to in future entries. For a minute and masterly analysis of the fugue, see the third appendix to Busoni's edition of the first book of Bach's *Well-Tempered Clavier*.

Beethoven worked long and hard at Opus 106, intending it to be his greatest sonata. Simultaneously he was engaged on his Ninth and greatest symphony. It is a coincidence that these are among the few works for which he personally provided metronome timings. The absence elsewhere in the sonatas of metronome marks is the less regrettable because in this case the tempo set for the first movement, $\flat$ = 138, is technically and musically far too fast; about $\flat$ = 104 would be more reasonable. When a composer of rank orders us to break our neck we should dutifully take the risk, provided that we can do so without breaking his neck too. The scherzo is also marked too fast, at any rate from the technical standpoint. Only the tempi of the Adagio and the fugue can be accepted with confidence and safety.

Sonata No. 30, Opus 109, E major. We find again in this sonata a beautifully balanced variety of moods; a sort of introspective amiability in the prelude-like *Vivace, ma non troppo*, alternating with graver accents in the twice intervening *Adagio espressivo;* decisive energy in the Prestissimo, a movement in compact sonata-form; and sheer euphony in the concluding set of variations, one of Beethoven's most divine inspirations. A curious little distortion of a sequence of imitations occurs in the Prestissimo, where the composer writes:

Ex. 75

Bülow's proposed emendation at*:

Ex. 76

satisfies the natural progression of voices better, though it is awkward pianistically. The only logical change would be more far-reaching:

Ex. 77

In Ex. 77 I have added the tremolo bass in order to show that the crossing of hands at °° presents no problem. But why presume to correct Beethoven?

In the variations, No. 1 should continue the mood and tempo of the theme. No. 2 breaks the legato of the melody into sixteenth-notes without disturbing the tranquil tone. Variations 3 and 5 save the movement from too cloying a sweetness by their sturdiness. Do not fail to notice that the melody and bass of the theme:

Ex. 78

are inverted in Variation 3:

Ex. 79

Variation 4, with its double imitations, is another conversation between two lovers like the rondo of Opus 90. Play the

Ex. 80

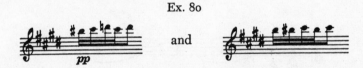

and

at the beginning of the second half like whispered interjections. In the coda (Variation 6) don't worry too much about the seemingly difficult trills; just concentrate on the melody and all will be well.

Sonata No. 31, Op. 110, A flat. One of the most continuously lyrical sonatas. The directions *molto espressivo* and *con amabilità* for the *Moderato cantabile* (in sonata-form) complement each other, requesting an expressive but not over-intense performance. Most pianists phrase the opening measures thus:

Ex. 81

Beethoven's solitary legato slur over the first two notes indicates the more correct reading:

Ex. 82

The passage in thirty-second notes must be taken trippingly; here the staccato marks are to be construed as light stresses. It would be tasteless to accent the first notes of the slurs (following a specious rule often laid down) in the phrase:

Ex. 83

Notwithstanding the apparent detachment of the phrasing, this serene movement should be played in long breaths. The *Allegro molto* is a scherzo in $\frac{2}{4}$ time and in dance form. The quality of Beethoven's humor is sometimes rather crabbed; this is a case in point, with a touch of intentional absurdity added by an allusion to a vulgar Viennese street song of the period:

Ex. 84

The trio, too, is a strange whimsey, incidentally very perilous to the fingers. D'Albert and Schnabel, in their respective editions, are at variance as to the scanning of the meter, the former asserting that the first measure of the Scherzo is obviously an upbeat, the latter retorting that it is obviously no such thing. While the authorities wrangle, the innocent bystander observes with amusement that, whichever way you foot it, you come to a point in the trio where Beethoven maliciously throws you out of step; you have to do a quick shuffle and start all over again.

Greatness banishes levity in the final movement, consisting of several distinct though connecting sections:

   (a) Introduction (from the fourth measure on a recitative), beginning in B-flat minor.
   (b) *Arioso dolente,* A-flat minor.
   (c) Fugue, A-flat major.

(d) Return of the Arioso in G minor.

(e) Return of the fugue, G major, at first in inversion of the theme, then in augmentation, diminution, double diminution, and stretto; leading to a brilliant free coda based on the fugue theme and returning to the tonic key of the sonata, A-flat major.

The *Urtext* unfortunately omits a significant direction at section (d), the return of the "sorrowful lay," where the autograph adds: *"Ermattet, klagend"*; that is to say, "Exhausted, complaining." Mentally restoring these words, the player will naturally sing the first appearance of the Arioso with full-voiced lament and subdue the return to a weakened echo, much to the advantage of his interpretation. Similarly, if we read the dynamics of the fugue carefully we first play it softly but not pianissimo, resorting to the soft pedal for the beginning of section (e). This fugue, unlike its giant cousin of the *Hammerklavier*, is bland and listenable, the friendliest of Beethoven's piano fugues. A layman entirely oblivious of its scholarliness may still take pleasure in its smooth melody and rise emotionally to the peak of splendor on which it ends.

Sonata No. 32, Opus 111, C minor. The stately series of sonatas ends here with the noblest of all. The eminent critic Henry E. Krehbiel wrote of this transcendent composition: "A musician's sonata it is, which discourses music rather than the charms of pianoforte tone. . . . Music, musical thought and its logical expression and development for the ends of beautiful art, is its be-all and end-all, and in his proclamation, especially in the Arietta, Beethoven becomes a seer, as truly transfigured in the spirit as John was on Patmos." The form is as simple as the conception is lofty. Enough to say that an exceptionally terse Allegro is prefaced by a slow introduction and succeeded by an air with variations beginning almost conventionally, straying (after Variation 4) into improvisation, then returning to the theme (at Variation 5) in an extended coda. Beethoven did not number the variations, nor was there any need. Nowadays we are not perplexed by the two-movement form, but Thayer tells us that the publishers, on receipt of the manuscript, wrote to ask if the copyist had forgotten to send a part of it, slyly adding: "they missed a rondo finale"! And Schindler, who aspired to be Beethoven's Boswell without the talents of Johnson's friend and biographer, densely advised the master to complete the work by a triumphant third movement.

The interpretation, like the form, is fundamentally clear and unmistakable. We have only to consult the directions, "majestic" for the introduction, "with fire and passion" for the Allegro, "very simple and singing" for the variations, to make sure of the right ideas. To express them adequately, however, is difficult indeed, for Beethoven's troubled soul seems to hurl its last grand defiance in the Maestoso, to endure its last struggle in the Allegro, to find at length the peace of God in the Arietta.

The Smaller Works

Most important among the smaller works of Beethoven for piano alone are the twenty-one sets of variations. They range in musical value from mere potboilers to the monumental *Eroica* and *Diabelli* Variations. Some of the former we may pass by without comment; of the others I shall speak in the order of their magnitude, beginning with the smaller sets.

1. *Six Easy Variations in G on an Original Theme.* A little piece charmingly adapted to beginners and children, and an ideal introduction to Beethoven's style; far better than the *Six Easy Variations on a Swiss Song*.

2. *Variations on Paisiello's "Nel cor più non mi sento."* A favorite teaching piece, more advanced than the "Easy" Variations, but still simple.

3. *Variations on Dittersdorf's "Es war einmal ein alter Mann."* Not much more difficult than the last mentioned, but much more valuable musically. A clever player can make it graceful and effective.

4. *Variations on Salieri's "La stessa, la stessissima."* The best of the smaller sets, showing great originality and maturity of style, particularly in the final *Allegretto alla Austriaca*, and deserving of a place on recital programs.

5. *Variations in F on an Original Air, Opus 34.* An especially interesting set, with the unique feature that after the theme has been announced each variation descends to the key a third below (from F to D, B flat to G, E flat to C minor) until the dominant is reached, affording a neat return to the tonic for the sixth variation, coda, and an embellished repetition of the theme. In addition to the changes of tonality, each variation has an individuality of its own; the first is a graceful fioritura, the second a scherzo, the third a little pastoral, the fourth a minuet, the fifth a funeral march, the sixth in rondo style. I

cannot recall that the fascinating key scheme has ever been duplicated.

6. *Variations on Righini's Arietta "Venni amore."* This neglected work might well be revived by an enterprising pianist ready to forsake the beaten track for an unhackneyed number. Wegeler tells a good story about it that is worth repeating. As a young man Beethoven was so impressed by the refined performance of the Abbé Sterkel at Aschaffenburg that he hesitated when invited to take his turn at the piano. The crafty abbé thereupon hinted that the *Venni amore* contained difficulties possibly beyond the composer's technique, and Beethoven was piqued into playing all the variations he could remember at the moment and improvising others no less intricate.

7. *Variations and Fugue on a Theme from "Prometheus."* These are known as the *Eroica* Variations, being based on the theme used by Beethoven for the last movement of his Third Symphony. They start with an introduction giving the bass of the theme in unison octaves followed by three variations in two, three, and four parts respectively. Only now does the melody itself appear. To this there are fifteen variations, the last a long, tuneful, and highly ornamented Largo. The bass recovers prominence as subject of the Fugue (*Finale alla fuga*), yielding again to the melody in the freely extended coda.

Notwithstanding the striking merits of the piece, it is thrown into comparative shade by the gorgeous orchestral version of the symphony.

8. *Thirty-two Variations in C minor.* Strictly speaking, this work should be called a chaconne, for the variations run into one another continuously throughout. "Thirty-two variations" threatens excessive length, but the theme contains only eight unrepeated measures, and the variations stay within the same limit until the expanded coda frees itself from so narrow a confine. The succession of small units might result in a scrappy effect did not many of the variations arrange themselves in larger groups; for example, Nos. 1–3, 10 and 11, 12–14, 15 and 16, 20 and 21, 26 and 27. Variety is further provided for by the combination of Nos. 12–17 into the equivalent of a slow movement. The coda really begins at Variation 31.

Beethoven's contempt of this grand composition is incomprehensible. We are told that he once found a young lady practising it, and after listening awhile asked: "By whom is that?" "By you," she returned wonderingly. "Such nonsense by me? O Beethoven, what an ass you were!" Musicians rank it among his finest works, and of all the variations it is the oftenest played and the best liked by concertgoers.

9. *Thirty-three Variations on a Waltz by Diabelli, Opus* 120. The publisher Diabelli, having composed a waltz, hit on the thought of inviting a number of contemporary composers to write variations on it. He carried out his plan, but Beethoven, not liking the theme, refused to collaborate. Later, however, he grew interested and contracted for a set of variations outnumbering the thirty-two already written by other composers (ultimately these grew to fifty). It is likely that he intended the piece to be his greatest in variation form, just as he planned Opus 106 to be his greatest sonata and the Ninth his greatest symphony. In any case it is written on a grand scale of dimension, style, and difficulty. Yet Beethoven's first misgiving about the theme was justified, so that with all the imposing workmanship lavished on it the composition suffers from the triviality of its origin and remains more attractive to the scholar than to the average listener. To comment on the variations one by one would be tedious. Monotony is averted by frequent changes of mood, tempo, and time signature. At one place a theme from Mozart's *Figaro* is introduced. Of course there is a fugue; curiously enough, it is placed not at the end but just before the last variation, a quiet minuet and coda.

It may be of historical interest to note that this work was once given at a concert of the Beethoven Association of New York[9] by a group of thirteen pianists and conductors[1] alternating at four pianos in the performance.

Very few of Beethoven's occasional pieces for piano solo reach the level of the sonatas or the best variations. Some, like the sets of écossaises and contradances, are so slight in themselves that they have given occasion for transcription in more effective form by Busoni, Seitz, and others. The second of the six small minuets has been annexed to the violin literature by Fritz Kreisler. A single E-flat Minuet, not included in the set of six, is better than they. The album leaf "For Elise," like the "Easy" Variations, is delightfully adapted to a child's technique and mentality. A number of other trifles may safely be ignored. The three sets of bagatelles, however, are truly Beethovenish, chips of marble from the workshop, some rough and unpolished, others

---

[9] The Beethoven Association was founded in 1918 under the presidency of Harold Bauer. For twenty years it gave concerts in New York, the participating artists receiving no remuneration and the proceeds being donated to various worthy musical objects.

[1] Bauer, Bodansky, Damrosch, Furtwängler, Ganz, Friskin, Hutcheson, Lhevinne, Merö, Moiseiwitsch, Randolph, Schelling, Stojowski.

fashioned with skill and affection. The composer himself had a high regard for them.

More ambitious are the Andante favori in F, a Polonaise, a Fantasia, the two rondos, Opus 51, and the *Rondo a capriccio*, Opus 129. We have already seen that Beethoven discarded the Andante in F from the *Waldstein* Sonata because of its length. We gain by a transplantation that turns our undivided attention to a lovely piece. The Polonaise in C, Opus 89, one may venture to say, is neither good Beethoven nor a good polonaise. Nor is the Fantasia, Opus 77, in Beethoven's best manner, though it throws some light on one type of his improvisations. Beginning in G minor, it roams through short sections in B flat, D minor, A flat, and D major, coming at last to rest in a longer coda, B major. The logic of the key succession is hard to perceive, and the thematic material makes no pretense to cohesion. To be blunt, it is a disconcerting and disappointing work.

The two Rondos, Opus 51, in C and G, find Beethoven on firmer ground. His genius was epic and manifested itself most naturally in forms allied to the sonata and symphony. One cannot imagine him writing successful nocturnes or mazurkas. The Rondo in G is an exceptionally graceful lyric, its gentle flow stirred to a more animated ripple in the middle section. The Rondo in C, not quite so fine, is a wonderfully instructive piece to study, calling for all sorts of niceties of tone, phrasing, rhythm, and style. Quite different is the *Rondo a capriccio*, Opus 129, bearing the strange subtitle "Rage over the lost Groschen, vented (*ausgetobt*) in a caprice." Here we have an unusually intimate personal glimpse of the master. One may picture him wildly hunting the lost coin, flying into one of his violent rages over the failure to find it, and then, suddenly realizing the absurdity of his temper, sitting down to "vent" it all in a tonal caprice full of humor and self-mockery. Bülow has written with charming understanding of this unique piece of program music.

The Chamber Music and Concertos

I can only lament the impossibility of giving space in this volume to Beethoven's sonatas for piano with violin or cello and to the pianoforte trios. The amateur will profit immensely by adopting a few of these into his repertory. He should readily find kindred spirits to join him in study of at least the F major Violin Sonata, the A major

Cello Sonata, and the C minor Trio, none of them extravagantly difficult. If he can add other sonatas and trios he will be the more fortunate. These chamber-music compositions equal the solo sonatas in beauty and power.

The five piano concertos cannot be so curtly dismissed. For the sake of completeness the Triple Concerto for piano, violin, and cello, and the Choral Fantasia, Opus 80, for piano, chorus, and orchestra must be listed, but the amateur will hardly feel a strong urge to study either of them, nor would he easily find opportunity to perform them. The Concerto in C, published as No. 1, Opus 15, is actually the second in order of composition. The Concerto in B flat, which should precede that in C, appears in print as No. 2, Opus 19. Both are strongly Mozartean in quality. Of late years they have figured prominently on symphony programs, particularly the C major Concerto, an attractive and brilliant piece with a Largo of inspired lyricism. For the first movement of this work the composer wrote no fewer than three cadenzas, the third so masterly as to seem disproportionately great; the tail, as it were, wags the dog.

The Third Concerto, Opus 37, in C minor, occupies a midway position, chronologically and musically, among the five. It is unquestionable Beethoven, though not yet the fully mature Beethoven of the two later concertos. All the movements show greater profundity than their predecessors. Noteworthy advances of style are evident in the opening theme of the first movement, sternly energetic:

Ex. 85

in the characteristically persistent development of the motive at (a), and in the novel entrance of the coda after the cadenza. Mysticism tinges the beauty of the Larghetto; virility replaces lightheartedness in the Rondo.

Whether you prefer the poetic G major Concerto, Opus 58, or the lordly *Emperor* in E flat, Opus 73, depends on your temperament. The prevailing moods of the two are so dissimilar that comparison is inevitable. One star differeth from another star in glory; both are masterworks. They both depart from the routine of the classic pattern by introducing the solo instrument in advance of the first long orchestral *tutti*, but in Opus 58 the piano dreamily foreshadows the main theme, while in Opus 73 it thunders forth a series of brilliant prefatory passages. The leading subjects, tender in the G major, pungently rhythmical in the E flat, preserve their distinctive features throughout the first movements. The finales are no less contrasted in feeling, the one light, wayward, and fanciful, the other assertive and imposing. The G major Concerto makes the impression of a piece of exquisite chamber music; the *Emperor* can only be thought of as a symphony for piano and orchestra.

We have seen again and again how careful Beethoven is to avoid monotony in his sonatas by a complete change of mood in their slow movements. He provides this relief in these two great concertos with even more than his usual fine sense of balance. As the basic quality of Opus 58 is gentle and visionary, severer accents are welcome in its *Andante con moto*. In this intensely tragic movement the strings issue and repeat iron commands, the piano responding only with pleading whispers. The soft answers of the soloist eventually turn away the wrath of the orchestra, which exits subdued. Now, however, the piano in turn is seized by agitation, flaring out in a passionate cadenza before it, too, exhausts itself. The strings finally rejoin the piano in an ending of dreary hopelessness. The last chord is softly prolonged until the gloom is magically dispelled by the *attacca* of the cheerful Rondo. In the *Emperor* Concerto, on the other hand, Beethoven's problem was to create a telling contrast to two movements of heroic power. Here, accordingly, the Adagio takes the form of an idyllic reverie, a hushed song in three strophes with the strings muted throughout and the piano improvising between verses without ever approaching a climax. The real end of the movement comes four measures before the sudden irruption of the Rondo after the change of key- and time-signatures. The last three measures of the Adagio are transitional, fragments of the coming rondo theme stealing into the consciousness of the dreamer before his slumber is completely broken. This haunting passage lends delicate emphasis to the peace of the Adagio while preparing by artful suspense for the crashing announcement of the imperious finale.

During Beethoven's lifetime the cadenza was already becoming a vexed problem of the classical concerto. Not all players were so gifted as to be able to display their virtuosity in improvisation without doing violence to the spirit of the composer. Add to this that the improvisor, once mounted on his hobbyhorse, too easily lost all sense of time and did not know when to stop. The cadenza therefore tended

increasingly to swamp the main movement with a long show of irrelevant dexterity. Beethoven bore the abuse patiently through his
first three concertos, and in the first movement of the G major still
unprotestingly allotted the usual space for a cadenza. In the last
movement of this work, however, he imperatively tells the player to
limit himself to a short extemporization: "*la cadenza sia corta.*" By
the time he wrote the *Emperor* he was determined to run no risk whatever. As it might have seemed startling to omit the customary invitation to the soloist entirely, he explained himself rather elaborately.
After bringing the orchestra to the time-honored fermata on the tonic
$^6_4$ chord near the close of the first movement, Beethoven instructs the
player "not to make a cadenza but to proceed immediately to the
following" ("*non si fa una cadenza, ma s'attacca subito il seguente*").
"The following" appears to be a short written-in cadenza of eleven
measures and a half ending with the usual long trill, but I myself
feel strongly that the character of a cadenza, though admittedly not
its form, is maintained for twenty-one measures more, through the
romantic entrance of the horns and up to the next marked *tutti,* where
the coda unmistakably sets in. The last movement of this concerto gives
no opportunity at all to interpolate a cadenza.

I offer several selections of Beethoven's piano works for reading
and study. The first is a fairly complete repertory of the best pieces
for children, assuming that our children are neither backward nor
in the prodigy class.

LIST A. FOR CHILDREN
Albumblatt: Für Elise
Bagatelles, Opus 33, No. 3, in F, and Opus 119, No. 1, in G minor
Two Easy Sonatas, Opus 49, G minor and G major
Rondo in A
Six Easy Variations in G

Of course it is sufficient for any child to learn one or two pieces
from this list; he should then be ready to advance. Nos. 3 and 6 of
the Variations need the octave stretch. The two sonatinas in G and
F often printed among Beethoven's compositions are excluded because
of their very dubious authenticity.

The next selection may be called an album for youth. A course of
study is doubly beneficial when well timed. There are pieces that
gain greatly if approached without undue sophistication; learned in

early years they are cherished through life, but if delayed too long the youthful naïvety of perception is lost. More commonly, works demanding mental and technical ripeness are permanently ruined for us if we attack them with a crude equipment. To illustrate, suppose we aim to play both the Sonata in A flat, Opus 26, and the *Appassionata,* it will be wise to study the two in that order, not reversely. In this way we give ourselves a reasonable chance to keep pace with the composer's own growth.

B. SUGGESTIONS FOR YOUTH
Minuet in E flat
Rondo in C
Sonatas in G, Opus 14, No. 2, and F, Opus 10, No. 2
Bagatelles, selected from Opus 33 and Opus 119
Variations on *"Es war einmal,"* or
Variations in B flat on *"La Stessa, la stessissima"*

There is every reason that the amateur should emulate one sterling virtue of the fine professional: namely, to familiarize himself with a much wider range of literature than the limited number of pieces that he can actually learn to perform. Thus you tap deep sources of experience and inspiration and bring to your work on any particular piece an accumulated wisdom. For my next recommendations, therefore, I propose alternatives of Beethoven's masterpieces.

C. FOR MATURE STUDY
Sonata in D, Opus 10, No. 3, or Sonata in C, Opus 2, No. 3
Sonate pathétique, Opus 13, or Sonata in E flat, Opus 31, No. 3
Sonata in C-sharp minor, Opus 27, No. 2, or Sonata in E minor, Opus 90
Variations in C minor, or Variations in F, Opus 34
Rondo in G, or Andante favori in F
Concerto in C major, or Concerto in C minor

A careful study of one or two sonatas of Beethoven goes far to initiate us into many simple but basic principles of taste and style. Too often the beginner, relying blindly on his teacher's instructions, learns to play detached passages correctly without understanding exactly *why* they are right. In this case his experience is useless for the future instead of being universally applicable. If the reader will have patience, I shall try to indicate a few at least of these elementary principles, taking two sonatas for my text.

SONATA IN G, OPUS 14, NO. 2

1. In beginning a piece or theme, it is all-important to set the listener right as to the meter; any wrong accent may throw him completely out. For instance, a stress at either of the points marked x in the following example would give a false beat.

Ex. 86

This does not mean that the metrical accent falling on the B of the motive need be bumped out violently. On the contrary, a faint swell toward the beat is preferable to a more localized emphasis.

Ex. 87

This gives the true upbeat character to the first three sixteenth-notes. No exercise could be more instructive than to play through the opening phrases of a great many different movements of Beethoven with this point in view, taking care to mark the beats clearly, however gently. In vigorous themes, of course, the stresses must be correspondingly stronger, amounting sometimes to a definite *sforzando*.

2. Whenever a short phrase is identically or quasi-identically repeated, it is advisable to make some slight change of tone to guard against monotony. Taste must decide whether the repetition had better be weaker, louder, or varied in some other way. In this case:

Ex. 88

it would be sufficient to omit the inflection (the rhythm now being established) at the second occurrence.

3. Similarly, melodic repetitions of the same note should rarely be played with equal tone; they may be either crescendo, diminuendo, or swelling toward the middle. Here—

Ex. 89

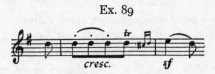

the *sforzando* E clearly requires a crescendo approach, as marked. The E is the climax of the phrase, and it is practically always safe to adjust the inflection to the climax, whether it falls on a high or a low note. For instance:

Ex. 90

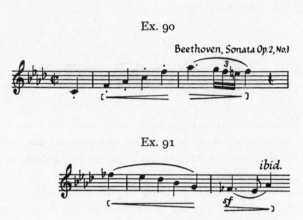

Ex. 91

The tyro's dearest vice is to begin crescendos like that in Ex. 88 too soon and too much. He may remember to advantage Bülow's maxim: crescendo means piano, diminuendo means forte. This is not a book on piano-playing; nevertheless I shall recommend one exercise in inflection that I have found invaluable.

Ex. 92

We might call this the *missa da voce* of the pianist. Do it with each finger in turn, grading the swell and decline of tone as evenly as possible. Then try eight notes to each rise and fall, making the range from *pp* to *ff*. If you are ambitious enough, end up with twelve notes each way; now you may have to help out as you near the fortissimo by dipping the hand to reinforce the finger action. If you master this exercise you will have acquired an enviable control of the technique of expression.

We might add to Bülow's rule, quoted above, its application to rhythmical nuance: accelerando means slow, rallentando means fast. In words of one syllable, if you wish to get loud, start soft; if you wish to get soft, start loud; if you wish to get fast, start slow; and if you wish to get slow, start fast. Few things in art can be reduced to axioms, but in these there is a goodly part of the law and the prophets.

4. Dissonances attract accents. This is particularly true of suspensions, as in those occurring at measures fourteen to twenty-two of this movement. Therefore play:

Ex. 93

The note of resolution is always softer. The rule holds even when the dissonance occurs on a weak beat of the measure; see the concluding measures of the first section. In such cases the accent is usually marked by the composer.

5. The only sure way of learning to play polyrhythms, especially in rapid time, is to train yourself to do them by ear. In a passage like the one beginning in A flat in the development section of this movement, it is a sheer waste of effort to attempt the "least common multiple" system often advocated by teachers. If, instead, you practise each hand separately, fully up to the tempo required, and then put them together, attending only to the beats where the hands synchronize and letting the other notes take care of themselves, I cheerfully guarantee that you will find little trouble. You only get into difficulty when you concentrate attention on the notes that do *not* come together. True, it is possible in a slow tempo to use the least-common-multiple idea for beginners, as in the following from Beethoven's Rondo in C:

Ex. 94

practising thus:

Ex. 95

but this mechanical method only postpones an evil day when you come to play three notes against four. Here you would have to count twelve, bringing one hand on every first, fifth, and ninth count and the other on every first, fourth, seventh, and tenth count, necessitating so slow a tempo that it would bear no relation whatever to the result desired. If you are not convinced, let me ask you to take a complicated polyrhythm, say seven against eight, for a test:

Ex. 96

counting only two to the measure, taking the hands alternately in moderate time and then playing them together with no thought beyond having them coincide at the two counts. You have an excellent chance of getting it right after a few trials. Now, even if you can already do it easily, try counting fifty-six and putting each note in its right arithmetical place. See how far you get! No: the ear triumphs easily where the mathematical sense abdicates. Note finally that all polyrhythms are easier fast than slow; hence it is common sense first to practise them in fast time.

SONATA IN A FLAT, OPUS 26

6. Whether a phrase consists of two notes or a hundred and two the last note is normally soft and unaccented. This is as natural as the drop of the voice at the end of a sentence in speaking. Look at the theme of the variations in this sonata. It easily scans in four phrases

of four measures each, then two shorter phrases of two measures each; the next six measures are indivisible, containing no cadence, and the theme ends with two more four-bar phrases. Every one of these phrases should be shaded off at the end, and of course the same procedure will be appropriate throughout the variations. All the phrases of the Scherzo require the same treatment. The rule is not invariable, for a phrase may end on a point of climax requiring an accent, just as the voice may be raised at the end of a sentence to signify a question or to give some exceptional emphasis. Nevertheless the habit of rounding off phrases to a tapering end is intuitive in musical persons and should be cultivated from the first stages of study.

We are ready now for another simple summary: dissonances, syncopations, and points of climax normally receive accents; upbeats, resolutions of dissonances, and ends of phrases are usually unstressed.

7. Among the minutiæ of rhythmical accuracy the observance of dotted values is one of the most important. First make sure to notice the difference between single- and double-dotted notes. (See for example the Adagio of the C minor Sonata, Opus 10, No. 1.) In the single-dotted rhythm the shorter note receives exactly a quarter of the beat; avoid the Scylla and Charybdis of ♪ and ♪. Yet we may make a fine discrimination between dotted notes in a lyrical context and those in martial rhythms. In the former avoid especially Scylla and in the latter Charybdis; for snippy performance destroys lyrical effect while a flabby one ruins the decision of the martial rhythm. If you err at all, err at least in the right direction. The first movement and the funeral march of Opus 26 offer a good opportunity to exercise this kind of discrimination.

8. Let me supplement these fragmentary remarks on interpretation by one piece of more solid advice. Always try to form a vivid mental conception of how you wish to play a piece or a theme, since no skill in the world will ever enable you to excel that conception. In doing this, give free rein to your own emotional reaction to the music, for good playing must be subjective as well as objective. Then try to make your conception come alive in tone. Last, intensify your performance sufficiently to carry it to your audience. Anglo-Saxon reticence is the bane of great art, and many feel deeply without ever expressing themselves convincingly. You must allow for the distance, physical and psychological, between yourself and your hearers, exactly as an actor in speaking his lines must reckon with the barrier of the footlights. No exaggeration (a morbid fear of many talented

players) is involved. It has been well said that to warm others you must be red-hot yourself. But even exaggeration is infinitely preferable to a cramped restraint, and it is far easier to curb an excess of temperament than to supply a deficiency of ardor.

This does not apply solely to the professional, for every amateur should play to an audience whenever possible—to a group of persons, to a single friend, or even to an altogether imaginary audience. Too much stress has been laid on music as a means of self-expression. As such it has a certain moral value; those who practise or play in solitude may acquire discipline and find emotional outlet. But it is easy to forget that music is above all else an art of communication. If you say to yourself: "I'm quite warm," you make a bald assertion. When you say to someone else: "I'm quite warm; feel my hands," you pass on a sensation of comfort besides testing the truth of the assertion.

Editions

1. The Breitkopf & Härtel *Urtext,* best edition of the sonatas, is based on the autographs and first editions and is therefore the most authoritative text. Happily it is now reprinted in the American edition of Edwin Kalmus. [Kalmus has also two volumes of variations, not the Urtext, and not well edited (Ruthardt). The six sonatinas are unedited.]

2. The best popular edition is that of Peters. It is reliable except for a few small details of phrasing and pedaling. The volume of variations is particularly useful. [The revised Urtext edition of Peters can be recommended (Carl Adolf Martienssen). Fingerings, Beethoven symbols, and pedal markings in evidence.]

3. Hans von Bülow's edition of the sonatas, beginning at Opus 53, forms part of Lebert's Cotta Edition, Lebert being responsible for the earlier sonatas. Far more trustworthy than in his editions of Bach, Bülow here offers many illuminating comments valuable to the student, but is still arbitrary and at times misleading. Some of the smaller works are included.

4. Eugen d'Albert's version of the sonatas, very similar in general plan to Bülow's, is on the whole better. D'Albert's fingerings are particularly noteworthy.

5. The Associated Board Edition of the sonatas, published by the

Oxford University Press, is by far the best annotated version. The text is fingered and sparingly revised by Harold Craxton. The most valuable feature of the edition, however, is the masterly preface and scholarly commentaries on each individual sonata written by Donald Francis Tovey. [The excellent English Associated Board Edition is now distributed by Mills Music, Inc.]

6. Alfredo Casella's revision of the sonatas in the Ricordi Edition, while elaborate, is scholarly.

7. Artur Schnabel, most recent commentator on the sonatas, overloads the original text with a quite bewildering prodigality of directions. One says this with regret, for Schnabel is a great artist and a great interpreter of Beethoven. I conjecture that he himself never uses anything but the *Urtext* and such facsimiles as are available of the autographs. [Artur Schnabel's death prevented the planned revision of his two scholarly and notable volumes of Beethoven sonatas of which he had spoken at times. He probably would have unloaded the large number of metronome marks during movements and would have changed some of the peculiar fingerings and phrasings.]

8. All the minor works are published in one volume by Augener. Breitkopf & Härtel has a less complete but excellent volume of variations, rondos, bagatelles, etc.

9. For the concertos, the best edition to use (next to the orchestral scores) is that of Steingräber, very thoughtfully edited by Franz Kullak, whose introductory notes are exceptionally instructive. The Schirmer reprint of this edition is trustworthy. These prints have the merit of giving Beethoven's own cadenzas in appendices.

10. For the chamber music with piano the Peters Edition is serviceable. [The new German Urtext edition of G. Henle Verlag of Munich is a commanding one. The music is untouched except for a few fingerings. The very informative text in three languages is excellent (two volumes). Also available in the Urtext are the thirty-two Variations in C minor (what a joy!), the *Andante favori*, and the Bagatelles, op. 33.

The Universal Edition has published (1960) a very fine volume of all the Beethoven variations in the Urtext (Vienna edition). It contains much interesting text in both German and English and a facsimile from a page of the master's sketch book, a delightful assembly of notes—if you can find them.]

CHAPTER SIX

Weber, Schubert, and Mendelssohn

T HE following chronological table places the contemporaries and successors of Beethoven in historical perspective. It includes only those composers who contributed extensively to the literature of the piano. The arrangement in order of death instead of birth gives a clear view of the transition from the classical to the romantic period.

CHRONOLOGICAL TABLE

Mozart	1756–1791	Mendelssohn	1809–1847
Haydn	1732–1809	Kalkbrenner	1788–1849
Dussek	1761–1812	Chopin	1810–1849
Weber	1786–1820	Schumann	1810–1856
Beethoven	1770–1827	Czerny	1791–1857
Schubert	1797–1828	Cramer	1771–1858
Clementi	1752–1832	Moscheles	1794–1870
Hummel	1778–1837	Liszt	1811–1886
Field	1782–1837		

Observe how memorable were the years 1809–11, when Beethoven was midway in his career. In 1809 Haydn died and Mendelssohn was born. 1810 saw the birth of Chopin and Schumann, 1811 that of Liszt.

Contemporaries of Beethoven

Before considering the three great composers whose names head this chapter let me give a short account of the lesser lights.

JAN LADISLAV DUSSEK (1761–1812) A Czech composer and pianist, celebrated in his time but now little more than a historical figure. Dussek is said to have been the first to place his piano sidewise to the audience in public playing.

MUZIO CLEMENTI (1752–1832) In the eighty years of his life Clementi made his mark as composer, pianist, teacher, and publisher. He wrote sixty sonatas for piano besides the sonatinas and that remarkable book of studies, the *Gradus ad Parnassum*. Beethoven admired the sonatas, but to modern taste they are exceedingly dry though excellently constructed. One of the best is the Sonata in B flat. Clementi played it at a historic contest with Mozart in 1781, both pianists acquitting themselves so well that no verdict was reached. The competition bore good fruit, for Clementi was so impressed by Mozart's taste and singing tone that he thereafter modified his own style of playing, until then mechanical, greatly to its advantage; and Mozart later made use of the first theme of the B-flat Sonata:

Ex. 97

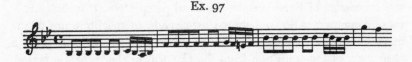

in his Overture to *The Magic Flute*.

It is a pleasure to turn from the heavy sonatas to the delightful sonatinas, full of charming ideas, spontaneous, and ideally suited to child study. It would be a pity if our youngsters ever became too sophisticated to enjoy them. As for the *Gradus ad Parnassum,* I own to a heretical opinion that the studies are too difficult to be really useful. Unless one already has a finished technique they cannot be played without stiffness and fatigue, and if one does have a finished technique, why not go straight to the études of Chopin and Liszt?

[The *Gradus ad Parnassum* of Muzio Clementi is still with us. Clever students will profit by conquering some of the difficult studies in the Tausig edition. The six pages of the F-minor Étude are as fine a task for finger dexterity and endurance as anyone could possibly wish for. Play the entire étude forte and then repeat it piano. Clementi technique prepares the student for Bach and Beethoven, while the rich collection of very varied études by Johann Baptist Cramer (page 148 below) direct the student toward the elegant, refined technique of Chopin. Schirmer's Bülow edition is recommended.]

Clementi must have been a first-rate teacher. He is credited with having introduced an idiomatic treatment of the piano as distinguished from the harpsichord. His best pupils were Field and Cramer.

JOHANN NEPOMUK HUMMEL (1778–1837) Once a famous composer, pianist, and teacher, Hummel is now remembered chiefly for his Piano Concertos in A minor and B minor, two of the four he wrote, and a *Piano School* in which he sensibly proposed to use the same fingering for recurring technical figures and to begin trills with the main note instead of the note above. Modern practice has accepted his rule of fingering with the addition that exceptions are no longer made when the thumb falls on a black key. Chopin seems in his teaching to have favored the concertos above those of Beethoven. Together with the tawdry *Bella Capricciosa* and the surpassingly dull Piano Septet they have passed into the limbo of forgotten things. Hummel was the teacher of Czerny, Ferdinand Hiller, Thalberg, and Henselt.

JOHN FIELD (1782–1837) Field was apprenticed to Clementi early in life and acted for many years as piano salesman in the warehouse of Clementi & Co., London. He and Cramer became Clementi's most illustrious pupils. Later he lived in St. Petersburg and Moscow and was known as the "Russian" Field to distinguish him from Henry Field, the "Field of Bath." His nocturnes have withstood the wear of time surprisingly well. No doubt Chopin's high estimation of them and adoption of the title for some of his own most beautiful creations have perpetuated their fame. Liszt, too, edited them with a laudatory preface. I cannot help finding them saccharine, and am content to hear them seldom. The best are Nos. 2, 3, 4, 5, and 11 of the Peters Edition, in the keys of C minor, A flat, A, B flat, and E flat. In playing these pieces Field used to improvise many graceful embellishments, a practice imitated by Chopin. Field's claim to our admiration may seem slim, but it was no small achievement to invent the nocturne type and to name it so happily.

FRIEDRICH WILHELM MICHAEL KALKBRENNER (1788–1849) This prolific writer of salon music is mentioned solely for the purpose of relating two amusing anecdotes. When Chopin went to Paris, he called on Kalkbrenner and played his E minor Concerto. Kalkbrenner thereupon made the amazing proposal that Chopin should come to him as a pupil, binding himself for a period of three years in order to become a good musician! Chopin was not so foolish as to accept the offer, but he received it with politeness, visited a few of Kalkbrenner's classes, and dedicated the concerto to him. On another occasion Kalkbrenner called on Adolf Marx, part founder of the *Berliner Allgemeine Musikalische Zeitung*, and to impress so important a personage "improvised" brilliantly for fifteen minutes. It happened next day, however, that Marx received a package of music sent from Paris for review. At the top of the parcel lay an *Effusio musica by Fred Kalkbrenner*, and in the printed music Marx instantly recognized the "improvisation," note for note.

CARL CZERNY (1791–1857) was a composer of colossal industry. His printed works run to nearly one thousand, comprising Masses and other vocal compositions, symphonies, concertos, chamber music, and arrangements of operas, oratorios, etc. Unfortunately the value of this stupendous output is in inverse proportion to its bulk. With the exception of the Toccata in C, everything but his studies has sunk into oblivion. These, however, are the best technical exercises ever written. Many of them contain fifty or more studies in a single opus number. When I was a student at the Leipzig Conservatory there was a legend, well invented if not true, that Czerny kept several desks in his workroom and that he would migrate from one to another while the ink dried on finished pages; he could thus juggle simultaneously with three or four compositions. He must have been a very able pianist; he was one of the world's greatest teachers; and his educational works have earned for him lasting fame. Beethoven was his teacher; Liszt and Leschetizky were among his pupils. It is said that Leschetizky, when interrogated about his much talked-of "method," was wont to reply: "I have no method. I teach piano as it was taught to me by my master Czerny"—a modest disclaimer, for every teacher of genius adds immeasurably to what he owes others.

Czerny never married—a circumstance that may have led Hermann Erler, author of a witty *Little Music Lexicon*,[1] to describe him as "a man of sour disposition who disliked children and therefore did nothing but write études."

JOHANN BAPTIST CRAMER (1771–1858) Famous in his day as pianist, teacher, and publisher, he is remembered chiefly for his études, eighty-four in number (in a later edition one hundred). He also wrote seven concertos and one hundred and five sonatas for piano, all now forgotten. In his studies he sought with considerable success to unite musical ideas with technical utility, paving the way to the complete fusion attained by Chopin and Liszt. They still enjoy a deserved popularity, stimulated in later years by Bülow's selected and annotated edition. Cramer by tuition and performance played an honored role in the formation of piano style. Beethoven admired him greatly as a

---

[1] Published under the pseudonym of Professor Kalauer. *Kalauer* is the German word for a pun.

pianist, on one occasion declaring that "all the others went for nothing."

IGNAZ MOSCHELES (1794–1870) More versatile than Cramer, Moscheles won success as composer, pianist, conductor, and teacher. Some of the compositions are faintly remembered, particularly the Concerto in G minor, Opus 60, and the Twenty-four Études, Opus 70. They held a place of honor in Chopin's teaching repertory, and many living pianists have included the Études in their course of study. His fame as a concert player rivaled that of Cramer. For a time he was conductor of the Philharmonic Society in London, where he had previously led Beethoven's Ninth Symphony with great credit. His friend Mendelssohn put him at the head of the piano department of the Leipzig Conservatory of Music and he taught there for twenty-four years until his death. He professed to play octaves with a stiff wrist, but Bruno Zwintscher, one of his best pupils, assured me that this was not so; the wrist was merely held very quiet, almost un-moving, but not rigid. In the preface to the Études, Moscheles gives a good deal of bad advice to students, and in spite of his extreme con-scientiousness it may be doubted whether he was an inspired teacher. He could never reconcile himself to Chopin's compositions or style of playing. This indicates a somewhat pedantic mind. It is said that having come into possession of one of Beethoven's penciled notebooks he carefully inked over the entire volume in order to preserve it!

Carl Maria von Weber (1786–1826)

WEBER's life was short but vivid. Dragged about from town to town in childhood by a nomadic father, he had little chance to get a decent education, musically or otherwise. In mature life, too, he wandered much until he secured conductorships, first at Prague for nearly four years, and then at Dresden for nine years. The extent and versatility of his accomplishments under such unsettled conditions are astonish-ing. Gifted with a singularly winning personality, he lost no oppor-tunity to improve his talents and his character. Greatest as a composer, he ranked in his day equally high as conductor and pianist. He was a skilled guitarist and wrote many songs to guitar accompaniment. In his youth he possessed a fine voice, which unluckily was seriously impaired by the accidental drinking of a glass of nitric acid by mis-take for wine. Always interested in literature, he wrote many musical criticisms, joining a secret society whose members adopted pen names

(Weber's was "Melos") like the future *Davidsbündler*. He thought of founding a musical journal, too, so that in this field also he partly anticipated Schumann. For a full account of his life the reader is referred to the excellent biography in *Grove's Dictionary*, fourth edition, by Philipp Spitta.

Weber's proper sphere was opera. From childhood he lived behind the scenes, fostering his native dramatic instinct and acquiring the intimate knowledge that later served him at Prague and Dresden, where he not only conducted but also took efficient charge of the details of stage management. As we all know, he created the German romantic opera and was the immediate precursor of Richard Wagner. His idea that opera should be a drama founded on a union of poetry, music, and descriptive art became the cornerstone of Wagner's philosophy. *Der Freischütz* remains the favorite opera of the German people; you hear it hummed and whistled in every field and village.

THE PIANO SONATAS

We need scarcely wonder that Weber's operas throw his piano works into the shade. Yet these latter have an importance of their own. Here as ever Weber was pre-eminently the virtuoso; almost all are difficult, beyond the technical range of even appreciative amateurs. The unusual size of his hand induced him to write extended chords, impossible to most players.

I shall always regret the loss of my boyhood enthusiasm for the four sonatas. Undeterred by my small hands and unformed technique, I seized on them avidly and took delight in their romantic and dramatic moods, in the rush of the dazzling menuettos and rapid finales. They are broadly conceived compositions, regular in form, pianistically exacting but extremely effective. Perhaps they are over-elaborate; greater simplicity would allow the musical values to stand out better. Three of them, those in C, D minor, and E minor, suffer from the comparative dryness of their first movements, a fact that has no doubt detracted from a wider popularity. The C major Sonata has a melodious slow movement with a dark, dramatic interlude, a fine Menuetto, and for finale the familiar *Perpetuum Mobile*. No. 2, in A flat, the most lyrical of the four, is the only one still occasionally played as a whole in public.

The five occasional piano pieces, a *Momento capriccioso*, Opus 12, a *Grande Polonaise* in E flat, Opus 21, a *Rondo brilliant* in E flat, the *Invitation to the Waltz*, and the *Polacca brillante* in E, have been far more popular than the sonatas. In order of merit I am inclined to put the *Invitation* first, the less-known *Momento capriccioso* second, the *Polacca* next, the *Rondo* fourth, the *Polonaise* last. The *Invitation* still preserves remnants of a vogue once tremendous and is known to symphonic audiences through the orchestral arrangements of Berlioz and Weingartner.

The *Momento capriccioso*, least often played of the shorter pieces, is a fine staccato étude with a choral-like middle section affording repose. An enterprising pianist might feature it as a quasi novelty, counting on success with his public and hoping for commendation from the critics.

We must not expect Polish sentiment in the polaccas and polonaises of Weber. *Polacca* is simply the Italian word for polonaise, but a shade of difference is commonly understood. *Grove's Dictionary*, fourth edition, tells us acceptably enough that "Polaccas may be defined as Polonaises treated in an Italian manner." The brilliant Italian style prevails in the Polacca in E, a work far superior to the earlier *Grande Polonaise* in E flat. Vivacious dotted rhythms:

Ex. 98

characterize the first theme and the piece as a whole, rapid sixteenth-note triplets giving variety of motion.

CONCERTOS AND THE CONCERTSTÜCK

The two Piano Concertos in C and E flat belong to a bygone period; we may pass over them in favor of the *Concertstück* in F minor for piano and orchestra. Now irretrievably hackneyed, the *Concertstück* long occupied a foremost place in the pianist's repertory and was a necessary part of every ambitious student's education. Much may still be learned from it, for it is a model of bravura style and a historical landmark. In form it is a fantasia in four connecting sections; a Larghetto in the tone of a lament, an Allegro passionato, a March for the orchestra alone except for a solitary glissando of the soloist, and an exuberant Finale, *Assai presto*. The sections are linked together by short transitional passages. The performer, dissatisfied with his inaction during the March, usually continues in fortissimo unison with the orchestra after his glissando.

Franz Peter Schubert (1797–1828)

One cannot read the story of Schubert's life without deep emotion. Rarely has genius struggled against odds so heavy or met so little material reward. Professor Otto E. Deutsch, a reliable authority, estimated that his total earnings from his compositions amounted to the paltry sum of £575. Audiences applauded singers to the echo and ignored the composer. The sordid behavior of his publishers is one of the disgraces of musical history. Too well aware of his necessity, they saw in it their opportunity, and in their bargainings beat him down without justice or mercy. As his reputation grew they offered less and less for his works. Probst bought the E-flat Piano Trio for less than one pound. Haslinger gave a florin apiece for some songs from the *Winterreise*. The memory of Diabelli should be pilloried in eternal infamy. This leading publisher of the time acquired the plates and rights of a number of songs originally published by private subscription for seventy pounds, pocketed near three thousand pounds in a few years from the sale of *Der Wanderer* alone, and persisted in exploiting the unfortunate composer throughout his short life with the rapacity of a vulture. In his youth Schubert was actually dependent on friends for music paper. At his death his belongings were officially appraised at sixty-three florins, including some five hundred manuscripts valued at ten florins![2] By contrast, the Vienna *Männergesangverein* in 1872 erected a monument to him at a cost of forty-two thousand florins.

Imagine an incurably shy, tongue-tied man, ill educated, not well-born and therefore obscure in aristocratic Vienna, undersized,[3] with dull, short-sighted eyes disfigured by steel-rimmed spectacles which he sometimes wore through the night, with no interest in life save music, yet of such compelling personality and kindliness that to know him was to love him. Newman Flower in his book *Franz Schubert, the Man and His Circle*, tells at length about Schubert's many devoted friends. While we appreciate their admiration, we can hardly comprehend why they allowed him to live in a continual privation that undermined his health, if he never literally starved. Some of them

---

[2] The Austrian florin or gulden was then worth about tenpence in English currency.

[3] His height was 5 ft. 1 inch.

were poor too. They were not stingy, however, and often extended practical aid, but no concerted effort was ever made to raise Schubert above the level of want. It must be admitted that to a great extent he had himself to blame for his misfortunes. He was lavish and improvident when in funds. He was recalcitrant and obstinate. Not the slightest concession would he make to publishers, critical friends, or public opinion. Once, when applying for a conductorship, he obdurately refused entreaties to simplify a difficult solo part by so much as a note, finally banging his score shut in a huff and ruining the opportunity. Though he occasionally accompanied his songs at this or that performance, he gave but one concert in his life; it was successful, yielding thirty-two pounds, but no urging could induce him to repeat it. Over and over again did he show blind indifference to his own advantage. Music sufficed him and he was seldom unhappy except at the end, when illness and lack of recognition affected his cheerful spirit. The poet Grillparzer wrote the celebrated epitaph:

> *Music has here buried a rich treasure*
> *But much fairer hopes.*
> *Franz Schubert lies here.*
> *Born January 31, 1797.*
> *Died November 19, 1828.*
> *31 years old.*

Controversy has not ceased to rage over the question whether Schubert had reached his full powers when he died. [It is said that during his last and fatal illness, Schubert told a friend: "If I come through this sickness I shall study again, study form and counterpoint."]

The most inspired song-writer of all time, Schubert possessed a gift for melody equal to that of Mozart. Any verses that came to his hand were good enough for a song. Schumann says that "he was the man for Telemann, who claimed that 'a good composer should be able to set a placard to music.'" More by happy chance than wise choice he composed music for hundreds of Germany's finest lyrics—72 by Goethe, 54 by Schiller, 44 by Müller, 19 each by Schlegel and Klopstock, 16 by Körner, 6 by Heine, and so on.

Words imposed a natural restraint on Schubert's "heavenly length"; without them he was apt to run riot. The piano sonatas, particularly in their finales, might have benefited by pruning. He wrote as fast as his quill would fly and never corrected. (The painstaking changes made in the C major Symphony were quite exceptional.) He had no patience with revision and little incentive to it, since many of his instrumental works were written without definite prospect that they would ever be published.

There is nothing novel in Schubert's piano idiom, no addition to the technical or tonal resources of the instrument. Except for a few impractical passages, instance the presto octaves in the last movement of the A minor Sonata, Opus 143, and the fatiguing excess of tremolo in the finale of the Fantasia in C, he wrote with extraordinary simplicity and directness. It has been well said that in listening to Schubert we forget the instrument he happened to be using at the moment and are conscious only of pure music.

This is true also of his orchestral style; of virtuosity there is no trace. Nor did he attempt innovations on forms already sanctioned. *Impromptu* and *Musical Moment* were new names for piano music, but the structure of the pieces themselves and of the ten sonatas follows strictly traditional lines.

Schubert was not a skilled pianist. He had a stubby hand, and from the reports of his tiring out after playing for any length of time we may infer that his technique was stiff and awkward. One might expect to read how he delighted friends with his sonatas and impromptus; instead he preferred to play the slighter waltzes and marches or to take a back seat as accompanist to the renowned baritone Vogl or others in their interpretations of his songs. At private performances of his string quartets, he would undertake the modest viola part though trained as a violinist. On occasion he improvised, but he is not mentioned as excelling in an art so generally cultivated by pianists and composers of the period. Always the same shy incapacity for showmanship!

[I should like to think that sometime, somewhere, there will be a complete Urtext edition of Schubert which will prevent students from having to look at certain existing editions immersed in dreadful fingerings.]

THE PIANO WORKS

The amateur's attention will inevitably be arrested first by the eight *Impromptus* and six *Moments musicaux*, or *Momens musicals* as Schubert named them in old-fashioned French. Two favorite pieces, the Impromptus in G, Opus 90, No. 3, and A flat, Opus 142, No. 2, require no dexterity whatever. The first is a pensive lyric demanding merely a warm singing touch and a pianissimo accompaniment. Originally written in the key of G flat, it was changed to the easier signature on the remonstrance of the publisher. The other is a sort of slow minuet and trio (or better, saraband), equally unpretending and melodious. Another piano favorite, the B-flat Impromptu, Opus 142,

No. 3, consists of a set of variations, the last calling for delicate finger-work. More difficult, though not extravagantly so, are the E-flat Impromptu, Opus 90, No. 2, the one in A flat, Opus 90, No. 4, and that in F minor, Opus 142, No. 4. The first of these three resembles an étude with a nobly passionate Intermezzo. The second really begins in A-flat minor; Schubert avoided a key signature of seven flats by the simple expedient of writing the minor third of the tonic chord, C flat, as an accidental. The F minor Impromptu, Opus 142, No. 4, sparkles with Viennese caprice; it should be played fancifully, without slavish rigidity of rhythm. The dainty episode:

Ex. 99

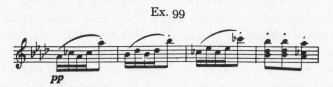

pp

forecasts Mendelssohn's fairy revels.

The first of the *Moments musicaux* is agreeable but not remarkable. All the others are gems, counting the rugged No. 5, in F minor, as a somewhat rough diamond. The shortest and most universally liked, also in F minor, takes only a minute and a half to play. No. 4, in C-sharp minor, a charming scherzo, is the trickiest of the set. The other two, both in A flat, are the most poetic. No. 2 in ₈ time, needs careful counting of the long-drawn dotted half-notes and a sustained cantilena. The last number, an expressive Minuet and Trio, gains by omission of all its repeats. These small compositions are tidbits for the musical epicure.

I advise the amateur to learn the "lesser" A major Sonata, Opus 120, and for the rest to satisfy himself by browsing on selected movements from the others. Opus 120 is a short sonata, technically easy but for the last movement, and a most gracious piece throughout. Professionals, however, have no excuse for neglecting a wonderland of beauty. To the best of my belief, none of the sonatas were played by Rubinstein, Liszt, or Paderewski. In more modern times Conrad Ansorge, Edouard Risler, and Artur Schnabel have brought to the public not just a few, but most or all of them. Opus 42, in A minor, Opus 53, in D, and two of the posthumous works, the "greater" Sonata in A and the exquisite Sonata in B flat, rival the finest of Beethoven's sonatas in wealth of invention and loveliness. With less of Beethoven's awe-inspiring magnificence and logic of thought, they show a more natural spontaneity. Opus 42 and the posthumous Sonata in B flat are in my opinion the grandest of all. Another A minor

Sonata, Opus 143, shorter than the four mentioned above, is hardly less impressive. Schubert plumbs unwonted depths of passion and drama in the first movements of Opus 42, Opus 143, and the posthumous Sonata in C minor. Divine beauty saturates the slow movements of Opus 42, Opus 53, Opus 143, and Opus 147 (in B major), infinite pathos those of the posthumous sonatas in A and B flat. The scherzos vary greatly in character, gay in the A and B-flat posthumous works, martial in Opus 53, restless (but with a serene trio) in Opus 42. Two sonatas have minuets instead of scherzos; four have neither minuet nor scherzo. The undue length to which Schubert often ran is most marked in the finales of the three posthumous sonatas.

It will be noticed that the theme of the slow movement of Opus 164 is almost identical with that of the Rondo of the greater A major Sonata. This is probably an example of Schubert's notorious forgetfulness. Once a piece was finished, he thought of it no more, immediately becoming absorbed in the next. Sir George Grove relates that Vogl, finding a new song too high for his voice, had it copied in a lower key. Two weeks later he took the copy to try it through with the composer. Schubert exclaimed: "I say! the song's not bad; *whose is it?*" Yet he seldom repeated himself unintentionally; to put his burning ideas down on paper was enough to get them out of his system.

The Fantasia in C, called the *Wanderer* Fantasia because an important theme from the well-known song forms the basis of its slow movement, is the most often played of Schubert's larger piano works. An outbreak of storm late in the slow movement, followed by radiant beams of melody suggesting a rainbow, has rarely been equaled in emotional effect, and the giant stride of the last Allegro is unforgettable.

The other so-called Fantasia, in G major, ought to be printed among the sonatas. It was intended for a sonata and entitled so by the composer, but the publisher Haslinger saw fit to issue it under the unwieldly name of *Fantasia, Andante, Menuetto, and Allegretto*, enumerating the several movements. It is far gentler and much longer than the dramatic *Wanderer* Fantasia; most judges consider it one of Schubert's most appealing works. I confess that the heavenly beauty of the first movement leaves me rather cold to the less interesting Andante and the diffuse final Allegretto. The Menuetto, however, is a little masterpiece, and anyone choosing to play it as an excerpt is fully justified.

Every good amateur enjoys playing four-hand music with a congenial friend. Beyond the social pleasure of it, three practical advantages are offered: useful practice in sight reading, the necessity of keeping time or breaking down, and the easy opening to knowledge of the vast literature of overtures, symphonies, string quartets, and so forth.

Schubert wrote more and better for this combination than any other composer. The Fantasia in F minor, the Andantino with Variations on French Motives, and Nos. 2 and 3 of the *Marches héroïques,* Opus 40, Book I, claim place among his best creations. The famous *Marche militaire,* first of the three in Opus 51, may be a trifle—but what a genial trifle! There are many other sweets to taste in the two large volumes of four-hand music.

The four major chamber-music works with piano are all of immortal beauty. The Rondo in B minor for piano and violin is exceptionally virile and effective. I leave it to the curious reader to discover for himself in it a strong resemblance to a theme from Beethoven's *Kreutzer* Sonata. The noble Piano Trios in B flat and E flat leave us wondering which we love most. The Quintet for piano, violin, viola, cello, and double bass, Opus 114, is more seldom heard because of the very unusual combination of instruments. Known as the *Forellenquintet* from the use of the song *Die Forelle* ("The Trout") in one of its movements, it is an example of faultless scoring. Incidentally, the insertion of the "Trout" variations is unnecessary and adds little to the value of the whole; the other four movements are complete in themselves.

These chamber-music compositions are difficult for the pianist and require skilled partnership of the strings. Easier and more practicable are the three delightful Sonatas or Sonatinas for piano and violin, Opus 137.

Characteristically, Schubert wrote no concertos. A concerto is by nature a display piece for a soloist, and display in any shape or form was alien to his retiring disposition.

Schubert's music has attracted many transcribers. The foremost of these was Liszt, whose settings of the songs and some of the waltzes (the latter under the title *Soirées de Vienne*) are familiar to every pianist. Before Schubert's fame became world-wide these arrangements helped substantially to bring his name to the general public. Many of them are superlatively fine. In others Liszt's obvious devotion to the original has not saved him from errors of taste such as his attempt to relieve the seeming monotony of the accompaniment in the G major Piano Impromptu by arpeggiating the harmonies at the reprise. Carl Tausig gave us an example of perfect transcription in his setting of the Variations on French Motives for two hands instead of four. This is infinitely finer than his arrangement of the *Marche militaire,* also reduced from four hands to two, transposed from D to D flat, and transmogrified from its pristine simplicity to an unbelievable bravura. Leopold Godowsky made piano versions of some songs, and his rewriting of the F minor *Moment musical* (No. 3) is highly ingenious and in its way admirable. Harold Bauer contributed an effective transcription of the *Rondo brillant on French Motives* (another four-hand piece) for two pianos.

Jakob Ludwig Felix Mendelssohn–Bartholdy
(1809–47)

Few musicians have enjoyed prosperity in life comparable to that of Felix Mendelssohn (we may immediately discard the extra names). Born of a well-to-do family, with every advantage of native endowment and careful education, successful and indeed lionized wherever he went and in whatever he undertook, he had a singularly happy lot. Beyond vexations connected with his temporary official position at the Berlin Academy of Arts he had no professional worries or disappointments. The only grave sorrows that came to him through deaths of family and friends are common to all men.

It has often been argued that if Mendelssohn had been less fortunate he would have been a greater man and musician. The presumption, for it is a mere presumption, is highly unfair. Sunshine does not stunt, but fosters growth. If any valid reason can be assigned that he might have become a greater composer, it would be that he scattered his versatile talent too prodigally. He wrote music from the age of twelve, producing the Octet for strings at sixteen and the Overture to *A Midsummer Night's Dream* at seventeen. At twenty-four he was conducting the Lower Rhine Festival and at twenty-six the famous Gewandhaus Concerts in Leipzig. He won early fame as pianist and organist. Later he showed marked capacity for organization by his business management of the Lower Rhine Festival and as founder of the Leipzig Conservatorium. Besides this he toured and traveled extensively, carried on a huge correspondence often enlivened by clever pen-and-ink sketches, and found time for watercolor painting, riding, swimming, dancing, billiards, and chess. One may, then, conjecture that by devoting himself, like Schubert, exclusively to composition he might have reached more lofty peaks. Why speculate? Our only regret should be that his incessant activity exhausted a physique sound but not robust and contributed to a premature death.

No doubt Mendelssohn was overrated during his lifetime. An inevitable reaction set in after his death, to the injury of his reputation. The pendulum, having swung too far both ways, has now gained a truer balance and we are able to appreciate him with impartiality.

Mendelssohn essayed all varieties of musical form: symphonies, oratorios, concertos, opera and incidental music, chamber music, songs including duets and part-songs, solo pieces for piano and organ. We may say of him, as Johnson said of Goldsmith, that "he left scarcely any style of writing untouched and touched nothing that he did not adorn." He was least successful in opera, but we can infer a potential gift for it from the stage propriety of the music to *A Midsummer Night's Dream* and still more from that amazing music-drama, *Elijah*. He wrote idiomatically for orchestra, solo voices and chorus, string quartet, organ, and piano, drawing from each a maximum effect without cruel demands on their technique or range. An unfailing sense of form was instinctive to him, so that his ideas are always presented in orderly sequence and proportion. The felicity with which he reintroduces themes is remarkable; typical examples occur at the reprises in "If with all your hearts" (*Elijah*), the entrance of the orchestra after the cadenza of the Violin Concerto, and in the last movement of the B-flat Sonata for piano and cello.

The spell of fairyland inspired Mendelssohn's imagination to some of its most entrancing flights. The magic of the elves, first depicted in the music to *A Midsummer Night's Dream*, reappears in later piano pieces; in the *Rondo capriccioso*, the E minor Caprice, Opus 16, No. 2, the "Spinning Song" of the *Lieder ohne Worte*, and the *Leicht und Luftig* of the *Characterstücke*, Opus 7. These pieces dart or hover on gossamer wings. Transformed into a dragonfly or hidden by an invisible cap, Felix must have stolen into meetings of the little people and recorded their proceedings unremarked. Or did the little people, trustful of his sympathy, admit him voluntarily to their mushroomed circle?

Mendelssohn's artistic tact often shows in small matters. Consider for instance Bottom's heehaw, interjected into the Overture, Scherzo, and Boor's Dance of the *Midsummer Night's Dream* music. Richard Strauss would probably have been taken roughly to task had he put an ass's bray into a symphonic poem. Mendelssohn got away with it uncensured because the jest is discreetly perpetrated and the element of the play that it recalls is essential to the wholeness of the picture.

No composer has ever done more imperishable service to his fore-runners than Mendelssohn. The revival of Bach's *St. Matthew Passion* in Berlin, at the age of twenty and against formidable opposition, was not a lonely instance. At Düsseldorf and Cologne he brought out Handel's *Israel in Egypt, Messiah, Solomon, Alexander's Feast,* and the *Dettingen Te Deum,* Masses by Beethoven and Cherubini, motets and cantatas of Palestrina and Bach, Mozart's *Figaro* and *Don Giovanni,* and the Sixth and Eighth Symphonies and the *Leonora* Overtures Nos. 1 and 3 of Beethoven. His first year at Leipzig was signalized by performances of Beethoven's Ninth Symphony, Bach's Three-Piano Concerto in D minor, and Mozart's Concerto in D minor "as written,"[4] himself seated at the piano. In 1838 the Gewandhaus series included four historical concerts, and we find in the programs the additional names of Gluck, Viotti, Haydn, Cimarosa, Salieri, Méhul, and others. Mendelssohn was famed for his masterly playing of Beethoven's sonatas and concertos when they were unfamiliar to the public. The resurrection of Schubert's Symphony in C, never heard as a whole by the composer and utterly forgotten until Schumann discovered the manuscript in Vienna, again attested his devotion to the genius of the past. It is all the stranger that while he furthered the interests of many contemporaries he was lukewarm in admiration of Chopin and Schumann. Trained exclusively in classical tradition and fastidious to a fault, he could not accept without reserve the harmonic boldness of the former or the rebellion against formal restraint of the latter.

Mendelssohn's best work stands out sharply above his less distinguished compositions. *St. Paul* cannot compare as a whole with the *Elijah,* nor the *Hymn of Praise* (a symphony with choral finale on the plan of Beethoven's Ninth) with the Scotch and Italian Symphonies, nor the piano concertos with the Violin Concerto, nor the "Trumpet" Overture with *Fingal's Cave,* nor the very poor piano sonatas with those for organ. Yet Mendelssohn was self-critical, often dissatisfied with what he wrote, and never complacent. Danger lurked, however, in a pen so facile and a market ready to print without question anything he offered to it. Those who condemn his music as sugary and sentimental have not looked beyond his weaker moments.

By his individual treatment of the piano Mendelssohn contributed largely to the development of a modern style of playing. His replacement of Beethoven's broken octaves:

---

[4] A hint that other pianists had made unauthorized changes of text. Later it is certain that Carl Reinecke felt justified in embellishing certain passages of Mozart's concertos.

Ex. 100

Beethoven, Opus 2, No.3

by the more practical and brilliant alternating octaves:

Ex. 101

Mendelssohn, Rondo Capriccioso

has been universally followed. Another novel feature is the distribution of a melody between two hands to an arpeggiated accompaniment:

Ex. 102

Etude in B-flat minor, Opus 104, No.1

or a corresponding division of the accompaniment, as in the "Spring Song" of the *Lieder ohne Worte*. He achieved Weber's brilliance with greater simplicity; hence his idiom is pianistically grateful and the technique, once mastered, is easily retained.

THE PIANO WORKS

The forty-eight *Songs without Words* are a happy hunting-ground for the amateur. It would be absurd to suggest a choice, since anyone can so easily read through them to make his own selection. Personally, my favorites are the following:

No. 3. *Molto allegro e vivace*, A major ("Hunting Song")
    5. *Piano agitato*, F-sharp minor
    6. "Venetian Boat Song," G minor
   12. "Venetian Boat Song," F-sharp minor
   14. *Allegro non troppo*, C minor
   17. Agitato, A minor
   18. *Duetto*, A flat
   22. Adagio, F
   23. *Volkslied*, A minor
   25. *Andante espressivo*, G
   27. "Funeral March," E minor
   34. Presto, C ("Spinning Song")
   37. *Andante espressivo*, F

To comment briefly on my list:

Few good hunting songs exist in piano literature; Mendelssohn's, with its horn flourishes, is one of the best. No. 5 is one of the few *Songs without Words* extending beyond simple song form and using a second theme. The volume contains three "Venetian Boat Songs"; the third, No. 29, in A minor, is inferior to the two I have chosen, both of which are charming. Nos. 14 and 17 speak with sincere passion, Nos. 22 and 25 with a truly exquisite lyricism. The *Duetto* is a skillfully contrived love song; antiphonal endearments lead to a *unisono* agreement, and a lingering coda tenderly confirms the understanding. Its sweetness contrasts with the power of the *Volkslied*. This is no ordinary folk song; one hears in it the anger of an oppressed people clamoring for redress of their wrongs, each verse rising in vehemence to a climax of moving intensity. The "Funeral March," curiously in $\frac{2}{4}$ time, wears its grief with stateliness. It was played at the funeral service for Mendelssohn. No. 34, known as the "Spinning Song," went in my Australian boyhood under the pretty title of "The Bee's Wedding." Another fairy piece! The *Andante espressivo*, No. 37, approaches but hardly comes up to Nos. 22 and 25 in pure melody.

I like others of the *Songs without Words* too, for instance No. 2, a simple *Andante espressivo* in A minor and No. 45, Presto, in C, a dainty bagatelle. And in over sixty years I have been neither able nor anxious to outgrow an old affection for the time-worn lyric in E, No. 9, and the "Spring Song."

One must love the *Songs without Words* to play them well. If you do not care much for Mendelssohn, better leave them alone.

The other piano works will be reviewed in the approximate order of their composition or publication.

Capriccio in F-sharp minor, Opus 5. Mendelssohn, who was addicted to the use of French terms, called this Capriccio *"une absurdité"*; he liked it and played it frequently, but it is now shelved in favor of more popular pieces.

Characterstücke, Opus 7. A set of seven pieces, four slow and three fast; it is doubtful if they were meant to be played in sequence, though it would be quite possible to do so. The best of the slow numbers is an excellent Fugue in A, headed "Serious and with rising animation." All three of the fast pieces are effective; the free Fugue in D, marked "Strong and fiery," a *Moto perpetuo* in A, "Fast and mobile," and the last of the set, a dainty staccato étude, "Light and airy."

Rondo capriccioso, Opus 14. If a piece is good enough, no amount of hackneying can quite kill it. Many hackneyed pieces, in fact, are hackneyed just because they are good. (Is the "Moonlight" Sonata any worse because it has been played so often?) No matter, then, that the *Rondo capriccioso* for more than half a century formed the coping-stone of every English maiden's pianistic culture. It may not be profound music, but it is a capital piece nevertheless, giving the player opportunity to show off his tone and technique and abounding in variety of touch, dynamics, and mood. I quote from the last episode (E major) a further example of Mendelssohn's tact in small things.

Ex. 103

Try this with the ritardando extended over the last three eighth-notes and observe how sentimentality is evaded by the apparently premature *a tempo*.

Three Fantasias or Caprices, Opus 16. The best of the three is No. 2, the Scherzo in E minor, originally named by the composer "Little Trumpet Piece." Here Mendelssohn's fondness for light staccato chords is in evidence. A fascinating trifle with an unexpected major ending; an ideal encore piece. The last Caprice, often called "The Rivulet," is placid, melodious, and unimportant.

Six Children's Pieces, Opus 72. With the exception of No. 5, an *Allegro assai* in G minor, the series (sometimes known as "Christmas Pieces") is neither especially suitable for children nor musically valuable. No. 5, however, is a captivating morsel, again prevalently staccato.

Fantasia in F-sharp minor, Opus 28, commonly known as the "Scotch Fantasia." Were it not for a rather insignificant middle movement, *Allegro con moto,* the Fantasia would rank high among Mendelssohn's piano works. A sustained mood of melancholy beauty ennobles the first movement and the *Presto* finale strikes real fire; the two merit a better intermezzo. Would it be allowable, I wonder, to play them without the middle movement?

Six Preludes and Fugues, Opus 35. Mendelssohn's talent for fugue-writing was pronounced, and we see him here in his most genial and original aspect. Usually a fast and prolific writer, he devoted himself almost exclusively to Opus 35 for the better part of an entire winter. In the scholarly A major fugue of the *Characterstücke* he had trodden closely in Bach's footsteps. Now he goes farther, modernizing his counterpoint, diverging at times into a harmonic style, and handling the form with a new flow and freedom. Schumann points out how successfully Mendelssohn adapted the fugue to modern taste, but goes too far in his enthusiasm when he declares that "the best fugue will always be that which the public takes for a Strauss waltz" and speaks approvingly of a "connoisseur of music who mistook a Bach fugue for a Chopin étude." Possibly Schumann's tongue was in his cheek when he wrote this; one notices that his article is signed *Jeanquirit.*

The first Prelude and Fugue of Opus 35, in E minor, has always been the most popular. The Prelude is typically Mendelssohnian, the Fugue a masterpiece, beginning quietly, working up through a long crescendo and accelerando to its climax, then breaking with superb effect into a majestic choral, finally subsiding to a serene return of the fugue theme and a pianissimo close. The diminuendo accompanying the rising scale in the third measure from the end:

Ex. 104

is a wonderful stroke of finesse. The only criticism of the piece that can conceivably be made is that there is no essential inner relation-

ship between the prelude and the fugue. In this respect No. 5, in F
minor, is superior; here prelude and fugue, the former sad and lovely,
the latter highly temperamental, are true soul mates despite all outward difference. The prelude of the third in the set (B minor) might
stand alone as a delightful staccato étude. Mendelssohn sets an example of reticence at the end of the companion fugue, where the
theme enters in a combination of direct and inverted position:

Ex. 105

Had he wished to display his knowledge of counterpoint in the tenth
and twelfth he could have written the sixteenth-notes thus:

Ex. 106

(The two E's marked x would be "free")

The fugue in D, No. 2, is better than its companion prelude. In No.
4 (A flat) prelude and fugue are well matched, both continuously
legato and cantabile. The prelude of No. 6 (B flat) is weak, but the
fugue is very spirited and well written.

Another Prelude and Fugue in E minor without opus number is
of later date but may conveniently be mentioned in connection with
Opus 35. It equals the others in merit. The prelude shows firm character and the fugue is particularly noteworthy for the bold downward leap of a major seventh with which the theme begins.

Ex. 107

Variations sérieuses, Opus 54. The title was no doubt a protest against the triviality of most variations of the period following the death of Beethoven, Weber, and Schubert. The work is certainly one of Mendelssohn's best piano compositions, perhaps the best of all, and seems destined to live as long as there are pianists to play it. Deep feeling pervades the theme and the slow variations. Mendelssohn wrote nothing lovelier than the end of Variation 14:

Ex. 108

The virtuoso variations never lose dignity.

> *Variations in E flat, Opus* 82.
> *Variations in B flat, Opus* 83.

These posthumous works[5] have beauties of their own, though surpassed by the *Variations sérieuses*. Opus 82 is very good indeed. The B-flat Variations suffer by a commonplace coda. This piece was duplicated by Mendelssohn in Opus 83[a], an arrangement for four hands.

Three Études, Opus 104. The first and best known of the three, in B-flat minor, is marred by its continuous cheap arpeggio accompaniment. The second, in F, more rarely played, is a *Moto perpetuo* in rapid $\frac{12}{8}$ time, very effective when performed with rippling ease. The last of the set, in A minor, and another Étude in F minor without opus number, are unimportant.

Scherzo a Capriccio in F-sharp minor (no opus number). This excellent piece, dexterous and animated, holds a deserved place on recital programs. Light staccato chords are once more a prominent feature of the technique.

It seems unaccountable that Mendelssohn's piano sonatas are so thin in quality compared with others of his works in large form. They are three in number, printed as Opus 6, Opus 105, and Opus 106. Only Opus 6, in E major, was published during the composer's life-

---

[5] All Mendelssohn's works after Opus 73 were published after his death.

time. Opus 105 is merely a boyish essay, but we might fairly expect more from the other two. All three, together with other compositions of small musical value, are included in the Supplement of the Peters Edition.

Mendelssohn's works for four hands are confined to the arrangement of the B-flat Variations, Opus 83ª, already mentioned, and an *Allegro brillant* in A, Opus 92. The two pieces are generally unknown, and lovers of four-hand music would do better by devoting themselves to the arrangements of the orchestral overtures, well transcribed and effective in this form.

The list of chamber-music compositions, too, is short. It comprises, however, three outstanding works, the two Piano Trios in D minor, Opus 49, and C minor, Opus 66, and the fine Sonata in B flat, Opus 45, for piano and cello.

The G minor Piano Concerto, Opus 25, is far the best of the five pieces for piano and orchestra. At that, it does not approach the great beauty of the Violin Concerto in E minor and after a long vogue is gradually disappearing from symphonic programs. Yet it has considerable intrinsic merit and is historically an important work. Breaking abruptly with classical tradition, the concise first movement discards the opening orchestral *tutti* and the cadenza completely. Short interludes connect the three movements. Needless to say, the scoring of the piano solo and accompaniment is brilliant and resourceful. The first truly modern concerto, it still remains on the "must" list for conservatory study. [The old G minor Concerto has had a distinct revival since its re-introduction into the concert hall by Rudolf Serkin. Even dated good music can create enthusiasm when played supremely well.]

The other piano concerto, in D minor, is a weak successor. There are also three concert pieces, the *Capriccio brillant* in B minor, Opus 22, the *Rondo* (or *Capriccio*) *brillant* in E flat, Opus 29, and the *Serenade and Allegro giocoso*, Opus 43. The B minor Capriccio, pleasant enough at a first hearing, soon wears threadbare; the others have long lost their interest.

Mendelssohn's piano style is extremely idiomatic; everything lies well under the fingers and the most difficult passages are never awkward. The road to good performance lies in strict observance of all directions. I had the good fortune to study the G minor Concerto with Carl Reinecke, who had studied it with Mendelssohn himself. Reinecke told me that Mendelssohn played every nuance in the work exactly as intimated by the marks of expression. I was told in Leipzig, too, that Mendelssohn's metronome marks represent the maximum speed of any given movement; this, however, I have not been able to verify. It is certain that he disliked rallentandos except when definitely prescribed by the author. We may be sure that his fortissimo was ample but that he never banged. The amateur will be wise to remember these points. In addition, he should cultivate variety of touch; the legato must be singing in melody, even and pearly in passage-work; and the elastic hand staccato, in which Mendelssohn excelled as a player and delighted as a composer, calls for a flexible and practised wrist.

CHAPTER SEVEN

Robert Alexander Schumann
(1810–56)

ALL too often does genius encounter tragedy. Beethoven's deafness, Schubert's grinding poverty and early death, Chopin's unhappy life—"an episode with no beginning and with a sorrowful end"—the blindness of Milton, the suicide of Chatterton when help was near, the broken heart of Keats—these are but a few of the historic catastrophes of art. With them we must place the insanity of Schumann, the ultimate disaster of a chequered life. Having lamed a hand and ruined his prospects as a pianist, he earned the gratitude of posterity by diverting his talents to composition. His fecund imagination gave birth to a long series of vivid works before it grew barren under the approaching decay of his mind.

The state of music immediately after the death of Beethoven, Schubert, and Weber was one of sad stagnation. Dry classicism was the order of the day; the composers then active met all the superficial requirements of sonata, rondo, and concerto without possessing the genius to give a higher meaning to the forms. As Schumann summed up the situation, Rossini reigned supreme in opera; little was heard on the piano except Herz[1] and Hünten;[2] and the influence of Mendelssohn and Chopin had not yet made itself felt. The time was ripe for revolt, and it fell to Robert Schumann to lead it by founding a new romantic school, shifting from worship of form for its own sake to insistence on significant ideas. To aid the propaganda for a serious view of music he joined with kindred spirits in the creation of a

---

[1] Heinrich Herz, 1806–88, execrated by students for his book of *Scales*.
[2] Franz Hünten, 1793–1878.

periodical, *Die Neue Zeitschrift für Musik,* which he directed for ten years. Many of the articles written for this magazine and others are reprinted in his *Collected Writings,* partly available in English under the title *On Music and Musicians.*[3] The essays and criticisms show remarkable insight, enthusiasm, and generosity. Such papers as those on Chopin and Brahms ring out like clarion calls proclaiming genius to the world. Others of lasting interest deal with Mendelssohn, Berlioz, Schubert, Lizst, etc. When his judgment was at fault it erred on the side of kindliness; he overestimated the talent of Field, Gade, and Sterndale Bennett. His consistent aim was to stimulate love of all that was sincerely artistic; he reserved severity for the unworthy and meretricious. In the main his opinions have been sustained by later criticism. If you read the collected essays be sure not to omit the "Rules and Maxims for Young Musicians," a friendly little guide full of penetrating wisdom.

Schumann made a late start on his musical career. Though he began to play piano and to compose at an early age, his precocity was by no means comparable to that of Mozart or Mendelssohn. The opportunities for musical education in Zwickau, his birthplace, were limited. His father, who died when Robert was only sixteen, might have encouraged his passionate wish to study the piano, but his mother saw no financial prospect in the arts, and under her influence he entered the University of Leipzig and then that of Heidelberg as a student of law. His distaste for jurisprudence was inveterate and he applied himself to it with neither zeal nor industry. The mother finally yielded to the inevitable and Robert began serious piano study under Friedrich Wieck in Leipzig. It was at this time that his resort to a mechanical contrivance to strengthen the weak fourth finger crippled his hand for life and put an end to his ambition as a concert player. Accepting his fate with fortitude, he turned to composition, choosing Heinrich Dorn, then conductor of opera in Leipzig, for his teacher. He had been living in Wieck's house and continued to do so after the injury to his hand. There he was thrown into the company of Clara, Wieck's gifted daughter, and the acquaintance ripened into the attachment that ultimately resulted in their happy marriage. Clara Wieck is the "Chiarina" of the *Davidsbund* and the *Carnaval.*

Schumann was always an irregular if indefatigable student. Dorn, recognizing his genius, allowed him to go his own way. It is a peculiarity of his development as a composer that he devoted himself

---

[3] A new edition of these essays, translated by Paul Rosenfeld and edited by Konrad Wolff, has recently been issued by the Pantheon Press.

at first exclusively to the piano, then (inspired by his love for Clara) took up song-writing, later ventured on to symphonies and chamber music, and finally gave most of his thought to choral works with orchestra. Two dramatic enterprises intervened in this cycle of activity: the opera *Genoveva*, unsuccessful as a stage piece, and the better known music to Byron's *Manfred*, also intended for the theater but heard only in concert performance. All the compositions from Opus 1 to Opus 23 are for piano solo. The *Spring* Symphony, first of four, is Opus 38. The three string quartets, the Piano Quintet, Piano Quartet, and two piano trios were all written in the year 1842.

Mendelssohn came to Leipzig in 1835 and the town leaped into musical prominence. It meant much to Schumann. The two became firm friends, and though Mendelssohn never did full justice to Schumann's genius, he invited him to teach piano and composition at the Leipzig Conservatory. Schumann, I fear, was a very poor teacher; at least I have not heard a word of praise for his instruction, however inspiring his enthusiastic personality may have been. But the rich fare of concerts and operas offered at Leipzig and the contact with the leading musicians of the time helped materially to foster his growth.

Father Wieck had opposed his daughter's marriage to Schumann from the beginning, and in spite of the composer's increasing fame still remained obdurate. At length Schumann was obliged to seek legal redress. After much delay the court found Wieck's objections baseless and trivial, and Robert and Clara were married in September 1840. The union has been generally accepted as an ideal romance, and in spite of doubts that have been raised as to her relations with Brahms, there is little reason to suspect Clara of infidelity to her husband. Brahms, no doubt, was deeply in love with her, and his devotion was convenient and agreeable to her, but her cool head and bourgeois morality were sufficient to protect her from an illicit affair. In such cases the underground service of history is often more reliable than documentary evidence, and the grapevine does not accuse Clara. To stick to facts, Clara was instrumental in making Robert's music popular. For a long time he was well treated by publishers and critics without winning the favor of the public. She, one of the great pianists of the time, played his compositions on all her concert tours and reaped a tardy harvest of applause for them. It is noteworthy too that Schumann's mastery of the larger forms was best shown in the period from 1841 to 1845, following his marriage.

In 1844 Schumann's health began to break down. His nerves were so shaken that he was forbidden to hear much music, and the family moved to Dresden, where in those days there was almost too little of it. He complained that he could not remember his own themes. This phase passed and he was able to resume hard work. In 1850 he was appointed conductor at Düsseldorf. At first happy and successful in his new post, he soon began to suffer from a growing melancholia. In 1854 he attempted suicide by throwing himself from a bridge into the Rhine. Insanity was now unmistakable and the last two years of his life were spent in an asylum near Bonn.

The piano was Schumann's natural medium of expression. His symphonies, overtures, and string quartets impress us by their wealth of feeling and imagination, not by any virtuosity of scoring. The choral works, even the *Scenes from Faust* and *Paradise and the Peri*, are products of a great musician rather than of a composer adept in handling massed voices. Most of the beautiful songs are in reality duets for voice and piano. The accompanying instrument does far more than furnish a background and reflection of the singer's mood; it takes an active part, sometimes indeed the more active part, in expounding the poem. It is significant that the piano works exceed in number the total of Schumann's other instrumental compositions.

A large proportion of Schumann's piano pieces contains personal and literary allusions and references. They abound in the *Papillons*, the *Davidsbündlertänze*, the *Carnaval*, and the *Kreisleriana*. It should be pointed out that, however interesting they may be to the musicologist, they have no bearing on the value or on the real understanding of the works. Sweep them entirely from mind and we should still stand exactly where the music itself puts us. Schumann himself was quite aware of this and sometimes, as in the *Papillons* and the *Phantasie*, after allowing his fancy to dally with fictional ideas, struck out all mention of them in the published versions. As for the descriptive titles of the *Phantasiestücke*, *Kinderscenen*, and others, the composer tells us that it was his custom to write the music first and invent the names later. They are not program music, and the titles serve merely to induce appropriate moods for performance.

The personal allusions in some pieces are unintelligible without some explanation of that unique secret society, the *Davidsbund* (League of David), and of Schumann's perception within himself of a dual, nay a multiple personality. He personified himself sometimes as Florestan, the ardent, hot-headed reformer, or Eusebius, the dreamer of dreams, or again as Raro, a sort of mediator between Florestan and Eusebius. Occasionally Florestan and Eusebius merge their identities in collaboration. Many articles in the *Neue Zeitschrift* and many numbers of the *Davidsbündlertänze* are signed by their names or initials. They were prominent in the membership of the *Davidsbund*—a membership existing solely in Schumann's fertile brain, to which he mentally elected some of his associates on the *Neue Zeitschrift* and any others, like Chopin, whose ideas were sympathetic to him. The function of the members was to wage war on the benighted Philistines.[4]

Schumann often amused himself by translating letters of the alphabet into their corresponding tones, a practice that probably originated when it was observed by Bach that his name could be spelled musically:

Ex. 109

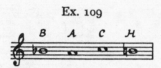

The letter H, often attributed to Byron; see the last three measures since B flat in German notation is equivalent to our B, while our B natural is called in German H. Schumann makes an extraordinary use of this device in his setting of Catherine Fanshawe's *Enigma:* of the song. A prettier instance occurs in the "Northern Song" of the *Album for Youth*, where the first notes spell the name Gade:

Ex. 110

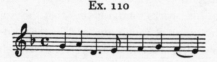

We shall find further examples in commenting on the *Abegg* Variations and the *Carnaval*.

Schumann's piano idiom is strikingly novel. In keeping with his abhorrence of anything unmeaning, he avoids the outworn accompaniments and Alberti basses of the classical period. Scales rarely appear in his compositions. The technique is chordal with exclusion of commonplace arpeggios. We note a fondness for interlocked chords to give unusual balances of tone, for instance:

---

[4] Philistine. "One temperamentally inaccessible to or afraid of new ideas, esp. to ideas whose acceptance would involve change: an active or passive opponent of progress or progressive ideas." *Webster's New International Dictionary*, definition 4. *Philister* is the German university students' opprobrious name for a townsman, implying lack of culture.

Ex. 111

from the *Phantasie,* and

Ex. 112

from the *Symphonic Études.*

Another feature of Schumann's style best observed in his piano works is his remarkable rhythmical ingenuity. The vitality of dotted rhythms attracted him strongly, and he often uses them with effective persistence. Syncopation is one of his favorite devices. We shall see when discussing his works individually that he sometimes carried persistence to the point of monotony and syncopation to such excess that the basic meter is endangered. He relies largely, as Beethoven did, on cross accents and irregularly placed *sforzandi* to express humor and caprice. In the use of the pedal Schumann is boldly experimental, constantly trying out new ideas of resonance and echo. Apart from a few inescapable Italian words he gives all his directions in German. The student should make particular note of his ritardandos. As a rule any indication of tone or speed is supposed to remain in force until supplanted by another. Schumann's retards, however, usually apply only to the exact places where they stand unless marks of prolongation (- - -) follow. We must not expect any corrective *a tempo.*

In the piano music of Schumann and Chopin we find an important departure from the classical notation of legato slurs. The two composers both seek to cover actual phrases by their slurs, pianistically a more appropriate method. Instead of closing the slur at every possible opportunity they go to the opposite extreme of ignoring minor interruptions of the legato. Take as a good example the *Aria* of Schumann's F-sharp minor Sonata. This is the way it is marked:

Ex. 113

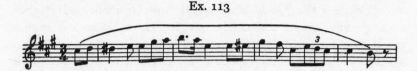

The classical notation might have been:

Ex. 114

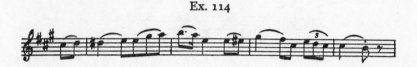

What the pianist plays is this:

Ex. 115

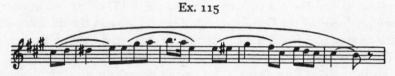

having due regard to Schumann's sub-phrasing as shown by the peculiar barring of the eighth-notes in the first and third measures and to the natural cesura in the second while preserving the sense of a long line. Of the three examples above, Ex. 113 is obviously the simplest and best notation to convey the composer's desire.

The Piano Works

It will be convenient to notice the works for piano in the order of their opus numbers.

The title of the *Variations on the name Abegg*, Opus 1, is explained by the dedication to Countess Pauline von Abegg and the first notes of the piece:

Ex. 116

Remember that B in German notation means B flat. The constant repetition of the rhythm ♩|♩ ♩ ♩|♩ is monotonous and ugly and the accompaniment to the theme is commonplace, but the four variations and the *Finale alla Fantasia* are ingenious and original, casting aside almost completely any fetters the tune and rhythm might have imposed. One may marvel how Schumann expected the accents on the tied notes, especially the last one, to be performed in the following passage:

Ex. 117

unless he had the old *Bebung* effect in mind. [The first two accents are produced by the sharp removal of the thumb and the third finger; the *fermata* G is heard if you take the damper pedal right on the beat. The same holds good for Example 120.]

In the *Papillons*, Opus 2, Schumann presents a number of short pieces in a sequence of ideas without any pretense at unity of form. It may be regarded as a preliminary sketch for the *Carnaval;* the six accented A's on the last page represent bell strokes, or a striking clock, signaling the end of a festival. This composition was inspired by the last scene, *Larventanz,* of Jean Paul's *Flegeljahre*. Schumann was a lifelong admirer of Jean Paul and was strongly influenced by his imaginative and eccentric writings; in mode of thought and artistic style musician and author had much in common. Originally the numbers of the *Papillons* referred to characters and episodes of the *Flegeljahre*. I give them as they appear on the program of a recital by Fannie Bloomfield-Zeisler:

1. *Larventanz*	7. *Das Umtauschen der Masken*[5]
2. *Walt*	8. *Geständniss*[5]
3. *Vult*	9. *Zorn*
4. *Masken*	10. *Enthüllungen*
5. *Wina*	11. *Forteilen*
6. *Vult's Tanz*	12. *Der forteilende Bruder*

[5] There must be a mistake here in the order of titles. No. 7 is evidently the "Avowal" and No. 8 "The Exchange of Masks."

They were not attached to the printed work and it is none the worse for the omission. Suggestions of spring in the air and glimpses of a masked ball account sufficiently for the captivating play of fancy. The Finale is packed with curious features. It begins with two separate phrases from the *Grossvaterlied,* an old song frequently sung in Germany at the end of wedding celebrations:

Ex. 118

Ex. 119

(Ex. 118 recurs in the finale of the *Carnaval,* where Schumann uses it as a symbol of the dense Philistines.) The theme of the Larventanz then returns and soon after the two motives are combined over an organ point on a bass D. Here Schumann had a prophetic vision of the future sostenuto pedal, for he requires the low D to be held under shifting harmonies for twenty-six measures. After the clock strikes six, the guests scatter and silence reigns. [The low D should be held with the damper pedal as indicated. Do not spoil this marvelous idea with the sostenuto pedal. Schumann did not worry about that perfectly good overtone E completing the grand orchestral sound. The long diminuendo is not easy to carry off. The people disappear in the distance while the clock strikes six times forte, not diminuendo, because it stays up in the tower.] A chord is made to disappear gradually, much in the manner of the passage from the *Abegg* Variations (Ex. 117):

Ex. 120

This time no accents are placed on the tied notes. We may be amused by the different notations of the rests, very inexact in Ex. 117, ultra correct in Ex. 120.

The six *Études on Caprices of Paganini*, Opus 3, need not detain us. Schumann had little talent for transcription and the series is interesting, if at all, only by comparison with the later set, Opus 10 and with Liszt's arrangements of the same or other caprices.

Opus 4 consists of six *Intermezzi*, mostly written in the simple form familiar to us in the *Phantasiestücke* and *Kreisleriana:* a main subject, an alternative section (sometimes two such interludes), and a return to the main subject—an expansion of the so-called A B A form. The fourth Intermezzo is an exception, being in simple song form. These pieces are worthy representatives of Schumann's early style, gaining when performed as a group. Yet they are seldom played. The theme of No. 5 is singularly tender and appealing:

Ex. 121

The *Impromptus on a Theme of Clara Wieck*, Opus 5, are really a set of variations. It is hard to discover any value in them, whether in the first or the second version.

Opus 6, the *Davidsbündlertänze*, is a work of very different caliber from the last, full of fire, poetry, and genius. We should not puzzle over the freakish title (literally "Dances of the Leaguers of David") but remember only that it implies a composition of Schumann's new romantic order, rich in content, as yet neglectful of form. The eighteen short pieces, few of which can properly be called dances, are a string of beautiful ideas connected only by an underlying uniformity of style. We could readily sign the slow, expressive numbers *Eusebius* and the temperamental ones *Florestan* for ourselves if Schumann had not initialed them. We can also ignore the *Motto by C. W.* (Clara Wieck, of course) at the beginning; it is merely an introductory phrase in compliment to the beloved and is never after referred to. The superscriptions to No. 9: "With this Florestan closed, and his lips twitched sadly," and to the last number: "Quite superfluously Eusebius added the following thought, great happiness shining in his eyes," will hardly help us to a musical interpretation. On the other hand, directions like "Inwardly," "Rather cockeyed,"[6] "Impatiently," "Very fast and introspectively," "Fresh," "Wild and merry," "With good humor," "As if from afar," are novel and instructive. The work is too long to be played as a whole, but it is easy to make effective selections from it. If Schumann did not know when to stop pouring out his wealth of invention, he did understand very well when each separate idea was complete, so that the *Davidsbündlertänze* is an album of tiny masterpieces. We can admire its pearls without care of the cord on which they are strung. There are two editions of the work. The changes in the second edition are inconsequential and most players prefer to follow the first readings.

The splendid *Toccata*, Opus 7, defers to classic principles, for it is written in fairly strict sonata-form. Most musical of all toccatas, it preserves the characteristics of its type and is a valuable technical study. The quiet end:

Ex. 122

is more satisfactory than any final bluster could be; few composers would have closed so circumspectly.

---

[6] *"Etwas hahnbüchen,"* an untranslatable German expression; "cockeyed" is the nearest English equivalent. [I have always understood the German dialect expression *"etwas hahnbüchen"* to mean "a bit rough, awkwardly so."]

Sandwiched between the *Toccata* and the *Carnaval* is the *Allegro*, Opus 8, a free fantasia of no interest whatever. Strange to find a piece of so little merit among Schumann's published compositions.

The *Carnaval*, Opus 9, though not the greatest, is decidedly one of the most original and representative of Schumann's works. It calls for detailed description, but once more I must warn the reader that all its literary and personal allusions, all its play upon letters, are irrelevant to its musical value, by which alone it should be judged. It is enough, for both performance and understanding, to heed the main title and the designations of the individual numbers.

The subtitle, *Scènes mignonnes sur quatre notes,* explains one aspect of the many-sided piece. It happened that Asch was the name of a small town in Bohemia, the residence of one of Schumann's girl friends, Ernestine von Fricken, and that a jumble of ASCH gives SCHA, the four letters in the name SCHumAnn that can be expressed by musical notes. The S is accounted for by E flat, in German *·Es.* AS can be reproduced separately (A, E flat) or by A flat, in German *As.* In one order or another the *quatre notes* are found at the beginning of most numbers of the *Carnaval.* In the *Pierrot* their entrance is half concealed in the tenor:

Ex. 123

Here Schumann permits himself the license of spelling his H (B natural) enharmonically as C flat. In the *Sphinxes* he indulges in further mystification by writing his cryptic notes in a long obsolete notation:

Ex. 124

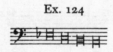

Some numbers, including the opening *Préambule* and the finale, make no allusion to the letters. [Why are pianists reluctant (or afraid?) to perform the three "Sphinxes"? Schumann must have had some reason

for placing those three fascinating figures in the way of the gay
celebrant, stunning him. Why not use your imagination? I used mine
by playing all three in three octaves in the bass, the first fortissimo,
the second mezzo-forte, the third pianissimo (hushed), all in very
slow tempo with long waits between them. I know that they are not
supposed to be played.]

The members of the Band of David have decided to attend the
masquerade. We meet specifically Eusebius, Florestan, Chiarina
(Clara Wieck), Chopin, Estrella (Ernestine von Fricken), and
Paganini. Doubtless others too are present, probably figuring in the
Papillons and *Lettres dansantes,* possibly also in the pair of lovers
to whom I shall shortly allude. In any case, the *Davidsbündler* gather
their forces at the end to march valiantly against the Philistines, who
are put to rout and fly in confusion to the strains of the *Thème du
XVIIème siècle.* This seventeenth-century theme is our old friend the
Grossvatertanz; we have already noticed that Schumann made use of
it in the *Papillons,* Opus 2.

The colorful scene would be incomplete without the leading
characters of the *commedia dell' arte,* or rather we should say of the
later French pantomime, *Pierrot, Arlequin, Pantalon et Colombine.*
Perhaps *Coquette* belongs to this group.

Finally, we can easily imagine a romantic couple dancing together
in the *Valse noble* and the *Valse allemande,* penetrating each other's
disguise in the *Reconnaissance* (the middle section of this piece is a
tender duet), confessing love in the *Aveu,* and immediately afterwards forsaking the glitter of the ballroom for a quiet *Promenade* in
the presumably moonlit gardens.

And now a few words about the music itself and its relation to the
title *Carnaval* and the headings of the movements. Above all, the
piece is animated by exuberant joy of life and interest in humanity.
The *Préambule* starts with stately decorum, *quasi maestoso,* but high
spirits soon carry it to ever increasing speed and happy excitement.
Much of its thematic material returns in the finale, and the two
numbers provide a brilliant frame for the scenes between. *Pierrot*
should not be buffooned. This is no circus clown, but the genial
spirit of pantomime, clever and freakish, everybody's friend. The
comical interjection of the three forte notes:

Ex. 125

resembles a cordial "how-d'ye-do" to neighbors as he makes his way through the crowd more than an unmannerly bumping into guests or a series of clumsy stumbles. The graceful leaps of *Arlequin* are charmingly depicted. The *Valse noble* and *Eusebius* are both beautiful. Florestan enters, impetuous as ever, calms down for a moment to recall a phrase from the *Papillons:*

Ex. 126

and makes a precipitate exit when he sees *Coquette* coming. Am I over-imaginative if I hear *Coquette* wielding her fan with flirtatious intent in this oft-repeated figure?

Ex. 127

And what does the *Réplique* to Coquette mean? Is it a remonstrance on her heartlessness? She seems, at all events, to soften under it; the fan stays quiet. The *Sphinxes* follow; Clara Schumann tells us wisely that they are not to be played. There is no connection between the *Papillons* of the *Carnaval* and those of Opus 2. These, truth to tell, strike us as somewhat heavy-winged insects. *Lettres dansantes* is dainty if enigmatic music. Both *Chiarina* and *Estrella* appear as energetic ladies, better possible mates for Florestan than for Eusebius. *Chopin* is an obvious imitation of the Polish composer's style. It may be objected that Chopin would hardly have written the *sforzandi* in the accompaniment or the doubling of the last notes in the cadenza-like measure at the end:

Ex. 128

Reconnaissance, difficult to play because of the repeated notes for the thumb, would be delightful under any name or in any collection. The capers of *Pantalon et Colombine* are amusing, no more, but the next piece, *Valse allemande,* is lovely. The waltz is startlingly interrupted by the apparition of *Paganini,* who has brought his violin with him to perform a short caprice. He sees Estrella listening and promptly compliments her by quoting her motive (see measure 25). At the end of this sketch Schumann introduces a bold and striking pedal effect:

Ex. 129

The *ppp* chord, touched very lightly, is drowned in the roar of the preceding *sforzandi* and only becomes audible after the pedal is changed. Needless to say, the directions must be exactly observed. Paganini vanishes as suddenly as he had entered and the *Valse allemande* is resumed. The B flat of the next to the last chord of the *Valse* (right hand):

Ex. 130

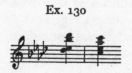

must be a misprint that has escaped correction, for it makes open octaves with the bass. G, supplying the missing third of the chord, would be the right note.

The *Aveu,* tiniest number of the *Carnaval* and one of the best, is closely related to the lovely *Promenade* that follows. Here the interwoven love story reaches a blissful consummation. The little ritornello of the *Promenade,* printed in small notes:

Ex. 131

may be construed as whispered responses to the ardor of courtship. Schumann is loth to break up the intimate scene; periods of lingering sweetness protract the end, and the short *Pause* barely gives the lovers time to rejoin their friends for the march against the Philistines. This *Pause* is badly named, for it is no interval of rest but a rushing introduction to the finale, a sort of call to arms. Its thematic material has already appeared in the *Préambule*. The *Marche des Davidsbündler contre les Philistins* opens heroically—with a touch of the mock-heroic, indeed, for Schumann's sense of humor tempers his adherence to the literary program. Amid the flight of the Philistines, strains of the *Préambule* reassert themselves, then predominate, to close in a matchless delirium of revelry. Perverted taste can make an orgy of this superb piece, but that is not Schumann's fault.

Opus 10 is another set of six *Études on Caprices of Paganini,* much finer than Opus 3 although one never hears them. Nos. 2 and 3 at least, both in G minor, deserve to be played. In Opus 3 Schumann had wished to emphasize the musical aspect of Paganini's ideas, which I think he overrated. Here he more logically transforms the Caprices into Études of some virtuosity, pointing the difference by calling the later set *Concert Études.* Particularly interesting is a comparison of the G minor Caprice, No. 2, with Liszt's version. Schumann did not see his way to an effective reproduction of the violin tremolo on the piano, so he substituted an accompaniment of repeated chords. To Liszt, however, the tremolo suggested the peculiar timbre of the Hungarian cimbalon, and he did not hesitate to transcribe it accordingly. Here is the first measure of the Caprice in the three versions:

Ex. 132

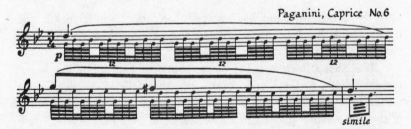

The two composers exchanged courtesies on this subject. Liszt put Schumann's arrangement above his own, measure for measure, in the first edition of his *Paganini Études* and Schumann wrote a warm eulogy of Liszt's dazzling settings.

The Sonata in F-sharp minor marks a new phase of Schumann's development. He now felt ready for the larger forms, and Opus 11 is the first fruit of his confidence.[7] The noble *Introduzione, un poco maestoso,* contains themes later utilized in the development of the first movement:

Ex. 133

---

[7] [Schumann's F-sharp minor Sonata easily ranks among the great sonatas for the keyboard. Others, after Beethoven's opus 111, might be the posthumous B-flat major of Schubert and the B minors of both Chopin and Liszt.]

and forming the substance of the *Aria:*

Ex. 134

and _____

Ex. 135

The *Allegro vivace* is built from two contrasting motives:

Ex. 136

These are expounded at considerable length before the reposeful
second subject enters. The development section is over-long and a

large portion is repeated in a different key with little other variation. This is a favorite practice of Schumann (see the Piano Quintet, etc.), but seems of doubtful propriety in the sonata-form, repetition hardly constituting development as we understand it. (The reference to the *Introduzione*, Ex. 133, in this section is of course quite in order.) The reprise of the first theme is hardly distinguishable from a further prolongation of the development. The second theme, on the other hand, unsupported by any episode or closing section, is too short in proportion to the whole. Its two occurrences together occupy only 59 measures in a movement totaling 368. These are merely formal objections, but the looseness of structure causes a surfeit of the rhythm ♪ | ♫♫ ♫♫ | ♪, in itself so vital and arresting. Unflagging energy sustains the movement and holds our interest despite the unequal balance of parts. Unclouded serenity sheds a blessing on the exquisite Aria, spiritually the finest part of the sonata. But Schumann must have been in a restless mood, for this is the last we hear of peace except for a few tranquil measures in the Finale. Eusebius has had his say and from now on Florestan takes over. The extremely animated Scherzo does not offer as usual the relief of a quieter Trio. Instead, it is interrupted by an Intermezzo marked *Alla burla ma pomposo,* a deliberate extravaganza much like a clown dancing a polonaise. The intentionally "wrong" accents:

Ex. 137

heighten its grotesque character. In the transition leading back to the Scherzo we find a grandiloquent recitative parodying the absurdities of Italian opera. It is a pity that the Scherzo ends fortissimo while the Finale starts at the same level of tone. The last movement is a very irregular Rondo, excessively repetitious of the vigorous first theme and of its most delicate episode:

Ex. 138

Ex. 138 gives us a good example of Schumann's rhythmical originality. The movement as a whole has tremendous sweep and fire. The coda, *Più allegro*, alludes briefly to a passage from the first movement. A curious notation of prolonging dots may be cited from it:

Ex. 139

The time-signature is $\frac{3}{4}$ and in this case each dot must receive the value of an eighth-note as if written:

Ex. 140

Inexact, maybe, but perfectly intelligible and a great saving of pen and ink.

I hope that I have not given a misleading description of this mighty work, vulnerable in form but glowing with genius. Pianists endowed with temperament plus discretion know how to mold it into consistency, bringing its beauties into high relief and artfully compassing its difficulties and lengthy stretches. Played so, it will enthrall any audience.

The *Phantasiestücke*, Opus 12, are probably the most popular of Schumann's piano pieces. All eight, except perhaps the vertiginous *Traumes Wirren* ("Dream Confusion"), lie within the capacity of the talented amateur. They are much played but have not become hackneyed. Eusebius speaks in *Des Abends* ("At Evening"), *Warum?* ("Why?"), in the wonderfully poetic interlude of *Traumes Wirren* and the reflective coda of *Ende vom Lied* ("End of the Song"). Florestan, always the more voluble partner, gives rein to his fancy in *Aufschwung* ("Soaring," literally "Upswing"), *Grillen* ("Whims"), *In der Nacht* ("By Night"), and the *Ende vom Lied*. We must be careful to reproduce the rhythm of the dreamy *Des Abends* correctly. This piece is in $\frac{2}{8}$ time, and the syncopated right hand:

Ex. 141

needs careful adjustment by the regular beat of the left on the fourth sixteenth-note so that it shall not sound as if the meter were $\frac{3}{8}$. At the beginning of *Aufschwung* and at the first re-entry of the theme most players are well advised to take over a few notes into the left hand:

Ex. 142

When the theme returns for the third time, this is not feasible; here it is expedient to make a slight change in the right hand, playing:

Ex. 143

The dotted rhythm ♩. ♫ ♪ must be exactly performed; too often it becomes a hybrid between the right thing and ♩ ♫ ♪ . An effective safeguard is to lift the hand distinctly between the last two eighth-notes: ♩. ♫ ′♪ . A canonic imitation in the B-flat section should not be overlooked:

Ex. 144

In *Warum?* an adorable miniature, the indicated crossing of hands after the double bar is awkward, unnecessary, and harmful to the smoothness of the left hand's phrasing. The title of *Grillen* ("Whims") and its many cross accents bespeak an appropriate interpretation. *In der Nacht* is among the finest of the set, a passionate nocturnal piece with a lull of the wind's moan in the F major interlude. We are free to attach our own meaning to the *Fabel* if we play it fancifully enough. Olin Downes aptly compared the *Ende vom Lied* to a shining golden staircase. The coda not only concludes this number but serves also as a poetic epilogue to the *Phantasiestücke* as a whole.

Schumann hesitated a long time about the title of the *Études symphoniques*, Opus 13. He considered in turn *Davidsbündleretüden* and *Études in Orchestral Character*, finally adopting the name by which we know them, with the subtitle *Études in form of Variations*. At no time did he call them simply *Variations*, yet that is what they really are. It is true that the theme plays a very small part in most of the variations and is entirely absent in others. Rarely do we hear more than its first few notes. Perhaps the composer did not realize that he was blazing a new trail for the variation form. Brahms and later writers often completely ignore the tune that first provoked their thought. "The melody of the theme," we are told in a footnote, "is by an amateur."[8] Fortunate dilettante who in a moment of inspiration gave birth to a theme of grave beauty and inspired a masterpiece! For the *Études symphoniques* is one of the peaks of the piano literature, lofty in conception and faultless in workmanship. Every so-called étude is dictated by musical thought; technique is held strictly in leash. In No. 2 the theme is heard in bass and tenor while a new melody floats above it. The influence of Paganini is traceable in No. 3, that of Bach in No. 8 and something of Mendelssohn's elfin lightness trips in Nos. 5 and 9. Nos. 7 and 10 are the only two of

---

[8] The adoptive father of Ernestine von Fricken.

pronounced bravura style. Mournful beauty haunts No. 11, the slow piece of the set. In the Finale, Schumann paid a subtle compliment to Sterndale Bennett[9] by quoting a song from Marschner's opera *Der Templer und die Jüdin* referring to the country of his birth:

Ex. 145

The Finale is a triumphant march, bringing the work to a brilliant climax. The original theme returns gloriously:

Ex. 146

though still in greatly abbreviated form.

Opus 14, published as a *Concert ohne Orchester*, with the preferable subtitle *Dritte grosse Sonate*, is the most perfunctory of Schumann's larger piano works. One misses his usual vividness and spontaneity, and the creative material falls far short of the plenitude of the other sonatas. Hence the looseness of form in the first and last movements is painfully felt. There were originally two Scherzos to the piece, one after the other, but the first was discarded. The slow movement, marked *Quasi Variazioni*, is based on an Andantino of Clara Wieck. Again the curious hesitancy to call variations variations!

I draw an essential distinction between the *Kinderscenen*, Opus 15, and the *Album für die Jugend*. The latter is written for young people to play. The *Scenes from Childhood* are viewed by a sympathetic observer of children poetizing about them with mature mind. The tender little finale, *The Poet Speaks*, sums up the difference of stand-

---

[9] The *Études symphoniques* were dedicated to the English composer.

point. Games, story-telling, make-believe, moods happy, sad, humorous, and pensive are touched on with inimitable grace and comprehension. In every number a gentle hand strokes a fair face. Schumann's imagination is at its best in this affectionate little work. Notice that the *Pleading Child* ends on a dominant seventh resolved in the next piece, where the request is granted to the child's *Perfect Happiness*. Another delicate point is the final nod of the sleepy head in *Kind im Einschlummern*. In this piece there is a curious resemblance to the slumber motive of Wagner's *Die Walküre*. The *Träumerei*, best of the *Scenes*, expresses its sensitive dreaminess in purest melodic line.

The *Kreisleriana*, Opus 16, is a set of eight fantasy pieces inspired by the character of Kapellmeister Kreisler in E. T. A. Hoffmann's book *Fantasiestücke in Callot's Manier*. One renews acquaintance with this author in Offenbach's opera *Tales of Hoffmann*. Conductor Kreisler is a quaint personality, eccentric, lovable, romantic. He likes to wear an E major cravat with a C-sharp minor waistcoat. Evidently a man after Schumann's own heart! Again we may conveniently forget that portrayal of a character gave impetus to the music, which ranks among the finest efforts of Schumann's genius. He never surpassed the searching beauty of the slow movements (Nos. 2, 4, 6) or the urgent passion of others (Nos. 1, 3, 5, 7). The mystic last number vanishes like a wraith, leaving us at an interrogation mark. The entire set is remarkable for richness of coloring and intensity of feeling. To appreciate it a high level of æsthetic intelligence is required, so that it will never be so generally popular as the *Phantasiestücke*, the *Novelettes*, the G minor Sonata, or the *Carnaval*. This is no facile music; there is severity alike in its beauty and its passion.

I add a few stray notes on the performance of the *Kreisleriana* by way of hint or warning.

No. 1. The middle section in B flat will sound best if the latent melody is brought out by holding the upper notes:

Ex. 147

without emphasizing them.

No. 2. The *sforzandi* of the first phrases should be very discreetly given. These are stresses of quality, not heavy accents. Follow the reading of the first edition.

No. 3. The passage at the end:

Ex. 148

is extremely difficult because of the awkward position of the left hand. No harm is done by transposing the left-hand notes an octave lower; similarly four measures later.

No. 4. The tempo at *Bewegter* is about twice as fast as the beginning, ♩=♪ . Usually this part is taken *too* fast.

No. 5. A slight rubato, which I mark by a comma, is needed in order to separate the short phrases of the middle section:

Ex. 149

No. 6. The thirty-second-notes in the sixth and following measures are to be played as *gruppetti*, not insisting on each separate note. At the ritard, however:

Ex. 150

take them slower and lyrically.

No. 7. The coda of this piece repeats the rhythm of its first phrase:

Ex. 151

fourteen times in succession. The pianist must use all his art to avoid monotony by subtle changes of quality and inflection.

No. 8. The continuous dotted rhythm presents the same pitfall that was mentioned in speaking of *Aufschwung* (see at Ex. 142). In view of the tempo it would be permissible to practise the sixteenth-notes like appoggiaturas:

Ex. 152

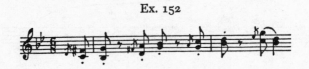

Be sure to observe the single legato slur.

In the magnificent *Phantasie*, Opus 17, Schumann found a medium much better suited to his temperament than that of the sonata. Freed from classical obligations, he chose to write an Allegro based indeed on the sonata-form but containing an interlude *Im Legenden-ton* that would have been out of place in the stricter mode, an imposing March definitely in dance form, and for finale a perfectly constructed Adagio. The unusual order of movements is explained by the fact that the *Phantasie* was composed as a tribute to Beethoven. A project was on foot to raise funds for the erection of a monument to Beethoven at Bonn, and Schumann proposed to contribute the *Phantasie* with the proceeds of its sale. With this in mind he named the three movements *Ruins, Triumphal Arch,* and *The Starry Crown.* The plan fell through and Schumann withdrew the titles. Instead, he prefaced the work by four lines of Friedrich von Schlegel as a motto:

> Durch alle Töne tönet
> Im bunten Erdentraum
> Ein leiser Ton gezogen
> Für den der heimlich lauschet.

The best translation I have seen is given in Philipp Spitta's article in *Grove's Dictionary,* fourth edition:

> Through all the tones that vibrate
> About earth's mingled dream,
> One whispered note is sounding
> For ears attent to hear.

Besides this, Schumann gave illuminating instructions to the player. The first movement is headed: *Durchaus fantastisch und leidenschaft-*

lich vorzutragen (To be performed throughout with fantasy and passion); the second *Mässig. Durchaus energisch* (Moderato, energetic throughout); and the third *Langsam getragen. Durchweg leise zu halten* (Adagio sostenuto, sempre piano). The *sempre piano* of the last direction must be taken with a grain of salt, for there are two stupendous climaxes almost calling for the full brass choir of the orchestra.

No words can describe the *Phantasie*, no quotations set forth the majesty of its genius. It must suffice to say that it is Schumann's greatest work in large form for piano solo. One must hear it often from eminent pianists to get an adequate idea of its grandeur.

The *Arabeske*, Opus 18, and the *Blumenstück* ("Flower Piece"), Opus 19, are two lighter compositions of quiet charm, the former more interesting than the latter. The peaceful *Arabeske* is an effusion of Eusebius and concludes with one of the expressive epilogues he knew so well to write. Florestan for once holds his tongue except for an occasional interjection in the second *Minore*.

Harold Bauer's contention that the title of Opus 20 should be in the plural, *Humoresken*, rather than the singular, *Humoreske*, is well founded. The piece easily divides into four numbers and a coda (*Zum Schluss*). The work cannot be considered one of Schumann's best. We are fatigued by the long procession of short sections and a monotony of tonality seldom ranging beyond B flat and G minor. There is less humor in it than we might reasonably expect, less freshness of invention, less distinction of character. After hearing it no single theme stands out as particularly memorable.

In the *Novelettes*, Opus 21, Schumann has recaptured his rapture. He says in a letter that they were written with enormous zest and that they are mostly gay and superficial "except when he got down to fundamentals." No. 1, a jolly march with a lyrical second theme, is the most popular. No. 2, a rapid bravura piece, persists characteristically in a rhythm that does not tire us because of its sustained vivacity and the relief afforded by the Intermezzo. The third is a merry waltz that might have come from the *Davidsbündlertänze*. No. 7 is brilliant, concise, effective. The finest is the last, No. 8, almost two pieces in one; the second, a sturdy Scherzo, begins at the *Continuation and End*. We find gaiety here without superficiality; Schumann evidently decided to "get down to fundamentals." The

Trio II of the first part starts out as a hunting song, quiets down to listen to a *Voice from the distance*, and ends with a meditative improvisation on the message of the Voice.

The Sonata in G minor, Opus 22, shows far greater control of form than either Opus 11 or Opus 14, and is quite free from their illogical ramblings. Yet it is as impulsive and spontaneous as anything Schumann ever wrote, making the impression that it might have been dashed off at one sitting. Actually Schumann worked on it intermittently over a period of five years and after a further interval of three years composed an entirely new Finale before publication. The rushing first movement is famous for the initial demand: "As fast as possible" and the subsequent insistences: "Faster" and "Still Faster." (The "still faster," however, can safely be ignored.) Slow movement and Scherzo are both short. The Andantino is romantic and lovely, the Scherzo full of snappy wit. Possibly the Rondo resembles the first movement too closely in tempo and mood, but I have not heard it criticized on that account. The continuous tremolo action makes it tiring to the player unless the arm is perfectly loose. In the second theme, *Etwas langsamer*, we find some shortlived retards placed apparently at random in a thrice-repeated phrase:

Ex. 153

I take these to mean that each phrase should be played rubato but with variation in the freedom, not stereotypedly.

The four *Nachtstücke*, Opus 23, bear little resemblance to the nocturnes of Field and Chopin. Only No. 4, everybody's favorite, is essentially lyrical. In this piece the arpeggios on the first and third beats at

Ex. 154

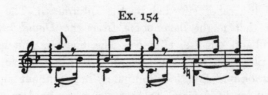

are best played downward to preserve the melodic lines, or alter-
natively the D and C marked *x* may be taken over by the left hand.
Besides the fourth I like the first *Nachtstück,* wistful and remote.
Its melody:

Ex. 155

is intimately related to the theme of the livelier No. 2. In playing it,
be sure not to shorten the quarter-note at the end of each measure.

The unbroken series of piano works ends with the *Nachtstücke.*
From now on the opus numbers alternate with other types of composition.

Schumann's six months' stay in Vienna, from October 1838 to
April 1839, failed in its chief objective to move the *Neue Zeitschrift*
to the Austrian capital, but enriched us by the *Faschingsschwank aus
Wien* (*Carnival Prank from Vienna*), Opus 26. Unlike the other
pieces in carnival style, this is a kind of loose fantasia in five movements headed respectively *Allegro, Romance, Scherzino, Intermezzo,*
and *Finale.* The Allegro, much the longest movement, consists of a
chain of waltz-like sections, the oft-repeated main theme being interspersed with many trios of varying mood. The tone of the whole is
humorous and robust. In one rather uproarious trio Schumann
played a joke on the Viennese censors, who had given him considerable trouble in his business negotiations, by sneaking in the
Marseillaise, then strictly banned from performance, in a thinly
disguised form:

Ex. 156

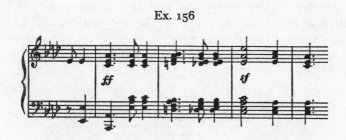

Indulgence in syncopation is carried to a vice in the Trio beginning:

Ex. 157

The rhythm of Ex. 157 is pressed relentlessly, almost throughout the section. Now syncopations like these baffle the ear when protracted without some corrective beat to measure them against; the listener begins to hear:

Ex. 158

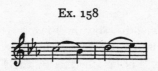

and the effect becomes hopelessly commonplace. The pianist can only do his poor best by striving to imitate strings, which could give a rectifying swell:

Ex. 159

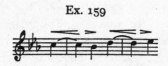

or to establish the beat artificially by an imperceptible gesture of head or body. (The pedal should be taken on the first of each measure.) Another rhythm ridden too hard in this piece is ♩ ♫♫, prevalent in the main theme and in the first and third Trios. This may sate the ear but at least does not confuse it. In the short Romance we find a lovely thought:

Ex. 160

again enfeebled by excessive repetition. The Scherzino is impish and fascinating. I cannot hear it without recalling the verbal suggestion of an amateur friend:

Ex. 161

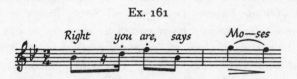

At one spot Schumann makes one of the worst musical jokes[1] on record by an appalling modulation from A to B flat:

Ex. 162

Short of adding the missing fifths to the chords, no first-term harmony student could exceed this willful crudity. The octaves at the end of the Scherzino may be divided between the two hands to facilitate the accelerando, though it is excellent showmanship to do them with the left alone. The Intermezzo, a noble surge of passion, is the chief glory of the *Faschingsschwank*. The Finale, with its pell-mell coda, reverts to the exuberant mood of the first movement. By no means equal to the *Carnaval*, this composition is true to Schumann and has its own measure of breezy invention. It is of medium difficulty.

No. 1 of the *Three Romances*, Opus 28, is good enough but not important. On the other hand the second, in F sharp, is one of Schumann's most endearing pieces, a perfect gem of poesy. The last, in B, runs through a medley of original and interesting ideas in the manner of the *Davidsbündlertänze*. It would be improved by elision of the second Intermezzo in E minor.

We may pass over the *Scherzo, Gigue, Romance and Finale*, Opus 32, to dwell awhile on the six *Studies for Pedal Piano*, Opus 56. The German title has *Pedal-Flügel*, meaning a grand piano with pedals. These *Studies* are in the form of strict canons, written with remarkable ease and flow. I know no canons more listenable. Schumann, a

---

[1] [A joke? No, a moment of inspiration!]

devoted admirer of Bach, spent much time on contrapuntal work, and his compositions abound in imitative passages, short canons, and fugatos. It is remarkable that his canons are superior to his fugues; he had an exceptional talent for the more difficult form. The later sets of *Four Fugues*, Opus 72, and *Seven Pieces in Fughetta Form*, Opus 126, can only be regarded as exercises in composition, whereas the canons of Opus 56 have real musical value. It is regrettable that they were composed for the pedal piano, condemning them to obscurity, especially as the difficulty of playing them on two manuals is quite trifling. The *Sketches for Pedal Piano*, Opus 58, have less significance. I shall not need to return to the Fugues and Fughettas if I point out here that the theme of Opus 72, No. 2, is openly copied from the B-flat minor fugue of Bach's *Well-Tempered Clavier*, Part I:

Ex. 163

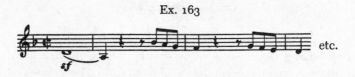

and that the theme of No. 3, in F minor, is almost equally clearly traceable to the first of Chopin's three posthumous Études:

Ex. 164

Nine tenths of the "teaching" pieces that flood the market might be thrown into the trash barrel without a pang to make way for that Golden Treasury of music for children, the *43 Piano Pieces for the Young*, Opus 68, familiarly known as the *Album for Youth*. What a blessing it would be to rid ourselves of the litter-ature of swing songs devoid of swing, cradle songs that don't rock, skating pieces, pop-guns, and what not! These are true teaching pieces in the sense that they are written to be taught, not played. They remind me forcibly of a remark made by an angling friend of mine about the array of lures displayed in a sporting-goods shop: that they are manufactured to capture not fish, but the eye of the fisherman. Schumann provides more tempting bait—first-rate music for young musicians, playable and attractive. Teachers should comb the *Album* diligently for suitable material, not stopping at the *Soldier's March* and *The Merry*

Peasant, noting the pieces calling for octave stretches and the ranges of difficulty from the *Little Étude* or the first *Melody* to the *Little Fugue.* Among my favorites are the *Little Hunting Song, The Wild Horseman, Sicilian Air, Knecht Ruprecht* (Santa Claus), *Erster Verlust* (First Loss), *Reaper's Song, Fremder Mann* (Stranger) and *Kriegslied* (War Song). Grownups need not disdain *May, dear May,* the two numbers in F marked only by asterisks, *Rundgesang* (Roundelay), the *Remembrance* of November 4, 1847 (the day of Mendelssohn's death), the Italian *Mariner's Song,* the *Little Fugue,* and the *Northern Song* to the letters of Gade's name. Observe that in the *Little Fugue* the theme is used both in prelude and fugue with a change of rhythm.

Schumann also wrote three *Piano Sonatas for Youth,* Opus 118ª, and a set of *Piano Duets for small and large Children,* Opus 85, which should be added to his library for youth.

Four sets of piano solos remain to be mentioned. The *Waldscenen* (*Woodland Scenes*), Opus 82, are charming pictures from glade and forest contained between an *Entrance* and a Mendelssohnian *Leavetaking. Einsame Blumen* (*Solitary Flowers*) and the well-known *Bird as Prophet* are the best, though the *Hunting Song* is as spirited as Mendelssohn's of the *Songs without Words,* and the *Haunted Place* properly spooky. In the *Bunte Blätter* (*Colored Leaves*), Opus 99, five numbers are listed as *Album Leaves,* not to be confused with the later Opus 124 of the same name. On the first of these Brahms wrote a set of variations. The third is a little waltz perhaps originally destined for the *Carnaval,* beginning:

Ex. 165

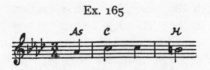

A fine *Novelette* in B minor is the most noteworthy of the *Colored Leaves.* No. 3 of the *Three Phantasiestücke,* Opus 111, has the old Schumannesque tang. A good selection from the *Album Leaves,* Opus 124, would be the *Waltz,* No. 4, the *Fantastic Dance,* No. 5, the *Slumber Song,* No. 16, and the tiny captivating *Elf,* No. 7—an Ariel putting a girdle round the earth in forty seconds.

Schumann contributed only slightly to the piano literature for four hands. A small volume contains the *Bilder aus dem Osten* (*Ori-*

ental Pictures), Opus 66, the *Piano Duets* for children already mentioned, and two groups of *Ball Scenes*. In his solitary work for two pianos, however, he added a valuable piece to a scanty literature—the Andante and Variations in B flat, Opus 46. It is beautiful, pianistically grateful, and universally popular. The same material exists in an arrangement for two pianos, two cellos, and French horn.

The Chamber Music and the Concerto

I remember that during my first year of study at Leipzig my teacher asked me if I were going to the *Abendunterhaltung* (students' concert) that evening. I told him yes, that I wanted to hear the Schumann Quintet. "Have you never heard the Schumann Quintet?" he asked—not too incredulously, for I was fifteen and had just come from Australia. And when I said no, he looked at me long and kindly. At last he said simply: "I envy you." Often since then I have reflected on the happiness of a music student's life. What an endless procession of joyful surprises awaits him! How dramatic the impact on a sensitive and ingenuous mind of masterpiece after masterpiece! Every encounter with new genius is a glorious adventure, a rebirth, and the growth of experience records itself in hours of indelible magic.

Such an event is one's first hearing of the Piano Quintet in E flat. You may discover later that chamber-music experts are inclined to deplore the frequent doubling of the piano and string parts, but this will not damp your just enthusiasm by a particle. Joy of creation exults in every measure and it is impossible for the listener not to be carried along with the tide. Hardly less exhilarating is the Piano Quartet in the same key. The slow movement may be a trifle sweet, but the Finale is even finer than that of the quintet. The Piano Trio in D minor, best of three, contrasts strongly with the ecstatic mood of the quintet and quartet. A brooding, gloomy Allegro is followed by an altogether tragic slow movement. The Scherzo wakes to rhythmic energy and the Finale comes like a burst of sunshine at the end of a dark day. Another beautiful piece is the Sonata in D minor for piano and violin, though the last movement is inferior to the yearning Allegro and the suave Andante. The other Violin Sonata, in A minor, is less interesting.

The first movement of the Piano Concerto in A minor was originally planned as a concert piece for piano and orchestra, the addition of two other movements to form a complete concerto being an after-thought. Such changes of intention rarely succeed. Here there is no patching of an incomplete work, but a perfect realization of unified thought. Schumann achieved a masterly work and we inherited the finest piano concerto since Mozart and Beethoven.

The first movement goes through all the gestures of sonata-form with a single theme, which takes various forms, functioning succes-sively as first and second subject, middle theme, cadenza, and coda. I quote some of the variations:

Ex. 166

The kaleidoscopic theme is skillfully interspersed with episodal matter to make a well-knit movement. Ex. 166e), a motive used extensively in the cadenza, may readily be traced back to the latter part of Ex. 166a). In the short Intermezzo, a delightful colloquy between solo and orchestra, a germ of Ex. 166a) is further developed:

Ex. 167

and still persists in the vigorous hunting flourish of the final *Allegro vivace:*

Ex. 168

The Intermezzo and the *Allegro vivace,* too, are subtly linked together by a phrase of the former:

Ex. 169

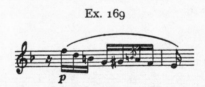

which in the latter becomes:

Ex. 170

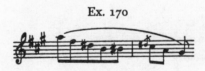

The beguiling second subject of the finale presents a new instance of Schumann's fondness for prolonged syncopation. There is danger here to the listener, for if he once begins to imagine the rhythm

$\frac{3}{4}$ ♩ ‿ ♩ | ‿ ♩ ♪ ⅄ ♪| as $\frac{3}{2}$ ♩ ‿ ♩ ⋮ ♩ ‿ ⋮ ♩ ⅄ ♪| the meter is transformed to banality.

The concerto as a whole is distinguished by its musical quality. Fortunately it cannot be misconceived as a show piece; technique is everywhere subordinated to artistic effect.

Besides the concerto Schumann wrote two concert pieces for piano and orchestra, an *Introduction and Allegro appassionato* in G, Opus 92, and a *Concert Allegro with Introduction* in F. The second of these, vague and unsatisfactory, may be ignored, but the first is a fine work and deserves more frequent hearing.

Clara Schumann's edition of her husband's works, published by Breitkopf & Härtel, is accepted as standard. It has now been reprinted in six volumes by Edwin Kalmus. Next best, probably, is the Peters Edition. [Regarding editions, it is unfortunate that the late Harold Bauer, a great Schumann player, permitted himself too many changes in the text without always indicating them (Schirmer). The Max Vogrich edition, also by Schirmer, is recommended. Urtext editions of many of Schumann's works are published by G. Henle Verlag.]

CHAPTER EIGHT

Frédéric François Chopin
(1810–49)

IN the person of Chopin we find a unique example of a composer writing almost only for the piano—little capable, indeed, of handling any other idiom—who yet is universally accorded a place among the great. It has already been observed that many famous writers of opera have limited themselves to that special field, but this is not a truly analogous limitation, since opera is in itself extraordinarily broad in scope and in the demands of its technique, both vocal and instrumental. Let us admit at once that Chopin shows complete ineptitude in the orchestration of his two concertos and the less-known concert pieces with orchestral accompaniment;[1] that his Trio for piano, violin, and cello as well as the Sonata and the Polonaise for cello and piano are undistinguished specimens of chamber music; and that his agreeable songs, some of which one still hears occasionally, are few and of slight value; in short, that his reputation must always rest solely on his compositions for the piano.

[I belong to the small minority of musicians to whom Chopin's orchestration in both concertos seems perfectly good and amply sufficient. You can hear the piano at all times, whereas the bombastic symphonic revisions of Xaver Scharwenka, Richard Burmeister, and others proved to be useless efforts interfering with the personal ideas of the Master. This is my opportunity to affirm my innate belief that Chopin was a man of strong, powerful mind and heart despite his frail physique. Yes, his lyric tenderness is often finely feminine, but

---

[1] The *Andante spianato and Polonaise,* best of these concert pieces, is usually performed as a piano solo.

it is a far cry from effeminate, as some people would like to have him appear.]

Other criticisms of Chopin's genius often urged are less important and more open to question. It is, I think, unjust to regard him, as he has sometimes been represented to the world, as a musical weakling with a creative power charming but hardly powerful. Too much has been made of his physical frailty, of the sensitiveness of his mental fiber, probably too of the lack of dominance in his relations with George Sand, a lover much stronger than himself.[2] It is hasty to attribute these characteristics to his music. The sheer tonal force packed into the first movement of the B-flat minor Sonata, or the B minor Scherzo, or the thirteen-measure Prelude in C minor, is enormous, to cite only a few random instances of a virility sometimes tragic, often tumultuous, but at its best altogether noble and controlled.

It has been observed with a greater show of truth that Chopin, admittedly excelling in the smaller forms of the prelude, étude, and the like, failed in mastery of more heroic structures and specifically of the sonata form. It is true that the two concertos are somewhat conventional in their conformity to an accepted type, but it might be argued that the composer was more embarrassed by his orchestra than by his form, and that if the works were better scored their architecture might well pass muster. The opening *Allegro maestoso* of the B minor Sonata is loosely knit and wavering, but it is not easy to take valid exception to the other movements of the piece; the Finale, indeed, is a masterpiece of cumulative effect. In the earlier Sonata in B-flat minor, the first movement is quite remarkably concise, and the daring omission at the reprise of the customary re-entry of the first theme is highly successful and logically justified by the insistent use of the first theme in the development section.

[To me, the powerful first movement of the B minor Sonata has perfect form. The fact that, especially in the B-flat minor Sonata, the expected recapitulation does not occur according to the established cliché is a matter of ingenious taste. I agree with Dr. Hutcheson that the "daring omission of the reprise of the customary re-entry of the first theme" is logical, a stroke of spontaneous craftsmanship.]

In any case, the sonata form is merely one of many, and by no means binding on composers since the classic period. Chopin's most valuable contributions to musical form took other directions, some of which deserve more than passing notice. While he did not create the prelude or the étude or the nocturne, he completely transformed and

---

[2] "And so she now loves a man who is inferior to her," wrote Balzac.

revivified them. He could not improve on the preludes of Bach, but he offered a modern equivalent of their beauty, perfection, and variety. The études of Moscheles were only a feeble indication of the immense possible difference between the purely technical study and the artistic type originated by Chopin. Similarly, the credit for the invention of the nocturne, given by Chopin himself to John Field, is an almost over-generous tribute to a minor composer who was fortunate enough to blaze the trail for an immeasurably greater successor.

The possibilities of the prelude and the étude were not exhausted by Chopin. One need only adduce the much later and entirely original preludes of Debussy and the more immediate development of the concert étude by Liszt and others. In the nocturne, however, Chopin reached a perfection of form and expression unapproached before or since.

We may next consider Chopin's enrichment of the dance forms as shown in his waltzes, mazurkas, polonaises, and scherzos. Long before, the older dance music of the pavane, sarabande, minuet, gavotte, gigue, and so on, had been diverted from its original purpose of simply providing an accompaniment to dancing. The early English composers, as well as Couperin, Bach, and others, had exploited all these dances as independent instrumental pieces. Chopin performed a like service for the waltz, the polonaise, and the mazurka. It is interesting to note that whenever this dissociation of the music from the actual dance takes place, there is a tendency to hasten the tempo very considerably. [It has been reported that Alfred de Musset and Meyerbeer reproved Chopin when he was playing some of his mazurkas at one of the renowned salon gatherings in Paris. They claimed that he was distorting the $\frac{3}{4}$ meters by playing them practically in $\frac{7}{8}$. How interesting! Could he possibly have over-accented the third, the mazurka, beat and prolonged it out of sheer patriotic enthusiasm?] Chopin's waltzes are a striking example of this, most of them being obviously quite undanceable because of their speed.[3] We shall come back to the matter of tempo later on; for the moment the important point is that Chopin created for these dances a new and modern form, establishing them in our concert repertory, and expressing all their spirit while shedding their physical steps. No further expansion of the polonaise or the mazurka has been made since Chopin. [Karol Szymanowski's four books of mazurkas, op. 50, are most beautiful contemporary

---

[3] At least undanceable as *waltzes*. Our modern dancers cheerfully undertake to give choreographic interpretations of anything up to symphonies.

expressions of the dance spirit of Poland. They emphasize the younger Polish master's position in music history as Chopin's worthy successor (1883–1937).] Nowadays, however, the concert waltz usually becomes either a valse-caprice or else a transcription of material from the inexhaustible wealth of Johann Strauss's dance music.

As for the scherzo (never a dance, though almost always written in dance form), it is well known that Beethoven substituted it for the minuet in most of his symphonies and sonatas. It was almost a creation of Beethoven's mind, so original was his conception of it and so complete his success in realizing the conception. It is no small achievement that Chopin was able to enlarge greatly the dimensions and the importance of a form modeled by so great a master. He expanded all the parts without sacrificing the symmetry of their proportion. The weight of the ideas, imperiling the appropriateness of the title *Scherzo*,[4] demanded this larger scope. Will it be objected that some repeated sections of these four magnificent pieces are sometimes omitted in performance without detriment to the composition? It is easy to retort that many repeats in the sonatas of Mozart and Beethoven are similarly and with equal justice ignored.

It remains to consider some of the larger pieces in which Chopin followed no model whatever but freely used the form that came most naturally to him. This group contains the ballades, the F minor Fantaisie, the Barcarolle, and the Polonaise Fantaisie. We should also include the Polonaise in F-sharp minor because of the strikingly unusual insertion of a Mazurka as middle section. Here we encounter complete absence of conventionality and finest adaptation of the structural plan to the expression of the composer's thought. If the essence of fine construction be that the form contain the thought and the thought fill the form, these works afford examples of extraordinarily beautiful and effective craftsmanship. Chopin acquired an uncanny talent for presenting a bewildering profusion of ideas, which first seem to run riot, only to resolve unexpectedly into perfect symmetry. The F minor Fantaisie is a case in point. In the main section themes and episodes tumble over one another, as it were, in their eagerness to obtain a hearing. A cold analysis of the succession of the themes as they alternate with the introductory slow march, with the dreamy interlude and the reminiscent coda, might look highly irregular on paper and would certainly give no conception of the spiritual growth of the Fantaisie, far less account for the sense of fully satisfied proportion remaining in our ears after the last chords

---

[4] Literally, "a joke."

have sounded. In the A-flat Ballade, the Polonaise Fantaisie, and the Barcarolle there is considerable diffuseness in the presentation of the material; but in each case the composer, by a brilliant coup, welds his elements into ultimate cohesion. [I must object to the word "diffuseness" as applied to the form of all the pieces mentioned. The old saying "The master can break the form if he can create a new one" is indeed splendidly supported in the case of Chopin by Debussy and Elsner (see the next paragraph).] The G minor and F minor Ballades effectively follow plans all their own; the second, in F major, is the only one of the four quite easy for any teacher of theory to explain by the usual book methods.

On the whole, we may well leave all cavil about Chopin's mastery of form to the critical analyst more intent on taking compositions apart to his own satisfaction than on comprehending the creative processes that gave them life. Truly, as Debussy says, "*La liberté de sa forme a pu tromper ses commentateurs.*" Let us rather, for our part, give ourselves freely to the enjoyment of an art singularly original, eloquent, and convincing. "Leave him in peace," advised the liberal-minded Joseph Elsner, whose operas are forgotten in the greater luster of his having taught Chopin counterpoint and composition. "His is an uncommon way because his gifts are uncommon. He does not strictly adhere to the customary method, but he has one of his own."

Chopin was a superb inventor of melody. It is sufficient to state the fact; elaboration is hardly needed. Every note in his music, essential or ornamental, is imbued with song. Let the unwary be warned against hasty acceptance of his passage-work as mere pianistic mechanics. On close scrutiny the runs will almost invariably reveal themselves as rapidly moving melodies. The fast thirty-second-notes toward the end of the F-sharp major Impromptu, the B-flat minor Prelude, and the main section of the "Minute" Waltz are striking though not unusual examples of this lyric fluency. It is especially interesting in this connection to make a careful examination of the études, where one might reasonably expect the technical element to be in the ascendant. Many of these are based on definite technical figures so consistently developed as to identify the pieces as true "studies" in the accepted sense. But wherever danger of a mechanical effect might threaten, a thematic idea is sure to assert itself, either predominatingly or insinuatingly, to bring relief. Consider the ingenious suggestions of musical line under the continuous ripple of the Étude in Thirds, or the outcry of the right hand in the "Revolutionary" Étude against the surging arpeggios below, or again, in the mighty A minor Étude,

Opus 25, No. 11, the implacable march of the left hand supporting the
dizzy swirl in the treble. In only two of the twenty-seven études, the
first of Opus 10 and the last of Opus 25, in C major and C minor
respectively, is the melody entirely latent in the figuration. More will
be said later on of these two pieces.

Today it is hard for us, who have survived so much modern dissonance, to understand how Chopin's harmonic progressions could
have seemed harsh to many of his contemporaries, including Schumann, Moscheles, Berlioz, Meyerbeer, Mendelssohn. It is true that
in harmony, as in everything else, Chopin strove to realize his avowed
intention "to found a new epoch in art." He often creates an extraordinary poignancy by a single accidental; consider for example the
unexpected B sharp in the fourteenth measure of the F-sharp major
Impromptu and the recurring use of the foreign D natural in the C-
sharp minor Nocturne, particularly at the thirteenth measure. Some
of his transitions are brought about by chains of infinitely beautiful
passing modulations. Jeweled harmonies of this kind may be found
in the *lento sostenuto* of the Fantaisie, in the measures immediately
preceding the *dolce sfogato* (not far from the *tempo primo*) of the
Barcarolle, and before the return of the main theme in the Largo of
the B minor Sonata.

It seems certain that Chopin frequently allowed himself to be
dissuaded, to his and our disadvantage, from boldnesses of harmony
and voice-leading that were part of his original thought. A very well-
known instance occurs in the last of the seven introductory measures
of the G minor Ballade:

Ex. 171

where the freely entering dissonant E flat at (a) is ingeniously though
indirectly resolved in the first phrase of the theme immediately following. Timid convention, in the form of the weaker version at (b),
won out in the early editions of the Ballade, but the melancholy E
flat, made more telling by the slight swell from the C and the arpeg-
giation of the chord, has long been restored to its rightful place. In

this connection the preface to the Oxford Edition says very pertinently: "Unfortunately, in the revision of his manuscript for publication, the composer permitted the intervention of two or three ill-advised counsellors, intimate friends of his, to whom he often entrusted the task of copying the music or of reading the proofs. And he, the great innovator in the domain of harmony, would sometimes accept the suggestions of these incompetent censors, who were entirely blinded by the all too original beauty of his writing. He would then water down his harmonies or even allow them to be modified by these paltry champions of supposedly intangible laws and jog-trot practice."

But—again unfortunately—the Oxford Edition puts itself quite out of court by the incredible readings it has sponsored as authentic. A more reliable authority is Saint-Saëns. In an essay describing the autograph of the F major Ballade, presented by him to the library of the Paris Conservatoire, he quotes some magnificently bold bass progressions from the coda which were softened down in the later printed version. "Possibly," he ventures, "some purist dropped a hint to Chopin that the left hand did not accord correctly with the right, a matter which, however, in a rapid movement like this, was no drawback at all." He concludes that the author had made "a regrettable correction."

In all the foregoing respects other composers may have equaled Chopin; even his melodic flow was certainly no more lovely and copious than that of Mozart or Schubert. Chopin's greatest distinction, the quality in which he outpointed all others, lay undoubtedly in the astonishing originality and appropriateness of his writing for the piano. He divined the soul of the instrument, and his every phrase, technical pattern, and ornament sounds inevitably proper to the chosen medium. Rarely does one find a trace of the orchestral suggestions abounding in Beethoven. The first of the waltzes begins with a sort of trumpet call, and the same instrument might take the theme in the trio (D major) of the A major Polonaise were the range somewhat higher; there is a strong hint of the cello in the slow C-sharp minor Étude, Opus 25, No. 7; one may pardonably imagine organ effects in the C-sharp minor Scherzo and both of the Nocturnes in G minor; and conceivably the opening of the Fantaisie could be scored for alternations of low strings and woodwind choir. But these are isolated cases, of small significance in proportion to the total output in which they occur. It is not surprising that Wilhelmj, encouraged by the tunefulness of the nocturnes, essayed an arrangement of them for violin; nor need we marvel that they successfully resisted transplantation, the over-familiar Nocturne in E flat being the only one to survive its change of habitat.

The utter originality of Chopin's genius has never been questioned. He had no predecessor and no successor. His indebtedness to John Field was almost purely nominal and limited at most to the nocturnes; certainly he thieved no giant's robe from the Irish composer. And if Scriabin was noticeably influenced by Chopin's lyricism in his earliest works, he quickly developed an entirely unrelated idiom. Chopin came and departed like a comet from remote space.

Every pianist anxious to play Chopin well would be wise to familiarize himself with the composer's own ideas as expressed in his instructions to pupils. Fortunately, fairly reliable accounts of his teaching have been transmitted to us, one of the most informative being contained in Carl Mikuli's preface to his edition of the piano works. In technical matters, we are told, Chopin insisted above all on flexibility. The various touches were thoroughly explored, with greatest emphasis on the full-toned legato. For scales he recommended the modern hand position, the wrist well out from the body and the hand and fingers bent inward from it to aid the crossings of thumb and fingers. He sought in scales a continuously even carriage of the hand and arm, ascending and descending, comparable to the motion of a glissando. He horrified the orthodox pedagogues of his day by using the thumb very freely on black keys and frequently passing it under the fifth finger. He was an adept at sliding a single finger from note to note (not necessarily from a black to a white key) without impairment of the legato effect. Among other innovations he greatly improved the fingering of scales in chromatic thirds. It is a disputed point whether he played with a flat or arched position of the hand.

On the musical side, Chopin directed his attention chiefly to matters of inflection, phrasing, and rhythm. Shadings were to be most carefully graduated. He disliked sharpness of accentuation, and this may profitably be remembered when observing the accents marked in his own pages. Bad phrasing was intolerable to him. It affected him as if someone were speaking in a language ill-understood, misplacing the natural stresses of words and syllables and even destroying the meaning by faulty punctuation.

The student is almost invariably astonished to hear that Chopin was "inexorable," as Mikuli puts it, in matters of rhythm, and that a metronome always stood on his piano. Even in the much discussed and badly misunderstood *tempo rubato,* for which he was famous, Chopin repeatedly stated that the left hand (meaning the accompaniment) should observe strict time while the right hand (meaning the melody) might exercise greater freedom, lingering behind or hurrying forward in languor or passion of utterance. "Let your left hand," he said, "be your conductor, always controlling the time." This is by no means a scientifically accurate theory of the rubato, and we need not unreservedly accept it; doubtless Chopin's practice, like that of many other musicians, was far truer than his theory. The attempted explanations of most writers are hopelessly confusing. A better conception is gained through Chopin's own metaphor of a tree whose trunk stands firm and unyielding while the smaller branches, twigs, and leaves are stirred by every passing breeze. I venture a general definition based on Chopin's image: rubato is the innate flexibility of rhythm which makes it responsive to emotion. This is true from Bach to Prokofiev. Rhythm is the pulse of music, and just as our physical pulse beats faster or slower in joy or sadness, in excitment or calm, so rhythm quite naturally adjusts itself to mood. A bad rubato resembles the irregular pulse of a fever patient. A proper rubato is just as rhythmical as the antithetical *tempo giusto,* and a metronomic performance of emotional passages is every whit as unmusical as an unmotivated rubato.

The Waltzes

There is a wide range of mood and tempo in the waltzes. About half of them, marked *vivo, vivace,* or *molto vivace,* are fast and brilliant; the others, variously marked *lento, moderato,* or *tempo giusto,* are of gentler tone and more sedate pace. A few, notably the fifth, Opus 42, in A flat, and the exceedingly graceful one in C-sharp minor, employ a *ritornello* episode with excellent effect. There is a splendor in the long undulations of No. 1, in E flat, and No. 2, in A flat, a whirl of unrestrained gaiety in the so-called "Minute Waltz," pensive sadness in the third, in A minor, while pure lyric beauty is concentrated in No. 9, another of several in A flat. The grace and courtesy of the Parisian salon are ever present. Schumann said of one waltz (Opus 42) that it is "aristocratic through and through. If played for dancers, half of the ladies should be countesses at least."

For all this it is a peculiar feature of the waltzes that Chopin, elsewhere meticulous in his attention to variety and subtlety of subordinate details, was here satisfied with left-hand accompaniments of the utmost harmonic and rhythmical simplicity. In some of these tum-tum basses Chopin comes as near the commonplace as his fastidious genius ever permitted.

Only the first eight waltzes of the volume as we know it were printed during Chopin's lifetime. All of these except the fourth, in F major, are very fine. Nos. 9–13 were published posthumously in 1855 as Opus 69 and Opus 70, while No. 14 did not appear until 1868 (without opus number). Of these latter the ninth, in A flat, and the fourteenth and last, in E minor, are also among the best.

Every pianist will wish to read through all the waltzes and to work more carefully at a few. Let us arbitrarily select three for special consideration.

1. *Grande Valse in E flat, Opus* 18. The introductory four measures are intended to arrest the attention. Play them forte diminuendo, with pedal so that the B flat resounds, and observing the accents. Chopin's original marking of the main theme:

Ex. 172

and the change in shading and phrasing in the answering phrase should be faithfully followed. The repeated notes in the next section are not really difficult; just hold the arm lightly suspended and shake the notes out of a free wrist. The D-flat theme invites greater repose and expressiveness, and the *dolce* (in G-flat major) just before the return to E flat may be taken still slower and rubato. The acciaccaturas of the B-flat minor episode may be played almost simultaneously with their main notes as long as the line of the melody stays clear. The effect of the whole must be extremely brilliant; a trace of ostentation would not be out of place.

2. *Valse in A minor, Opus* 34, *No.* 2. By some incomprehensible freak of publication this piece appeared with two companions under the general title of *Trois Valses brillantes.* As a matter of fact, it is elegiac in mood, slow in tempo, and might appropriately be called a *Valse triste.* Confessing to a preference for the gentler type of waltz, I consider this the most beautiful in the book. It has all the grace and sway that distinguished the waltz as a dance before it became a *Grande Valse brillante* or a *Valse de concert* and so lost something of it finer virtue. The alternation of melody between the two hands is entrancing

and should be properly featured. Play the A major section with no-bility, *forte ma dolce,* and the succeeding transposition to the minor mode like a saddened echo. Give special attention to the last of the alternating sections, starting with a new melody in the left hand and developing into a duet between left and right. This is the perfection of poetry; only Keats could duplicate it.

3. *Valse in C-sharp minor, Opus* 64, *No.* 2. In this favorite of artists, amateurs, and public there is the nicest imaginable balance of three ideas, the main theme occurring twice, the ritornello three times, and the middle theme (in D-flat major) once. In the main theme the first motive of two measures should be played *espressivo,* the second answering motive *leggiero.* In spite of Chopin's injunction of *"tempo giusto"* some freedom of rhythm is quite permissible. Here is the best fingering for the *leggiero* motive:

Ex. 173

Use the same fingering for measures 4, 7, and 8. Make the sixteenth-rest perceptible in spite of the legato slur over it. Chopin's rests must always be regarded as breathings, but all the melody *notes* of this composition are strictly legato. The ritornello offers a tempting op-portunity to vary the repetition by emphasizing the thumb notes of the right hand at the last of each measure as well as by observing the prescribed pianissimo. The *più lento* of the middle theme (D-flat major) invites a full singing tone.

If you add to my selections the Waltz in D flat, Opus 64, No. 1, DON'T try to play it in one minute. It simply can't be done, even if you race through the lyrical middle section without slackening speed —which would be criminal. Nevertheless, the piece will always re-main a kind of stunt for flying fingers.

The Polonaises

The polonaise is not, properly speaking, a dance, but rather a stately processional, a sort of march in $\frac{3}{4}$ time with a touch of pageantry. It is an aristocratic "showing off" in movement and gesture. Were it not too irreverent, one might suggest that it is the courtly equivalent of the lowly cake-walk. It has also a curious approach to a more popular style in the possibility of "cutting-in," somewhat as in modern American dancing.

Many descriptions of the polonaise have been written, varying from the dry report given in *Grove's Dictionary*, fourth edition, to the highly colored rhapsody, doubtless from the pen of the Princess Wittgenstein, in Liszt's book on Chopin. The best account that has come to my attention is that of Casimir Brodziński, poet and critic, quoted in part in Niecks's life of Chopin.

The polonaise preserves a dignified tempo, with an extreme range of about ♩ = 76 to ♩ = 100 and a basic rate not far from ♩ = 80. There is little difference of speed between the most brilliant and the most melancholy specimens. The resplendent Polonaise in A flat is commonly played far too fast; even the virtuoso octaves of the left hand in the middle part should not degenerate into a display of wrist technique. Those of us who remember Paderewski will not forget the majesty with which he clothed these gorgeous compositions. That majesty was largely one of tempo. [How is it possible that some artists distort the theme of the great A-flat Polonaise into a supposed-to-be exciting, though questionable, error of taste? The original writing of the inspired theme emphasizes the singing legato.

Ex. 174

Example (a) 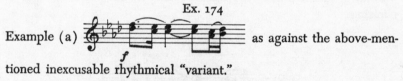 as against the above-mentioned inexcusable rhythmical "variant."

Example (b)  .]

Minor characteristics of the Polonaise are:

1. Frequency of an accompanying rhythm: ♪♫ ♫♫ or ♫♪ ♪♩ ♪.

2. A tendency to place a long note on the second beat of the measure (See the Polonaises in E-flat minor, A major, and A-flat major).

3. "Weak" endings in all the cadences.

Chopin's polonaises easily fall into two sets, those in A major, A flat, and F-sharp minor constituting a brilliant, spirited, and manly group while those in C-sharp minor, E-flat minor, and C minor are characterized by gloom and melancholy. The three posthumous examples, printed as Opus 71, add nothing to Chopin's reputation and need not here be considered. The Polonaise Fantaisie, one of the master's loveliest works, is in a class by itself, and so is the less valuable but extremely pianistic Polonaise in E flat, to which Chopin added a prefatory *Andante spianato* of much grace and an orchestral accompaniment so insignificant that it can be and usually is omitted without regret.

I propose for special study the Polonaises in C minor and A major. The two are typical expressions of Chopin's strongly pronounced patriotism, that in C minor picturing the tragedy, the other the glory of Poland.

Polonaise in C minor, Opus 40, No. 2. The chords of the preliminary two measures should set a somber background for the dark oppression of the octave theme in the left hand. The gloom is not lessened by the louder repetition. Take heed of the phrasing; above all, do not neglect the important sixteenth-rest after the first note. At the end of each eight-bar period the right hand becomes melodically prominent. The outbreak of passion in the second section introduces the polonaise rhythm: ♫♪♩ , which should be well marked. The following measure has been maltreated by the editors, who have too often distorted Chopin's difficult but eminently correct phrasing:

Ex. 175

losing sight of the fine contrast with the continuous legato six measures later when the bass begins to sing again. (Compare this passage with another victim of editorial indiscretion, the episode in triplet quarter-notes concluding each section of the first movement of the B-flat minor Sonata.) The yearning theme in A flat gives occasion to practise the utmost possible legato in repeated chords. This is a theoretically impossible feat often demanded by Chopin, best accomplished by a kind of blocked touch in which the keys are never allowed to rise to their normal surface between chords. A formidable addition to the pathos of the piece occurs at the return of the main subject by the addition of the counterpoint:

Ex. 176

This should be thundered forth like a knell of doom. Note incidentally how skillfully the effect is prepared in the four measures
preceding.

Polonaise in A major, Opus 40, No. 1. A pæan of triumph,
ringing with pomp and circumstance. Good performance of it hinges
largely on keeping the stately polonaise time; few compositions can
be so badly cheapened by too fast a tempo. There is such a preponderance of forte that every opportunity of avoiding noisiness should be
grasped. With this in mind, watch the differences between *f*, *ff*, and
fff and realize them in tone. Observe, too, the crescendo and diminuendo signs, remembering that every crescendo implies a comparatively soft start. There are many of these marks in the original and
later editions, some versions wisely suggesting an occasional piano.
Careful attention to the indicated legatos and staccatos will afford a
change of quality even where the intensity is unchanged. All prevailingly loud pieces should be treated similarly, for, while the ear
will contentedly absorb many pages of soft or varied tone, a protracted and unmitigated forte becomes painful.

The Mazurkas

The mazurkas are rightly regarded as among the most characteristic of Chopin's works. His nationality speaks even more unmistakably in them than in the polonaises. The romantic susceptibility
of the Polish temperament, marked by abrupt transitions from energy
to lassitude, gaiety to melancholy, exaltation to morbid depression,
finds here its fullest and most intimate expression. Not that this range
of feeling is exhibited in each and every mazurka, for there are
many, especially among the shorter ones, that offer fugitive glimpses
of a single mood. Nevertheless it is true of the type as a whole that
a gay thought may equally provoke a plunge into despair or another cheerful idea in the next breath. The unexpected is always
happening and when it happens always seems natural and inevitable,
however wayward.

The novice must not be disappointed when he often fails to notice the "strong accent on the third beat of the measure" so confidently promised for the mazurka by the dictionaries. In some cases it is prominent enough; in many others (as in Nos. 5, 20, 24, and 41) the prevailing accent favors the second beat rather than the third; while again (as in Nos. 10, 13, 31) the beat is obviously quite variable.

The mazurkas are too numerous for individual review. There are fifty-one, placed in all complete editions in the order of opus numbers,[5] so that they are easily identified by the serial numbers. The best, in my opinion, are Nos. 1, 5, 7, 10, 13, 20–7, 31, 32, 35, 38, 40, 41, 45, 47, and 49. Among these the general character is gay or animated in 1, 5, 10, 20, 23, 31, 38, mournful or plaintive in 13, 17, 22, 26, 40, 41, 45, 47, 49. No. 24 is gentle, No. 23 (known as the "Clap" Mazurka) boisterous. Only a few are long. None are technically difficult, some easy enough for a beginner, but musically most are beyond the reach of players not endowed by birth or intuition with an understanding of their Slavic nature. The amateur is advised to make his first selections from Nos. 1, 5, 22, 24, 40, 41, 45, and 47. These are among the easiest to interpret. Later, of course, he may choose his own favorites.

Harmonically the mazurkas are extraordinarily daring and advanced. Either Chopin's well-meaning conventional friends did not dare interfere when his foot was on his native heath, or he was firm in resisting any suggested changes. The facile accompaniments so common in the waltzes are extremely rare; when they occur at all, as in the B-flat Mazurka, they are apt to give way to altogether original effects like the following:

Ex. 177

Drone bases of this kind abound in the mazurkas. [Observe the very original and "advanced" long Chopin pedal of Ex. 177, totally ignored in one otherwise admirable recording.]

---

[5] The last ten are posthumous works, but late opus numbers have been given to them for convenience.

In the very first Mazurka Chopin indulges his fondess for chromatic sequences:

Ex. 178

They are present, too, in No. 49, his last piece, written when he was too ill to try it over at the piano. Near the end of the C-sharp minor Mazurka, No. 21, there is a riot of seventh chords moving chromatically downward without regard to their consecutive fifths and octaves. At the other harmonic extreme is the "Clap" Mazurka, deliberately rustic and reminiscent of Weber in its bald tonic and dominant chords.

Contrary to the general practice in dance forms, the tempo of Chopin's mazurkas must often be taken much slower than that of the dance from which they originated. This is particularly true of some of the most beautiful and pathetic; for instance, those in A minor, No. 13, B-flat minor, No. 17, and E minor, No. 27.

The Nocturnes

It is in the nocturnes that Chopin fully reveals himself as the poet of the piano. The moods inspired by night are expressed by them in matchless songs of rest and peace, tears and anguish, dreams, romance, and storm. It would be hard to extend their gamut.

The essentially pianistic type of melody invented by Chopin shows prominently in these works. Seldom is the line vocal, yet nothing more truly lyrical can be imagined. Try to sing the first half-page of the first, eighth, twelfth, thirteenth, or sixteenth Nocturnes, and you will see at once how utterly unsuited they are to a human voice of any imaginable range or *tessitura*. Except for brief moments they are hardly more appropriate to any other instrument, even the violin. Only the piano, that so-called "percussive" instrument, can sing them to advantage.

Chopin's accompaniments are for the most part as untranslatably pianistic as the melodies, depending for their effect on the sustaining quality of the pedal, without which their widely spread chord figures cannot even be played legato. Look at the first, seventh, eighth, twelfth, and sixeenth Nocturnes for illustrations of this point, and notice how often the left hand covers two octaves or more of sound, affording a rich harmonic background in spite of the thin appearance to the eye.

There is infallible instinct in this as well as art, for not only are the harmonies held and the overtones of the strings freed (a normal result of using the pedal), but the melodic tones are continually fed by fundamentals in the bass. To get an idea of this, try the experiment of silently holding the first melody note F of the D-flat Nocturne while you play the introductory measure for the left hand alone with the pedal down; now take your left hand off the keys and lift the pedal, and you will distinctly hear the unstruck F sounding. Your first melody note, therefore, has been partly created before you play it at the beginning of the second measure. Of course Chopin is not the only composer to exploit this property of the piano; he does so, however, to an unusual degree and with remarkable effect.

Most of the nocturnes are constructed of a main section, an intermezzo (sometimes calmer, oftener more agitated), and a return to the original thought. Their form, while quite simple, is a faultless vehicle for their depth of feeling.

1. *B-flat minor, Opus 9, No. 1.* Beautiful enough in itself, the first Nocturne hardly counts among the best. To me its melancholy sounds a little affected, ornamentation overloads the sentiment, and the accents in the D-flat major section do not fall quite naturally. The irregular groups of notes in the second and third measures, etc., need not worry the student; it is not necessary to execute them as true polyrhythms against the left hand, and they may be divided conveniently according to taste. The twenty-two notes of the third measure, for instance, might be played 4, 3, 4, 3, 5, 3 to the six beats. This kind of liberty is in good taste and belongs, in fact, to Chopin's characteristic rubato.

2. *E flat, Opus 9, No. 2.* The only nocturne in simple song form, and the only one that might conceivably have been written by Field. So popular for many a long day that it became one of the most hackneyed pieces in the literature, it now enjoys a much needed rest.

3. *B major, Opus 9, No. 3.* Most players tend to take the rondo-

like theme too slowly and seriously; Chopin's instructions—"Allegretto, $\rule{0pt}{0pt}$ = 66," and "*scherzando*"—are all correct. This is the most light-hearted of the nocturnes; even the agitato interlude suggests energy rather than unrest. But the light grace of its general mood is not easy to convey. Entrancing in the hands of a master, it can hardly be recommended to the amateur.

4. *F major, Opus* 15, *No.* 1. Like the Ballade in the same key (*q.v.*), the F major Nocturne presents an alternation of ideas of the "flower-storm-flower" kind. Here, however, the storm enters only once and the flower remains unharmed. The simplicity of the main section is in its way just as difficult to express as the technically exacting outburst of the interlude. The melody should be treated very gently, with no attempt to force a full tone and with only moderate inflection. In this piece we have occasion to admire Chopin's mastery of smaller form; it contains not one superfluous or insignificant note.

5. *F-sharp major, Opus* 15, *No.* 2. A favorite number that has fallen deserving heir to the lost popularity of the E-flat Nocturne. It is a much finer piece though perhaps a trifle over-ornate. Again, as in the first Nocturne, the irregular little cadenzas (here printed in small type) need not be played too literally but may be divided into convenient groups; rather than hurry, let the left hand pause on its last eighth-note to allow the right hand to catch up. The descending chromatics in the eighteenth and twentieth measures should sound as much as possible like a vocal portamento, the tone gliding down from E sharp or F sharp to A with the intermediate notes hardly recognizable. At the *Doppio movimento* we meet a modern instance of variable dot values:

Ex. 179

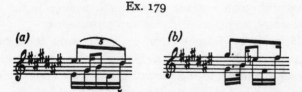

The dotted D sharp marked *x* is obviously intended to receive a fifth, not a quarter value of the beat, and the complicated-looking notation at (b) becomes simply two triplets. The important thing is to observe the change of rhythm from even quintuplets to triplet rhythm, at the ninth measure. The whole passage is simpler than it appears in print, for the holding of the lower and inner parts may safely be ignored by the fingers and entrusted to the pedal.

6. *G minor, Opus 15, No. 3.* This curious nocturne sounds more like an improvisation than a finished composition. Starting with a melancholy theme, it goes over to a modulatory episode rising to a climax and then subsiding to introduce an entirely unrelated section, *religioso,* in the key of F. The *religioso* subdivides into two parts, the first suggestive of the organ, the second:

Ex. 180

hinting at orchestral effect, with the long notes sustained by trumpets and horns. The last four measures return to G minor, but end on a *tierce de Picardie* (major triad). I find the piece extremely interesting musically, and as it is very easy technically I can hardly understand why it is not a favorite of the amateur.

7. *C-sharp minor, Opus 27, No. 1.* An atmosphere of morbid pessimism, heavy and oppressive, enshrouds this masterpiece. The spirit struggles heroically at the *più mosso* to rise above despair, relapses into gloom, and finally attains resignation and perhaps a wan hope at the closing measures in the major mode. The first section must be played with great restraint of tone and shading; in the interlude, on the contrary, no height of climax can be excessive.

8. *D-flat major, Opus 27, No. 2.* If we were asked to name a piece typical of the serenity of night our choice would probably fall here. What a contrast to the preceding nocturne! Now the soul is at peace with itself and with a starlit world. This ideal lyric gives wonderful opportunity for the display of expressive touch and perfect legato.

9. *B major, Opus 32, No. 1.* A piece of calm mood, not especially important. Its most remarkable feature is the unexpected dramatic recitative at the end, turning to the minor mode. The last chord contains a D natural wrongly "corrected" by many editors to D sharp.

10. *A-flat major, Opus 32, No. 2.* The melodic line is more vocal than usual, barring a few idiomatically pianistic cadenzas. The inter-

lude in $\frac{12}{8}$ time becomes more agitated and leads to an appassionata reprise; the fortissimo here, however, should be lyrically moderated and may be reduced to piano after eight measures. At the sixth measure from the close the theme should be softly stressed, so that it vibrates through a light haze of embellishment.

Ex. 181

(The upturned stems and "stamps" of Ex. 181 are added to the original text.)

11. *G minor, Opus* 37, *No.* 1.   This is a good nocturne for the student to begin on, its easy technique allowing him to concentrate his whole attention on style and phrasing. It is a mournful little piece with a hymn-like interlude. The latter may be played as if on the organ, not emphasizing the melody too much and using the "swell" for the crescendo. The natural cesuras at the end of each line of the hymn justify slight pauses, not so long as those later prescribed by Chopin.

12. *G major, Opus* 37, *No.* 2.   This, the most graceful of the nocturnes, might equally appropriately be named a barcarolle, for it has the undulation of a boat song both in the rippling double notes of the main subject and in the swaying motion of the alternating theme. The frequent modulations in both themes are unusually interesting and original. The form differs from that of other nocturnes because of the repetition of the second theme in a new cycle of keys and a last echo of it in the exhalation of the concluding measures. It is a question how best to finger the tricky thirds and sixths; the first motive, often repeated, may be taken with either of the alternatives shown in Ex. 182.

Ex. 182

(Chopin invented the occasional use of the fingers $\frac{5}{1}$ in scales and passages of thirds; Tausig added the slide of the second finger from

a black to a white key. Both devices should be used liberally to ensure a strict legato.)

13. *C minor, Opus 48, No. 1.*   A masterpiece, nobly tragic, perfect in every line. The impressive first theme is more declamatory in
character than lyrical, the frequent rests lending passion to its speech.
The interlude in C major, starting with quiet majesty, ascends to an
overwhelming climax when the interrupting octaves reach a fortissimo.
Doppio movimento at the resumption of C minor seems an ill-considered
direction; *tempo primo ma agitato* would better express the intention.
We find in this section a peculiarity of notation at

Ex. 183

and elsewhere. This looks as if Chopin wished the chords and melody
to be played together, not two against three; all the same, the melodic
eighth-notes must sound as duplets. The right effect will be gained
by playing approximately as follows:

Ex. 184

[*Doppio movimento* means that the triplets in eighths are the same as
the sixteenths of the preceding bar. I disagree with Dr. Hutcheson's
suggestion of grace notes in Ex. 184.]

14. *F-sharp minor, Opus 48, No. 2.*   Here is one of those cases
where the first pages look thin in print, only one note being allotted
to each hand except for the two introductory measures. The pedal,
however, gives the effect of four-part harmony. A pensive melody,
reinforced later by octaves in the right hand, leads over to a noble,
richly harmonized theme in D flat, $\frac{3}{4}$ time. Seven measures before
the return to F-sharp minor a mistake occurs in the first edition,
which, though obvious, has been perpetuated in every reprint I have
seen except that of the Breitkopf & Härtel revision. Two measures later
many editions misrepresent the rhythm. The two places in question
should read:

Ex. 185

The recapitulation of the first theme is greatly curtailed, partly because it was amply expounded in the former statement, partly to make room for a coda of haunting sweetness ending in F-sharp major.

15. *F minor, Opus 55, No. 1.* Youthful aspirants to concert fame have played this number at so many debuts that it is popularly known as the "Prodigy's Nocturne." In truth it is suitable for a talented child, though grownups need not disdain its charm. Again the repetition of the first part is shortened in favor of an interesting coda.

16. *E-flat major, Opus 55, No. 2.* A long strain of purest lyricism, very improvisational, and exhibiting all the characteristics of the best nocturnes, including a coda of added delicacy. Chopin always ends beautifully, and just when we are most sure that he has exhausted the entrancement of his themes he is apt to surprise us by a surpassing afterthought.

17. *B major, Opus 62, No. 1.* The fragrance of this nocturne calls for utmost delicacy of touch. We should recognize two varieties of singing tone in Chopin: a delicate but penetrating tone oftenest marked *dolce* and a full-throated cantabile for which the composer's favorite word is *sostenuto*.[6] Here, for instance, the middle section is marked *sostenuto* in contrast to the *dolce legato* of the beginning. The original melody is beautifully adorned with chain trills on its return; once heard, this exquisite passage is not easily forgotten. The coda offers a good example of Chopin's pianistic type of melody.

18. *E major, Opus 62, No. 2.* This is one of Chopin's sostenuto melodies, warm and luscious like the G string of a violin. After the main theme comes an episode, first leading to an *agitato* middle section and afterwards returning at greater length as coda.

19. *E minor, posthumous work.* The mournful mood is tempered with resignation. Though not in a class with the great nocturnes, the piece is true to its genre and alluring in its tunefulness. At the second

---

[6] Chopin habitually writes *sostenuto* in reference to breadth of *tone*, whereas Brahms almost always uses the word to indicate breadth of *time*.

measure of the episode marked *aspiramente* the trusty revised edition of Breitkopf & Härtel is for once in error: the C sharp in the right hand of the last beat should be C natural (enharmonic for B sharp), and in the parallel place ten measures from the end, F sharp should be corrected correspondingly to F natural (= E sharp). Most editions give the right version.

The Ballades

The four ballades and the four scherzos demand so finished a technique and such powers of interpretation that the amateur should think twice before attempting them. By frequent hearing and diligent reading he can put himself in the pleasant and easier position of criticizing the performance of great artists when they fail to agree with his conception of the pieces. But I would not seek to deter any gifted player, amateur or professional, from essaying these splendid pieces. They are essential to the education of every advanced student.

Chopin told Schumann that he had been "incited to the creation of the Ballades" by the poetry of his compatriot Adam Mickiewicz. He gave the titles of the poems that inspired the first three, not vouchsafing that of the last. The G minor Ballade, No. 1, was suggested by *Konrad Wallrod*, the F major by *Le Lac de Willis*, and the third by *Undine*. Few of us, I suppose, know these poems, so they do not help us much. Nor do we need them, for Chopin, though he often had a "program" in mind, very seldom thought it necessary to put it into words.

Schumann thought the G minor Ballade, Opus 23, "the most spirited, most daring work of Chopin," but at the time of writing he had only the earlier compositions before him for comparison. The first theme should be played in two separate phrases:

Ex. 186

---

[7] [The first two measures of Ex. 186 should have been quoted as appearing in Chopin's unusual and musically important way:

as indicated, the two motives answering each other. The first *agitato* must not be anticipated, as it usually is, four measures sooner than marked, and the *sempre più mosso* immediately afterwards need not be rushed. Don't sentimentalize the second theme at the *meno mosso* or the episode marked *sempre pp*. After this the excitement mounts steadily to a climax. There is a momentary lull before the final *Presto con fuoco* in common time (it should be *alla breve*). The pianist may help himself out in this difficult coda by transferring a few notes to the left hand, thus:

Ex. 187

Anton Rubinstein gave this interpretation of the Ballade in F, Opus 38:

"A field flower, a windstorm, the wind caressing the flower, resistance of the flower, stormy fight of the wind, pleading of the flower —the flower lies broken. Or, paraphrased, the flower can be regarded as a country lass, the wind as a knight."

Saint-Saëns reports that Chopin "played the opening Andantino without any nuance whatsoever except the two indicated, and these he accented strongly." As there are more than two nuances indicated, this is rather puzzling, but doubtless the reference is to the inflections over the repeated phrase:

Ex. 188

The pathetic end, where the flower lies broken, is as heavenly as anything Chopin ever wrote. The player must find the right contrast between the tender simplicity of the first theme and the stormy interruptions of the *Presto con fuoco*. This ballade was dedicated to Schumann, who for some reason liked it less than the first.

The A-flat Ballade, Opus 47, was for a long time the most popular of the four. It is the least difficult technically and its interpretation is fairly obvious. We should avoid a sentimental accent on the F of the opening phrase:

Ex. 189

The crescendo stops at the C, and there is no break in the legato. The descending motive (a) persists through the ballade, as a careful examination shows, at many different intervals and sometimes in upward inversion. At the ninth measure it is taken over by the left hand; later it is decorated by trills; and it is still present in a new theme in F major:

Ex. 190

This theme is too often played jauntily instead of lyrically. Chopin's pedaling is faulty, and I have ventured to change it in the quotation. It is a common error to hurry the three eighth-notes at the end of the second and fourth measures of Ex. 190; no rubato of any kind is called for. The ballade should be played songfully, rather wanderingly up to the change of key to C-sharp minor. Then it turns dramatic and can be worked up to a convincing climax, ending with all possible brilliance.

Lovliest of all is the Ballade in F minor, Opus 52. "Its witchery is irresistible," says Huneker. The motives of the first theme:

recur so often, especially (a), that the inflection must be artfully varied to avoid monotony. Just how these nuances should be applied—for instance, whether the repetition of (a) should be fainter or stronger in any particular place—can hardly be determined beforehand; a good pianist had best trust the inspiration of the moment to give the right flexibility to his performance. This will accord with the extremely intuitive character of the piece, which is a fine example of Chopin's power to shape a perfectly satisfactory whole from a form that on the surface seems disjointed. It is advisable to start the coda (immediately after the five long pianissimo chords) quite moderately in time and force, increasing the speed when you feel safe. An accelerando of this kind is easy and effective, whereas it is humiliating and ineffective to begin at top speed and be obliged to slacken. A broadening of tempo should always sound intentional, never as if forced by technical difficulty.

The Scherzos

The scherzos diverge widely from the merry character implied in the name. No wonder that Schumann asked: "How is gravity to clothe itself if jest goes about in dark veils?" The first three of these works, at least, are wildly tempestuous in mood. Only the fourth, in E, is amiable, if not noticeably humorous. They are all written in much expanded but easily recognizable dance form. This involves an amount of repetition that to many artists is disagreeable; accordingly, some repeated sections of the B minor and B-flat minor Scherzos are often omitted without detriment; and it is both possible and advantageous to make a long cut in the trio of the E major Scherzo. The one in C-sharp minor is the best formed and most concise of the four; here no interference can be tolerated. The difficulty of these compositions lies in combining the required abandon of style with the technical control needed to preserve clarity. The tempo is so rapid that the count is always one to the measure; four of the fast measures can conveniently be thought of as a longer unit.

Of the four scherzos, that in B minor is probably the finest in theme and character, though it suffers a little from excessive repetition of the chief subject. Ushered in by two crashing, imperious chords, the piece plunges immediately into a vortex of fierce agitation. It is demoniac, *boiling* music. Then, what a contrast in the quiet section! Some magic quells the spirit of turmoil, and we are transported as from Klingsor's castle to the garden of the flower maidens. An Elysian song lulls us to repose, the turmoil is forgotten, when lo! the two imperious chords cut sharply in to shatter the mood. All is turbulence once more, driving urgently to a delirious end. We have touched the extremes of passion and peace.

The trio:

Ex. 192

sotto voce e ben legato

goes very much slower than the main section. Here the latent melody

Ex. 193

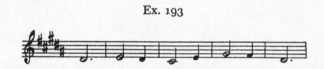

may be faintly breathed but not emphasized. The coda at the end of the piece is a page of finest frenzy.

The second Scherzo, in B-flat minor, gives occasion for much bad playing, especially in the rhythmical sense. Paderewski, who certainly understood Chopin well, took the opening almost metronomically exactly, so that the time-values were clear to the listener; his example should be followed. The cadenza-like passages of the trio (printed in small notes) are also best played without accelerando and of course *delicatissimo*, as marked. There is a long development of the material of the trio before the return of the main section. At the actual reprise comes a striking example of Chopin's finesse: the original motive

Ex. 194

is changed by prolongation of its last note to:

Ex. 195

On no account overlook this subtlety. At the end of the piece two *più mossos* are directed by Chopin; the first must allow for still greater speed in the second. This brilliant, temperamental composition wavers in tonality, beginning in B-flat minor and ending in D flat.

No. 3, in C-sharp minor, easier than the other scherzos except for the inevitably finger-breaking coda, needs clean octave-playing and fluent arpeggios. It is virile, organic, and less vertiginous than its predecessors. In the trio there is a suggestion of a choral played on the organ. The first twenty-four measures are introductory, the first subject entering with the fortissimo octaves. Authoritative editions read as at Ex. 196 (a)

Ex. 196

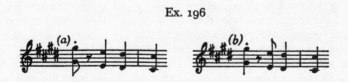

not as at (b), often found in other prints. In the trickling descending figuration of the trio (at the change of key to D flat) keep time, and take care to play the left hand as accurately as the right. The effect to be aimed at is:

Ex. 197

The trio is heard again after its appearance as a middle section. It reappears in E major, then mournfully in E minor, and ends in a fine peroration in C-sharp major leading into the tumultuous coda.

One hears the last Scherzo, in E, comparatively seldom. As I have said, it is gentler in mood than the others. Unfortunately it suffers from its loose, wandering form, so that the player has trouble in lending shape and coherence to it. Yet it contains much beautiful material and elegant passage-work.

The Preludes

Much has been written about the preludes. Louis Ehlert compared them to small shooting stars dissolving into tones as they fall. Rubinstein spoke of them as the pearls of Chopin's works. James Huneker turned the warm light of his intelligence on them; Alfred Cortot essayed to supply them with descriptive titles. Schumann shows the insight we should expect of him, writing:

> "I must signalize them as most remarkable. I confess I expected something quite different, carried out in the grand style of his Studies. It is almost the contrary here; these are sketches, the beginning of studies, or, if you will, ruins, eagle's feathers, all strangely intermingled. But in every piece we find in his own hand—'Frédéric Chopin wrote it.' One recognizes him in his pauses, in his impetuous respiration. He is the boldest, the proudest, poet-soul of his time. To be sure, the book also contains some morbid, feverish, repellent traits, but let everyone look in it for something that will enchant him. Philistines, however, must keep away."

And long before the preludes were conceived, Kit Marlowe had described them to perfection in six words: "Infinite riches in a little room."

Opus 28 contains a prelude for every key, major and minor, arranged so that each major key is followed by its relative minor—C, A minor, G, E minor, D, B minor, and so on through the circle. Most of them are very short. Only six of the twenty-four exceed fifty measures, sixteen are under forty. But they are packed with meaning, and in at least two (Nos. 9 and 20) grand conceptions are expressed in twelve or thirteen bars.

Occasionally one hears the preludes played in succession as a long concert number. This, I submit, is unwise, if only because of the preponderance of slow tempo. Not that the slow preludes outnumber the fast (the reverse is the case), but they take much longer in performance. The ear tires of slow playing more quickly than of brisk movement; hence in a sonata or symphony the proportion of the latter is normally three to one. We should respect this natural predilection of the ear, I think, and limit ourselves to judicious selections of these small masterpieces.

Emulating the brevity of the pieces themselves, I shall reduce my comment and advice on the preludes to a minimum.

1. *C major.* Spirited, nervous. The preferred reading begins each measure of the right hand with a sixteenth-rest, not changing the rhythm anywhere.

2. *A minor.* Extremely morbid, very uncertain in tonality. The voice-leading of the left hand indicated in the first two measures should be preserved throughout.

3. *G major.* It takes fairy fingers to compass the sun-kissed ripples of the left hand, but don't forget the melody above them.

4. *E minor.* An infinitely sad lyric. Huneker thinks this gem alone would immortalize the name of Chopin as a poet. Trust the piano to carry the long melodic notes, for they lie in a favorable register; and stress the melancholy harmonic changes slightly but clearly.

5. *D major.* Chopin is seldom in such a happy, carefree mood.

6. *B minor.* This, not No. 15, is the famed "Raindrop" Prelude. The slow beating of the repeated notes in the right hand should resemble a *"Bebung"* effect, every second eighth-note barely audible. The important thing, however, is the complaining cello-like melody of the left hand.

7. *A major.* A tiny exquisite song in two sentences.

8. *F-sharp minor.* One of the finest preludes; a good example of Chopin's use of chromaticism. The melody demands a highly expressive thumb.

9. *E major.* Chopin in the grand manner; a lordly theme supported by magnificent rolling harmonies. Shortest of the preludes (twelve measures).

10. *C-sharp minor.* An elfin trifle, tricky to play but fascinating.

11. *B major.* Amiable, distinguished by ease and charm.

12. *G-sharp minor.* Restless, urgent, and powerful; by no means easy.

13. *F-sharp major.* A dreamy miniature nocturne. One of the few preludes with a middle section.

14. *E-flat minor.* Fantastic and spectral, recalling the last movement of the B-flat minor Sonata.

15. *D-flat major.* Longest of the preludes, with a developed interlude in C-sharp minor. A true nocturne, and very popular.

16. *B-flat minor.* A fiery virtuoso étude of headlong impetuosity, very difficult.

17. *A-flat major.* A tuneful, well-developed Gondoliera. The accompanying repeated chords must be carefully subdued, using that kind of repressed touch in which the keys are always held half down. In the coda the deep bell strokes on the low A flat should be mellow notwithstanding their *sforzandi*.

18. *F minor.* In the style of a passionate recitative, dramatic, almost grandiloquent. Difficult.

19. *E-flat major.* An attractive short étude in extended arpeggios. Very difficult for hands of small span; it takes a pianistic chamois to play it infallibly.

20. *C minor.* Another fragment in the grand manner, suggesting the atmosphere of a cathedral. Beware the pitfall at the last chord of the third measure; every knowing ear will be cocked to hear you play correctly E natural or wrongly E flat. Try to make the second contrast between piano and pianissimo as effective as the first between fortissimo and piano. The last measure is an Amen on one chord.

21. *B-flat major.* An ideal song without words. Chopin gives amusing proof that he knew little about old ornaments by writing a *long appoggiatura* in the second measure as a small quarter-note:

Ex. 198

If we go strictly by rule, deducting the full quarter-note value of the appoggiatura from its main note, no time whatever is left for the E flat. Evidently Chopin accepted the common formula of giving the appoggiatura half the value of the main note, and we are meant to play two equal eighths. The joke is that since the F is a consonance no composer of any period had the slightest occasion to resort to an appoggiatura of any kind.

22. *G minor.* Chopin in a rage, venting it in thunderous left-hand octaves and angry right-hand chords.

23. *F major.* Rippling and calm. Another "flower between two abysses" (Nos. 22 and 24), added to the garland of the preludes. Notable for the ending, extraordinary in its day, on a dominant seventh-chord.

24. *D minor.* Unbridled, maniacal fury; a terrifying piece, tremendous in its strength and passion. Huneker says that the three *fff* notes at the close "sound like the clangor of overthrown reason."

One more Prelude, a solitary piece in C-sharp minor numbered Opus 45, must be added to the set of twenty-four. It is musing and improvisational, slow lulling waves of arpeggios breaking to melody at their crests.

The Études

The études will always rank among Chopin's most masterly writings. In spite of the great technical difficulty of many, the amateur may still find some suitable material for browsing or study. The third, sixth, and ninth of Opus 10, the first, second, and seventh of Opus 25, and the first and second of the three posthumous studies involve one in no serious technical trouble. Opus 10, No. 3, contains one awkward passage in "stretchy" diminished sevenths; the left hand of Opus 10, No. 9, has extensions easily compassed by an agile, even if small, hand; the wide-spread arpeggios of Opus 25, No. 1, are not very difficult; and the only problem in the two posthumous studies mentioned is rhythmical, not mechanical.

Next a group may be considered that is of no more than moderate difficulty to a good player. For a large hand the eleventh in Opus 10 may be placed in this set; small hands, however, must shun it. The third, fourth, and fifth of Opus 25 belong here. No. 3 requires accuracy in the execution of the dominating figure

Nota bene, it is *not*

analogously with the left hand. No. 4 looks open and easy, but the left-hand skips are quite treacherous. In No. 5 the different settings of the theme on its various recurrences call for some honest, rewarding work; it is a beautiful piece of music.

All the others must be accounted difficult. Nos. 1, 2, and 4 of Opus 10 and the last three colossi of Opus 25 exact the highest degree of virtuosity and are best left to the professional. Far be it from me, however, to discourage any good player from attempting such universal favorites as the "Revolutionary," the "Butterfly," and the "Black Key" études (it would be pedantic to avoid the popular titles). They have one advantage in common; they are quite short, so that a good deal of work can be put on them without much expenditure of time. The last of the posthumous set is deceptively simple in appearance; I place it in the difficult category because of the finical labor needed to bring out the different touches in the right hand accurately and beautifully. The A-flat Étude, Opus 10, No. 10, and that in D flat, Opus 25, No. 8, are much easier to players blessed with good stretch between the inner fingers than to those with less flexibility. In the former of these it is far from easy to make the frequent changes of accent, rhythm, and phrasing stand out. The latter is an excellent musical study in double notes, and one may follow it up with Opus 10, No. 7 and (calling on all one's ambition) with that most celebrated of all studies in thirds, Opus 25, No. 6.

The arpeggios with passing-notes of Opus 10, No. 8, in F major, are difficult chiefly because of their speed, and this leads me to comfort the amateur with the information that many of Chopin's études are marked considerably too fast. In Opus 10 alone, Nos. 3 to 9 inclusive and No. 12 suffer musically and often technically too if the metronome instructions are followed. I think that all pianists are agreed on this point. The explanation usually offered is that the mechanism of the pianos of Chopin's time was extremely light, encouraging a facile speed. It is possible, too, that Chopin (like Mendelssohn) habitually prescribed the maximum speed rather than the average. It is curious, however, that the two *slow* études of Opus 10, those in E major and E-flat minor, are especially badly mistimed ($\flat$ =100 and $\downarrow$. =69), as a trial with the metronome will immediately prove.

It has seemed proper, in speaking of the studies, to consider their technical demands with some minuteness. Yet it must not be forgotten that none of these works has a mechanical value only; in many of them the musical importance is obviously paramount. Were the E major Étude called a nocturne, the E-flat minor a dirge, and the slow one in C-sharp minor an elegy (it suggests a duet between cello and clarinet), no one could take much exception to the titles. Nos. 1, 2, and 6 in Opus 25 are zephyr-like creations. Schumann spoke of the first, in A flat, as "a poem rather than a study." "Soft as the song of a sleeping child," he remarked of the second, in F minor. Mechanism is relegated to the background, too, in the posthumous études, of which the middle one, in A flat, may well be played as a reverie. In some of the greatest of these wonderful pieces, —for example, the "Winter Wind," Opus 25, No. 11, and that tornado of octaves with the entrancingly tender major intermezzo, Opus 25, No. 10—technique and music join hands on the highest level of art. The first of Opus 10 and the last of Opus 25 deserve special mention. To the eye they may seem the most gymnastic of all Chopin's works. But masterly playing brings out in the former a noble architectural line. As to the latter, even poor playing can scarce conceal the grand manner of its writing; the steep two-handed arpeggios are too epic for the honey of melody.

I recommend three of the études for inclusion in the repertory of the amateur.

Étude in E major, Opus 10, No. 3. Chopin himself thought that he had never written a lovelier melody than this. Sing it, then, with all the lyricism of your soul. This is one of the cases in which the right hand has to play both the melody and part of the accompaniment, of course properly subordinating the latter. At the *poco più animato,* don't plunge at once into a much faster tempo. There should be a gradual increase of time and tone, which does not reach its full climax until the *forte con bravura.* It is a good plan to practice the next eight measures slowly and without pedal in order to get them perfectly clean. The excitement should not suddenly drop at the first subsequent piano; it is better to let it subside by degrees, recovering complete calm with the return of the theme at the *a tempo*. The shortened reprise may be played more dreamily than before, as if in retrospect.

Étude in A flat, Opus 25, No. 1. One can best learn how this "Æolian Harp" song should be played by reading Schumann's description of Chopin's own performance of it. "It would be a mistake to suppose that he allowed us to hear every small note in it; it was rather an undulation of the A-flat major chord, brought out more loudly here and there with the pedal, but exquisitely entangled in the harmony; we followed a wondrous melody in the sustained tones, while in the middle a tenor voice broke clearly from the chords and joined the principal melody. And when the étude was ended, we felt as though we had seen a lovely form in a dream and, half awake, we strove to seize it again." It would be impertinent to add to this.

Étude in C minor, Opus 10, No. 12 ("Revolutionary" Étude). Whether the story that Chopin wrote this piece on hearing of the capture of Warsaw by the Russians in September 1831 be true or well imagined, the piece is bursting with revolt and defiance, justifying Karasowski's comparison with the thunderbolts of Zeus. Its thorny progressions must be approached with the utmost courage, courage supported by willingness to work hard at its detail. Of course it presupposes a strong, enduring, and skillful left hand, but by judicious shading, undue fatigue may be avoided. The bold theme is given entirely to the right hand, and if the player will take the trouble to read the composer's directions exactly, he cannot go wrong in the interpretation. After nine measures and a half of introduction the principal subject enters *appassionato*. Attend to the forte of the first short motive, the piano of the answering motive, to the crescendos and *sforzandi*, and especially to the rest at

Ex. 199

(here a thunderbolt is cast—and strikes). Many pianists culpably fail to notice the *sotto voce* starting the repetition of the first period. All the momentary drops to piano really serve to enhance the boiling agitation of the music. Toward the end the fury seems to exhaust itself, only to break out again in a final blast of rage.

The Sonatas

Professionals deplore the fact that they have only two sonatas of Chopin to play (the early one in C minor, published posthumously, does not count, being a perfunctory student composition). Chopin is one of the few piano-writers offering sufficient interest and variety to justify one-composer programs. But every good program needs the backbone of at least one work in large form, a sonata or some equivalent, and in this respect the public player would welcome a wider choice. The amateur can easily forgo the sonatas, for he has a wealth of Chopin's finest pieces at his disposal and need not consider the building of recital programs.

Sonata in B-flat minor, Opus 35. This poem of struggle and death is a sustained tragedy, though the first three movements all have their moments of assuaging tenderness. Even the Scherzo is fateful and gloomy. The *Marche funèbre* forms the emotional climax of the work; the enigmatic last movement must be regarded as an epilogue. The tragic note is struck immediately in the four introductory *Grave* measures by the stern motive:

Ex. 200

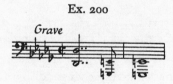

and the panting agitation of the first theme, *Doppio movimento:*

Ex. 201

These compelling ideas are combined with overpowering effect in the development section:

Ex. 202

where the two motives are worked out for a stretch of twelve measures. It is proper here for the performer to thunder out the left-hand theme with utmost force, doubly so because the entrances may be completely missed by superficial listeners. The funeral march should be played like a dirge, its trio like a song of hope and aspiration, centering attention on the spiritual expression of grief and consolation, not on any such imaginary externals as rumbling wheels or the measured tramp of feet. The spectral epilogue has been variously interpreted: haunting ghosts; a mind tortured by remorse; the wind moaning over a grave. A poetic idea helps the pianist; only let him not try to impose it literally on his audience. Certainly anything is better than to rattle off the Finale like a study in unison playing.

The correct reading at measures thirty-five to thirty-seven is:

Ex. 203

Most editions unwarrantably change all the G flats to G natural.

Sonata in B minor, Opus 58. Because of its exceedingly rambling form the first movement of this sonata is difficult to shape intelligibly. The themes themselves are striking and beautiful; everything sounds well by itself, but nothing hangs firmly together and the weakness is especially marked in the development section. At the reprise Chopin again uses the device so successfully employed in the B-flat minor Sonata, of eliminating the re-entry of the first theme, but this time there is not the same good reason for it, and all it does is to save undue length at a sacrifice of clear form. The delightful Scherzo, on the other hand, is short and concise, and stands out conspicuously as the only really gay scherzo Chopin ever wrote.

Editors have got badly tangled in the trio of this movement by the many tied notes. The most logical versions are given in the revised edition and that of Kullak, both now difficult to obtain; most others tie repeated notes that should properly be played.

The Largo, beautifully placed in the sonata, has the character of a dreamy nocturne. One might think that it would sound well if played by itself, but it loses half its charm when detached from its surroundings. The middle section may wisely be taken considerably more flowingly than the rest; it easily drags if one lingers on its phrases. The Finale, as already remarked, is a well-built rondo, gaining a wonderful cumulative effect from the quickening accompaniments of the main subject (first eighth-notes in both hands, at the next return three eighths against four to the beat, finally with sixteenth-notes in the left hand) and by the extraordinarily brilliant coda, which brings the work to a thrilling conclusion.

The Miscellaneous Works

Fantaisie in F minor, Opus 49. This is the greatest of Chopin's miscellaneous pieces and one of his most inspired works. As it offers many nice problems of interpretation I shall discuss it at some length. Its peculiarities of form have already been noticed. Like the B-flat minor Scherzo it fluctuates between two central tonalities, beginning in F minor and ending in A-flat major. The introductory *Marcia* is solemn, but not in the nature of a funeral march; andante would be a better time direction than "grave." It is correct to phrase the first two notes legato, following here the original rather than the revised edition, which unaccountably marks them detached. On no account let the dotted rhythms degenerate into triplets. Observe the subtle diminuendo on the ascending progression of Ex. 204:

Ex. 204

the differences between ♩. ♪ and ♪ 𝄾 ♪ , and the new slur covering the last two notes. The *poco a poco doppio movimento* leading to the main movement is an unusual expression to denote an accelerando; after the third fermata begin slowly again and hurry as before. The syncopated first theme of the fantasia proper begins at the *agitato*. Only nine measures later comes an episode in A flat:

Ex. 205

Here it is finer to place the accent on the first beat of the second measure, not on the preceding high C. In any event, avoid breaking the phrase at the high C; the line remains uninterrupted until the end of the first legato slur. Rapid episodes follow, which should not be unduly raced; their inherent excitement is sufficiently thrilling, and something must be held in reserve for the fortissimo climax with its awkward octaves in contrary motion. The entrance of the quick-step in E flat, shown at A of Ex. 206 after the final chords of the preceding section, is badly marked.

Ex. 206

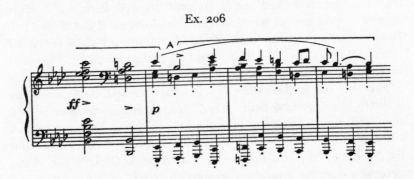

The legato slur at least, if not the piano also, should not begin until the *second* beat at A. It is essential, though not easy, to play the march melody legato and the accompanying chords staccato, like the bass octaves. Above all, take the quickstep on this its first occurrence softly and without increase of speed; when it returns later in the key of A flat Chopin tells us distinctly that he wants it *più mosso* and *sempre forte*. In this parallel place, incidentally, the faulty phrasing of Ex. 206 is corrected.

The dreamlike middle section, *Lento sostenuto*, should sound as if from afar. The breath after the sigh of the first two notes:

Ex. 207

is vital to the idea; lift not only the hands but the pedal too, in spite of Chopin's explicit direction. I venture to say that in this case Chopin was clearly wrong. Note the indescribably lovely harmonic successions at measures nine to seventeen. And linger on the final hold before shattering the dream by the rude *sforzando* introducing the recapitulation. Near the end of the piece the dream motive recurs momentarily fortissimo; the little cadenza that follows may be whispered like the faintest of echoes. Finally, do not strain for overwhelming force in the last two chords; it is sufficient to play them with dignified finality.

Barcarolle, F sharp, Opus 60.   The barcarolle style was congenial to Chopin, though this is the only piece so named. The second, third, and fourth Ballades and the G major Nocturne contain long sections that should be played with the slow, easy swing of a boat song. This Barcarolle is a beautiful piece of music, melodious and ingratiating in every measure and exceptionally clear in form. Chopin wrote into if some of his most inspired harmonic progressions, for instance:

Ex. 208

and

Ex. 209

In the second measure before the change of key to A major the correct text is:

Ex. 210

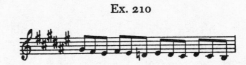

Later editions have altered the three E sharps to the more commonplace E natural, but Chopin is right and we have no business to tamper with him, especially as both the original and the finally revised editions read E sharp.

Variations brillantes on the Ronde de Ludovic, Opus 12. A good enough piece, but Chopin has composed better.

Berceuse, Opus 57. This ideal cradle song will probably always hold a place in our affection. From the formal standpoint, it is written in four-bar periods, each period a miniature variation, over a ground bass of only one measure. In playing it, forget the rocking of the cradle (it will creak if you give too much attention to it) and think only of the mother's cooing endearments. [It is interesting that the two introductory measures of the Berceuse are not in the manuscript. Did Chopin happen to add them after hearing some customary "till-ready" measures of a Bellini aria?]

Impromptu in A flat, Opus 29. Du Maurier went wildly astray scientifically and imposed on our credulity when he made Svengali hypnotize Trilby into singing this piece. It is another example of Chopin's pianistic type of fast-moving melody. Though agreeable and flowing, with a rather dramatic intermezzo, it hardly represents Chopin at his best.

Impromptu in F sharp, Opus 36. The most poetic of the impromptus, opening dreamily, interrupted by a martial episode, improvising on the first theme, then leading unexpectedly to a coda of new material in rapid thirty-second notes, finally recalling the dreamy mood. It is important to make the dotted notes of the martial episode (in D major) sharp and decisive, and on the other hand to play the coda sensitively (the forte marked in some editions is incorrect), not like a mechanical finger study. We may well question whether the two concluding fortissimo chords are in keeping with the prevailing spirit; most pianists choose to play them softly. [The two chords are an inspiration of the manliness of Chopin. A noble *f* should satisfy all interpreters.]

Impromptu in G flat, Opus 51. The esoteric quality of this piece excludes it from general popularity, yet it is very fine, showing Chopin in wise control of deep emotion. Again it is permissible to doubt the propriety of the indicated fortissimo ending. [A noble *f* will suffice to do justice to Chopin's deeply forceful "Amen," or "So Be It."]

Fantaisie-Impromptu in C-sharp minor (a posthumous work, but numbered as Opus 66). For all its effectiveness, this familiar concert piece is somewhat facile in its bravura, a little sentimental in the cantabile interlude. Chopin wrote many works less showy but of greater musical value.

Tarantelle, Opus 43. Effective when surpassingly well played, but only then. It is more musically conceived than most tarantelles, but not very typical of the Italian dance.

The amateur may safely leave out of consideration the Rondo, Opus 16, the Bolero, Opus 19, the Concert Allegro, Opus 46, and the three posthumous polonaises. The *Ecossaises,* another posthumous set of three short pieces, are rather trivial; only the first has charm.

Chopin wrote no four-hand music and only one piece for two pianos—the Rondo in C, an unimportant composition of the master and pupil type, with an easy part for the second pianist. Lee Pattison has made an arrangement of the Rondo, distributing what interest it possesses more equitably between the two players.

The chamber-music works would probably never have been undertaken but for Chopin's friendship with the violoncellist Auguste Franchomme, who doubtless saved Chopin from glaring awkwardness in writing for strings. Two movements from the Sonata in G minor for cello and piano are the most one ever hears of these inferior compositions.

The two piano concertos are astonishingly fine piano pieces ruined by incompetent orchestration. No orchestra, no conductor can pretend enthusiasm for them or perform them willingly, though they may still show occasional complaisance to some famous virtuoso reluctant to abandon them. Even the material for good scoring is lacking, for the ideas are unorchestral by nature. Hence the efforts of Tausig, Burmeister, and Granados[8] to amend them in this respect have been unavailing. It is a thousand pities, for their themes are lovely and their pianism superb. The F minor Concerto, less spectacular for the soloist than the earlier one in E minor, is musically superior. [As I said earlier, I consider Chopin's orchestration in both concertos perfectly good and amply sufficient.]

The other concert pieces with orchestra are never played with the exception of the Polonaise in E flat, sometimes performed as a solo (see under Polonaises).

In the course of this chapter I have made many suggestions for study. Perhaps, however, it may be helpful to recapitulate and group the various works as follows:

A. FOR CHILDREN

Waltz in A minor
Nocturne in G minor, Opus 37, No. 1
Nocturne in F minor, Opus 55, No. 1
Prelude in A
Impromptu in A flat (more advanced, for larger hands)
Mazurka in C, Opus 33, No. 3
Polonaise in C-sharp minor (contains some polyrhythms, two
  against three, not very easy)

B. FAIRLY EASY

Selected Preludes (for example, those in C, B minor, B, D flat,
  C minor, B flat)
Mazurkas in F-sharp minor, Opus 6, No. 1; G-sharp minor, Opus
  33, No. 1; A minor, Opus 41, No. 2; F minor, Opus 63, No. 2;
  C-sharp minor, Opus 63, No. 3; A minor, Opus 67, No. 4
Polonaises in E-flat minor, A, C minor
Nocturnes in E flat, Opus 9, No. 2; F sharp, Opus 15, No. 2;
  G minor, Opus 15, No. 3; B, Opus 32, No. 1; E minor (post-
  humous)

---

[8] Tausig rescored the E minor Concerto, Granados the F minor, Burmeister both. Nicodé, for some reason best known to himself, made an arrangement of the Concert Allegro, Opus 46, for piano with orchestra.

Waltzes in C-sharp minor, Opus 64, No. 2; A flat, Opus 64,
   No. 3; A flat, Opus 69, No. 1
Impromptu in G flat
Études in E, Opus 10, No. 3; E-flat minor, Opus 10, No. 6;
   A flat, Opus 25, No. 1; F minor, Opus 25, No. 2; C-sharp
   minor, Opus 25, No. 7

C. DIFFICULT

Other waltzes, mazurkas, polonaises, nocturnes
Preludes and études
Berceuse
Fantaisie-Impromptu
Ballades
Scherzos
Barcarolle
Fantaisie in F minor

The grading of these lists is perforce based chiefly on technical
difficulty, and at that is very rough. Many of Chopin's works are
technically extremely simple but can only be played even acceptably
by students and amateurs of real talent. Personal taste counts for a
great deal in successful performance; within reasonable limits any
child or adult will play a difficult piece that he loves better than an
easier one to which he is cold or indifferent. The one indispensable
requirement for good Chopin-playing is an intuitve feeling for beautiful phrasing.

Editions

The most authoritative edition of Chopin is the *First critically revised collected edition* of Breitkopf & Härtel, edited by Bargiel,
Brahms, Franchomme, Liszt, Reinecke, and Rudorff, and published
in large format like the other complete editions of the firm. To the
best of my belief this is no longer procurable, and few of my acquaintances possess copies. Nothing is added to the composer's text
and markings; many errors of early copies are corrected and the few
that remain are at least inherited from authentic original publications.
(Chopin, for all his neat handwriting, was notoriously careless in the
revision of his manuscripts and proofs.) For all ordinary purposes
the Peters Edition serves excellently. The *Édition classique* of Durand,

revised by Debussy, is fairly reliable. If the student should desire a highly revised text with innumerable suggestions for phrasing and inflection, he may be referred to Carl Klindworth's edition. While this belongs to the category of over-edited versions, which in general I find objectionable, it must be conceded that Klindworth knew his Chopin thoroughly, though not a pupil of the master, and did little violence to his style. Joseffy's edition (Schirmer) would without doubt have been excellent had he lived to complete it, for he was an ideal editor, never changing the composer's original marking and adding only occasional hints on pedaling and fingering. His fingerings are always highly ingenious and pianistic. Unfortunately his death occurred while he was still revising the edition, and many glaring errors remain uncorrected in some of the volumes. The best of the highly annotated editions is that of Kullak, which offers a very reliable text. The edition of Ignaz Friedman (Breitkopf & Härtel) is also highly regarded.

[Regarding the Joseffy edition (Schirmer), it is good as far as the text is concerned but as to its fingerings, I beg to disagree with Dr. Hutcheson. They are often abnormal, illogical, and awkward. The Arthur Friedheim edition of the Études (Schirmer) is carefully made, though overedited, but can be used to advantage. The new Chopin books edited by Alfred Mirovitch (Schirmer) are of good use in the studio. The old Oxford Press edition of the complete works of Chopin as well as Schirmer's by Mikuli (pupil of Chopin) of the sonatas, are close to the Urtext. The Kalmus edition is also near to the Urtext. It was reprinted from a publication by a board of musicians of which Liszt was the active chairman. The final, most authoritative word of editing the magnificent legacy of Chopin's genius is said in the so-called "Paderewski Edition" sponsored by the government of Poland. It is excellently made, and the accompanying text regarding general performance is of major interest. The two Polish musicians whom Paderewski had appointed, Dr. Ludwik Bronarski and Professor Jozef Turczynski, must be congratulated for the thoroughness of their painstaking research work and the clairvoyance of their results. I personally recommend this edition above all others.]

CHAPTER NINE

Johannes Brahms
(1833 – 97)

WE have seen in Schumann a duality of character harmonious but incoherent ending in disruption of life and art. In Brahms we find a contradiction of personality leading to a subjugation of temperament by craftsmanship. The former was the greater genius, the latter the more polished artist and the better architect. To Schumann, strive as he might, form always remained merely a vessel for thought; to Brahms it was an end in itself. Starting out as a romanticist deeply impressed by the spirit of Schumann, Brahms put a curb on his imagination instead of giving rein to it. Progress to him meant progress along classical lines, which, as Beethoven had shown, did not exclude romance. But new departures reaching into the future were congenitally repugnant to him. He had no use for the operas of Wagner, the program music of Liszt, for Bruckner's symphonies or Hugo Wolf's songs. We can imagine how he would have hated Debussy and loathed all ultra-modern music.

In his life the conflict of ideas took the form of a struggle between bourgeois and idealistic tendencies. He hankered after a secure position and a home. These he might have had almost at any time; he did in fact hold honorable positions at Detmold and Vienna and lived in the Austrian capital permanently from 1862 until his death; but he was bitterly disappointed because no appointment was offered by his native city of Hamburg. The desire for home, wife, and children could also have been easily gratified, for he made a good income at an early age, received ample financial return from his compositions, and fell in love repeatedly. He could not, however, bring himself to suffer any loss of independence, and this undoubtedly was the leading motive deterring him from fixed responsibilities and marriage. After the death of Schumann no obvious impediment remained to a union with Clara Schumann, but he took no steps to fulfill the grand passion of his existence.

The Brahms of later years lost the personal attractiveness of his handsome youth. After he began to cultivate a beard and gruff manners his rudeness became proverbial in Vienna, where they circulated a story of his apologizing to a company on leaving "to anyone whom he might have neglected to insult." Yet friends clung to him, discerning a good heart under the shell of harsh behavior. Economical to the point of stinginess in expenditures for food and clothing, he was generous in aid of his family and of many needy fellow artists— good done by stealth, for he was careful to keep such transactions secret. He was devoted to children and when likely to meet them would stuff his shabby pockets with sweets.

The contradictory elements in Brahms's nature show themselves curiously in his music. In his symphonies, concertos, and chamber music he attained a mastery of sonata form not surpassed by Beethoven, and since his time no tonal architecture has approached his logic and symmetry. Though he won this supreme mastery, however, his later compositions exhibit a surprising restriction of ambition. Why did he cease to write large orchestral and choral works after the Fourth Symphony, the *German Requiem,* and the *Gesang der Parzen?* Why did he not follow up the piano sonatas and the great variations by others of equal dimensions instead of confining himself to the long list of short capriccios and intermezzos? There was certainly no diminution of power or inspiration, as the continuing series of chamber-music works and the quality of the songs and piano pieces convincingly prove. Perhaps he felt, being both self-critical and modest, that his orchestral style was not particularly idiomatic. This is true; there is a general grayness of scoring, a lack of brilliance only intermittently relieved by such flashes of genius as the sunny entrances of horn and flute preceding the finale of the C minor Symphony or the exquisite introductory horn measures of the B-flat Piano Concerto. In any case, he soon turned his back on the "new paths" predicted for him, forswore the famous *Sturm und Drang* of his adolescence to put himself through an intense study of the classics, and strove for perfection of form and style rather than subjective expression of beauty. He gained much by this unbending self-control. Perhaps in the same process he cramped the free growth of a larger genius.

A striking feature of Brahms's composition is his love of folk song. Now, a folk song is ordinarily not a folk song if we can name its author. With Brahms the rule does not hold; he had the peculiar gift of writing simple tunes that would be accepted anywhere as genuine expressions of a people's untutored feeling. This agreeable talent is freely exercised and crops up again and again to delight us with its freshness. Brahms was also strongly attracted by the Hungarian idiom. The *Hungarian Dances* for four hands are improvisations on Hungarian airs, and the *Gypsy Songs* and movements like the finale of the G minor Piano Quartet are full of Magyar flavor. His warm sympathy with the popular strain in music is again evident in the Waltzes, Opus 39, and the *Liebeslieder Waltzes*, Opus 52 and Opus 65, the latter written for piano duet and obbligato vocal quartet—a unique combination handled with amazing deftness. If Brahms's style sometimes seems heavy and his coloring somber, we shall do well to remember the daintiness and transparency of these winsome pieces.

Purists who frown on all transcriptions are thrown into some confusion by mention of the Three B's. Bach, Beethoven, and Brahms felt no shame in recasting their works for other instruments. Brahms changed his plans on many occasions. The most conspicuous instances are the F minor Piano Quintet, originally a Quintet for strings, then a Sonata for two pianos before assuming its final form, and the Variations on a Theme of Haydn, scored first for two pianos and later still more successfully for orchestra. It is not generally known that the Piano Concerto in D minor was the ultimate result of sketches for a two-piano sonata. The Waltzes, Opus 39, and the *Hungarian Dances* were rearranged for one player from the better versions for piano duet. Brahms drew on other composers for a group of Etudes for piano, amplifying an étude of Chopin by double notes, transferring the passage-work of Weber's *Perpetuum Mobile* and Schubert's E-flat Impromptu most unnecessarily to the left hand, setting Bach's Chaconne for left hand alone, and offering two alternatives of the same composer's Courante from the G minor Suite for Violin. It must be confessed that these Études tend to justify objection to transcriptions. Very tasteful and attractive, on the other hand, is the arrangement of a Gavotte in A by Gluck.

Brahms, as we have seen, preferred not to be an innovator. His treatment of the piano resembles in general that of Schumann, holding to a harmonic scheme and eschewing scales and ornamental figures. That he might have added novel technical effects is shown in the Paganini Variations, but this is his one essay in virtuosity. He liked doublings of melody in two or three octaves accompanied by thirds and sixths; passages like the following are characteristic:

Ex. 211

I believe he was the first composer to use double slurs systematically for the indication of sub-phrasing, for instance:

Ex. 213

Here he set a precedent that might profitably be followed. Some of his technique is awkward and unpianistic to such a degree that Harold Bauer had the temerity to revise the F minor Sonata with the idea of making it more easily playable. [Brahms is supposed to have said to performers of his music: "I have never written anything awkward or unusually difficult. Just take the time to play intelligently." Harold Bauer's editing of certain parts in all movements was well meant, but is to be deplored because the changes are not according to Brahms's text.]

The student should hold it a duty to analyze Brahms's music with care. Otherwise he may too easily overlook such fine points as the concentration on a two-note motive throughout the Intermezzo in B-flat minor, Opus 117, No. 2:

Ex. 214

and the changing lengths of periods (five, six, and four measures) in the Ballade, Opus 118, No. 3, and the Rhapsody, Opus 119, No. 4.

Possibly Brahms did his best writing for piano in his chamber music. The partnership of piano and strings has always been one of the composer's hardest problems. Brahms succeeded admirably in blending the refractory elements. No other writer has achieved a like perfection in this respect, all the more remarkable because of the thematic beauty and masterly development of the works themselves.

The Piano Sonatas and Variations

The three sonatas are early compositions, their opus numbers 1, 2, and 5. Opus 2 was the first in order of writing, Opus 5 is by all odds first in order of merit. The Sonata in C, Opus 1, opens with a forceful motive reminiscent of Beethoven's *Hammerklavier:*

Ex. 215

The same idea reappears with altered rhythm as first subject of the Finale:

Ex. 216

The Andante, a short set of Variations, is based on a charming old German folk song. The theme of the Scherzo has already been quoted (see Ex. 211).

Schumann's influence makes itself felt in the F-sharp minor Sonata, Opus 2. One sees it at once in the first measure:

Ex. 217

and can trace it throughout. The Finale, however, closes with a cadenza of trills and scales quite foreign to either Schumann's or Brahms's usual manner. [The trills and scales of the last page of the Finale may stem from the closing measures of the F-sharp minor Nocturne of Chopin.] Though they are now increasingly played in public, I cannot find in these two sonatas much more than a fair promise of better things to come.

That promise is nobly made good in the Sonata in F minor, Opus 5. The opening *Allegro maestoso* is powerful and concise, the themes well contrasted, the development section hardly marred by the unorthodox introduction of new material. I may say in passing that the change to $\frac{6}{4}$ time (for one measure only) near the end of this movement is a clerical error; $\frac{6}{4} = \frac{3}{4} \times 2$ and is therefore no change at all. $\frac{3}{2}$ would be perfectly intelligible and was doubtless the unconscious intention.[1] Brahms prefixes to the Andante three lines of the poet Sternau:

---

[1] It is astonishing how often good composers get mixed up between $\frac{6}{4}$, a duple meter, and the triple $\frac{3}{2}$.

Der Abend dämmert, das Mondlicht scheint,
Da sind zwei Herzen in Liebe vereint
Und halten sich selig umfangen;

and never was a "program" more beautifully expressed in music.
Which of its long succession of romantic themes is loveliest?— the
love song of the beginning:

Ex. 218

or the following episode (*ben cantando*); the soft interchanges of the
Poco più lento:

Ex. 219

or the sacred hush of the *Andante molto* (used here incorrectly for
"very slow") before it rises to passionate climax? The mood of the
lovers, at first idyllic, deepens in feeling as the tempo slows down to
a lingering end. Energy reasserts itself in the Scherzo, and the Trio
sweeps on majestically in long melodic curves:

Ex. 220

Now comes the unexpected; after the Scherzo an Intermezzo or
Rückblick (Retrospect) is inserted, reverting to the theme of the
Andante. Ths bliss of the Andante turns to profound gloom (cf.
Ex. 218):

Ex. 221

while inescapable hints of drum rolls and peals of orchestral brass suggest a funeral march. Too evidently the course of true love has not run smooth. Thus the sonata calls insistently for a tragic finale. Hope and trust have turned to ashes in the *Rückblick* and a "happy ending" is dramatically unnatural. Brahms, however, did not see that he had committed himself. It is true that the last movement begins appropriately to the preceding mood, but the first episode wanders into a Mendelssohnian sweetness, and the dignified middle theme in D flat:

Ex. 222

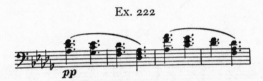

immediately tempts Brahms into canonic imitation, later leading to gay diminutions in a double coda culminating in an outburst of joy and triumph. The contrapuntal work is sometimes dry, but well sounding and ingenious in the following passages:

Ex. 223

Ex. 224

No one will question the effectiveness of this finale. Nevertheless its inconsistency with the previous movements and the looseness of its form combine to lessen its purely musical value.

The Variations on a Theme of Schumann, Opus 9, are interesting though they have never been popular. The theme is taken from the first Album Leaf of Schumann's *Bunte Blätter*. Variation 9 closely follows the second Album Leaf of the same group, and Variations 2, 6, and 16 faithfully reproduce Schumann's style. Three of the numbers are contrapuntal exercises, No. 8 an incomplete canon in the octave between soprano and tenor, No. 14 an incomplete canon in the second between alto and soprano, and No. 15 a complete canon in the sixth between soprano and bass. Notice, too, the inversion of soprano and bass in No. 10. The piece ends mysteriously in the manner of Eusebius at Variation 16 with no finale or coda.

Opus 21 contains two sets of Variations, one on an Original Theme, the other on a Hungarian Song. The second has the peculiar double time-signature of $\frac{3}{4}$ C, measures of $\frac{3}{4}$ and common time alternating in the theme and the first eight variations. Neither set shows Brahms at his best. [It is strange that Dr. Hutcheson does not think of Brahms "at his best" in the two variations works, Opus 21. The original theme of the first set is one of his most beautiful utterances. The "Hungarian" set is a brilliant work, a *must* for students eager to know the manifold idioms of Brahms's music. Though the pieces are technically very interesting, the difficulties of both sets are mostly musical.]

Next to the sonatas the Variations and Fugue on a Theme of Handel and the Paganini Variations, called by Brahms *Studies for Piano*, are the longest and most important of the piano works. Handel's theme comes from the Ninth Suite, in B flat, where five simple variations are attached to it. The student will be amused by comparing their naïveté with the sophistication of Brahms. The later composer preserves only the periodic structure of his text (two phrases of four measures, each repeated) and the original harmonic cadences in dominant and tonic respectively. Within this narrow frame he writes a series of twenty-five companion pictures with little or no aural relationship to Handel's melody, though careful analysis discovers frequent traces of its presence. [The Handel theme is strictly present in the grace notes of the G-minor Variation.] The massive fugue, of course, frees itself to follow its own path, which leads through inversions, augmentations, and clever organ points to a stately coda where counterpoint yields to full harmonies.

Clearly this method of constructing variations is formal in the extreme, but Brahms's fancy often ran freest under self-imposed restrictions that would have killed imagination in other men. One may be sensible of the length of the piece (many players omit many or all of the repeats), but cannot accuse it of monotony, so well are the miniatures contrasted in feeling, tempo, and modes major and minor. It has been lavishly praised by experts, yet the composition is more of an intellectual feat than a work of beauty. Poetry is for the most part latent, proclaiming itself unashamed only in the "Hungarian" variation, No. 13, and the wonderful chromatics of No. 20.

The Paganini Variations, Opus 35, Books I and II, are written precisely on the same formula. Here the theme and all the variations are contained within a rigid block of twenty-four measures including repeats. The codas of both sets are composite variations of greater length. It is a mistake, I think, to play the two books together; the pianist feels obliged to repeat the theme before entering on the second set, and the first coda becomes purposeless. On the other hand, when only one book is played, the performer will be obliged to omit some of his special favorites. Probably the best solution lies in a judicious selection from both books. Paderewski adopted this expedient, to my mind with distinguished success.

Brahms called these pieces *Studies for the Pianoforte,* and if the Handel Variations are an intellectual feat the Paganini Variations must be classed as a technical *tour de force.* And no mean one, unexpected as this may be from Brahms. Once in each book we find a lonely gem departing refreshingly from the étude type—No. 11 in the first book, No. 12 in the second. These two should be included in any selection.

Admitting without reserve Brahms's superlative mastery of the variation form as he defined it to himself, admitting too that the definition conforms to classical tradition, we may still be glad that it was not accepted by modern writers as a model. Else we should have been deprived of such grand works as the *Istar Variations* of D'Indy, the *Enigma Variations* of Elgar, and Strauss's tone poem *Don Quixote,* to mention only a few from the orchestral literature.

The Shorter Piano Works

One of the best specimens of Brahms's "storm and stress" period is the early Scherzo in E-flat minor, Opus 4. The turbulence of the main theme and the motive in the left hand at measures 10–14:

Ex. 225

marcato

show traces of Chopin's Scherzo in B-flat minor; Schumann's influence betrays itself in the use of two trios and in their style; and there is much of Beethoven's manner in the thematic development. A subsidiary phrase is lifted bodily from Marschner.

Ex. 226

Marschner, Overture to HANS HEILING

p

For all these slight reflections, the piece is thoroughly original. Its symmetrical structure, vitality, and pianistic effectiveness warrant a wider popularity than it enjoys.

We see a quite different aspect of Brahms in the poetical Ballades, Opus 10, four in number. The first of these was inspired by the old Scottish ballad *Edward*,[2] and we can easily imagine either the original words or their German translation accompanying the first phrase:

Ex. 227

Why dois your brand sae drap wi bluid, Ed-ward, Ed-ward?
Dein Schwert wie ist's von Blut so roth, Ed-ward, Ed-ward?

The tense horror of the poem is marvelously brought out in Brahms's piano setting. Edward's evasive answers, the final confession

---

[2] See Percy's *Reliques of Ancient English Poetry*. Brahms found a German version in Herder's *Stimmen der Völker*.

of guilt and his denunciation of the mother, the remorse and despair
of the parricide, are read in the music as simply and shudderingly
as in the language that instigated it. Am I too carping if I call attention
to the thinly veiled parallel octaves at the climax:

Ex. 228

a bad progression forced on Brahms by the lack of the lowest B flat on
his piano? Today we should fearlessly restore the correct bass, given
at measures 8–9, by changing the octave D of the left hand to B flat.
The Second Ballade, in D, begins and ends in beautiful serenity, and
the B major section, *quasi pizzicato* chords surrounding a *quasi corno*
middle pedal note:

Ex. 229

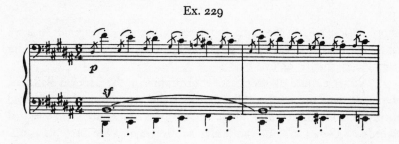

is piquant and original. We may complain that the motive of the B
minor section:

Ex. 230

not particularly interesting in itself, is developed with boring monotony
of rhythm. Extremely Puckish is the Third Ballade, in B minor. Its

tricky passages in sixteenth-notes entangle any but skilled fingers.
The last of the ballades starts peculiarly on the minor third of the key,
B major:

Ex. 231

We may regard the D natural if we wish as a synonym for C double
sharp. The piece breathes a vague, austere atmosphere of beauty.

We should be misguided to expect any freedom of form in the two
Rhapsodies, Opus 79. The second, indeed, is actually in sonata-form.
Even Brahms's states of ecstasy must be sternly controlled. He emulates
neither the improvisational quality of Bach's fantasias nor the
dithyrambic rapture of Liszt. The Hungarian Rhapsodies of the latter
and these pieces are poles apart. Let us forget the name and be
satisfied with two fine, well-ordered compositions, temperamental but
guarded in their passion.

The remaining works for piano solo consist of twenty-eight short
pieces almost invariably named *Intermezzo* or *Capriccio*. They appear
in five sets with the general titles of *Piano Pieces* (Opus 76, Opus 118,
and Opus 119), *Fantasias* (Opus 116), and *Intermezzi* (Opus 117).
Some are unaffectedly simple songs without words, the larger number
are cast in the familiar A B A form (first section, alternative section,
repeat of the first section), and others can best be described as in
double song form. It will be impossible to comment on so many items
one by one. But it is also not easy to select one's favorites or name the
best without mentioning all, so rich is their store of beauty, varied
mood, and persuasive musicianship. Playing or listening to them, we
find compensation for Brahms's desertion of the larger forms. Here
he reached his long-sought perfection, and lovely ideas are expressed
with utmost economy of means. The intermezzos are as a rule slow
and poetic, the capriccios fast and vigorous. Opus 118 includes a
Ballade and a *Romance*. Opus 119 ends with a *Rhapsody* more
rhapsodic than its namesakes of Opus 79; writing his last piano piece,
Brahms actually let himself go! The six numbers of Opus 118 lend
themselves well to performance as a group, and the eight pieces of
Opus 76, varied in style and tempo, might also be played together
with good effect. Very few are too difficult for a gifted amateur, who
may indulge his taste for lyric, gay, somber, energetic, or subtle, in-

definable moods in a wide range of choice. He should examine all of Opus 76, at least Nos. 4 and 6 of Opus 116, the first two intermezzos of Opus 117, all but No. 4 of Opus 118, and again all of Opus 119, before making his decisions, and to these he may fitly add the Ballades, Opus 10. If he wishes to touch the extremes of sentiment let him look up the B minor Capriccio, Opus 76, No. 2, and the C major Intermezzo, Opus 119, No. 3, for humor and lightness and the dirgelike E-flat minor Intermezzo, Opus 118, No. 6, for depths of tragedy. Players of small technical ability but sound musical instinct will discover suitable material in such gems as Opus 76, Nos. 4 and 6, Opus 116, No. 6, the second Intermezzo of Opus 117, and the romantic Intermezzo, Opus 118, No. 2.

Brahms's works for piano duet and two pianos offer further temptations that ought to be irresistible to the student and amateur. The original version for four hands of the Waltzes, Opus 39, is preferable to the adaptation for two hands, and the same is true in still greater degree of the Hungarian Dances (without opus number). These delightful compositions charm by their naturalness and ease. They are among the happiest products of Brahms's flair for folk music, the Waltzes saturated with the grace and swing of the Viennese waltz and the German *Ländler,* the Hungarian Dances with the carefree abandon of the gypsy. The *Liebeslieder* Waltzes, Opus 52 and Opus 65, still have power to charm if played without the obbligato vocal quartet, though of course they lose by the omission. More serious are the Variations on a Theme of Haydn known as St. Anthony's Chorale. These are hardly less fine in the setting for two pianos than in the later orchestral score, and are much more easily playable than the formidable Handel and Paganini Variations for two hands, which they resemble in their strict adherence to the frame of the theme. In the case of the Haydn Variations, however, the rigidity of the form is much less apparent because the theme itself is so diversified in rhythm. The first section contains two periods of five measures each; the second part starts with two four-bar phrases and ends with an expanded period of eleven measures, subdivisible if you choose into four + seven. I have already remarked in Chapter IV on the freedom of Haydn's periodic structure and need only add that Brahms treats the irregularity with unfailing humor and understanding. The Finale of the piece takes the shape of a Passacaglia, a modification of the theme serving as the *basso ostinato.*

The two-piano Sonata in F minor, Opus 34[bis], is superseded by the much finer version of the Piano Quintet. Note, however, that the martial third movement acquires greater force in the two-piano arrangement, since neither pianist need exercise restraint in mercy to the strings.

[For some reason Dr. Hutcheson failed to mention one of the arrestingly beautiful works of Brahms. It is the duet *Variations on a Theme by Robert Schumann,* op. 23, Augener edition. Supposed to be one of Brahms's last musical thoughts, it is a divinely lyrical theme, followed by a few measures of the first variation, whence Brahms continued. There is an excellent transcription for two pianos by Theodor Kirchner.]

The Chamber Music

I can do no more than barely list Brahms's splendid works for piano in combination with other instruments; I should be completely at a loss to suggest a choice between such masterpieces. From a practical standpoint the amateur will more easily enlist the co-operation of one or two artists than of three or four. Hence the sonatas and trios will prove more viable than the quartets or the quintet. One is unusually blessed if one can count a clarinetist or horn-player among his musical friends, but the Horn Trio sounds remarkably well when a cello is substituted and the clarinet sonatas are often played by a viola instead of the wind instrument. Notwithstanding this reluctant advice, it must be said that the pianist who has never taken part in a study or performance of the F minor Quintet has missed something in life.

LIST OF THE CHAMBER MUSIC WITH PIANO

a) Three Sonatas for piano and violin:
   1. Opus 78, in G
   2. Opus 100, in A
   3. Opus 108, in D minor
b) Two Sonatas for piano and cello:
   1. Opus 38, in E minor
   2. Opus 99, in F
c) Two Sonatas for piano and clarinet, Opus 120:
   1. F minor
   2. E flat
d) Three Trios for piano, violin, and cello:

      1. Opus 8, in B
      2. Opus 87, in C
      3. Opus 101, in C minor
  e) Trio for piano, violin, and horn (or viola, or cello), Opus 40, in E flat
  f) Trio for piano, clarinet (or viola) and cello, Opus 114, in A minor
  g) Three Piano Quartets:
      1. Opus 25, in G minor
      2. Opus 26, in A
      3. Opus 60, in C minor
  h) Piano Quintet, Opus 34, in F minor

The Concertos

The two piano concertos differ markedly from each other in style. Brahms wrote the first at the age of twenty-five, the second twenty-two years later. After what has been said of his artistic development we can readily understand the contrast. The earlier D minor Concerto, Opus 15, is still full of storm and stress. Defiance thunders out in the opening *tutti* of the first movement:

Ex. 232

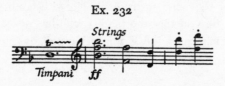

at the reprise, and again in the coda. The second theme, for all its cantabile, is still urgent; not before a fragment from it is softly repeated by the horn do we enjoy a brief interval of peace:

Ex. 233

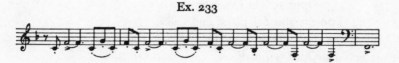

For sustained calm we must wait until the Adagio, about which Brahms wrote to Clara Schumann: "I am painting a lovely portrait of you." The autograph of this movement bore an inscription:

Ex. 234

withdrawn before publication. The Rondo is once more restless, partly defiant, partly humorous. The development introduces a fugato, and there is a short cadenza toward the end. The work was originally conceived as a symphony, and a draft was made for two pianos; it is Brahms's first orchestral composition and betrays at times a lack of skill in the scoring.

The Concerto in B flat, Opus 83, was written in Brahms's full maturity, after he had composed the first two symphonies and the Violin Concerto. As might be expected, it bears every evidence of serene mastery. This work adds to the customary three movements of the concerto a fourth in dance form, really a scherzo with trio although headed only *Allegro appassionato*. When called to account for this anomaly Brahms is said to have replied that he needed a strong, temperamental piece between two movements as "simple" as the first and third. A strange idea of simplicity, especially when applied to the massive *Allegro non troppo*! Brahms must have had the exquisite horn opening:[3]

Ex. 235

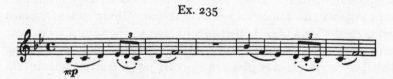

in mind and forgotten most of the rest. He might have advanced a more cogent reason: without the scherzo the concerto would present three successive movements in the same key, B flat, and it was better to add another than to transpose the Andante. Besides, why *not* four movements? The convention that deprives the concerto of a feature common to the symphony, the sonata, and chamber music, is logically indefensible.

---

[3] To emphasize the "simplicity" the answering phrases of the piano solo are omitted in this quotation.

The B-flat Concerto pursues a long, unhurried way through paths of beauty. Were we not speaking of Brahms I might dare to call the first movement diffuse; it holds an astonishing wealth of thematic material combined into a dignified whole, impressive without the least recourse to soloistic display. The impassioned scherzo shuns the violence of the first concerto; gaiety breaks out in its D major section. Sheer beauty pervades the peaceful Andante. The first *tutti*, with its cello solo and the imitations between oboe and cello, and the ineffably tender duet of piano and clarinet at the later *più adagio* attest Brahms's progress in the art of orchestration since the D minor Concerto. In the finale, *Allegretto grazioso*, a lighter mood prevails; a Hungarian relish gives piquancy to the A minor episode:

Ex. 236

The form is somewhat irregular; we might think that throughout the concerto Brahms was less intent on perfect structure and more willing than usual to let his ideas roam at will. The movement carries us through a succession of ingratiating themes and leaves us happy after forty-five minutes of absorbed listening.

The concertos are formidably difficult, yet the player who seeks in them a vehicle for technical showmanship exposes himself to grievous disappointment. No one could call them pianistically effective. They have been described as symphonies with piano obbligato, but this does scant justice to the importance of the solo part. "Symphonies for piano and orchestra" would be better. In any case, the performer must treat them symphonically, must set aside all thought of self-glory in grappling with their problems, must play as a musician rather than as a pianist. He will have little success if he performs them for his own sake instead of for theirs. This is more or less true of all Brahms's piano works, but one must insist on the necessary abnegation of display more particularly in the concertos because the very name suggests the quality of show pieces.

Editions

The early compositions of Brahms were published by Breitkopf & Härtel, all the later works by Simrock. The Universal Edition later took over the Simrock publications. After the expiration of the copyrights the firm of Peters produced the complete piano works edited by Emil Sauer. This is almost an ideal edition, for Sauer gives an accurate, ungarnished text, adding only a few directions for fingering and pedaling; it is accessible to American students in the reprint of Kalmus. Sauer's arrangement of the orchestral tuttis in the concertos for the second piano alone, instead of distributed between the two pianos as printed in the first two-piano edition, is very serviceable.

[It is peculiar that the Universal Edition entrusted the brilliant Liszt disciple, Emil von Sauer, with the editing of the piano works of Brahms. The edition is not ideal. Typical Brahms fingerings are Chopinized and ossias are indicated to facilitate solving of technical problems which do not exist. I have been told that Emil von Sauer never played Brahms in public. Peters and Kalmus later on took over this Universal Edition. Good recent editions are Schirmer's three volumes, excellently edited after the Urtext by Eusebius Mandyczewski. The complete piano works of Brahms, also in two volumes, are published, unedited, by the International Music Co. Both editions are highly recommended.]

CHAPTER TEN

Franz (Ferencz) Liszt
(1811–86)

[ERNEST HUTCHESON's chapter on Franz Liszt is so remarkably complete that it would be futile to try to disagree with or contradict any of his statements. I fully share his admiration for the nineteenth century's greatest pianist, who was also a most generous, unselfish colleague and a fearless propagandist for the new and the not-yet-recognized. On my first professional visit to Budapest, I made many friends who seemed to be pleased with my part-Lisztian programs. The then well-known organist and all-round musician Desiderius Demenyi was much interested in a statement of mine about the extent to which Lisztian themes, especially from the early *Années de Pèlerinage* and the Sonata, had reappeared in Wagner's operas. In fact, I have always believed that even Chopin's chromaticism had some influence on the man from Bayreuth. Only a few years ago I finally read in a book on Liszt that Wagner used to ask his guest, once dinner was over: "Please play some Chopin for us." A charming story relating to the so-called "Dresden Amen":

appears in Liszt's oratorio *The Legend of Saint Elizabeth* and plays quite a part in *Parsifal*. Bülow was conducting the prelude to *Parsifal* at a rehearsal at which both Liszt and Wagner were present. When the

"Amen" resounded in its Wagnerian splendor, Richard nudged Franz and said: "We have heard this before, have we not?" "Yes," Liszt answered, "but at least it is being performed now."]

When Franz Liszt first played in public at the age of nine, a group of Hungarian noblemen were so struck by his talent that they clubbed together to pay the expenses of his education for six years. He went to Vienna and studied piano with Czerny and theory with Salieri. After two years he appeared in Vienna and received universal acclaim, Beethoven joining in the chorus of praise. Shortly after this he sought admission to the Paris Conservatoire, but his foreign birth made him ineligible and Cherubini was unable to relax the rule in his favor. He therefore studied privately under Reicha and Paër. In 1824 and 1825 young Franz visited England, playing in London. In the latter year one of his first compositions, a one-act operetta, *Don Sanche,* was produced in Paris. Tours in England and Switzerland followed. In 1827 his father died and simultaneously the six-year guarantee came to an end. Obliged now to provide for himself and his mother, he settled in Paris, where he became acquainted with Berlioz, Chopin, Victor Hugo, George Sand, and Lamartine. His success in Paris caused him to embark on a virtuoso career. In 1834 he met the Comtesse d'Agoult, who wrote under the pen name of Daniel Stern. From their irregular union, which lasted ten years, three children were born, one of whom was the celebrated Cosima, later wife of Bülow and then of Wagner.

The period of Liszt's greatest concert activity was from 1838 to 1848. During these years he traveled almost incessantly, playing all over Europe and establishing himself as the greatest pianist in history. It is interesting to read the record he kept of the pieces he played. Public taste at that time did not stand high, and though we should now criticize any pianist indulging in so many transcriptions of orchestral works and songs, we must honor Liszt for his efforts to win appreciation for the best in music. We should remember that many of the arrangements were undertaken to spread a knowledge of neglected masterpieces; no self-seeking artist would have performed symphonies of Beethoven at piano recitals. On Liszt's repertoire we find overtures by Mozart, Beethoven, Weber, and Berlioz; movements from the Fifth, Sixth, and Seventh symphonies of Beethoven, and Berlioz's *Symphonie fantastique.* He played the "Goldberg" Variations, the Chromatic Fantasia and Fugue, and the organ fugues of Bach; the suites of Handel, the greatest of Beethoven's sonatas, the C minor and E-flat concertos, the trios and the violin and cello sonatas; Schubert's trios, fifty (!) transcribed songs, an unspecified sonata and the *Wanderer*

Fantasia; Mendelssohn's concertos, trios, fugues, and the *Variations sérieuses;* the *Carnaval,* F-sharp minor Sonata, and Phantasie of Schumann; waltzes, polonaises, mazurkas, preludes, études, ballades, scherzos, nocturnes, impromptus, and both concertos of Chopin; and of course a large number of his own original pieces and transcriptions. There are curious omissions in the list of important works that he must surely have played—for instance, the *Waldstein* Sonata and the sonatas and Fantaisie of Chopin. Most of his own best works, too, are missing, not always because they were written in later years. It is much to be regretted that the list was not continued after 1848.

In spite of his unique successes, it is doubtful if Liszt's heart was set on public performance. As a boy he had wished to enter the priesthood—a desire discouraged by the family and by a wise confessor; he had adopted the virtuoso career with some reluctance, and he abandoned it in 1848 for the permanent position of conductor at the Court Theater of Weimar with the purpose of devoting himself to the interests of rising composers. He held the post for twelve years, raising the little town to a musical eminence comparable to the literary fame it had enjoyed in the time of Goethe and Schiller. He had known Weimar for some years, and the second great attachment of his life, to the Princess Karolyne zu Sayn-Wittgenstein, had been formed in 1847. At their residence, the Altenburg, a stately mansion, he and the Princess assembled the most progressive spirits of the day. Weimar became the center of German musical life. Here too he found increased leisure for composition. Factious opposition to the production of Cornelius's opera *The Barber of Bagdad* eventually led him to resign from the Court Theater and move his headquarters to Rome, where again he inevitably became the focal point of musical activity. The breach with Weimar was healed by an invitation to conduct the Beethoven festival there in 1870, and thenceforward his life was divided between Rome, Weimar, and Budapest. Pope Pius IX made him an abbé in 1866; later he received the tonsure and minor orders. We may wonder at the assumption of the cassock by so accomplished a courtier, lover, and man of the world, but there is no reason whatever to question the genuineness of Liszt's devotion to the Catholic religion. We find the best evidence of its fervor in his numerous sacred works.

In every affair of life or art Liszt had the grand manner. He could not enter a room without arresting all eyes. Princes courted him; women adored him. A lady of unimpeached respectability confessed to me that she would gladly have surrendered to Liszt had he ever made advances. He had only to take his seat at a piano to throw his audience into a state of hypnosis. His pupils, many of whom traveled with him from city to city, are credibly said to have worshipped the very warts on his face. I knew a lady who until her death wore in her bosom the stump of a cigar that he had smoked in her home. It may be doubted that people fainted from excitement at his recitals, but the report was current for many years. In public he sometimes played to the gallery, and to appreciate his supremacy over other pianists, Reinecke told me, one had to hear him in a smaller circle of friends and musicians.

Liszt's generosity was regal. His biographers have recorded the large sum he raised by giving concerts to relieve victims of the inundation of the Danube in 1837; his insistence that a fund collected to erect a monument to himself in Budapest be turned over to a needy Hungarian sculptor; his payment out of his own pocket of the amount needed to complete the Beethoven monument at Bonn; and his continuous ungrudging assistance to the ever indigent and clamorous Richard Wagner. Though he made a considerable fortune from his tours before 1847, these benefactions were by no means easy gifts from large resources; he straitened himself for any worthy cause and was often imposed upon by dishonest claimants. The last concert he gave for his own benefit took place in 1847, when nearly forty years of life and possible riches lay before him. After that he played exclusively for the benefit of others. He spent himself no less freely than his money. His magnanimity toward other composers, few of whom ever did anything for him in return, yielded historic results. It is within common knowledge that *Lohengrin* was first produced under his baton at Weimar. Other works accorded first performances or important revivals there were the *Flying Dutchman*, *Tannhäuser*, the *Benvenuto Cellini* of Berlioz, Schumann's *Genoveva* and music to *Manfred*, and Schubert's *Alfonso and Estrella*. He popularized dozens of composers, classical and modern, by transcribing and performing their works, and his influence secured publishers for music new and as yet little known and positions for young conductors and teachers.

Not least among Liszt's contributions to musical progress was the formation of a class for pianists at Weimar for which with habitual generosity he refused all remuneration. The world's best talent flocked to him, and while his good nature often led him to accept mediocre students, a long line of illustrious pianists, including Bülow, Tausig, d'Albert, Friedheim, Siloti, Rosenthal, Sauer, Joseffy, Reisenauer, Lamond, Stavenhagen, and Sophie Menter, drew inspiration from his instruction and example. Amy Fay in her *Music Study in Germany* describes very pleasantly the atmosphere of these classes. It should be added that their tradition was carried on after Liszt's death by Stavenhagen and Busoni. The latter, though never a pupil of Liszt, became one of his most ardent disciples.

Liszt's kindly impulses were sometimes tempered by humor. Once when a poorly advertised concert in Leipzig attracted a mere scattering of listeners, he invited the audience to leave the hall with him and proceed to his hotel, where he hospitably played his program to the delighted group. On another occasion an unscrupulous young woman had announced herself for a recital as a "pupil of Liszt," blissfully unaware that the master happened to be in town. Imagine her astonishment when he called on her unbidden, asked her to play to him, proffered some advice, and on leaving remarked blandly that she might now *truthfully* appear under his auspices!

Liszt's reputation as a composer might stand higher had he written less. The most complete catalogue of his works is contained in Peter Raabe's authoritative book *Liszt's Leben und Schaffen*.[1] Raabe, scholarly curator of the Liszt Museum at Weimar, was able through diligent research and access to the archives and manuscripts of the museum to document almost every statement he made. The catalogue was begun by himself and completed by his son, Dr. Felix Raabe. It lists the astounding number of 659 items, exclusive of unfinished works. When one sets against the numerous repetitions because of different versions of the same material the fact that such collections as the nineteen Hungarian Rhapsodies and the twenty-six pieces of the *Années de Pèlerinage* are allotted a single number, one gains some idea of Liszt's immense productivity. Critical discernment will discard much of this output as ephemeral or unworthy and yet leave an impressive corpus of the best. Pianists no longer rave about the *Rigoletto Fantasie* or the *Galop chromatique*. The bulk of the ambitious choral works, sacred and secular, has already fallen into oblivion. Liszt's nature was too dramatic for expression of his religious feeling through the channels of oratorio and cantata. Even the *St. Elizabeth*, finest of the vocal compositions with orchestra, is more convincing on the stage than in concert performance. Yet with the exception of the boyish *Don Sanche* and the sketches for *Sardanapalus* he made no attempt at opera. His fame rests chiefly on

---

[1] The book is unfortunately not available in English. Its publication in 1931 was made possible after long delay by a partial contribution toward the expense from members of the faculty of the Juilliard School of Music in New York.

secular works for orchestra, songs, and pieces for piano and organ. The founder and leading exponent of modern music, he invented the symphonic poem and for the first time made conscious, systematic use of "leading motives" subject to what he called the "transformation of themes." Perhaps I should here explain that composers recognize three principal methods of developing thematic material: (1) by varied repetition (of which transformation is an offshoot); (2) by prolongation and contraction of melodic units, best exemplified in Beethoven; and (3) by imitation or fugal treatment, as in Bach. Great composers avail themselves liberally of all three methods. Liszt was no exception; long passages originating in his leading motives are built up by the classic expansion of phrase and he is equally at home in the fugal idiom. Wagner was quick to perceive the boundless possibilities of leading motives for opera and made no bones about adopting them from Liszt; he, too, constructs long passages of consecutive thought derived from them, but notwithstanding his gorgeous counterpoint he is remarkably weak in fugal writing. Using a medium so plastic, both Liszt and Wagner were incapable of producing the orderly succession of themes and episodes on which the classical symphony and sonata are organized.

Liszt's genius was best adapted to the creation of program music. His imagination reacted spontaneously to the stimulus of a poem, a sculpture, or a painting, to stories epic or dramatic, or to scenes from nature. Thus the *Sposalizio* and the *Hunnenschlacht* were inspired by pictures, *Il Penseroso* by a statue, *Les Préludes* by lines of Lamartine, the *Faust* Symphony and the *Mephisto* Waltz by Goethe's play and Lenau's poem, the *Dante* Fantasia (*Après une lecture du Dante*) by *The Vision*. Frequently Liszt quoted the source of his impressions at length, for those were the young days of program music, and explanation was deemed advisable. It would be a mistake, however, to suppose that he was altogether dependent on suggestion from without; the two concertos and the great piano Sonata are no less program music because no program is or could be stated in words. Of all "programs," in fact, a purely musical one is the best, for there is no irreconcilable difference between good program music and good "absolute" music, whereas there does exist an irreconcilable difference between bad program music and bad absolute music.

Liszt excels as a writer of songs. In these beauty of lyric invention is undisturbed by any alloy of showmanship; the voice is treated with knowledge and insight; exceptional consideration is given to the natural accent and inflection of the words; and the artistic accompaniments are neither thick nor self-assertive. In many of them leading motives are employed to advantage. It is a pity that Liszt's pre-eminence in piano-writing has to a great extent diverted attention from the songs.

Some of Liszt's organ compositions also count among his best; fortunately he published several in equally fine piano versions. Outstanding examples are the Fantasia and Fugue on B A C H, the Grand Variations (not the Prelude) on "*Weinen, Klagen,*" and above all the magnificent Fantasia and Fugue on the Choral "*Ad nos salutarem undam*" from Meyerbeer's *Le Prophète.*

Liszt's writing for the piano is commonly described as orchestral. This is true only in the sense that he extended the sonorities of the instrument to orchestral proportions. But the writing is above all pianistic. Strongly influenced at first by Chopin, he possessed in abundance that composer's gift for melodic line and ornamentation. He went much farther than Chopin, however, in exploring the resources of keyboard technique; indeed, he exhausted them. Impressed by Paganini's miraculous feats on the violin, he resolved to transfer them to the piano. Beginning by copying the great violinist's wizardry in the six Paganini Études, he later took an independent path in the twelve *Études d'exécution transcendante.* The dazzling Hungarian Rhapsodies, too, touch heights of virtuosity unknown before his time, though modern students make light of their difficulties. He had a genius for using the piano tone to musical effect. No one better understood the values of its different registers. Consider the judicious placement of the following melodies:

Ex. 237

Après une lecture du Dante

ppp dolcissimo con amore

Ex. 238

cantando

Consolation No.3

Ex. 239

Sonetto 123 del Petrarca

Ex. 240

dolce con grazia

Ex. 241

pesante

and the contrast between the sustained low pitch of *Il Penseroso*, never rising above middle B flat, and the high level of *St. Francis' Sermon to the Birds*, for page after page not descending below middle A. The filigree treble of the Polonaise in E on the return of the main theme after the Trio shows another effective use of the upper registers. Again, observe the easy skill by which the whole compass of the piano is covered in Ex. 242:

Ex. 242

Contrary to the general belief of students, the problems of Liszt's music are musical rather than technical. This is not to deny that much of it bristles with difficulties of the mechanical sort, but once the hard passages are mastered they stay well in the fingers and can be recalled after long intervals of time with little effort. Too often, however, the technique is assiduously practised while the musical quality is slighted. I have known more than one girl to whom the third *Liebestraum* meant nothing beyond its seductive title, but who would cheerfully spend hours of labor on the two unessential cadenzas. The E-flat Concerto suffers in most performances from exaggerations of speed and bravura to the detriment of its character and well-wrought form.

Liszt's harmonization displays boldness and originality. His modulations often surprise us by their unexpectedness and felicitous returns to the main key. He puts altered, doubly altered, and "foreign" chords to new and ingenious uses. It was natural that he should favor the Hungarian minor scale:

Ex. 243

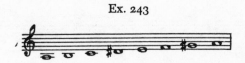

and exploit its colorful augmented intervals (see particularly the 13th and 19th Hungarian Rhapsodies), and that his religious moods should find expression in modal style; stranger, though, that we catch occasional anticipations of the whole-tone scale.

Certain peculiarities of Liszt's notation deserve remark. It will be seen from Exs. 238–241 that he was by no means scrupulously correct in his use of legato slurs, often closing them at the end of the measure in the manner of the classics, regardless of the phrase. In other respects he was more consistent. No other composer except Beethoven made so accurate a distinction between dots (···) and wedges (❚❚❚) to indicate different degrees of staccato. Beethoven's wish to reserve dots (under a slur) for the portamento touch has never been respected, not even in the *Urtext*. Liszt writes dots alone for a moderate staccato, wedges for a very sharp detachment. He makes a clear distinction too between lighter stresses (> > >) and heavy accents (Λ Λ Λ or in the lower staff V V V). The following notation is quite individual to him:

Ex. 244

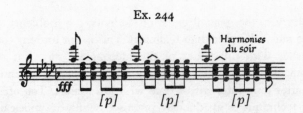

Here the emphasis must be spread over the chords marked   , the repetitions at the second and fourth beats being played lightly (the bracketed *p*'s are mine). It is always necessary to treat repeated chords like those in Ex. 244 with discretion; otherwise they sound cheap and noisy. Liszt was overfond of this effect; in the second *Légende,* for instance, *St. Francis Walking on the Waves,* a fine piece is marred at its climax by the ordinariness of the left-hand accompaniment. Liszt himself, we are assured, never thumped, and we may take it for granted that he knew how to produce these grandiose effects without blatancy, perhaps by such touch modification as I have suggested.

Another characteristic habit of notation is the unorthodox direction of Liszt's stems; he preferred to turn them up or down without reference to their position on the staff wherever the part leading could be made clearer. In Ex. 245 the stems are turned down because the bass carries the melody; in Ex. 246 they are turned up to indicate a tenor voice:

Ex. 245

Ex. 246

The Lyrical Piano Pieces

I shall make no attempt to discuss all of Liszt's works for piano. Felix Raabe's catalogue enumerates 113 original compositions, counting many entire collections as single items, and 182 arrangements of orchestral works, songs, and so on, by over fifty different composers. The concertos and concert pieces, as well as 84 numbers for four hands and two pianos, mostly arrangements, are not included in the list. On artistic grounds I shall omit mention of everything superficial or merely flamboyant. On the other hand I shall try to do justice to the best of Liszt's output and shall not fear to defend some part of it, including the Hungarian Rhapsodies, often assailed by critics with undue severity. Although Liszt made a point of not attaching opus numbers to his works, identification is usually easy because of his very distinctive titles. Complete or nearly complete editions have been faithfully edited by Sauer (Peters Edition) and Busoni (Breitkopf & Härtel). Joseffy's editing of selected pieces (Schirmer) is equally trustworthy, since he never tampers with the text and confines his additions to hints on fingering or pedaling and correction of obvious misprints.

We may begin by reviewing the large number of purely lyrical pieces.

The six *Consolations* are altogether devoid of technical adornment. Simple and sensitive, they afford a valuable introduction to Liszt's melodic style and careful workmanship. All are good.

The three *Liebesträume* or *Nocturnes* were first composed as songs and later transcribed for piano. The original words preface the piano versions. The first is possibly saccharine and the third certainly hackneyed to death, so I recommend No. 2 to the amateur, who should have no trouble in bringing out its broad singing quality. The *Consolations* and *Liebesträume* are conveniently reprinted in a volume of the Schirmer *Library of Musical Classics*. They contain many examples of the delicately adjusted accompaniments and harmonic originality characteristic of the composer. Note, for instance, how skillfully the accompaniment of the second *Consolation* is diversified in figuration and rhythm. The introduction of the foreign chords, especially the A minor chord, in the key of A flat (*Liebestraum* No. 1) is also typical:

Ex. 247

In these pieces we may also notice the extension of Chopin's ornamentation into the ingenious cadenzas so familiar to us in Liszt.

Like the *Liebesträume*, the three *Sonetti del Petrarca* were written for voice and afterwards arranged for piano. Here too the words of the sonnets (Nos. 47, 104, and 123) are prefixed. I cannot pretend to admire the first *Sonetto*, but the second interprets the antithetical

moods of the poem finely and the third is exquisite, ending in subtle
harmony with Petrarch's last lines:

> And Heaven unto the music so inclined,
> That not a leaf was seen to stir the shade,
> Such melody had fraught the winds, the atmosphere.
>
> Nott[2]

The Petrarch sonnets will be found in the second book, *Italie*, of
the *Années de Pèlerinage*. The same volume contains three other pieces
that should be mentioned here: the *Sposalizio*, *Il Penseroso*, and the
Canzonetta del Salvator Rosa. The last is a light, humorous song
befitting its easygoing text, which is quoted under corresponding notes
of the music. *Il Penseroso* was inspired by Michelangelo's *Meditation*,
a heroic statue of Giuliano de' Medici. Its tone is grand and severe,
suggesting granite rather than marble; otherwise it is remarkably
simple for the player. The *Sposalizio* is one of Liszt's loveliest pieces.
It owed its inception to Raphael's painting of the betrothal of the
Virgin Mary in the Brera Gallery at Milan. The picture represents the
ceremony taking place on the high steps of a church, adoring onlookers
standing below and a swinging bell in the church tower surmounting
the scene. Liszt's composition is based on a few leading themes; a
bell-motive:

Ex. 248

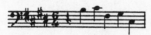

plays an important part, subsequently figuring in diminution as accompaniment to what might be called a theme of affiance.

The first book of the *Années de Pèlerinage, Suisse*, has many easily
playable numbers, but none compare in value with those of *Italie*
except the graceful *Églogue* and the brilliant *Au bord d'une source*.
The latter cannot suitably be counted among the lyrical pieces;
amateurs should look on it as an étude of refined technique.

The three pieces constituting the *Supplément à l'Italie* include the
popular and fairly easy *Gondoliera*, a favorable specimen of the better
type of salon music. The coda, when we hear a deep-toned bell striking across the water, redeems the piece from triviality and reminds us
forcibly of the end of Chopin's Prelude in A flat.

I have never been able to wax enthusiastic over the last book of

---

[2] Nott's translation is almost literal but deviates from true Petrarchan strictness by using three instead of only two rhymes in the sestet.

the *Années de Pèlerinage*. Little of it ever appears on recital programs, so I may assume my lukewarmness to be shared by others.

Among the *Harmonies poétiques et religieuses* are two more compositions of small difficulty, the simple *Ave Maria*, bracketed with the more imposing *Invocation* preceding it, and the *Bénédiction de Dieu dans la solitude*, a beautiful piece if too spun out in length.

The second of the three *Valses oubliées* is a tender, pensive trifle usually ruined by being rattled off too fast. One must play it in a quite moderate tempo to get its delicate flavor. The other two waltzes are in truth "*oubliées*." For greater gaiety we must turn to the Valse-Impromptu in A flat, deliciously light, disdaining the brilliance of the "concert waltz," and original in the absence of either Polish or Viennese idiom.

The short but extremely fine Prelude on "*Weinen, Klagen*," not to be confused with the Grand Variations on the same theme of Bach, brings to an end my selection from the lyrical compositions. We may next examine the pieces of the étude type with the understanding that they too are often prevailingly songful and that they are segregated chiefly because of their greater difficulty. The Concert Étude in D flat and the *Harmonies du soir*, for instance, are fully as lyrical in conception as any pieces we have yet considered.

The Études

Most popular among the six *Paganini* Études are the second, in E flat, *La Chasse*, and *La Campanella*. The first is hardly ever played. Nos. 1, 2, 3 (the *Campanella*), and 4 are really difficult. *La Chasse* is easy, allowing that one may execute the glissando sixths with two hands, and No. 6, for all its black looks, not so very hard. Nowadays, when perfect technique has become an almost unregarded prerequisite of every pianist's equipment, we can hardly understand the amazement created by the publication of these and others of Liszt's études. Schumann thought them and the *Études d'exécution transcendante* well-nigh impossible. Modern students take them in their stride. Their quality is not altogether mechanical: No. 1 has melodic flow, Nos. 2 and 5 elegance, No. 4 an airy caprice—merits inherent in the violin originals. The celebrated *Campanella*, taken from Paganini's Rondo of the same name, is musically the least valuable of the set, but there is no need to handle it brutally. Remember that it supposes a *little* bell; play the introductory D sharps as if you were testing the tone and pitch before beginning; and you will be in a fair way to ring its changes without offensive "stunting." No. 4, in E major, looks simple in its notation on one staff but treachery lurks behind the rapid crossings of the left hand over the right. Liszt's equivalent for the violinistic device of arpeggios on four strings is uncannily clever:

Ex. 249

The unpretentious theme of the last étude:

Ex. 250

has proved a veritable magnet to composers. Liszt, Brahms, and Rachmaninoff were all attracted by it. Brahms and Rachmaninoff piled mountainous variations on the molehill; Liszt was satisfied to treat it lightly. I like this piece best of the *Paganini* études.

Of the three *Études de concert* the first, in A flat, is least played. The second, in F minor, one of Liszt's best piano pieces, calls for great delicacy of finger; it begins and ends quietly and slowly, rising to a climax in the middle but throughout avoiding the spectacular. The time signature, at first $\frac{3}{4}$, changes imperceptibly to $\frac{4}{4}$ with occasional interpolations of irregular meter. Its delicate tracery charms the hearer; the rippling chromatics, distinctly Chopinesque, are employed with consummate taste. The melodious D-flat Étude, last of the group, has been played to excess. If you care to try it, you may accept Alexander Siloti's assurance that the bass note of the chord immediately preceding the first cadenza should be A natural, not A sharp, as it stands in other editions; and by all means thank him for adding, after the second cadenza, the six measures of restful chords that Liszt himself inserted:

Ex. 251

These three études had subtitles in the original edition: the first *Il Lamento,* the second *La Leggierezza,* and the third *Un Sospiro.* They all depend on musical effect rather than technical display.

Two excellent pieces, the *Waldesrauschen* and the *Gnomenreigen,* are also known as Études de concert. The graceful *Waldesrauschen,* recommendable to advanced amateurs, was suggested by a poem of Carmen Sylva (pen name of Queen Elizabeth of Rumania). The *Gnomenreigen,* while more difficult, is again written more from the musical than from the bravura standpoint. Both are deservedly popular.

At first glance the twelve *Études d'exécution transcendante* scarcely seem formidable. No. 1, properly designated Prélude, is short, brilliant, and playable by the average piano student. The second, in A minor, has no special name; while not at all easy, it presents no great difficulty and no particular attraction. The *Paysage,* next in the book, is an étude only by courtesy; a study, if you will, in legato and portamento, like some of Chopin's, entirely innocent of passage-work, but essentially a lyric that might have come from the *Années de Pèlerinage.* The "execution" begins to be transcendent in *Mazeppa,* a real war horse of the professional. What a difference between the tremendous bravura of *Mazeppa* and the delicate refinement of *Feux-Follets!* This entrancing will-o'-the-wisp is a priceless gem of the étude literature, the kind of thing one can work on for weeks without tiring of it. *Vision, Eroica,* and *Wilde Jagd (Le Chasseur Maudit)* are too consciously "transcendent" for my taste, as is also the last of the twelve, *Chasse-Neige;* these are among the works rarely heard. *Ricordanza,* better known, may be criticized for its salon style, for the ornate elaboration of the melodic line and some commonplace arpeggio accompaniments. No. 10, in F minor, otherwise unnamed, is a splendid étude, impassioned and heroic. It should not be confused with the gentle *Étude de concert* of the same key. Liszt's metronome mark, I think, is too fast for dignity and expressiveness. *Harmonies du soir*, a richly colored poem, covers the range of piano sonority from softest breath to resounding fullness.

The Rhapsodies

To qualify as a critic of piano music it is fashionable to adopt a sneering attitude toward Liszt's Hungarian Rhapsodies. This may be because the critic must needs maintain a superiority to public taste, and public taste in its ignorance adores the rhapsodies, applauding them frenetically whenever they are performed. The young recitalist, ever in search of that elusive phantom the "effective end piece," finds it incarnated in these dazzling works. For near a century the world's best artists have not disdained to play them. They would fascinate if only because of their highly interesting national character; in this respect they are analogous to the mazurkas of Chopin. Hungarian, or rather Magyar, music consists mainly of instrumental tunes and dances, though Béla Bartók has collected a large number of authentic folk songs. The csárdás or czardas, chief of the national dances, has two contrasting parts, a *lassú* or *lassan*, a slowish, usually melancholy movement, and a lively *friska*. The meter is always square, as in our American jazz; $\frac{3}{4}$ and $\frac{6}{8}$ times are unknown. Outwardly the music is characterized by capricious, prevalently syncopated rhythms, sometimes hardly susceptible of exact notation, and by the frequent use of the harmonic minor scale with raised fourth. Abrupt changes of tempo often occur, but must be played in the correct idiom, not with unbridled license. Gypsy performers added a curious and profuse ornamentation of their own, and Liszt adopted this mannerism to such an extent that his rhapsodies are as much gypsy as Hungarian. The proper instrument for this music was the cimbalon, a variety of dulcimer.

Hungarian influence is traceable in Bach, Haydn, and more markedly in Schubert, but these composers translated it incongruously into classical terms. Strangely enough it was the unbending Brahms who first captured its spirit. Credit for this must be given partly to the violinist Reményi, who became acquainted with Brahms and charmed the great man by his playing of the Magyar tunes. Liszt's interest in his native music seems to have lain long dormant. Only after his wildly acclaimed return to Budapest in 1840, nearly twenty years after leaving for study in Vienna and Paris, did the cosmopolite suddenly turn patriot. The rhapsodies, fittest medium for the expression of gypsy abandon, were all written after he had forsaken his career as a professional pianist. They endow the improvisational essence, the violent extremes of gloom and gaiety of untutored folk utterance with form, musicianship, and supreme mastery of piano effect.

I have no indiscriminate praise for the rhapsodies. Nos. 1, 3, and 7 are comparatively insignificant, but we may note in No. 3 a very early combination of major and minor thirds in one triad:

Ex. 252

calando

This mixed harmony should not astonish us unduly; we hear it in the overtones of any well-tuned bell. Busoni and the ultra-modern Olivier Messiaen, among others, use it very freely. The Fifth Rhapsody, *Héroïde-élégiaque,* is a stately funeral march and has been scored for orchestra by Frank Damrosch. The famous No. 2, striking as it is, offends in the final section by its strong suggestion of the circus; one can almost hear the crack of the ringmaster's whip, almost see the equestrienne leaping through paper-covered hoops. The *Carnaval de Pesth,* No. 9, seems pretentious and on the whole tiresome. The *Rákóczy March,* No. 15, dubiously classified as a rhapsody, sounds singularly ineffective in its two-hand piano version after the stirring orchestral setting of Berlioz. The last four rhapsodies are almost unknown to musicians, even to pianists, and two of them, Nos. 16 and 17, call for no special comment.

No. 4 is one of the few rhapsodies beginning and ending in the same key, in this case E flat, and one of several in which the customary *lassú* is replaced by another kind of slow movement, andante or allegretto. It gives the impression of a preliminary sketch for the

far more brilliant Sixth Rhapsody. The latter starts in D flat and
ends in B flat. Its *lassú* is preceded by a stately *tempo giusto*, usually
played much too fast, and a short sprightly presto. The extremely
brilliant working up of the octaves in the *friska* has made it a favorite vehicle for players with supple and untiring wrists. Musically
the *lassú* is the best part of it. Better to my mind than any of its
predecessors is No. 8, in F-sharp minor and major. Here we have a
fine variety of moods: the melancholy of the *Lento a Capriccio,* the
grace of the Allegretto, and the joyous outburst of the *Presto giocoso.*
Note the lavish ornamentation and the hint of cimbalon effects in
the Lento. Better still is No. 10, somewhat obscurely subnamed
Preludio. This piece is especially interesting pianistically because of
the successful imitation of the cimbalon at:

Ex. 253

and, immediately following, the happiest use of ascending and descending soft glissandos to be found anywhere in the literature.

The Eleventh Rhapsody, shorter, more intimate, less dazzling than
many of its companions, makes a strong appeal to the musician. It starts
in A minor and ends in F sharp. At the outset there is another direct
imitation of the cimbalon:

Ex. 254

The effect comes out better if the tremolo is divided between the
two hands thus:

Ex. 255

A swell to the middle is permissible.

The Twelfth Rhapsody, as celebrated as the Second, is musically superior to the earlier piece. The form reminds us that as originally danced the czardas changes from slow to quick movement by indication from the bandmaster. The themes are characteristically Hungarian and it goes without saying that they are varied, alternated, and developed with utmost skill. Artistically, however, the most important of the rhapsodies is No. 13. This was Liszt's own favorite, and in his later years he liked to play it publicly. The native flavor is as strong as ever, but Liszt adds a more personal feeling, as if he were playing with his own children rather than those of a neighbor. It is more aristocratic than any other rhapsody except the Nineteenth.

Liszt wrote the Fourteenth Rhapsody, with unimportant changes of key and material, in three versions: one for piano solo, one for orchestra, and one for piano with orchestra. The last, named *Hungarian Fantasia*, is the most effective and the best-known setting, and it will be appropriate to speak of the piece later in connection with the concertos. No. 18 is extraordinarily short; it may be played in three minutes and is not difficult. Though hardly more than a sketch, it is worth looking at. You will find in it interesting anticipations of one of the motives of No. 19. The last rhapsody, the Nineteenth, is long, almost completely neglected, but to the initiated as fine as the Thirteenth. The catchy tunes of the early rhapsodies are conspicuous by their absence; so are the elaborate ornamentation and the virtuoso technique. The piece takes the form of a meditation or improvisation on two short motives in which Liszt concentrated the essence of Hungarian feeling:

Ex. 256

Probably Liszt never wrote anything less calculated to strike popular fancy.

Passing mention should be made here of the *Spanish Rhapsody*, a brilliant composition introducing the familiar *Jota Aragonesa*. It is no sacrilege to consider Busoni's arrangement for piano and orchestra an improvement on the original.

Some Larger Works

The original edition of the *Funérailles*, seventh among the *Harmonies poétiques et religieuses*, bore the date "October 1849." It is a moot point whether the work was written in commemoration of Chopin, who died during that month, or of other friends who lost their lives in that year of unrest and revolution. Lina Ramann, a careful biographer, upholds the latter theory and is supported by the Hungarian idiom of the work. In any case, the *Funérailles* remains the most eloquent funeral oration ever pronounced by a solo instrument. It is excelled only by Wagner's music to Siegfried's death. In this piece we have a striking example of the composer's so-called "orchestral" style. Liszt accomplished the incredible when he combined Beethoven's gift of orchestral suggestiveness with Chopin's inevitability of pianistic fitness. The *Funérailles* opens with a clangingly despairing introduction leading to a funeral march, proceeds to a tenderly reminiscent Trio, and then surprisingly enters on a new, martial episode. After this has culminated in a tremendous climax, the main subject returns, fortissimo, to be followed by a faint echo of the Trio. A short reference to the martial episode brings the piece to a darkly mournful close.

Liszt's two *Légendes, St. François d'Assise: La prédication aux oiseaux* and *St. François de Paule marchant sur les flots*, are true program music. Critically regarded in this light, I confess to a preference for the *Sermon to the Birds*. In *St. Francis Walking on the Waves* there is a certain direct imitation of the physical, far less fine to my mind than the non-imitative suggestion first of bird-chorus, then of hushed attention to the saint's address, in the first legend. Yet the second is by far the more generally popular of the two. In a long preface to it Liszt admits his indebtedness to a drawing by E. J. von Steinle representing St. Francis crossing the Strait of Messina. The sketch, a gift from the Princess Wittgenstein, stood on Liszt's writing-table at the Altenburg in Weimar.

The *Mephisto Waltz*, another example of avowed program music, is based on an episode from Lenau's *Faust*. Since few pieces gain so much from a knowledge of the author's poetic intention, I give the "program" as set forth by Liszt; the preface containing it is omitted in many reprints:

Mephistopheles, in hunter's garb, arrives with Faust at a village tavern where a gay crowd is dancing. Faust is inflamed at sight of a black-eyed beauty but does not dare approach—he who had not feared to make a compact with the infernal powers. Mephistopheles, bored with the stupid music and the rustic propriety of the waltz, seizes a violin and maliciously provokes the company to a mad whirl of excitement. The emboldened Faust pairs up with his inamorata. Still dancing, they cross the garden and disappear into the neighboring forest while the tones of the magic violin grow ever fainter to them. Plunged in amorous delight, they listen to a nightingale singing from the fragrant woods.

Those who see nothing to admire in Liszt will decry the splendor, the knightly pageantry of the Polonaise in E major. Yet it is an outstanding specimen of its type. If you do not like it, neither can you consistently like the A-flat Polonaise of Chopin. Hardly Liszt at his greatest except in pianistic quality, it shows one more aspect of his amazing versatility.

The Ballade in B minor, too, is written in the grand manner. According to your viewpoint you will laud it as intensely dramatic or denounce it as theatrical. Broadly planned, with many passages of great beauty, it may justly be criticized for a rather grandiloquent climax.

The most ambitious of Liszt's programmatic works for piano is the final number of the Italian volume of the *Années de Pèlerinage*, *Après une lecture du Dante, Fantasia quasi Sonata*. Impressions of the *Inferno*, *Purgatorio*, and *Paradiso* are so clear that the title alone fully describes content and form. Each division is preceded by a "motive of entrance." On its first appearance one cannot help thinking of the line "All hope abandon, ye who enter here";

Ex. 257

Andante maestoso

at the gates of paradise it sinks to a hushed awe:

Ex. 258

It is eminently characteristic of Liszt that by appropriate modifications he makes all the motives available throughout; even in hell the lost souls chant an *Ave Maria* and in heaven itself echoes are heard of a purgatory absolved. The passage partly quoted in Ex. 237 is said to have been inspired by the episode of Paolo and Francesca da Rimini; if so, Liszt has charitably transferred the lovers from the *Inferno* to the *Purgatorio.* I quote the *Ave Maria,* used as a theme of salvation, from its appearance in the *Paradiso* division:

Ex. 259

The B minor Sonata, dedicated to Schumann, is one of the mightiest peaks in the literature of the piano. It makes exceptional demands on the listener's attention, partly because of its great length, partly because there is no pause between movements. The form departs so widely from the sonata tradition that it might aptly be called a symphonic poem. Nevertheless, the various sections suggest with some definiteness an extended first movement, *Allegro energico,* a lyrical slow movement, *Andante sostenuto,* and a Finale, the fugato preceding the final section taking the place of a scherzo. Alternatively, we may regard the composition as a sonata in one movement with the following general scheme:

    I. Statement of thematic material

    II. Development, into which the slow section is inserted

    III. Recapitulation and coda.

Richard Wagner wrote to the composer his opinion of the sonata as "beyond all conception beautiful, great, lovely; deep and noble; sublime even as thyself."

The structure of this monumental work is so intricate that a chapter would be needed to analyze it. I must be satisfied to quote in their simplest form the few pregnant motives on which it is based:

Ex. 260

Ex. 261

Ex. 262

Ex. 263

Ex. 264

Ex. 265

Exs. 260–262 are immediately announced in a short introduction. The combination of the motives in Exs. 261 and 262 corresponds to the first subject of a regular sonata-form:

Ex. 266

Ex. 264, to the second subject. Ex. 265 is the main theme of the lyrical slow section; associated with it are a preliminary phrase:

Ex. 267

recurring later at the climax of the section, and a subsidiary motive of considerable importance:

Ex. 268

In the ten-measure theme of the fugato, Exs. 261 and 262 are both used.

It takes careful study to follow the motives through their in- genious transformations of rhythm and character. Obvious as it looks on paper, comparing note with note, the identity of

Ex. 269

and

Ex. 270

with Exs. 261 and 262 has eluded many a musical ear. Still more subtle is the left-hand accompanying figure:

Ex. 271

an inversion of the first notes of Ex. 261. As instances of Liszt's workmanship I give three further examples derived from Ex. 266:

Ex. 272

Ex. 273

Ex. 274

ff fuocoso assai

The student is advised to scrutinize minutely everything that has the appearance of ordinary passage-work. Often, as Exs. 272 and 273 show, he will find that it is really a part of the thematic development.

THE CONCERTOS

Of the two concertos the first, in E flat, is far the more popular. It is highly effective even when badly played—and, unfortunately, it suffers more from a prevalently wrong interpretation than almost any other piece of its kind. Under this misconception pianists and conductors usually conspire to ignore Liszt's tempo marks: the first section is played *allegro vivace* rather than *maestoso*, losing all its dignity; the *Allegretto vivace* becomes a rapid scherzo; and the final section, oblivious of the intended gradual accelerando, is taken at a mad scramble from the B major passage following the pompous trombone motive:

Ex. 275

to the end. All this is the more reprehensible because, at least until recently, pianists were still living who had heard the concerto from the composer or studied it with him and observed a correct tradition. Approximately right metronome markings would be:

Allegro maestoso, ♩ = 100; the same for all returns of the main theme, including the coda. The piano should start its grandiose opening cadenza still more broadly.

Quasi adagio, ♩ = 60. This is usually played in accurate tempo, but the transition to the third section, where the piano starts a long series of trills and the flute announces a new theme:

Ex. 276

is often hurried unmercifully. It is true that a *più mosso* (say to ♩ = 92) is needed here, though none is prescribed, but it should not be exaggerated.

Allegretto vivace, ♩ = 126.

Allegro marziale animato, ♩ = 132; the trombone entries and the answering piano octave passages noticeably slower; several indicated accelerations toward the end provide a climax of speed.

At its best the E-flat Concerto is more a bravura piece magnificently scored than a work of deep musical value. Liszt is said to have evaded questioners who pestered him for a "meaning" to it by putting words to its first theme:

Ex. 277

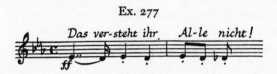

A catchy triangle rhythm, ♪♪ ↱ ♪ | ♪; introduces the *Allegretto vivace*. In the arrangement for two pianos this is cleverly transcribed as follows:

Ex. 278

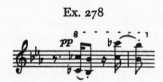

It is profitable to compare the form of the concerto and its various transformations of themes with those of the B minor Sonata, though the latter is an immeasurably grander work in every respect.

The A major Concerto, No. 2, though much less popular than its predecessor, contains beauties and refinements missing in the other. Substantially it is based on a single protean motive first enunciated by the clarinet:

Ex. 279

There are contrasting episodes, but the leading thought always prevails. Its last manifestation, *marziale, poco meno allegro,* is easily vulgarized unless performed very broadly, *much* rather than "a little" slower. One regrets the rather cheap glissandos in the piano part a few pages from the close. The scoring of the quiet sections is peculiarly beautiful, at times partaking of the delicate nature of chamber music.

The *Hungarian Fantasia* for piano and orchestra, already mentioned as identical in subject matter with the Fourteenth Rhapsody, is another piece too easily ruined by cheap performance or by the mutilated versions of some radio broadcasts. This is a good occasion to repeat and emphasize my former remark that Liszt's music offers musical rather than technical problems. In a very real sense it is easy technically and difficult musically: the hardest passages always lie well pianistically and, once mastered, are easily retained by the fingers; but the very brilliance of the piano writing misleads too many pianists into superficiality, and few come anywhere near the beauty and grandeur of conception attained by Liszt himself.

The first theme of the *Hungarian Fantasia* is hardly susceptible of exact rhythmical notation. Liszt writes it thus, giving the nearest possible approach:

Ex. 280

but no Hungarian would play it so: he would shorten indefinably the eighth-notes marked *x*, and some others occurring later he would lengthen. Formally, the piece consists of a Lassú, alternately melancholy and heroic in mood and interrupted by many free cadenzas and an episodic *Allegretto alla Zingarese*, and a shorter Friska. The chief requirements for a fine rendering are good taste and knowledge of the Hungarian idiom. Bernhard Stavenhagen used to play it marvelously, and I have heard John Powell do it with beauty and distinction.

The *Todtentanz*, a paraphrase or set of variations on *Dies Irae*, is a curious piece, powerful, recondite, and no favorite of the public. Since the death of Alexander Siloti, who published an intelligent edition of it and played it with masterly conviction, I know of no pianist who includes it in his repertory. Amateurs and all but the most aspiring students may safely pass it by.

Liszt also made arrangements for piano solo and orchestra of Schubert's *Wanderer* Fantasia and Weber's *Polacca brillante*, Opus 72. The first is well known, but in my opinion adds nothing valuable to the original. A few other early works of this kind need not be mentioned.

The following list summarizes the works of Liszt most suitable for the browsing amateur:

ORIGINAL WORKS

Consolations

Liebesträume

Années de Pèlerinage, Vols. I and II, especially the latter, and the *Gondoliera* from the *Supplément à l'Italie*.

Valse oubliée, No. 2

Valse-Impromptu

Prelude on *"Weinen, Klagen"*

Paganini-Caprice No. 5 (*La Chasse*)

Waldesrauschen

Bénédiction de Dieu dans la solitude

Ave Maria (from *Harmonies poétiques et religieuses*)

Prélude, Ricordanza, and *Harmonies du soir* from the *Études d'exécution transcendante*

TRANSCRIPTIONS

Alabieff	*Le Rossignol*
Chopin	*Chants polonais*
Mendelssohn	*On Wings of Song, Zuleika*
Schubert	*Du bist die Ruh'*
	Serenade (*Hark! Hark! the Lark*)
	Sei mir gegrüsst
	Frühlingsglaube
	Am Meer
Wagner	Elsa's Prayer
	Bridal March

[There are all kinds of editions of the piano music of Franz Liszt, outstanding among them the unfortunately out-of-print complete works published in several volumes by Breitkopf & Härtel. Consult public, college and university libraries. The evolution of both sets of the Transcendental Études and the Paganini Caprices from their original settings to their final forms is immensely interesting and informative as to the Master's continuous greater technical demands and increasing virtuosity. After hearing Paganini, Liszt is supposed to have stated: "What he has created for the violin, I shall endeavor to do for the piano." The two volumes by the Liszt Society Publications can be secured through the Associated Music Publishers. A Liszt album and two volumes of *Christmas Tree* in the Peters edition are recommended.]

CHAPTER ELEVEN

French Piano Music[1]

Franck, Saint-Saëns, Fauré, and Others

AFTER the flourishing days of the old opera and the great clavecinists France suffered a long period of musical unproductiveness. This applied to all branches of composition. Even in the early part of the nineteenth century, when opera had been kept alive by

---

[1] [Dr. Hutcheson justly realized that the chapter on French Piano Music was "too brief." He should have mentioned in the first line the name of France's most important clavecinist, Jean-Philippe Rameau, the father of modern harmony. In the earlier editions of the present book, this great master was passed upon in a few lines, curious as that may seem. In a note in Chapter II, I have mentioned his contribution to keyboard literature, and the very welcome recent Urtext editions of his complete works. Rameau was not "before Bach"! True, he was born two years before the German master, but he survived him fourteen years. The two were contemporaries. Rameau, Bach, Handel, and Domenico Scarlatti all were born in 1683 or 1685, and each of them achieved greatness in his respective country of birth or adoption: Bach in Germany, Scarlatti in Italy and Spain, Rameau in France, and Handel in England (which he reached from Germany via Italy).

1683 Rameau 1764
1685 Bach 1750
1685 Scarlatti 1757
1685 Handel . . . . .1759]

Grétry, Méhul, and Halévy, Paris was refusing recognition to Berlioz and depending for piano music on the foreigners Chopin and Liszt. But a new generation was rising and in the latter half of the century began to take its rightful place. Bizet, Offenbach, Gounod, Thomas, and a little later Massenet and Charpentier restored the glory of French opera; and while these composers, like most dramatic writers, completely neglected the piano, César Franck, Saint-Saëns, and Gabriel Fauré bestowed at least a part of their genius on it. Berlioz thought only in massed combinations. There is no saying what Bizet might have done had he lived longer, and we can enjoy his two *Arlésienne* Suites in arrangements for two pianos. Delibes, author of light operas and the fascinating ballet *Coppélia,* is known to piano students by a few excerpts from his stage works, such as the little Passepied from *Le Roi s'amuse,* and Dohnányi's concert transcription of the Waltz from *Naila.*

Mention may be made in passing of the salon music of BENJAMIN GODARD (1849–95), HENRI RAVINA (1818–1906), VICTOR DUVERNOY (1842–1907) and CÉCILE CHAMINADE (1857–1944). The *Guirlandes* and *Le Chevalier fantastique* of Godard, the twelve *Études de style* and the D-flat *Nocturne* of Ravina, the two-piano *Feu roulant* of Duvernoy, and the *Scarf Dance* of Chaminade, are fair specimens of their manner. The more classical writers deserve much greater consideration.

[CHARLES-HENRI-VALENTIN ALKAN (real name Morhange, 1818–88) was a modernist whose piano works are extremely difficult and full of original writing: note-clusters, major-minor combinations, impressionistic cadenzas. His major variation set, the *Fables of Aesop,* is a tremendous repertory piece. The étude *Le chemin de fer,* written in 1840, is a real tour de force. The *Étude à mouvement semblable et perpetuel* has been republished by Schirmer, Isidor Philipp being the editor. As most of the music of Alkan is not presently obtainable, it is useless to cite others of his works which one might consider of importance in the literature of the piano. That Alkan was well known and admired is attested by the dedications to him of the Fifth (big brother to the Fourth) Piano Concerto of Anton Rubinstein, of the *Hexameron Variations* by Liszt, and of Bülow's only significant symphonic piece.]

HENRY-CHARLES LITOLFF (1818–90) Alsatian-English composer born in London. Composed five "concerto-symphonies" for piano and orchestra.

CÉSAR AUGUSTE FRANCK (1822–90) Born in Belgium, Franck is usually grouped with French composers because of his long residence and activity in Paris. In his life often slighted, frowned on by the powerful Conservatoire, and officially ignored on his death, he yet made a deep impress on the music of his time and is now universally honored for the nobility of his work and character. Many eminent composers studied under him, among others d'Indy, Duparc, Pierné, Ropartz, Chausson, and Lekeu. His piano compositions, few in number, are remarkable for their serious beauty, rich harmonization, and the "cyclic" form associated with his name. Pianists narrowed down to a choice of solos between the equally fine *Prélude, Choral et Fugue* and *Prélude, Aria et Final*, both difficult, sometimes resort for a change to the easier *Prélude, Fugue et Variation*, an organ work sympathetically transcribed by Harold Bauer.[2] It must be deplored that Franck wrote no short pieces for the benefit of modest pianists; the little *Valse (Danse lente)* is not at all representative. The amateur is best advised to essay the lovely Sonata for piano and violin, than which no purer music exists, or the *Variations symphoniques* for piano and orchestra, a concert piece of high musical value. The gorgeous Piano Quintet suffers to some extent from Franck's fondness for piling up a succession of climaxes. *Les Djinns*, another work for piano and orchestra of programmatic intention, should not be neglected; the impassioned prayer of the middle section is very fine.

[Peters has published a small volume of easier piano pieces, some of which are pleasant material for younger students. The word "amateur" in the seventeenth line of the above paragraph is misplaced. The beautiful Violin and Piano Sonata, the masterly Piano Quintet, and the two unusually brilliant works for piano and orchestra belong only to the mature and completely equipped professional musician.]

In Franck's "cyclic" form themes introduced in the first movement reappear at any later time and are often ingeniously combined. Both the *Prélude, Choral et Fugue* and the *Prélude, Aria et Final* furnish examples of such melodic combinations; in the former the theme of the Chorale is joined at the climax to that of the Fugue; in the latter the complete coda of the Aria appears together with the complete theme of the Prelude toward the end of the Finale—an astonishing example of counterpoint deeply premeditated yet doing no violence to the absolute simplicity of either melody:

---

[2] To this pianist belongs the credit of having first made the three works named familiar to American audiences.

Ex. 281

and so on for fifteen measures more. In Ex. 281 the leading voices are quoted for greater clearness without bass or accompaniment.

EMMANUEL CHABRIER (1841–94) The best of Chabrier's small output for piano consists of the *Idylle* and *Scherzo-Valse* from the *Pièces pittoresques* and the *Bourrée fantasque*. His style is brilliant and incisive, strongly flavored with daring harmony and rhythm. The natural violence of his temperament comes out at times in his compositions. His piano-playing has been described as accompanied by "a fireworks display of snapping strings and broken keys." The student should remember, however, that as a teacher he insisted on scrupulous observance of every detail of tempo and accent. Besides the solo pieces he wrote three *Valses romantiques* for two pianos. The orchestral *España*, faithfully transcribed for two pianos by the composer, is an exciting concert number. For further particulars the reader should consult Alfred Cortot's essay on *French Piano Music*.

CHARLES-MARIE WIDOR (1845–1937) Noted organist and composer, whose works for piano include two concertos, a fine Suite in B minor, Opus 58, and a Carnaval, Opus 61.

ERNEST CHAUSSON (1855–99) studied with César Franck, whose influence is traceable in most of his works. He is mentioned here for his Concerto for piano, violin, and string quartet, often performed with string orchestra. [To the Concerto should be added the Piano Trio in G minor and the full-sized and extremely effective Piano Quartet in A major.]

CAMILLE SAINT-SAËNS (1835–1921) It is surprising that so few

of Saint-Saëns's piano solos have become popular favorites, for he
was a composer of great talent and facility, and a master of the piano
idiom. The best-known are the *Étude en forme de Valse*, the charming
Alceste de Gluck; of real interest also are the Twelve Études, Opus 52
and Opus 111, and the Six Fugues, Opus 161. He made a number of
musicianly arrangements of movements from Bach's violin sonatas
and church cantatas and a transcription of the *"Chorus of Dervishes"*
from Beethoven's *Ruins of Athens.* Much more important are his concertos and works for two pianos. The Piano Concertos in G minor and
C minor were popular until quite recently; they are so well written
and graceful that we may possibly see a partial revival of their vogue.
The Fifth Concerto, in F, contains an extremely original movement
in Moorish style. The concert piece *Africa* for piano and orchestra (in
an alternative version for piano alone) also shows the influence of his
trips to Algeria. The Scherzo, Opus 87, the Variations and Fugue on a
Theme of Beethoven, Opus 35, and the arrangements of his own
symphonic poems *Danse macabre* and *Le Rouet d'Omphale* are valuable contributions to the two-piano literature. The Piano Trio in F
is perhaps the best example of his chamber music. [The excellently
written and brilliant Violin and Piano Sonata in D minor also deserves
the most careful attention.]

It cannot be disputed that in his compositions Saint-Saëns lacks
depth. Too often he is more concerned with skillful development of
material than with the merit of the ideas themselves. Classical in his
own writing, he was a pioneer of progress, actively and successfully
encouraging performances of the modern French symphonists. Later
he became more conservative and, when the new era that he had
predicted actually set in with Debussy and Ravel, his sympathy
failed. Early in life he came under the influence of Liszt and adopted
the symphonic poem as a form without sacrificing his own fastidious-
ness of taste or economy of orchestration. Liszt proved a true friend;
when *Samson et Dalila* was rejected by the Paris Opéra, it received a
hospitable première at Weimar.

Saint-Saëns was an admirable pianist, and his concert tours helped
to make him famous. I heard him play his G minor Concerto when
he was well over seventy years old with impeccable technique and
all the finesse of the French school of pianism. He had literary talent
too; the *Outspoken Essays* on musical subjects are well worth reading.
Finally, he performed a great service to music by his edition of the
complete works of Rameau, published by Durand.

The amateur should not deprive himself of the pleasure of looking over the *Carnaval des animaux* (*Grande Fantaisie zoologique*). The piece, composed for two pianos and a small group of orchestral instruments but playable by two pianos alone, is one of the wittiest skits ever penned, so unique that I make no apology for giving some space to it. Saint-Saëns indulges in barefaced but amazingly clever imitations of animal sounds and movements—the lion's roar, the crowing of cocks and cackling of hens, the donkey's bray; the fleetness of wild asses (*Hémiones*) and the sluggishness of the tortoise, the uncouth gambols of a waltzing elephant, and the eccentric leaps of the kangaroo. These antics are relieved by numbers of real beauty —the notes of a cuckoo coming from deep woods, the sweetly confused sounds of an aviary, a suggestion of an aquarium, and the gliding swan (cello solo). The "animals" include two pianists who interrupt the proceedings to practice the dullest imaginable finger exercises, scales, and thirds, and a group of *Fossiles* humorously represented by three old French tunes and Saint-Saëns's own *Danse macabre*. By a marvelous touch of fun the poor elephant is made to waltz to the *Dance of Sylphs* of Berlioz and a fragment from Mendelssohn's *Midsummer Night's Dream* music. The tortoises crawl along in exaggeratedly slow tempo to two volatile themes from Offenbach's *Orphée dans l'enfer*. The Finale brings the animals together in a Noah's ark parade.

GABRIEL FAURÉ (1845–1924) This distinguished composer and teacher was active on the faculty of the Paris Conservatoire for many years and succeeded Théodore Dubois as director of the institution in 1905. Among his many prominent pupils were Enesco, Roger-Ducasse, Ravel, Florent Schmitt, and Nadia Boulanger. Best known for his lovely songs, he also wrote prolifically for the piano. For a detailed description of the piano pieces I again refer to Cortot's volume on *French Piano Music*. They include six impromptus, thirteen nocturnes, thirteen barcarolles, a Theme with Variations, and some *Romances sans paroles* and *Valse-caprices*, all noticeable for their lyrical invention and refinement of taste. Fauré had a peculiar talent for enriching his smooth phrases by some unexpected turn of line or harmony that at a stroke conferred distinction on them. If any criticism can be urged, it would be that of a lack of force in his ideas. If you play too many of the barcarolles and nocturnes, one will in the end come to sound much like another. In addition to the piano solos there is a sympathetic little children's Suite for four hands entitled *Dolly* and an early Ballade for piano and small orchestra. I suggest the Impromptu in F minor and the Barcarolles in G and A flat as typical of Fauré's style and workmanship. It is in the chamber music, however, that he reveals himself to the best advantage. The two piano quartets, in particular, show power and originality; they are real ornaments to the literature. The amateur will find pleasure in the A major Sonata for piano and violin; it will be worth his while to master the tricky rhythms of its charming Scherzo. One of the most famous songs, *Après un Rêve*, has been simply and well transcribed for piano by Guy Maier.

VINCENT D'INDY (1851–1931) D'Indy's importance in musical history must not be measured by his works for piano, which with the exception of the *Symphonie sur un chant montagnard français* (for short *Mountain* Symphony or in French *Symphonie cévenole*, from the Cévennes) are almost completely neglected. The music of d'Indy is permeated with unswerving idealism; he was utterly disregardful of popularity. His influence on the younger generation of French composers, exercised through his foundation of the Schola Cantorum of Paris, his teaching at the Conservatoire, his biographies of Beethoven and Franck, and the monumental *Cours de composition*, was profound. The little-played piano pieces include a Sonata, Opus 63, a *Thème varié, fugue et chanson*, and collections of smaller works with opus numbers 68, 69, 73, and 74, some for children. The piano part of the *Mountain* Symphony is more than an obbligato, less than a solo. [D'Indy conducted the "Mountain Symphony" for me at one of my concerts in Berlin. He thought my tempo of the finale too fast and punished me by writing on my score "To Rudolph Ganz and his twenty fingers, with my admiration." To me this major work is perfection in form and content and as transparent as a Mozart concerto.]

PAUL DUKAS (1865–1935), famed for the orchestral scherzo *L'Apprenti-sorcier* and the opera *Ariane et Barbe-bleue*, wrote little for piano beyond a sonata and an interesting set of Variations on a Theme of Rameau. JOSEPH ROPARTZ (1864–1935), a disciple of César Franck, may be mentioned for his two-piano *Pièce*. [ALBERT ROUSSEL (1869–1937) and GABRIEL PIERNÉ (1863–1937) made very worthy contributions to the repertory of the piano. Of Roussel there are the Piano Concerto, Piano Trio, Suite op. 14, Sonatina op. 16, and a number of smaller pieces that need first-class pianism. Pierné's outstanding work for the piano is his Variations in C minor, a large-scale concert repertoire piece. There is also an effective *Poème symphonique* for piano and orchestra, a Barcarolle for two pianos, an early Piano Concerto and the popular *Marche des petits soldats*.]

Claude Achille Debussy (1862–1918)

DEBUSSY's life was extremely uneventful. He entered the Paris Conservatoire as a boy of eleven, studied there until he was twenty-two, spent a summer at Moscow and two years in Italy as winner of the Conservatoire's Prix de Rome, then settled down to a quiet life in Paris interrupted only by short visits to London and Bayreuth and trips to various European capitals for the purpose of conducting his own works. Very retiring in disposition, he never held any official position and rarely showed himself in public as either pianist or conductor. The labor of composition was occasionally varied by articles written for newspapers and periodicals. A selection of these essays, *Monsieur Croche antidilettante*, appeared posthumously in 1921. [These essays were splendidly translated by the eminent New York critic, Lawrence Gilman. They are extremely interesting and at times amusing or shocking on account of the master's strange personal views.] During his last years Debussy suffered from ill health and did little work of any kind.

If Debussy cannot be considered a truly great composer, his works are phenomenal in their originality, mastery of technique, and power of suggestion by what in the arts we call impressionism. In his hands harmony takes on new hues, often expressed through the whole-tone scale and chords derived from it or adept use of the higher harmonics. Sometimes he becomes enmeshed in a purely tonal idea and elaborates it for its own sake without much other significance. He is a master of innuendo, of subtle implication avoiding direct statement, and it is this quality that makes his opera *Pelléas and Mélisande* so uniquely appropriate to the text of Maeterlinck. The orchestral technique of *L'Après-midi d'un faune* and *Fêtes* is superb. It is impossible to derive his mature works from any former tradition. Even his early compositions, before he had cast off the shackles of the Conservatoire, are scarcely imitative, granted that traces of Chopin and Fauré are discernible in them. If he owed anything to the influence of Mussorgsky, who had already discovered possibilities in the whole-tone scale, it was not through his visit to Russia but because of his later immersion in the piano score of *Boris Godunov*. A callow enthusiasm for Wagner was soon converted into violent opposition, inevitable in one who took pride in calling himself *musicien français*. We know that he was fascinated by the Javanese and Annamese bands of the Paris Exposition in 1889 and that he was always interested in Oriental decorative art. Eastern music, more than that of any one composer, colors a good deal of his writing. Finally, he must have acquired his surprising command of the Spanish idiom by sheer instinct. [Debussy was a truly great composer. He was the father of impressionism, which will go down in music history as a distinct renaissance of values. *The Prelude to the Afternoon of a Faun* expressed fascinating true music ideas with a reduced orchestra—no trumpets, no trombones, no percussion—while Mahler's Eighth Symphony ("of the 1000") represented oversized post-Wagnerian orchestration.]

Debussy made no attempt to create new forms, or to modify, still less enlarge, those familiar to him. His personal tastes were narrow and prejudiced. He and the convenient, flippant, ironical M. Croche object equally to Italian and German opera, to the sonata form, to program music and the leitmotiv. A few brief extracts from their opinions may amuse the reader. Bach, "a benevolent god to whom musicians should pray before starting to work," is "bearable only when he is altogether admirable" and wrote "hundreds of pages through which we must wander between long rows of dreary bars." Beethoven's sonatas are "very badly written for the piano," and only the *Choral* Symphony receives unqualified praise. Gluck, a special target of dislike, is merely a "court musician," and Mendelssohn a "facile and elegant notary." Some songs of Schubert are "inoffensive, like dried flowers"; the "Unfinished" Symphony "cannot decide once and for all to remain unfinished." No opportunity is lost to take a fling at Wagner, evidently regarded as the arch-enemy of French composition. Wagner is "beautiful, singular, impure, seductive." *Parsifal*, though the drama and characters are derided, is admitted to be "one of the loveliest monuments of sound ever raised to the glory of music." Of Brahms I find no mention except a description of the Violin Concerto as "a bore." In Verdi's *Traviata* the listener "travels from ballad to ballad." Grieg is "no more than a clever musician, more concerned with effects than with genuine art." Liszt, Richard Strauss, Stravinsky, Mussorgsky, and Albéniz come in for praise not altogether unmixed. Weber is the only German opera-writer for whom there is a good word; "his work had a sort of dreamy melancholy" and "he was master of every known means of interpreting the fantastic in music." Some of Debussy's compatriots fared hardly better than foreigners. Berlioz "is so enamored of the romance of color that he sometimes forgets music" and "has always been the favorite musician of those who do not know much about music." Saint-Saëns's later works are held up to scorn, and Charpentier's *Louise* is "so silly that it is pitiful." One observes with some amusement the cautious admiration of Gounod and Massenet. What composers did Debussy really like? Apparently Mozart, "a great artist," Chopin, whose "charming soul," he thought, "directed the passion of *Tristan and Isolde*" (!), Couperin and Rameau, as is every Frenchman's duty, Franck, Dukas, d'Indy, Lalo, and Satie. No wonder that Edward Watson, writing in *Grove's Dictionary*, fourth edition, says that "his world may have been small," adding however that "within it he was a great man, and sometimes he saw beyond it."

Debussy's music delights, fascinates, amuses. I have not heard its most ardent admirers claim that it ennobles. The piano pieces are numerous and thoroughly representative of his style. To a performer versed only in the classics they call for a readjustment of ideas, for new nuances of tone and balance, new conceptions of pedaling. One must know some French to understand his titles and directions, and one must learn to interpret unusual indications of prolonged tone:

Ex. 282

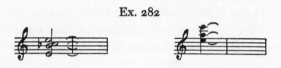

and oddities like these:

Ex. 283

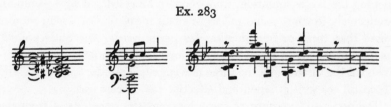

Again, one must be watchful to correct errors of notation—for instance, thirty-second-notes where sixty-fourths are intended (see *Poissons d'or*). Debussy makes liberal use of the "stamp," — or $\cdot$-, to denote melodic or other stresses not amounting to accents. In his later works he frequently employs three staffs to facilitate the reading of complicated passages. His instructions to the player are elaborate and precise in matters of phrasing, shading, and rubato; on the other hand he gives no fingering whatever and not a single pedal mark in the twenty-four preludes and many other pieces, so that modern editors will doubtless get in their dirty work when the copyrights expire. [Most Debussy pedals are clearly indicated by the length of the bass notes. French pianos have no third, or *sostenuto*, pedal. The performer must learn to adjust himself to the sounds that the composer's sensitive imagination created.]

PIANO WORKS

The earlier piano compositions are at best innocuous, revealing little of the marked personality of the riper works. Nevertheless the two *Arabesques*, the *Rêverie*, and the *Suite bergamasque* possess a charm of their own and may be recommended as starting-points for the amateur's appreciation. The popular *Clair de lune* of the *Suite bergamasque* has the defect of falling throughout into blocked-off two-bar periods, but it is spontaneous and tuneful. I care less for the *Romance*, the *Nocturne*, and the *Valse romantique;* they might have been written by any gifted youngster. There are faint premonitions of the future *Fêtes* in the lively *Danse*, originally called *Tarantelle illyrienne*. This is the only one of the immature works comparing favorably with the later *Masques*, an inferior piece of the same type. For a whole decade, 1890–1900, Debussy's piano was silent; during those ten years he produced *Pelléas et Mélisande, L'Après-midi d'un faune*, the *Nocturnes* for orchestra, and a string quartet. Incongruous as it seems to compare him in any imaginable way with Brahms, Debussy duplicated the history of the German composer by abandoning the larger ambition; from 1900 on he restricted himself almost exclusively to short piano pieces in small form, few of which require more than three or four minutes for performance. The *Suite pour le piano*, intermediate in style, shows increased confidence in its treatment of the instrument; the three movements, Prélude, Sarabande, and Toccata, are well grouped and effective for concert use.

Debussy's full mastery of the impressionistic genre dates from the fine *Estampes*, published in 1903. In the three pieces of this group, *Pagodes, La soirée dans Grenade*, and *Jardins sous la pluie*, his exceedingly individual style is developed to perfection. *Pagodes*, less popular than its two companions, makes liberal use of the Oriental five-tone diatonic scale without any pretense of genuine Chinese idiom. The quickening rhythms may be taken to suggest tiers of rising height. To my personal fancy there is a possible reminiscence of the Javanese music that delighted the composer and a foreshadowing of Godowsky's *Gamelan* in it. *La soirée dans Grenade*, best of the *Estampes*, brings before us the twinkling lights of a city settling down to the quiet of evening, its inhabitants already refreshing themselves with song and dance; in the distance a serenader begins to thrum his mandolin. All this to the sensuous motion of a habanera. Manuel de Falla pronounced it "characteristically Spanish in every detail," an extraordinary acknowledgment because at the time of writing it Debussy had never set foot in Spain. Economy of technique and assurance of touch give distinction to this little masterpiece. *Jardins sous la pluie* is more opulent. Rain and wind sweep over thirsty gardens; in a lull of the storm heavy drops fall from wet bushes; at the end the sun burst forth and the flowers rejoice to see it again. Two children's songs dexterously woven into the piece have been identified by Oscar Thompson in *Debussy, Man and Artist* as *Nous n'irions plus au bois* and *Do do, l'enfant do*.

The *Images* were issued in two series, each containing three pieces. The finest of them are *Reflets dans l'eau* and *Poissons d'or*, first and last of the six. *Reflets dans l'eau* bears out its title admirably besides justifying Debussy's claim that it discovers the newest in "harmonic chemistry." Consider, for example, the subtle chord successions:

Ex. 284

The arpeggiated ornamentation looks deceptively simple until one analyzes the harmonies from which it is derived and observes the breaking up of the first chords (a) into (b) later on:

Ex. 285

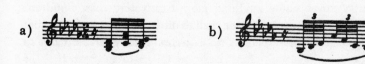

Both the pentatonic and the whole-tone scale are used. ["*Reflets dans l'eau*" to me is like a supremely conceived elongation of the Chopin *Berceuse*. It connects two eras very sensitively.]

The origin of *Poissons d'or* is commonly ascribed to a piece of Oriental lacquer or embroidery in Debussy's possession representing a leaping water faun. I venture to dissent and, without wishing to impose an individual interpretation on others, offer my own conception of the piece for what it is worth. I imagine, then, real goldfish in a real goldfish bowl. To an accompaniment of fluttering fins enters a "gulping" motive of two notes:

Ex. 286

from which the whole piece is developed. Someone takes up the small net lying by and dips it into the water, whereupon the fishes skirmish in wild panic; the net is withdrawn and the little creatures ("*en s'apaisant*") circle the bowl in glad relief. From such concrete things, at least, Debussy was wont to draw his shadowy musical inspirations.

The other numbers of the *Images* can hardly be thought equally successful. *Hommage à Rameau* is not nearly so good a sarabande as that of the *Suite pour le piano*. [To me the "*Hommage à Rameau*" is Debussy's most valuable and masterly piano piece. There is passion in it, and the form is well-nigh perfect.] *Mouvement* plays fantastically with technical patterns; there is little or no music in it. *Cloches à travers les feuilles* and *Et la lune descend sur le temple qui fut* have never become favorites of players or audiences.

Masques and *L'isle joyeuse*, published as separate pieces, were at one time announced as movements of the forthcoming *Suite bergamasque*. *Masques* has already been passingly mentioned. I must leave it to the reader to form his own opinion of *L'isle joyeuse*, for it is unsympathetic to me, while others admire it greatly. Brilliant, gay, and effective, it is a pleasure-seeker's revel.

Debussy never wrote anything more captivating than *Children's Corner*. For once he overcame his dislike of dedications and inscribed the little suite *A ma chère petite Chouchou, avec les tendres excuses de son Père pour ce qui va suivre*. Chouchou, five years old when thus immortalized, was the daughter of his second marriage. The English titles are usually taken to suggest the supervision of an English governess. They betray an imperfect acquaintance with the language: on the dedication page we find *Sérénade [sic] for the doll*, in the text *Serenade of the Doll*, and in the French translation more correctly *Sérénade à la poupée*. And *Jimbo's Lullaby (Berceuse des éléphants)* should surely read *Jumbo*. The suite contains six charmingly understanding pieces, tender and humorous. In *Doctor Gradus ad Parnassum* the child practises her study with fitful attention, by turns fast and conscientiously slow, ending in gleeful haste and some hearty thumps as the study period comes to an end. She sings her toy elephant (pictured in the cover design) to sleep in *Jimbo's Lullaby* and makes love to her doll in the *Serenade*. *The snow is dancing* may express pleasure in winter outdoors or impatience for better weather, as you construe it. *The little Shepherd*, his sheep presumably reposing in their toy box, whiles away an idle hour by playing melodiously on his pipe. The suite concludes with *Golliwogg's cake walk*, a merry romp before bedtime. *Children's Corner* may confidently be recommended to the amateur for its taste, humor, and moderate difficulty.

The two books of *Préludes* each comprise twelve numbers. The twenty-four pieces, varying considerably in musical value, power of expression, and technical demand, are all characteristic in one way or another of Debussy's impersonal art. Here, as always, we see in him an acute observer of life and nature rather than an active participator in human drama or emotion. In this respect they afford a startling contrast to the preludes of Chopin. In the first book any competent amateur with sensitive ear and touch and a good instinct for pedaling should be able to play with ease *Danseuses de Delphe, Voiles, Les sons et les parfums tournent dans l'air du soir, Des pas sur la neige* [a tenderly sensitive piece of deeply felt music to which only an artist can do justice], *La fille aux cheveux de lin, La Cathédrale engloutie*, and *Minstrels*. The others, *Le vent dans la plaine, Les collines d'Anacapri, Ce qu'a vu le vent de l'Ouest, La sérénade interrompue*, and *Le Danse de Puck*, are technically harder. The finest numbers are in my opinion *Les collines d'Anacapri, Des pas sur la neige, La sérénade interrompue*, and *La Cathédrale engloutie*. Snatches of folk music break into the sunny *Collines d'Anacapri*, which resembles a small tarantelle. *Des pas sur la neige* gives a vivid impression of desolation and frozen landscape; it is one of Debussy's closest approaches to program music. *La sérénade interrompue* shows a delicious sense of wit; nothing could be more felicitous than the disconsolate resignation of the unlucky serenader's exit. A truly Gallic dramatization of not very deep emotions! *La Cathédrale engloutie* was inspired by an old Breton myth according to which the sunken cathedral of Ys rises to view on certain clear mornings from a translucent sea; bells chime, priests chant, until the mirage disappears again below the waters. The piece would be still more effective musically had not the composer brought it to two climaxes, the second much weaker than the first. *Danseuses de Delphe, Les sons et les parfums,* and *La fille aux cheveux de lin* have lyrical charm, and *Minstrels* abundant humor. Debussy must have found entertainment in the Negro minstrel shows of the music halls, for here interlocutor and end men crack their jokes with infinite gusto. I think M. Cortot mistaken in imagining a group of English clowns.

Voiles (meaning Sails, not Veils) is merely an exploitation of a whole-tone pattern, clever enough but superficial. If you insist on reading something deeper into it, think of Turner's paintings and etchings of boats in the haze of the English Channel as a mental stimulant. I cannot find much value in *Le vent dans la plaine,* and the dotted rhythms of *Le Danse de Puck* seem to me more irritating than exhilarating. The stormy sweep of *Ce qu'a vu le vent de l'Ouest* presents a difficult problem to the interpreter, who is often hard put to it to suggest more than an obscure rumble of sound. The wind is there, sure enough, but what on earth does he see?

When the second book of *Préludes* came out in 1913, Debussy's powers were already on the wane. He who had never imitated others began to repeat himself, and to repeat himself less well. Compare, for example, *Bruyères* with *La fille aux cheveux de lin*, "*General Lavine*"—*eccentric* with *Minstrels, La Puerta del Vino* with *La soirée dans Grenade*. There is little essentially new in *Brouillards, Feuilles mortes,* and "*Les Fées sont d'exquises danseuses*" beyond a freer but no finer use of dissonance. [*"Feuilles mortes"* contains a stunning example of Debussy's distinct polytonality (second page, last line). The twelve études are beginning to be heard in the concert hall. Most of them are splendidly conceived technical and tonal problems that need careful study and much imagination in performance.] Few persons will be moved to laughter by the *Hommage à S. Pickwick Esq. P.P.M.P.C.*, granting that the quotation of *God Save the King* points to an Englishman; but we may notice the clever suggestion of a man whistling at:

Ex. 287

pp lointain et léger

on the last page. *Les tierces alternées* is still more artificial than the *Voiles* of Book I and lacks the atmosphere of the earlier piece; *Canope* is better but unimportant. Enthusiasts will probably reject these criticisms in whole or in part; they will admit, however, that the works I have mentioned are seldom played except for the bright and attractive *General Lavine* and *La Puerta del Vino.*

Three of the later *Préludes* must be ranked with Debussy's best work and have incontestably added to his reputation. *La terrasse des audiences au clair de lune* finds Debussy in his tenderest mood. This lovely nocturne is suffused with the dreamy romance of the night. *The Moon Holds Her Court* is a good English equivalent of the lengthy title. At the beginning a few notes of the popular tune *Au clair de la lune* are quoted. The next piece, *Ondine,* is another musical gem of impressionism, true to the spirit of a capricious and seductive water sprite. Very different is the quality of *Feux d'artifice,* a virtuoso *tour de force* of the first order. In an astounding display of pianistic effect Debussy succeeds in conveying irresistible suggestions of Catherine wheels throwing sparks afar as they whirl, startling jack-in-the-boxes, and soaring rockets. At the end of the show a few notes of the *Marseillaise* blown on a distant trumpet put a neat finishing touch to the picture.

You will notice that in both sets of *Préludes* the titles are given at the end of each piece instead of at the beginning—a harmless if futile invitation to the reader to guess for himself a suitable name before being confirmed or more likely corrected.

The twelve Études, Debussy's last works for piano, are sadly disappointing. No student resorts to them for technical profit and few players seek repertory material in them. They deal with patterns of five- and eight-finger exercises, thirds, fourths, sixths, octaves, chromatics, ornaments, arpeggios, and chords. One étude, *"pour les sonorités opposées,"* promises a more musical scheme. The series is dedicated to the memory of Chopin. [Mention should be made of the fine two-piano suite *En Blanc et noir* and Debussy's own two-piano transcription of the *Prélude à L'Après-midi d'un faune.*]

Maurice Ravel (1875–1937)

RAVEL, of Basque origin, was born in 1875, showed early signs of musical talent, went to study in Paris at the age of twelve, and entered the Conservatoire in 1889. In 1905, when already well known as a leader of modern French composition, the authorities of the Conservatoire flunked him at the preliminary examinations for the Prix de Rome, bringing on themselves a storm of indignation in which friends and opponents joined. Romain Rolland was one of the most disinterested protestants. "L'affaire Ravel," as it came to be called, created such a scandal that Dubois, director of the Conservatoire, was forced to resign, Fauré replacing him. Throughout the newspaper war the composer remained unmoved, but he was deeply hurt by the injustice and in later years three times rejected the decoration of the Legion of Honor offered by the government. Success was slow but sure, and long before his tragic end Ravel was honored the world over. He traveled extensively, conducting and playing his own works. In 1928 he visited the chief cities of the United States, Florent Schmitt guaranteeing the tour financially. In 1932 he suffered a blow on the head from a taxicab accident, which may have caused or aggravated the brain trouble that shortly afterwards began to manifest itself in intense depression, lack of physical co-ordination, and difficulty in speaking. By slow degrees the malady deprived him of all power to work. The fact that to the last he never lost his mind and was fully conscious of his state adds unspeakable poignancy to the tragedy. He died in 1937. Mrs. Madeleine Goss has written an exceptionally well-informed and understanding biography under the title of *Bolero: the Life of Maurice Ravel.* Her pages compel our respect for the incorruptible artistic integrity of the composer and the moral courage of the Frenchman who refused to countenance any ban on German music during the first World War, and reveal by a hundred intimate details the endearing qualities of a character strangely compounded of sophistication and childish incapacity in some of the most ordinary concerns of daily life. We learn that he loved children, animals (especially cats), fairy tales and mechanical toys, walking, night clubs, smoking Caporals, jazz and Spanish music. We learn too of his inveterate unpunctuality, absence of mind, and foppishness in dress and seem to like him better for these human foibles.

The chief influences in Ravel's musical development were Chabrier, Saint-Saëns, Debussy, Liszt, and the Russian masters of orchestration. But while he was willing to work from models, as he advised younger composers to do, his own finished product seldom bears the remotest trace of imitation. When writing the *Tzigane* he begged a violinist friend to hurry to him with her violin and the *Twenty-four Caprices* of Paganini. Similarly, he consulted the concertos of Saint-Saëns and the études of Liszt when scoring or composing for piano. It was inevitable that he should have much in common with Debussy, who like himself flew in the face of classic tradition. At first the two men were close friends, but as time went on they were forced into the position of competitors or rivals, though never losing their appreciation of each other's music. The differences between the two, however, are more striking than the superficial resemblances. Debussy was a voluptuary, Ravel an ascetic. Debussy owned to an occasional *"besoin de s'encanailler"* and indulged it in art and life; Ravel always preserved an aristocracy of mind. In writing for voice, piano, and orchestra they pursued different methods. Ravel had greater respect for form than Debussy; the latter could never have written a piece like the *Sonatine*.

[Maurice Ravel is indeed not an imitator of Debussy. At the time when he had composed *Jeaux d'eau* and the *Pavane pour une infante défunte*, the only published important work of Debussy was the *Suite pour le piano*. It pays to compare these works. The second piece in *Gaspard de la nuit,* a fantastically original pianistic painting entitled *Le Gibet* (The Gallows), is no doubt the most precious contribution from Ravel's pen. No one has the right to touch the three masterpieces of *Gaspard* without having become intimately acquainted with the fascinating texts by Aloysius Bertrand. The third number, *Scarbo,* happens to be dedicated to me and I treasure this touching gesture. Ravel's piano style is unique and demands much study in sounds. He mentioned to me one day that "People can hardly realize the hours I have spent at times to perfect just a few measures." The "blues" in the Violin and Piano Sonata is a charming greeting from his visit over here. If anyone doubts that Ravel could write red-blooded music, let him study the second movement of the monumental trio, the *Passacaille*, with its orchestral climax.]

Ravel felt a passionate compulsion to file any work he undertook to the sharpest point of perfection. He delighted in setting himself problems of extraordinary difficulty to solve them with triumphant success. The celebrated *Bolero*, for instance, was the outcome of a long-harbored determination to write a long piece on a single theme and with one long, very gradual crescendo. There is obvious artificiality in such a scheme, and Ravel correctly thought the *Bolero* a stunt, "orchestral tissue without music." "Once the idea of using only one theme was discovered," he said, "any Conservatory student could have done as well." And again, "whatever may have been said to the contrary, the orchestral writing is simple and straight-forward throughout, without the slightest attempt at virtuosity." Ravel was fated to achieve the greatest popular success of his career by one of his least important works.

Considering the long period of his activity and his early emergence from immaturity, Ravel's output is remarkably small. Most of his works for orchestra are transcriptions of his own piano pieces, some movements of Debussy's and Mussorgsky's *Tableaux d'une exposition*. The two *Daphnis et Chloé* suites, best of the original orchestral compositions, were adapted from the ballet of the same name, commissioned by Diaghilev. *La Valse* (*Poème chorégraphique*), the *Rapsodie espagnole*, and the early overture *Schéhérazade* exhaust the short list. The only stage piece is the delightfully witty comedy-opera in one act, *L'Heure espagnole*. A solitary string quartet was one of the first compositions to bring him fame.

PIANO WORKS

The published works for piano are rather more numerous; they are as follows, those which were orchestrated by Ravel himself being marked by asterisks:

Menuet antique (a very early work)
Jeux d'eau
Pavane pour une Infante défunte
*Sonatine
Miroirs
  1. Noctuelles
  2. Oiseaux tristes
  3. Une barque sur l'océan
  4. Alborada del gracioso
  5. La Vallée des cloches
*Ma mère l'Oye (for four hands, with a very easy part for a child)
  1. Pavane de la Belle au bois dormant
  2. Petit Poucet
  3. Laideronette, Impératrice des Pagodes
  4. La Belle et la Bête
  5. Le Jardin féerique

Gaspard de la Nuit
 1. *Ondine*
 2. *Le Gibet*
 3. *Scarbo*
Menuet sur le nom d'Haydn
*Valses nobles et sentimentales
A la manière de . . .
 1. Borodin
 2. Chabrier
Prélude
Le Tombeau de Couperin
 *1. Prélude
 2. Fugue
 *3. Forlane
 *4. Rigaudon
 *5. Menuet
 6. Toccata
Frontispice (four hands)
Sonata for violin and piano
Trio for piano, violin, and cello
Concerto in G for piano and orchestra
Concerto for piano, left hand, and orchestra

If we wish to select only the best, we may discard the *Menuet antique,* the two pieces in the manner of Borodin and Chabrier, the Prélude, and the *Frontispice.* Neither the chamber-music works nor the two concertos represent Ravel at his finest. The left-hand Concerto was composed at the request of Paul Wittgenstein, who had lost an arm in the war. The G major Concerto seems trivial except for the slow movement, which I think should be played much more romantically than Ravel intended.[3] The last movement is frank jazz.

The first of the mature works, beginning with the Pavane, at once show a departure from the methods of Debussy. The Pavane, sincere and deeply felt, offers a striking proof that Ravel could be modern within the limits of simple diatonic progressions. It is one of his virtues that by adding new harmonic combinations to chords familiar to the classics he enriched the resources of the composer. Others less wise, obsessed by love of their innovations, too often harped on novel dissonances to the exclusion of any harmony that could conceivably

---

[3] The impressionist movement was essentially a revolt from romanticism. Yet there is much truth in a remark once made by Harold Bauer that, try as he might, Ravel remained "incurably" romantic.

have been written by Beethoven and succeeded only in creating monotony—for we tire quickest of pungent flavors. The whole-tone scale is already as dead as Queen Anne.

Jeux d'eau quotes a line of Henri de Régnier: *"Dieu fluvial riant de l'eau qui le chatouille,"* by way of subtitle. Here again we find long passages purely diatonic opposed to remarkable new harmonies and suggestions of polytonality. The piano idiom, accustomed as we now are to it, caused amazement when the piece appeared. Today we can appreciate it better for the delicious shimmering and plashing intimations of laughing waters and a "tickled" god of the rivers.

[The "new harmonies" are mostly chords of the ninth and eleventh. Regarding the "cadenza" on the second page before the end in *Jeux d'eau*, probably few people realize how closely related the keys of

Ex. 288

C major and F sharp major are. They have two notes in common: E and B flat (A sharp). See the exercises at the conclusion of the appendix on "Technique."]

The *Sonatine* is a masterpiece of form; it should be analyzed carefully before study at the keyboard. A two-note motive, occurring as a rising or falling fourth or fifth, appears in every movement:

Ex. 289

Ex. 290

Ex. 291

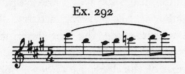

A larger part of the phrase at Ex. 289 changes in the Finale to:

Ex. 292

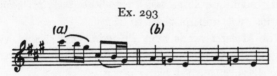

Another motive of the first movement (Ex. 293[a]) is transformed in the last to a carillon chime (Ex. 293[b]).

Ex. 293

(a)   (b)

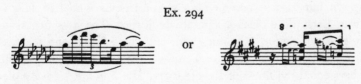

Slight as it is, the *Sonatine* is beautifully developed and may justly be called a classic. It opened up new possibilities for this smaller type of sonata and instigated many composers to revalue the form; a fine later example is the Sonatina of Beryl Rubinstein. Carlos Salzedo made a well-sounding transcription of the work for flute, harp, and cello.

Miroirs contains some of Ravel's most individual thought. *Oiseaux tristes* and the *Alborada del gracioso* are the favorites among the five numbers. The first avoids direct imitation of nature; no bird ever sang:

Ex. 294

   or

and the persistent

Ex. 295

is merely symbolic. The title itself is a flight of imagination, for mournful birds are silent. The cadenza near the end of this exquisitely refined piece is much in the manner of Liszt. The *Alborada* shows how thoroughly Ravel had absorbed the allure of Spanish music. The rapid repeated notes and the glissandos in fourths are difficult and the composition as a whole is not easily made clear to a listener.

In *Gaspard de la Nuit*, three *Poems for piano* inspired by words of Aloysius Bertrand, the literary texts are quoted in full and should by all means be read. The simple titles *Ondine, Le Gibet,* and *Scarbo* are, however, sufficient in themselves provided we know that Scarbo is a dwarfish nocturnal imp, an elusive will-o'-the-wisp. In this suite Ravel reached the high point of his pianistic artistry. It is interesting to contrast *Jeux d'eau* with *Ondine,* the first descriptive of water itself as an element, the second portraying in its seductive long-drawn melody a wooing spirit of the deep. *Le Gibet,* a somber piece written with incredible power and simplicity, induces shivers of horror by its masterly realism. *Scarbo* is probably Ravel's most difficult piano work; to master its technique alone is a formidable task, let alone to bring its imagination, wit, and mischief to life.

The little *Menuet sur le nom d'Haydn,* very simple, very charming, thoroughly Ravelian, can be specially recommended to the amateur. This is Ravel's shortest piano piece.

Chronologically the *Valses nobles et sentimentales* follow the Minuet on Haydn's name. This is Ravel's longest piano piece. We might well expect to discover here an entirely novel treatment of the waltz, but we could hardly be prepared for such infinite delicacy of texture, such sublimation of the dance's spirituality. Only a pianist commanding the last refinements of tone and pedaling can hope to do justice to these sensitive creations. Ravel arranged the work as a ballet entitled *Adélaïde, ou le langage des fleurs.*

Le Tombeau de Couperin was composed not only in tribute to Couperin but also in commemoration of friends who had fallen in the war. Each piece bears a separate dedication. The suite begins with a Prelude and Fugue, continues with old dance forms, and ends with a Toccata. The Fugue may be thought a trifle strained but the other numbers equal the finest of Ravel's work. The *Forlane,* a lovely piece, rather long considering its unvarying slowish rhythm, introduces a favorite dance of Italian gondoliers. Pianists find in the Toccata a brilliant concert number of great originality.

Most of Ravel's piano pieces demand a virtuoso technique, but the amateur will not be troubled by the *Pavane, Oiseaux tristes* of the

Miroirs, the *Minuet on the Name of Haydn, Le Gibet,*[4] and the *Forlane,* Rigaudon, and Minuet from *Le Tombeau de Couperin.* He should not overlook the four-hand suite *Ma mère l'Oye,* and he may well include the Minuet of the Sonatine. More ambitious ventures will depend on individual ability and discretion.

After Ravel

During the lifetime of Debussy and Ravel and since their death French composers have gone farther but often fared worse. Many have exceeded them in temerity of harmonization, none has equalled their inventive genius. This applies particularly to piano composition, though it should be remarked that some have attempted to revive a style of greater simplicity. The merits of ERIK SATIE (1866–1925) have been much disputed. He succeeded in impressing Debussy and Ravel; the former orchestrated two of his *Gymnopédies* (a coined word intelligible enough) and on one occasion the latter organized a whole concert of his works. Though not a member of the group of Six (to be mentioned shortly), they looked on him as their prophet, and Milhaud became his literary executor. It was not until he was forty years old that he entered the Schola Cantorum for serious study under d'Indy and Roussel; previously he had left the Conservatoire after a year's stay, restive under its criticism of a pupil who rebelled against learning the fundamentals of composition. A deliberate mocker, he raised laughter by inventing grotesque titles such as *Pièces en forme de poire, Pièces froides, Véritables Préludes flasques, En habit de cheval, Croquis et agaceries d'un homme de bois.* Milhaud has said that "we need perhaps fifty years or more to know how far Satie is the great benefactor of us all." I, for one, am willing to wait.

The group of *Les Six,* dissenters from the school of impressionism, was formed with the purpose of furthering performances of each other's works. There was little cohesion of ideas among them and the informal organization soon disbanded. The Six were:

[ARTHUR HONEGGER (1892–1955), see "Swiss Composers," Chapter XIII.

LOUIS DUREY (1888–   ), who wrote little for solo piano. A Piano Trio of his is still performed.

---

[4] [I would like to meet the amateur who can conquer *Le Gibet* without hanging himself.]

GERMAINE TAILLEFERRE (1892–   ), who has written a Piano Concerto, a Concerto for Two Pianos, one for voice and orchestra, an opera, and a ballet, a Concertino for Harp and Orchestra, a string quartet, two violin sonatas, and piano pieces, and is well known for her suite for two pianos, *Jeux de plein air*.

DARIUS MILHAUD (1892–   ), an eminent, prolific composer and pianist, has written a great number of works in every genre. Among his experimental efforts are two string quartets (Nos. 14 and 15) that can be performed singly or, together, as an octet, also some works for electronic instruments, some twelve operas, eight symphonies for large orchestra, five for small orchestra, and concertos for all kinds of instruments including marimba, harmonica, and percussion. For the piano: four concertos, a *Ballade, Cinq Études, Le Carnaval d'Aix* for piano and orchestra, a Concerto for Two Pianos, *Second Sonata for Piano* (1950), *Bal Martiniquais,* and *Carnaval à la Nouvelle-Orléans* for two pianos, Concerto No. 3 for piano and orchestra (1951), a concerto and a suite for two pianos and orchestra, and many shorter pieces, among them the popular *Saudades do Brazil.*

GEORGES AURIC (1899–   ), best known for his ballets and film music. Many pieces for the piano, especially a charming *Sonatine.*

FRANCIS POULENC (1899–1963), brilliant composer and pianist, operas, ballets, cantatas, a Mass, a Stabat Mater, much chamber music, many songs, and a large number of piano pieces.

Other recent French composers of importance are:

FLORENT SCHMITT (1879–1958), best known for his large-scale Piano Quintet, composed some brilliant pieces for piano solo.

ISIDOR PHILIPP (1863–1958), an admirable pianist and internationally known master teacher. His *Feux follets* is a delightful encore number. A Concerto for Three Pianos without orchestra has had many performances. Philipp's large number of technical books, transcriptions, and editions have been in use everywhere.

GABRIEL GROVLEZ (1879–1944), best known for his three piano works: *A Child's Garden, L'Almanach aux images,* and *London Voluntaries.*

JACQUES IBERT (1890–1962), whose writing combines Impressionism with neo-classicism most felicitously: five operas, many ballets, several symphonic poems, among them the often heard suite of three movements entitled *Escales* and the very popular and witty *Divertissement,* and much chamber music. For the piano: the *Dix Histoires,* containing the charming and much performed *Le petit âne blanc,* who is the piano student's friend, *Les Rencontres* (five pieces), and *Petite Suite en quinze images.*

ROBERT CASADESUS (1899-1972), famous pianist, but also noted composer: a piano concerto, one for two pianos and orchestra, two sonatas, 28 preludes, a set of études, all written in brilliant style for the instrument.

ANDRÉ JOLIVET (1905–   )—two splendidly written piano sonatas, the second of which is in the idiom of the illuminated avant-garde.

OLIVIER MESSIAEN (1908–   ), outstanding contemporary composer and most original theorist whose music is both strongly religious and exotic. Among his important works for the piano are: *Vingt Regards sur l'Enfant-Jésus, Cantéyodijayâ,* many shorter pieces, and *Sept Visions de l'Amen* for two pianos, a fascinating but difficult work for ambitious two-piano teams. Most original, but decidedly difficult in their unusual technical demands, are the two "bird" concertos—*Réveil des Oiseaux* with large orchestra and *Oiseaux exotiques* for small symphonic accompaniment. See also Chapter XV.

JEAN FRANÇAIX (1912–   )—for piano a full-sized sonata, brilliant in its French *esprit,* and shorter pieces, especially the delightful two-page *Scherzo,* a very charming Concertino for piano and small orchestra (twelve minutes), and a Concerto in D major (1953), frolicking and appealing.

PIERRE BOULEZ (1925–   ), whose Second Sonata, and especially the not yet completed Third, put him in the front rank of aggressive contemporary avant-garde composers. His *Structures* for two pianos are difficult to perform in their constant changes of meters and sudden changes between extreme dynamics. See also Chapter XV.]

CHAPTER TWELVE

Russian and Polish Composers

The Russian Schools

BEFORE the nineteenth century no native art music existed in Russia. Catherine the Great had imported Italian opera in the eighteenth century, and by the beginning of the nineteenth century French opera had gained a foothold and visiting artists were welcomed, but Russian composers were still to seek. A vast store of folk song, however, had accumulated through the ages and the liturgical music of the Greek Catholic Church had developed a distinctive character. The strength and beauty of this folk song and the gorgeous imagination of the Russian fairy tales lay ready to the hand of a genius capable of utilizing them; and after the Napoleonic invasion had aroused flaming patriotism and the writings of Pushkin had provided dramatic material, the time was ripe for the establishment of a national school of music. With Glinka's *A Life for the Tsar* (1836) Russian opera leapt into life. The epoch-making work met instant success, and Liszt rightly hailed Glinka as a "prophet-patriarch." The nationalistic movement quickly spread to other fields than opera when Balakirev gathered together the group of the *Russian Five*, consisting of himself, Borodin, César Cui, Mussorgsky, and Rimsky-Korsakov. There are obvious dangers in carrying nationalism too far, and later many composers, among them Tchaikovsky, Arensky, Rubinstein,

Rachmaninoff, and Medtner (the last of German origin) followed a more cosmopolitan trend. Recently the artistic policy of the Soviet government has encouraged the assertion of native ideas with marked if variable success.

Russian Piano Music

MILI BALAKIREV (1837–1910) was the only one of the Russian Five who was a trained musician. It is an astonishing fact that four of these men began their artistic careers as amateurs. Cui was an authority on military science, Rimsky-Korsakov a naval officer, Borodin a surgeon of repute, Mussorgsky an army officer. Balakirev himself in his youth studied law. He founded a Free School of Music at St. Petersburg in 1862. His compositions are few in number, the most popular of those for piano being the Oriental fantasy *Islamey*, a favorite bravura piece, and a transcription of Glinka's song *The Lark*.

ALEXANDER BORODIN (1834–87) This composer's masterpiece was the opera *Prince Igor*. He might be entirely unknown to pianists but for his colorful short piece *Au couvent*, first number of a *Petite Suite*.

CÉSAR CUI (1835–1918), least virile, least typically Russian of the group of Five, wrote prolifically. His works comprise operas, choral works and songs, and chamber music, all more noteworthy for their lyrical quality and taste than for intensity or dramatic power. *Grove's Dictionary*, fourth edition, gives a fairly long list of small piano works, no one of which can be cited as representative of his style. A Waltz contributed to the collection of *Paraphrases* is charming. *Paraphrases* had its origin at a gathering of musicians where Borodin, Cui, Liadov, Rimsky-Korsakov, and Stcherbatchev were guests. A young daughter of the host complained that all the music was too serious; why couldn't they play something that a little girl might enjoy? *Her* idea of a nice piece was *Chopsticks*, known to her in this form:

Ex. 296

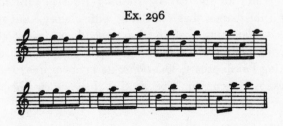

The composers took up the idea and proceeded to write a set of paraphrases on the babyish theme, lavishing incredible skill and humor on their task. You should know the piece, for it is a marvel of talent and resourcefulness. You will find in its pages a Minuet, two Waltzes, a Polka, a Galop, a Mazurka, a Gigue, and a Tarantella as well as a *Carillon*, a *Cortège triomphal*, a *Requiem*, a *Fughetta on the name of Bach*, and a *Fugue grotesque*, all written as a substratum to the ridiculous, unvarying tune. [A new edition of the *Paraphrases* was published by Alexander Tcherepnin, with added contributions, including one by Liszt. Amateurs and professional duettists should be interested.]

NIKOLAY RIMSKY-KORSAKOV (1844–1908) was a past master of orchestral technique, and his book on instrumentation has become a standard work. The orchestral suite *Schéhérazade* and the opera *The Golden Cockerel* (Coq d'or), based on a poem of Pushkin, are perennial favorites in America. His piano compositions are negligible except for the Concerto in C-sharp minor, Opus 30, a pleasing though shallow piece.

MODEST MUSSORGSKY (1839–81) This ill-fated composer never knew success. After resigning from the army in 1859 to devote himself entirely to music he led a life of constant poverty. His morbid nature and intemperate habits aggravated his misfortunes and he died miserably. In his art he failed to acquire the technical mastery of his colleagues, yet he surpassed them all in genius. Rimsky-Korsakov, for all his skill and knowledge, rescored the wonderful opera *Boris Godunov* only to its disadvantage. Mussorgsky's sympathy with the common people, his love for children, and his strong realism are seen in his numerous songs. He was the only one of the Five to write a piano work of first-class importance. This is the *Tableaux d'une exposition*, in which Mussorgsky recorded his musical interpretations of drawings by his friend Victor Hartmann, the architect. The piece is so amazingly modern and unconventional, so vivid in imagination, that it merits a detailed account. A *Promenade*, frequently recurring, suggests a visitor to the gallery strolling from picture to picture. *Gnomus* is a misshapen dwarf walking with clumsy, dragging steps. *Il vecchio castello* brings before us a troubadour singing at a castle gate. *Tuileries* (*Dispute d'enfants après jeux*) explains itself. *Bydlo* is a lumbering Polish oxcart. The *Ballet de poussins dans leurs coques* shows chickens dancing in glee as they leave their shells; Harold

Bauer informs us in his edition that the drawing was made for the ballet of *Trilby. Samuel Goldenberg und Schmuyle* cleverly sketches two Polish Jews, the one rich and pompous, the other poor and whining. The next scene represents *Limoges, le marché,* where market women are haggling volubly over their wares. In the *Catacombæ sepulchrum Romanum* Hartmann views by lantern light the catacombs of Paris. The second part of this number, entitled *Con mortuis in lingua mortua,* touches a climax of fantasy. Mussorgsky wrote of it as follows: "The creative spirit of Hartmann leads me to the skulls and apostrophizes them—the skulls glow with a soft luminousness from within." *La Cabane sur des pattes de poule* is the hut of *Baba Yaga,* a witch of Russian legend. The impressive Finale, *La Porte des Bohatyrs de Kiev,* inspired by a design for an entrance to the city, suggests marching hosts, chanting priests, and pealing bells. Russians are acknowledged to be able linguists, but I can hardly explain why Mussorgsky found it necessary to use French, Italian, German, Russian, and Latin in his various subtitles. I have quoted them faithfully, however, from the accurate reprint of Augener. [It is difficult to obtain the original Russian edition, and the new "authentic" one, published by the International Music Corporation, is therefore doubly welcome. Harold Bauer's edition often deviates from the text; Vladimir Horowitz's own version is augmented, very orchestral, and superlatively exciting, but he refuses to publish it.] The piece has been orchestrated by Ravel.

PETER ILICH (or Ilyich) TCHAIKOVSKY (1840–93) Tchaikovsky's orchestral works are so well known to every concertgoer and the events of his life so familiar through Rosa Newmarch's biography, her translation of his brother Modest's *Life and Letters,* and the recent authoritative *Tchaikovsky* of Herbert Weinstock that I need not dwell on them here. It has already been remarked that Tchaikovsky held aloof from the nationalistic movement. By far the most important of his piano compositions is the Concerto in B-flat minor, a splendid and original piece broadly designed on classic lines and the most popular work of its kind since Brahms and Liszt. The main theme of the first movement:

Ex. 297

is borrowed from a folk tune. The Concerto in G is seldom played and the one in E flat never. Next in value to the B-flat minor Concerto comes the Trio in A minor, inscribed "to the memory of a great artist" (Nikolay Rubinstein). This work has moments of fine inspiration, but is long and diffuse, with arid spaces of development; some cuts are often made, to its benefit. Usually it turns out to be more interesting to the performers than to the audience. The brilliant piano writing of the concerto and trio leads us to expect much from the numerous solo pieces, but here we are disappointed, for among them all there is not a single work of great value. The Sonata in G is weak and many of the short pieces sound no better than potboilers, as perhaps they were. The Variations in F and the Valse Caprice in D show care in workmanship and the amateur will enjoy attractive trifles like the *Chant sans Paroles* in F, *Chanson triste*, *Humoresque* in G and *En Troïka* (from *The Seasons*) and more serious numbers like the F minor *Romance*, Opus 5, and the G minor *Barcarolle*, Opus 37, No. 6. Tchaikovsky also wrote a pretty *Album for Children*, Opus 39.

ANTON RUBINSTEIN (1830–94), next to Liszt the most eminent pianist in history, suffered in his compositions from a too facile pen and an incapacity for self-criticism. He composed many operas and oratorios (or Biblical operas), six symphonies, five piano concertos, chamber music, songs, and piano solos. His concert tours took him all over Europe and once, with the violinist Henri Wieniawski, to America. The greatest achievements of his life were the founding of the St. Petersburg Conservatory in 1862 and his series of historical recitals, given in the chief cities of Europe as a farewell tour in 1885–6. Albert Lockwood[1] and Catherine Drinker Bowen[2] have done a useful service by reprinting in full the programs of the seven historical recitals.

Of the piano concertos that in D minor, Opus 70, is best; the one in G major has been played frequently by Josef Hofmann, a devoted pupil, and that in E flat by Josef Lhévinne. The pieces for piano alone include some famous numbers: the *Valse-Caprice* in E flat, with the crazy leaps often missed by Rubinstein himself, the *Melody* in F, Opus 3, No. 1, the *Romance* in E flat, Opus 44, No. 1, the *Barcarolles* in A minor and G, the *Rêve angélique* (Portrait 22 of the col-

---

[1] Albert Lockwood: *Notes on the Literature of the Piano* (University of Michigan Press).
[2] Catherine Drinker Bowen: *"Free Artist."*

lection *Kamennoi-Ostrov*), and the *Staccato Étude* in C. I like some other pieces as well: the *Romance* in F, Opus 26, No. 1, the *Barcarolle* in F minor from Opus 30, the Gavotte in F sharp, Opus 38, No. 5, and another *Valse-Caprice* in F, a better piece than its more celebrated namesake. All the piano works have gone out of fashion, but the amateur cannot yet afford not to know some of the best. He will find all he wants in the two Rubinstein albums of the Schirmer Library.

NIKOLAY RUBINSTEIN (1835–81), younger brother of Anton, was declared by the latter to be the better pianist—an opinion not concurred in by the world. Nicolay was a fine teacher and conductor; Taneyev, Siloti, and Sauer studied with him. He founded the Imperial (now the State) Musical Society of Moscow in 1859, and it in turn founded the Conservatory of Moscow, of which he was the first director. Anton included two of the piano pieces in his last historical recital, but they have since fallen into neglect. [He pronounced the Tchaikovsky B-flat minor Concerto to be a "concerto against the piano" and refused to accept the dedication. Hans von Bülow became acquainted with the concerto while in Moscow, was enthusiastic about it, and took it along on his American tour. This explains the unusual fact that its *première* took place in Boston rather than in Moscow.]

ANTON ARENSKY (1861–1906) Apart from his piano compositions Arensky's work is unfamiliar to us in America. None of his operas or symphonies, as far as I know, have succeeded in crossing the Atlantic. His musical taste seems to have been cosmopolitan rather than Russian, his style lyrical rather than dramatic. He wrote about one hundred pieces for piano, many of them beautiful and some curious. To the latter category belong the *Sketches on Forgotten Rhythms*, Opus 28 (*Logaèdes, Péons, Ioniques*, etc.). In the fine *Basso ostinato*, Opus 5, No. 5, Arensky skillfully opposes a bass of six quarter-notes to a time signature of $\frac{5}{4}$:

Ex. 298

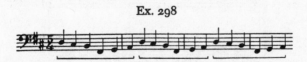

By this device the first beats of bass and measure coincide after a period of six measures. Each such cycle contains a new variation above the "ground."

I recommend to the amateur the two *Esquisses* in F and F minor, Nos. 1 and 3 of Opus 24, the Etude in F sharp, Opus 36, No. 13, the *Basso ostinato,* and the set of six pieces, *Près de la mer,* especially the fourth and fifth. Also the Piano Trio in D minor, Opus 32, an attractive and fairly easy chamber-music work. The suites for two pianos, Opus 15 and Opus 33, and the *Silhouettes,* Opus 23, are indispensable to the duo-pianist repertory. A Concerto in F minor and a Fantasia on Two Russian Airs for piano and orchestra lack depth and need not be considered.

ALEXANDER SCRIABIN (1872–1915), apostle of mysticism, studied at the Moscow Conservatory, where he afterwards taught for a few years, made his name as a touring pianist, withdrew from other work in 1904 to give his whole time to composition, and died prematurely at the age of forty-three. In his early years he was influenced by the piano style of Chopin and the orchestration of Wagner, but later on he dissociated himself from every known trend of composition and attained a striking originality of thought. To express his esoteric ideas he invented a "mystic" chord based on the upper overtones (the ninth, tenth, eleventh, thirteenth, and fourteenth), usually disposed in order of fourths:

Ex. 299

and available in many alterations and inversions. Here is a simple example of its use:

Ex. 300

While this was not his only harmonic innovation, it was sufficient to stamp all his later music with an unmistakable quality. Scriabin

experimented in combining tone and color; *Prometheus: the Poem of Fire* was scored for orchestra, piano, organ, chorus, and color keyboard. He intended to summarize his religious convictions in a *Mystery*, an oratorio-opera composed of "music, speech, gesture, scent, and color," but did not live to complete his sketches for it.

Apart from a few symphonic poems (the *Poème d'extase* is the best-known) Scriabin expressed himself most fully in his writings for piano. The ten sonatas cover the successive periods of his artistic development, the first four illustrating the early and intermediate phases, the fifth dominated by the "mystic" chord and manner, and the others entering into trances beyond normal understanding. [Of the ten sonatas, the grandiose fourth and the very orchestral fifth are the most powerful and most popular. The ninth and tenth are in his final style, built entirely upon his mystic chord (Ex. 299). The two Poems, op. 32, are works that will best acquaint you with this fantastic composer (International Music). A Siloti edition of No. 1 is not good. Two pianistic gems are the Albumleaf, op. 58, and *Le Désir*, op. 57. The former is a close cousin to the *Träumerei; Le Désir* is a very sensitive, fascinating study in polychromatics. The early Études contain excellent material for students and amateurs. Scriabin's last

Ex. 301

Études, op. 65, featuring fifths, seventh, and ninths are for piano-gourmets, as are the five Preludes, op. 74. In the fourth Prelude appears the simultaneous meeting (to others, clash) of major and minor, establishing a precedent that now is a commonplace in contemporary music.]

If we ignore Scriabin's philosophy completely, we can enjoy his music better. The student cannot fail to be enticed by the lyric and pianistic value of the preludes, études, and so forth, of the earlier and middle period, and should cultivate at least a bowing acquaintance with a few of the more occult. I submit a selected list covering all the aspects of his art.

Easier Pieces:
Étude in C-sharp minor, Opus 2, No. 1
Étude in B-flat minor, Opus 8, No. 11
Prelude for the left hand alone, Opus 9, No. 1
Twenty-four Preludes, Opus 11, especially Nos. 3, 9, 10, 14, 17
   (No. 14 is in the unusual time of $\frac{15}{8}$)
Poème, Opus 32, No. 1
Quasi Valse, Opus 47
Le Désir, Opus 57
More Difficult:
Nocturne for the left hand alone, Opus 9, No. 2
Études, Opus 8, especially Nos. 5, in E, and 12, in D-sharp
   minor
Étude in C-sharp minor, Opus 42, No. 5
Sonata-Fantaisie in G-sharp minor, Opus 19
Very Difficult:
Étude in D flat, Opus 8, No. 10
Poème satanique
Vers la flamme, Opus 72
Sonata No. 4, F sharp

SERGEI RACHMANINOFF (1873–1943) It is hard to believe that this eminent composer and pianist is no longer with us. After 1917 he spent most of his time in New York, traveling and concertizing throughout the United States, second to none in popularity with our symphony orchestras and public. Like Tchaikovsky, he refused to join the nationalist movement headed by Rimsky-Korsakov and remained all his life a classicist. His early years were marked by the success of the one-act opera *Aleko* and the celebrated Prelude in C-sharp minor and the failure of his First Symphony and piano concerto. At this time he was active as conductor of the Grand Theater in Moscow. By the turn of the century, after the production of the Second Concerto, in C minor, his fame began to spread abroad, and he went to Dresden to give all his time to composition. It was in Dresden that he wrote his finest orchestral work, the symphonic poem *Island of the Dead,* after the painting of Böcklin. In 1909 he made his first tour of America. He has left us a whole library of piano compositions rich in melodic invention, harmonic warmth, and unsought effectiveness. The Concertos in C minor and D minor and the later *Rhapsody on a Theme of Paganini* are outstanding contributions to the literature. The first has become the most popular concerto since that of Tchaikovsky in B-flat minor. The rhapsody, more modern in style, is a set of variations on the theme already used by Brahms and Liszt, with the addition of a very effective introduction of the *Dies Irae* in the course of the piece. A Sonata for piano and cello is the best example of his chamber music. Rachmaninoff's piano solos show uniform excellence of musicianship and intimate acquaintance with the instrument. Some of the earliest offer fine material to the amateur, for instance the *Elegy, Polichinelle,* and *Serenade* from Opus 3 and the *Barcarolle* and *Valse* from Opus 10. The C-sharp minor Prelude is a typical example of a piece that became hackneyed simply because it was extremely good. The twenty-three other preludes, ten in Opus 23, thirteen in Opus 32, vary more in difficulty than in merit. Few are as demanding as those in B flat, G minor, and E-flat minor of Opus 23, none more beautiful than the easier ones in E flat of Opus 23, and G major, B minor, and G-sharp minor of Opus 32. The G minor Prelude, Opus 23, No. 5, has been played since its publication oftener than the one in C-sharp minor. The very difficult E-flat minor Prelude, Opus 23, No. 9, is marked at an appalling speed. The *Études-Tableaux,* Opus 35 and Opus 39, differ little from the preludes in type, but have never been so popular. I cannot imagine why the fascinating *Polka of W. R.* is so seldom played; true, it is very far from easy. The Sonata in B-flat minor, too, deserves more attention than it receives; the finale in particular is extremely effective. Rachmaninoff also wrote two suites of pieces for two pianos; *Les Larmes* and the *Tarantelle* will give you a good idea of them.

[I find the Prelude in D major, op. 23, to be the most lyrical and pianistically most interesting one of both sets. I used to play the epic B minor and the graceful B major of op. 32, bracketed like brother and sister, and closed the group of four or five Preludes with the one in A minor from the same opus. The B-flat minor Sonata, op. 36, is a monumental work and has its place with the great sonatas of the classical and romantic periods. I played this sonata at two Carnegie Hall recitals, four months apart. The press received it with strong reservations at first, but became very enthusiastic after the second hearing. Rachmaninoff published a new copyrighted edition of it, facilitating certain extremely difficult passages and making some cuts. I still prefer the original version. Three of the *Études-Tableaux* are warmly recommended: the ghost-like E-flat minor, followed by the triumphant E-flat major of op. 35. In the op. 39, you find the most powerful and dramatic of them all, the one in E-flat minor, the pianist's challenge. The two Suites for two pianos are excellent music and give audiences as much listening pleasure as the performers can derive from their own playing. Among them *Les Larmes* and the *Tarantelle* are two especially attractive numbers. International Music Co. has published the twenty-five Preludes in one volume and has combined the *Études-Tableaux*, op. 33 and op. 39, in another single volume.

A charming anecdote should not be withheld from my readers. At a dinner in Dr. Frederick Stock's home, Rachmaninoff was "toasted" for his magnificent playing of his own second and third concertos and invited to perform the first and fourth the following season. I was curious and suggested that he play the fifth, which I gathered was in the offing. He retorted in his Russianized English: "There *is* no fifth—the depression is everywhere"!]

Those of us who knew Rachmaninoff learned to respect his incorruptible artistic integrity as highly as we admired his creative and pianistic genius. I cannot refrain from relating an experience, trivial enough in itself, that went far to reveal the utter sincerity of his nature. I was sitting with him and two other famous pianists in the judges' box at a contest in Carnegie Hall. We had all arrived early and the piano events had not begun, so that we were condemned to listen for some twenty minutes to the execrable sounds of two competing brass bands. The others ridiculed the performance, but Rachmaninoff sat like a stone, the saturnine mask we knew so well on his face. Finally he turned to me and whispered: "If they knew *how hard* it is to train a band" (a pause, then:) "they would not laugh."

SERGE PROKOFIEV (1891–1953) ably upheld the genius of Russian music and wrote many important works for piano. He was, first of all, an admirable example of the immense fecundity of Russian art. Such vitality is in itself no mean virtue. In many countries music has languished or been almost crushed by the forces of war and destruction, but through thick and thin, through war and peace, Russia has continued to pour out the treasures of its spirit to a nation and a world hungry for more than bread. But Prokofiev's merits go much further; to his astonishing wealth of original ideas and unlimited power to say what he means, he added versatility and knew how to temper the frequent crassness of his style with many moments of true beauty and tenderness. One of his most amiable characteristics was his appeal to the mind of childhood, exemplified in the ballet *Peter and the Wolf* and the *Music for Children*, Opus 65, a charming set of twelve easy piano pieces. Technical difficulty puts many of the sonatas and other works beyond the reach of any but advanced students. Some of the *Visions fugitives*, however, the twelve pieces, Opus 12, which include a Prelude in C written for harp or piano, a March in F minor, and a Gavotte in G minor, another Gavotte in E flat from Opus 77, and a few transcriptions from the orchestral works are not discouraging to modest players. The *Music for Children* offers a welcome besides easy introduction to modern idiom.

[The piano concertos in D-flat major (No. 1) and C major (No. 3) are valuable contributions to the repertoire. In the first eight sonatas, the *Visions Fugitives*, op. 22, and the *Suggestion Diabolique*, Prokofiev experimented successfully with polytonality, but he was too resourceful a harmonist to restrict himself long to any one scheme.

The piano concertos No. 1 and No. 3 have become popular. In fact, the latter is rapidly moving into place as the Grieg A minor of our era, and for good reasons. It is brilliant and powerful, lyrical in the slow movement, and ends in fury. The composer was heard in the United States in the Fifth and I well remember baptizing it the "Emperor Jones" Concerto after the first hearing. Prokofiev wrote a ninth Sonata, which I feel is not very sympathetic. No. 7 is his masterwork as to both his lyrical and technical craftsmanship. Who could possibly resist the climax of the exciting finale? No. 3 and No. 6 appear often on programs. The Toccata, op. 11, is meant for athletic performers who enjoy endurance tests using bicep resources.

Other Russian composers who have contributed to the literature of the piano include:

ANATOL LIADOV (1855–1914), composer of many good lyrical pieces of moderate difficulty. A little gem is the *Tabatière à musique*.

VLADIMIR REBIKOV (1866–1920), a somewhat mild experimenter in old modes and new tonalities.

SERGEI LIAPUNOV (1859–1924), who, having been a great admirer of Liszt, dedicated his twelve *Études d'exécution transcendantes* to the master's memory. They are difficult but rewarding. Two of the best known are *Lesghinka and Carillon*. They were written for aspiring young pianists.

ALEXANDER GLAZUNOV (1865–1936), who wrote two piano concertos, two sonatas, a suite for two pianos, and many smaller works, outstanding among them the Variations in F sharp minor.

NICOLAS TCHEREPNIN (1873–1945), father of Alexander—a piano concerto and an especially worthwhile quintet for piano and strings.

REINHOLD GLIÈRE (1875–1956)—twenty-four preludes in all keys.

SERGEI BORTKIEVICZ (1877–1952)—four piano concertos, most notably the one in B-flat minor, and smaller pieces.

NIKOLAI MEDTNER (1880–1951), three piano concertos, several sonatas. His *Fairy Tales* and two of the concertos were performed by Rachmaninoff, who admired him greatly.

NIKOLAI MIASKOWSKY (1881–1950), a remarkable composer who wrote four sonatas, of which No. 2 and No. 4 are outstanding. It is the music world's loss that he is not better known.

VALERY JELOBINSKY (1912–1946), whose Six Études, op. 19, was performed by Vladimir Horowitz in recital. There is also a set of *Scenes of Childhood*.

ARAM KHATCHATURIAN (1903–   )—two symphonies; a violin concerto; a cello concerto; much chamber music; for the pianist two good sonatas (No. 2 and especially No. 3), the somewhat acrobatic and exciting *Toccata,* and finally the Piano Concerto in D-flat major, a showpiece for well-equipped performers.

DMITRI KABALEVSKY (1904–   ), whose contributions to the literature of the piano are considerable: three piano concertos, the second of which is often heard. The third one, a *Youth Concerto,* should easily become very popular, especially with young pianists. Extremely interesting and powerful in both lyrical and dramatic expression are the *24 Preludes* (1943).

DMITRI SHOSTAKOVICH (1906–   ), who has written, in addition to several operas and ballets, eleven symphonies, a violin concerto and much chamber music, two piano concertos. The first of the piano concertos has become popular. Its score calls for piano, trumpet, and string orchestra. His most important contribution for solo piano is *Six Preludes and Fugues* (1951), a major work though not very interesting throughout and looking backward stylistically, whereas the two books of Bach's *Well-Tempered Clavier* are pointing forward.]

Polish Composers

IT seemed as if Chopin had exhausted the Polish talent for piano writing. A long gap of years intervened between him and his next successors, none of whom have yet approached his genius.

XAVER SCHARWENKA (1850–1924) Xaver, like his elder brother Philipp, composed a large number of works now forgotten. The Piano Concerto in B-flat minor is a fine piece with an exceptionally brilliant and taking Scherzo. Another Concerto in F minor contains very musicianly work, and exceptionally has five movements. A set of *Polish Dances* and a little Minuet in E minor used to be popular. Scharwenka wrote well but had nothing new to say.

MORITZ MOSZKOWSKI (1854–1925) Light music has a legitimate place in art not to be disdained by the intellectual. Hence our perennial enjoyment of the Gilbert and Sullivan operettas, which are liked equally by Arnold Schönberg and the man in the street. Is not first-class light music preferable to dreary classics? Moszkowski had a happy flair for writing salon music of the highest order, tuneful, witty, and polished. Some of his best pieces deserve and find an occasional place on the concert platform. Josef Hofmann features the *Caprice espagnole*, and I have heard him play *La Jongleuse* three times in succession to a clamorous Carnegie Hall audience. For some seasons Josef Lhévinne performed all four of the Études from the *School of Double Notes*. Moszkowski always succeeds in creating a maximum of effect with a minimum of difficulty. His passages "lie" naturally under the fingers and flatter the pianist's estimate of his own technique. He is particularly adroit in dispersing runs between the two hands.

KAROL SZYMANOWSKI (1883–1937) may prove to have founded a new school of Polish music, so individual is his style, so free from outside influence or tradition. The lamented Polish violinist Paul Kochanski did much to make his compositions for violin known in America, but so far no one has done the same for the piano works, which are rhythmically, technically, and harmonically intricate. Nine Preludes, Opus 1, and four Études, Opus 4, are easier and serve as an introduction to his very modern style. The twelve later Études, Opus 33, were intended to be played without pause. [One can hardly understand that a highly gifted creator of so much original good music should be nearly totally neglected by conductors (three symphonies) and pianists (three sonatas, Variations on a Polish Folksong, three extensive poems called *Masques*, four books of mazurkas, op. 50, and especially the grandiose *Symphonie Concertante* for orchestra and piano). Arthur Rubinstein is the only one among the great pianists who has championed his countryman's music. Szymanowski's place in music history is of universal significance, and we can easily call him Chopin's national successor. His music is difficult to perform, but rewarding in the finest sense of the word.]

LEOPOLD GODOWSKY (1870–1938) This distinguished pianist and composer wrote only for his own instrument. He has left us a large number of original compositions, mostly in small form, and many remarkable transcriptions. Of the former, the *Triakontameron*, thirty pieces in $\frac{3}{4}$ time, the *Phonoramas*, musical reminiscences of Javanese music, and the *Miniatures*, twenty-four short pieces for four hands, the treble part quite easy, are well known. *Alt Wien, Nocturnal Tangier*, and the *Ethiopian Serenade* from the *Triakontameron* may be selected as excellent specimens of charming and musicianly trifles. The *Phonoramas* are more elaborately worked out; the *Gamelan*, No. 1 of the set, imitates the sonorities of the percussion instruments of the Javanese orchestra. The *Passacaglia*, taking for its theme the opening eight measures of Schubert's "Unfinished" Symphony, builds up a masterpiece of variation form. There are also many interesting pieces for the left hand alone.

Godowsky's transcriptions, almost as numerous as the original works, show a phenomenal mastery of polyphony. The long series begins with over fifty arrangements of Chopin's Études. In the *Bandinage*, the two G-flat études (that on black keys and the "Butterfly") are cleverly combined. The *Renaissance* clothes old pieces of Schobert, Rameau, Couperin, and others in modern dress. The revision of Rameau's *Tambourin* is especially popular. Six transcriptions of Bach's sonatas and suites for violin and cello show reverence for the great master and emulation of his immense contrapuntal skill. Some arrangements of waltzes by Johann Strauss excel any except those of Tausig in fine workmanship, but are so forbiddingly difficult that they tend to defeat their purpose of entertainment. Paraphrases of songs by Schubert and various piano pieces must be added to the list; among the happiest of these are the *Tango* of Albéniz and the little *Moment Musical* in F minor of Schubert.

Godowsky was a pianist's pianist. His colleagues used to sit at his feet, marveling while he practised or played to them for hours at a stretch—for it was easier to start than to stop him. He had the knack of doing apparently impossible things with the utmost simplicity and ease. To bring out three different rhythms, counterpoints, or gradations of tone with one hand was child's play to him. Curiously, however, he was often less effective in public performance, owing partly to his utter lack of showmanship, partly to the fact that extreme subtlety is apt to be lost in a large auditorium.

[Godowsky's large size *Passacaglia* is followed by an equally extended but remarkably written double fugue. Unfortunately, Godowsky altered the opening theme of the "Unfinished" Symphony by adding an upbeat, an F sharp eighth-note before the half-note B in the first measure. Thus the quiet classical beauty of the inspired thought was destroyed, a strange, hardly explicable error of taste and judgment. My greatly admired late colleague insisted that a passacaglia needed an upbeat. Well then, chaconne would have been the proper designation.]

IGNACE JAN PADEREWSKI (1860–1941) As a composer Paderewski is best known for his melodious and graceful pieces of superior salon type, beautifully written for the piano. The Nocturne in B flat, the Melody in B from the *Chants du voyageur*, the Caprice in G and the celebrated Minuet in the same key, represent this phase of his work. More important are three sets of variations, the *Thème varié* in A, the Variations and Fugue in A minor, and, above all, the Variations and Fugue in E-flat minor, Opus 23. The last is a piece of imposing dimensions and great merit, unjustly neglected by pianists. The still larger works are a Concerto in A minor, now considered old-fashioned in spite of its beautiful *Romanze*, a *Polish Fantasia* for piano and orchestra, and an ambitious but almost unknown sonata.

It seems unnecessary here to speak of Paderewski's career as pianist and statesman. Before he had made his first successes in Paris and London, someone asked Leschetizky, his teacher, whether he would become famous. "Without the slightest doubt," was the answer. "Oh! is he then such a talented pianist?" "He is that," said Leschetizky, "but he would succeed in any case because he is such an accomplished diplomat." The word could only be applied to Paderewski in its finest sense. It was not diplomacy, but nobility of soul that carried him to the heights he attained. No one ever spoke with him for as much as ten minutes without being conscious of meeting a prince among men, an overwhelming personality, and an artist to the core in music and in life.

[I enjoyed the intimate friendship of this "aristocrat of our profession" for many years. His warm performances in the grand manner plus the magnetism of his personality account for his unique success before large audiences that usually went wild in their hero-worship. As a man, Ignace Paderewski was simple, kind, and generous, but firm of character.]

[SIGISMOND STOJOWSKI (1869–1946) was a finely sensitive pianist and musician. His well-written Second Piano Concerto was played by Paderewski in New York with much success, and his beautiful, lyrical *Chants d'amour* has been popular and should not be neglected.

JOSEF HOFMANN (1876–1957), sometimes known as the "giant of the piano," wrote five concertos for his instrument, but was unable to score any lasting success with them. He then adopted a pseudonym, M. Dvorsky, and earned more appreciation for a rather charming set of piano pieces that are more progressive in character.

ALEXANDER TANSMAN (1897–   )—prolific composer: two operas; seven symphonies; a large number of chamber works; for the pianist two concertos, a suite for two pianos and orchestra, two sonatas, and four albums for piano, *Pour les enfants.*]

CHAPTER THIRTEEN

Piano Music Since Liszt

Modern German and Austrian Composers

IN this chapter it is first necessary to consider some contemporaries
and successors of Liszt who contributed to the piano literature without creating anything remarkably new. We can then go on with a
clear conscience to the more important pathfinders, Richard Strauss
and Arnold Schönberg.

SIGISMOND THALBERG (1812–71)   This great pianist, who for a
time disputed the laurels of Liszt, composed a large number of salon
pieces, all now consigned to oblivion. I suppose, however, that thousands of older persons remember his variations on *Home, Sweet Home*.
And pianists of a former generation used to struggle valiantly with
the *Théme original et étude* in A minor, a difficult repetition study
played by Rubinstein in his historical recitals. A story is told that
when Thalberg introduced the piece at a recital, so many publishers
asked for it that he made appointments with them for the same day
and hour, and on meeting the astonished group proceeded to auction
it off to the highest bidder. As a player Thalberg was distinguished
by his singing tone and legato. He transcribed a set of twenty-two
pieces with the title *L'Art du chant appliqué au piano*. [It is most interesting that in his transcriptions Thalberg had the melody notes in
both staffs printed in larger size than those of the accompaniment,
thus intensifying for both the eye and ear of the performer the importance of the singing quality. Chopin followed this fine idea in the
so-called "Aeolian Harp" Étude, op. 25, No. 1.]

CARL TAUSIG (1841–71) After a pianistic career of extraordinary brilliance Tausig died prematurely in his thirtieth year, universally lamented. His playing, when he had shed some youthful eccentricities, was noble and impassioned, supported by an infallible technique. Of all the claimants to be the "favorite" pupil of Liszt he was the only one acknowledged as such by the master. His repertoire embraced the whole literature of the piano from Scarlatti and Bach to his contemporaries.

Tausig had a singular gift for transcription. Often as the waltzes of Johann Strauss have been adapted to concert use, the two *Valse-caprices, Nachtfalter* and *Man lebt nur einmal,* are still unexcelled. The arrangements of Bach's organ Toccata and Fugue in D minor, of five Scarlatti sonatas, of Schubert's *Andantino and Variations on French Motives,* and of Schumann's rollicking song *Der Contrabandiste* are admirable. The *Marche militaire* of Schubert, more of a stunt than the others, was popular for many years. The original compositions are fewer and less interesting. Once the *Halka Fantasia* was a great favorite, but no one plays it now. The two *Études de concert,* however, especially the first, in F sharp, are fine pieces.

Tausig also published a condensed edition of Clementi's *Gradus ad Parnassum* and a valuable book of *Daily Exercises.*

ADOLF JENSEN (1837–79), a skillful and melodious but not over-original composer, is best known to piano students by one of his lesser works, the easy *Wanderbilder,* containing the faithfully turning *Mill.* A Barcarolle in A flat and the *Dryade,* Opus 43, No. 4, are better, and the *Erotikon,* a collection of seven pieces including *Galatea, Elektra,* and *Eros,* represents him at his best. Jensen is more famous for his songs, one of which (*Murmuring Zephyrs*) has been neatly transcribed by Walter Niemann.

JOACHIM RAFF (1822–82) It is a thousand pities that a composer capable of writing the *Lenore* and *Im Walde* symphonies, whose marked talent won the admiration and friendship of Mendelssohn, Liszt, and von Bülow, should have wasted his life turning out potboilers. Many of Raff's piano pieces, like the *Polka de la Reine,* are not even good salon music. Others are superior, for instance *La Fileuse, Märchen (Fairy Tale)* and the *Rigadon* in D and *Tambourin* in B flat from the Suite, Opus 204. A much more serious effort is the D minor Suite, Opus 91, largely molded, and graced by the *Giga con Variazioni,* Raff's best concert piece.

ADOLF HENSELT (1814–89) A famous pianist of his time, Henselt achieved his greatest successes in Russia, where he spent most of his mature life. He was noted for his playing of widely extended arpeggios and is said to have spent hours daily practising stretching exercises for the fingers. His compositions, all in a vein of old-fashioned languishing romance, are not entirely forgotten. The most important, two books each of twelve études, contain the delicate *Si oiseau j'étais*, Opus 2, No. 6, and the *Love Song*, Opus 5, No. 11. The *Spring Song*, Opus 15, is a tuneful piece and the *Toccatina*, Opus 25, may also be recommended. Henselt had a genuine melodic gift, which shows well in the slow movement of his once famous Concerto in F minor. He wrote ingenious additions for a second piano to some of Cramer's études. [A resemblance between one of the themes of the slow movement of the concerto and the C-sharp minor Prelude of Rachmaninoff is interesting. After all, Rachmaninoff was only seventeen when he wrote his world-renowned piece.]

CARL REINECKE (1824–1910), Reinecke's compositions for piano include three concertos, that in F-sharp minor being the best, a *Ballade* in A flat well known in its day, and a welcome addition to the two-piano repertory, *Impromptu on a Theme from Schumann's Manfred*. A cycle, *From the Cradle to the Grave*, also deserves mention. The *Six very easy Sonatinas*, Opus 127ᵃ, *Toy Symphonies*, and many other pieces for children, all charming, may possibly have been inspired by the musical needs of his own large family. Reinecke is probably best remembered for his forty-two cadenzas to classical concertos, a very useful aid to students and teachers. As a pianist he inherited the elegance but not the fire of Mendelssohn, his teacher, and was admired for his performances of Mozart's works and his taste as a player of chamber music. I have never heard a better accompanist. For many years he was the conductor of the famous Gewandhaus concerts in Leipzig. [I remember Reinecke's delightful playing of the Mozart "Coronation" Concerto as if it had occurred a week ago. I was fourteen then.]

MAX REGER (1873–1916) Howard Brockway aptly dubbed Reger the "champion heavy-weight composer of modern times." Endowed with all possible facility of technique and command of form, Reger's music is always meritorious. He had an extraordinary flair for fugue-writing and his modulations are highly ingenious. But he is usually dull, often turgid. Many of his numerous works are very long. Little interest is shown in his piano compositions. The sole right of performance of the F minor Concerto was granted for a year to the pianist Frieda Kwast-Hodapp, putting it at some disadvantage in spite of her accomplished interpretation. The amateur will probably be satisfied by a perusal of the *Bunte Blätter*, Opus 36, and the two volumes *Aus meinem Tagebuch (From My Diary)*, Opus 82, both published in the Universal Edition. [Rudolf Serkin has tried in vain to revive the Piano Concerto in F-sharp minor.]

EUGEN D'ALBERT (1864–1932), first making a name for himself as an instrumental composer, turned to writing operas and after the success of *Tiefland*, the first, devoted himself exclusively to the stage. His Second Piano Concerto, in E, is a splendid work in Lisztian form. It was frequently played by himself and by Teresa Carreño, with whom he contracted one of his and her numerous marriages.[1] The fine Piano Suite in D minor, Opus 1, strictly after Bach's model but harmonically more modern, was written in d'Albert's teens. The *Allemande* and *Gavotte and Musette* from it, though only parts of its general excellence, became especially popular. Other good solo pieces are the brilliant Scherzo in F sharp, Opus 16, No. 2, the *Ballade* in C minor from Opus 29, and an altogether delightful *Serenata* in B. One must not forget the transcriptions of Bach's organ Prelude and Fugue in D and the great Passacaglia in C minor.

D'Albert was a magnificent pianist, excelling alike in his interpretations of Bach, Beethoven, Chopin, Schumann, Brahms, and Liszt. In later years he was too preoccupied with composition to practise and his technique fell off lamentably. He was almost the first to program pieces of Debussy in Berlin, and I can remember his amused look when they were hissed by part of the audience.

[Some lesser German and Austrian composers whose music is still performed are:

FERDINAND HILLER (1811–1885) (German). His Concerto in F-sharp minor still is performed in music schools. It is not very difficult, but is effective.

JOSEPH RHEINBERGER (1839–1901) (German from Liechtenstein). His best-known work for the piano is a skillfully written Prelude and Toccata in G minor.

MAX VOGRICH (1852–1916) (Austrian). His *Staccato-Caprice*

---

[1] An imaginary appeal from Teresa: "Please come, Eugen, your children and my children are quarreling with our children," went a merry round in Berlin.

enjoyed real popularity. His most important contribution is his Schumann edition (Schirmer).

MORIZ ROSENTHAL (1862–1946) (Austrian). One of the famous pianists of the post-Liszt era. Wrote a light virtuoso piece called "Papillons" and thought it necessary to play Chopin's "Minute" Waltz in double thirds, a decidedly doubtful achievement artistically.

ERICH KORNGOLD (1897–1957) (Austrian). Wrote two good sonatas in his later teens, but his *Fairy Pictures* were written and published when he was eleven.]

RICHARD STRAUSS (1864–1949) This revolutionary genius, so famous for his symphonic poems, operas, and songs, has unfortunately written very little for piano. The most important work is the *Burleske,* a concert piece with orchestra, not extravagantly difficult, effective and rewarding. The title misleads most pianists into rushing hastily over its beautiful lyrical stretches. Next in value is the fine Sonata in E flat for piano and violin, one of Strauss's few essays in chamber music. Here he shows mastery of the sonata form he so seldom uses. I often heard him play it in his early days at Weimar and have wondered since why so well equipped a pianist did not give more of his talent to the instrument. The accompaniments to his songs are masterly, and there is an idiomatic piano part in the small orchestration (for only thirty-seven instruments) of *Ariadne auf Naxos.* The *Music to Tennyson's Enoch Arden,* a melodrama for narrator with piano accompaniment, should also be noted; Strauss often played it with Ludwig Wüllner reciting the words. The only solo pieces of any moment are the *Stimmungsbilder,* Opus 9, containing the romantic little *Träumerei.*

Strauss was the legitimate successor of Liszt and Wagner. In his opera *Elektra* (too gloomy ever to be widely popular) he carried the use of leading motives to its last possibility, and in later works, notably in *Der Rosenkavalier,* relaxed the rigor of the system.

ARNOLD SCHÖNBERG (1874–1951) This distinguished composer has undergone astonishing transformations, beginning by carrying romanticism to a new peak in his *Verklärte Nacht* for string sestet (also arranged for string orchestra) and outdoing Wagner in the tremendous score of the *Gurrelieder,* abjuring romanticism completely in the Chamber Symphony and *Pierrot Lunaire* to adopt atonality, and finally creating the "twelve-tone" system of his later works.

Even in an essay on piano literature it is necessary to attempt some

explanation of the twelve-tone system of construction, especially
because Schönberg's Three Pieces, Opus 11, Six Little Piano Pieces,
Opus 19, and Five Piano Pieces, Opus 23, the Suite, Opus 25, and the
Two Pieces, Opus 33, illustrate its evolution.

In modal music, tones are arranged in relation to a Greek or
church mode, in classical music in relation to a given key or tonality as
represented by its tonic chord and diatonic scale. The twelve-tone system offers a substitute for the idea of key-relationship. The composer
uses for each piece a pattern or "row" in which he arranges the
twelve tones of the chromatic scale in a chosen order. All themes or
motives and the harmonies of the piece are derived from adjacent
notes of the pattern, which may be used in its direct form, in inversion, in the "crab" (the "row" read backwards), and in the inversion
of the "crab." For instance, the pattern for the Passacaglia in the
first act of Alban Berg's opera Wozzeck is:

Ex. 302

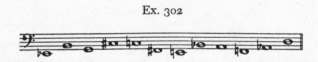

The first five notes (a) of the inversion of the series, (b) of the crab,
and (c) of the inversion of the crab, are given below:

Ex. 303

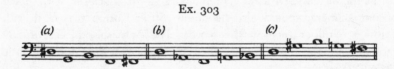

Berg based his entire opera Lulu on a single twelve-tone pattern!

The tones may be set in any octave of pitch (not necessarily within
the limits of one octave) and in any desired rhythm to form motives,
and the spelling will vary enharmonically as a matter of convenience.
As it is a main object of the system to escape the limitations of tonality, it would obviously be inappropriate to construct a series containing two successive consonant intervals or an order of tones such
as D, F sharp, C, both instantly suggestive of key relationship.

The twelve-note system offers a perfect vehicle for atonality.
Schönberg protests against the term "atonal" as meaningless, pro-
posing "pantonal" instead. But atonality (absence of key) is a good
noun and atonal a correct adjective accurately defined by Webster's

Dictionary.[2] The system is no more complicated or empirical than the polyphony of a Bach fugue or the harmonic and formal structure of a Beethoven sonata, though it has been accused of being involved, mechanical, and cerebral. It is simply a technique of composition, and works written within it must, like all others, be judged primarily by the value and perceptibilty of their ideas. Schönberg's music is debatable because it has not yet established its perceptibility either to schooled ears or to the untrained listener; to most it is still unacceptable. Time must decide whether it leads into a blind alley or opens a new gospel. Schönberg is an artist of immense talent, originality, and discipline, and he has able disciples to carry on his work, among them Alban Berg, Anton von Webern, Egon Wellesz, and the American Adolph Weiss. [Many musical people now will find the word "unacceptable" dated and no longer would apply it to the music of Schönberg. The man is gone, but he left his heritage for music history to accept it complete, or in part. Schönberg is one of the great musical figures of the first half of the twentieth century. His musicianship, his uncanny craftsmanship, his honesty in expressing himself are the elements of the undeniable influence he has had upon the evolution of music. His most famous disciples, the late Alban Berg, the late Anton Webern, and Egon Wellesz followed in his footsteps, but transformed their master's ways and means by their own newer conceptions:

ANTON WEBERN (1883–1945) (Austrian). His contributions to the piano repertory are a slight, short set of extremely dissonant Variations (twelve tone) and an early piano quintet. Unappreciated during his early lifetime except by a circle of friends, his chamber music and symphonic works later began to attract the attention of the profession and the press. He was fêted by the avante-grade at some of the European festivals. I happened to be present at the famous concert-hall scandal of the Salzburg Festival in 1923, when some ill-behaved anti-twelvetoners interrupted the performance of the Webern String Quartet. Police had to clear the hall and the concert did not continue. A major International Webern Festival presenting practically all of his music took place in Seattle, Washington, in May 1962. A recently published book, *The Death of Anton Webern,* by Hans Moldenhauer, is the clarifying tribute to a composer whose forceful but sensitive creative ability, unhappy life, and tragic death finally have found the sympathy

[2] Observe that omission of a key signature does not in itself indicate atonality; often it is a wise expedient to simplify the notation of accidentals. Walter Piston's Sonata in F minor for violin and piano, for instance, bears no key signatures.

and understanding of our generation. During the last years of Webern's life he dropped the "von" from his name.

ALBAN BERG (1885–1935) (Austrian). Early influences of Wagner and Mahler can be heard in his only works written for the piano; the Sonata, op. 1. Its constant chromaticism and restless lyrical expression demand elasticity of musical and pianistic execution. Berg became world-renowned through his opera *Wozzeck*, one of the most dissonant but powerful operas ever written.

PAUL HINDEMITH (1895–1963), born in Germany, one of the leading composers of the twentieth century. His contribution to opera, the symphony, oratorio, and chamber music was enormous. For the piano he wrote two concertos, the *Four Temperaments* for piano and orchestra, three sonatas, a sonata for two pianos, the *Suite 1922*, twelve Easy Pieces, Seven Waltzes for four hands, a piano quintet, sonatas for each orchestral instrument with piano, and, finally, the *Ludus Tonalis*, a very important if not always inspired imitation of the preludes and fugues of *The Well-Tempered Clavier*.]

Hungarian Composers

Hungary has recently produced several notable composers. Béla Bartók discovered new methods of expression, and Zoltán Kodály follows him in a milder spirit. Egon Wellesz and Alexander Jemnitz are disciples of Schönberg. Ernst von Dohnányi conforms to classical tradition; he and Bartók are by far the more generous contributors to the piano literature.

STEPHEN HELLER (1813–88) Without any good reason Heller is sometimes listed as an English composer. He was born in Hungary and died at Paris, was educated in Vienna, settled in Augsburg, toured in Germany, lived and taught a great deal in Paris, and during his life made only two trips to England, where his Studies and refined salon pieces became immensely popular. Schumann praised his talent, Liszt and Chopin were among his friends. The most familiar of his many books of Studies are Opus 45, Opus 46, and Opus 47. The *Art of Phrasing*, Opus 16, is musically more valuable, containing among other numbers a Nocturne in C-sharp minor equal or superior to any of Field's. The *Promenades d'un solitaire* and the easy Tarantelles in

A flat and A minor were at one time played all over the world. Heller wrote exclusively for the piano, and the melodiousness and very moderate difficulty of his works made him the delight of the amateur. One finds not the slightest trace of nationalism in his writing.

BÉLA BARTÓK (1881–1945) The most prominent representative of his country, Bartók is doubly distinguished by his compositions and by his untiring researches into the origins of Hungarian music. His book, *Hungarian Folk Music*, published in 1931, effectually dispelled the long-standing confusion between the genuine Magyar lore and the gypsy incrustation. His compatriot and collaborator Kodály aided in the collection of thousands of peasant folk songs and dances, a labor of many years. As a musicologist, therefore, Bartók is already firmly established. His compositions are more open to dispute and must await the verdict of time. Original, nationalistic, and deeply convinced, they often sound so bitter that it is difficult to hear them with enjoyment. It is impossible to classify them or to associate them with any school of thought, though they are influenced by the intricate rhythms of Stravinsky and a fondness for polytonality. Their melodic and harmonic substance is strong but primitive. The most important works are six string quartets and abundant piano music. Bartók also wrote an opera, a ballet, and orchestral pieces, but produced no one great composition by which he is universally known.

Bartók came to America in 1940 and at the time of his death was pursuing his researches in folk music at Columbia University as honorary professor.

The piano music exhibits all Bartók's qualities. They are seen at their best and worst in the six volumes of the *Mikrokosmos,* a set of 153 progressive pieces intended as an introduction to modern idioms of harmony and rhythm. Here teacher and student have at their disposal elementary five-finger sketches, simple folk songs and dances, essays in polytonality, diversified rhythms—pure melody rubbing shoulders with clashing discord. Many of the set are extremely charming and as a whole it is a refreshing change from the run of stupid teaching literature usually fed to our youth.

Many pieces of Bartók are technically quite easy and none are very difficult. The *Eighty-five Little Pieces for Children* and the *Ten Easy Pieces* are suitable for beginners. A large part of the *Mikrokosmos* is designed for first- and second-year study. More advanced but within the reach of the average player are the *Fourteen Bagatelles,* Opus 6, the Sonatina, and the *Fifteen Hungarian Peasant Songs.* The

Bear Dance and *Allegro barbaro* are good concert pieces, interesting and intelligible in spite of their clangor. The *Music for two pianos and percussion*, often played by Bartók with his wife, is one of the latest and most debatable works.

[It is interesting to compare Dr. Hutcheson's evaluation of Bartók with the position this pathfinder and experimenter in new sounds occupies now. I personally have known Bartók's style of music since 1909, when I played in Berlin five of the *Ten Easy Pieces* written in 1908. I believed in him then, and I consider him now the most consistent writer of our era. His dissonant style is always logical. He composed for every branch of musical literature: opera, ballets, three piano concertos, a sonata, two violin and piano sonatas *Music for two pianos and percussion* (not debatable any more!), the Suite op. 14, the Sonatine, the two Romanian dances, etc., etc. The early "Bear Dance" and the later "Diary of a Fly" are musts for every young player. The *Mikrokosmos* is his gift to the learning youth of today. The Chicago Fine Arts Quartet programmed for their last European tour all of the Beethoven quartets and the six quartets of Bartók. As to his symphonic masterwork, played all over the world, it is the Concerto for Orchestra. This marvel of invention and orchestration alone stamps him as one of the great of our time.]

ERNST VON DOHNÁNYI (1877–1960)   In striking contrast to Bartók, Dohnányi is the least nationalistically modern of Hungarian composers. Most of his work might be that of a German; the influence of Brahms is distinctly apparent, and in some early pieces he forgetfully borrows whole themes from Schubert. He has written a ballet, a one-act opera, and symphonies, but is best known for his piano compositions. The latter include Four Pieces, Opus 2, a fine Passacaglia, Opus 6, Four Rhapsodies, Opus 11, *Winterreigen* (*Ten Bagatelles*), Opus 13, *Humoresques,* Opus 17, and Six Concert Études, Opus 28. The Concerto in E minor has not held its own, but the delightful *Variations on a Nursery Song* (*Ah! vous dirai-je, maman*) for piano obbligato and orchestra rank with the best pieces of the kind. The Quintet in C minor and the Sonata for violin and piano, Opus 21, are excellent chamber music. Dohnányi writes skillfully, pianistically, and with humor, in classic form. For the Hungarian element in his music we must turn to the *Variations on a Hungarian Theme*, Opus 29, the *Ruralia Hungarica*, Opus 32ª, and the Second Rhapsody, in which are found cimbalon effects. None other of the rhapsodies resembles in the least those of Liszt; the last takes for its theme the *Dies Irae*.

Dohnányi's most popular pieces are the Capriccio in B minor, No. 4 of Opus 2, the Second and Third Rhapsodies, in F-sharp minor and C, and the last Étude, a Capriccio in F minor. A charming and adept concert arrangement of the Waltz from Delibes's *Naila* also deserves mention. None of these are easy, so they are recommended to advanced amateurs only.

Bohemian Composers

Two Bohemians, neither of whom wrote extensively for piano, demand special attention.

BEDŘICH (Frederick) SMETANA (1824–84) made it his mission in life to produce a series of works expressing the Czech spirit; these included eight operas, of which *The Bartered Bride* is familiar to American audiences, and a cycle of six symphonic poems entitled *My Country* and containing *The Moldau*, also well known. In his later years he was afflicted with deafness and nervous disorder; he died in an asylum. His piano pieces are all in small form. The best of them are probably the *Czech Dances* (without opus number) and the concert étude *By the Seashore*, Opus 17.

ANTONIN DVOŘÁK (1841–1904) carried on the efforts of Smetana to form a national school of Czech music. Largely self-taught through study of classical scores, he remained comparatively immune to modern influences. His work is prevailingly happy and naïve. Among his important compositions are operas, the Czech oratorio *St. Ludmilla*, the *Stabat Mater*, and the overture *Husitzka*. Brahms befriended him and helped to secure German publishers for his music. He spent some fruitful years in America, teaching at the National Conservatory of New York, urging the adoption of Negro folk song as a foundation for a school of American music, and composing his famous *New World* Symphony, in which he added example to precept.

Dvořák's most characteristic piano music will be found in the *Slavonic Dances* for four hands, the *Humoresques*, Opus 101 (No. 7 of these became almost as popular as *Songs My Mother Taught Me*), and the Piano Quintet. The last-named introduces a *Dumka* (*Lament*), imported as an art form from Little Russia. [The difficult Piano Concerto in G minor, op. 3, has been revived during the past few years with considerable success. It is good music, nationally influenced, vital, and appealing.]

Swiss Composers

[EMILE R. BLANCHET (1877–1943) was a first-class pianist and a composer of considerable originality. Some of his works are difficult for the average performer (especially the exotic *Turkish Pieces*). Two *Conzertstücke* and a Ballade for piano and orchestra are brilliant and effective numbers. His many Études are full of interesting polyphonic and polyrythmical problems, and the fourth book of his "*64 Préludes*" (Eschig) is devoted to last-word exploitation of the left hand (which the French have baptized "*gauche,*" meaning "clumsy, awkward"). Clever students and young as well as some older pianists might take the trouble to invert all of these ingenious exercises symmetrically for the right hand.

OTHMAR SCHOECK (1886–1957), well known in Europe for his six operas, violin concerto and sonatas, string quartets, choral works, and, especially, his several song cycles and many separate songs, wrote little but well for the piano. Recommended are two pieces, the finely lyrical two-voiced *Consolation* and a stunning *Toccata*. There is also a set of *Ritornelles et Fughettes*.

ARTHUR HONEGGER (1892–1955), born in Le Havre, France, of Swiss parents. Though he lived most of his life in Paris, he retained his Swiss citizenship until his death. He wrote a charming, witty Concertino for piano and orchestra. Among his many pieces for solo piano, the most important are Toccata and Variations, the Prelude, Arioso and Fughetta on the name of Bach (a must for young pianists), *Sept pièces bréves and Le Cahier romand* (Colombo, formerly Ricordi). Curious duettists might look into his arrangements for four hands, one piano, of some of his symphonic works, especially *Pacific 231,* the sensational railroad piece of 1924.

WILLY BURKHARD (1900–1955). In addition to his violin-piano and cello-piano sonatas, he wrote Six Preludes, op. 99, and "Eight Easy Pieces" (Bärenreiter), all very much recommended.]

Scandinavian Composers

EDVARD GRIEG (1843–1907) Norwegian folk music found its greatest exponent in Grieg. Lyrically highly gifted, he wrote many songs of real beauty and many small piano pieces which in their day were enormously popular. Had his application been equal to his talent he might have left us greater works of lasting value. But his studies at the Leipzig Conservatory bore little fruit; he never mastered the larger forms, and one might think he did not care to take them very seriously, judging by the loose structure of his Piano Sonata in E minor and the three for piano and violin. The Piano Concerto, still a favorite with the public, is much better except for the last movement, which is disfigured by a sickly middle theme and a bombastic coda. The ambitious *Ballade* starts well with a melancholy theme typically Scandinavian, but like the Concerto goes rampant at the end. The smaller pieces are charming, for Grieg is at his best when simple and unassuming.

[I must disagree with Dr. Hutcheson regarding the Concerto in A minor, written in 1861, which has had an unusual revival during the last few years. If well played as to its spirit, proportion, and continuity, its classical though limited sonata form is bound to please. The "sickly" middle theme of the last movement is a well-known and beloved Bavarian folk song. As to the coda, is the Grieg the only concerto with a bombastic ending? To me, neither the Concerto nor the Ballade goes rampant. Grieg may not be a great composer, but after eight measures from his pen you know who the author is. There are dozens of attractive gems in the ten sets of *Lyrical Pieces*. In Book 3 you will find "Butterfly," "Erotikon," and "To Spring," in Book 5 "The March of the Dwarfs." Three of his best repertoire numbers are to be found in Book 6, op. 57: "Secret," "She Dances," and "Nostalgia." The Nocturne in C and the *Norwegian Bridal Procession* are also popular. Grieg himself arranged the *Holberg* and *Peer Gynt* symphonic suites for piano solo.]

Other Scandinavian composers who should be listed are:

NIELS GADE, Danish (1817–90) Schumann's high opinion of Gade was never justified; the Trio in F, *Novelettes*, and *Aquarelles* (the last formerly used as easy teaching pieces) are pale reflections of Mendelssohn. Apart from Grieg, in fact, Scandinanvian music has remained too firmly under Teutonic influence to gather much strength of it own.

EMIL SJÖGREN, Swedish (1853–1918), wrote two sets of piano pieces, *Auf der Wanderung* and *Erotikon*, and sonatas for piano and violin, showing more individuality than most of his countrymen.

CHRISTIAN SINDING, Norwegian (1856–1941), was very prolific, and there was a time when every amateur played the *Rustle of Spring* or the *Marche grotesque*. His Piano Quintet raised a sensation by a theme in consecutive fifths and octaves occurring in the finale, a very daring reversion to the style of the *Organum* for its time. Sinding told me a pretty story of his relations with the firm of Peters in Leipzig, who published most of his works, acquiring some early pieces for nominal sums. When he lived in Berlin he ordered large quantities of scores and sheet music from Leipzig without ever receiving a bill. After several years he wrote requesting an account and remarking that he must owe thousands of marks. On this the house duly rendered a bill that did indeed reach some such figure, but with a notation that the debt was "canceled in view of the large profits from the sale of the *Rustle of Spring*." How different from the scurvy treatment of Schubert by Diabelli!

[I had heard that on the occasion of the millionth copy sold Peters sent Sinding a specially decorated copy of the *Rustle* with thanks instead of a check for 50,000 marks. Sinding wrote a piano concerto, a violin-piano sonata, and one for piano solo that he dedicated to me. Unfortunately these larger works were written under such influence of Wagner that their performances in public would have encouraged discouraging thoughts by the press. Grieg and Sinding studied in Leipzig at the same time. Whereas the latter could not resist the power of Wagnerian themes, Grieg was satisfied with adopting their chromaticism while remaining himself.

JEAN SIBELIUS (1865–1957). Although ten attractive piano pieces were published, they failed to attract much attention. His *Valse Triste* and the Romance in D flat became very popular and still are.

SELIM PALMGREN (1878–1951) composed a great deal for the piano. *May Night, The Swan*, the very original *Bird Song*, and *The Sea* are often heard in the conservatory studios. His ambitious and sympathetic piano concerto, *The River*, has seldom been heard in the United States.]

Italian Composers

The Italians have always been lovers of opera and song. Since the days of the old clavecinists they have accomplished little in composition for the piano, though the instrument was invented by an Italian. In the classical period, as we have seen, Clementi enjoyed a moderate reputation, but it was far surpassed by Rossini and other writers of opera. In modern times, too, no writer for piano has approached the genius or fame of Verdi and Puccini. It is to be noted, moreover, that many of the composers now to be mentioned have contributed more to dramatic and sacred music than to the literature of the piano. Most of them have been conservative in style, and only in Busoni, Malipiero, and Casella do we encounter advanced tendencies and originality of thought.

GIOVANNI SGAMBATI (1841–1914) wrote a piano concerto and elegant pieces like the *Gavotte* in A-flat minor and the *Vecchio Menuetto*. He transcribed Gluck's flute melody from *Orpheus* and the *Chant lituane* of Chopin.

MARCO E. BOSSI (1861–1925) is known for many children's pieces.

GIUSEPPE MARTUCCI (1856–1909) was to some extent influenced by Brahms. His work is conventional and lacks distinction. Ricordi publishes several volumes of his compositions, the first and best containing twenty études and concert pieces.

FERRUCCIO BUSONI (1866–1924), though born in Italy, spent almost all his life in Germany. His original compositions are puzzling in the extreme. Scholarly, modern, finely constructed, they yet fail to sound well and give the impression of being more sought than inspired. The piano works vary in complexity from the simple *Little Ballet Scene* in F and the Sonatina in C to the huge *Fantasia contrappuntistica* and a concerto that calls for a final chorus. [Busoni's Piano Concerto is a colossal work of seventy-five minutes' duration. It demands of the pianist both the possible and the quasi impossible. Whatever Busoni wrote for the piano is pianistically supremely interesting and at times very original. I felt very honored when he dedicated his First Sonatina to me.] Busoni is less likely to be remembered for any of these than for his admirable transcriptions of Bach's organ pieces and Chaconne for violin. Here he comes near saying the last word in the art of arrangement; one may read with profit his remarks on the subject appended to his edition of *The Well-Tempered Clavier*. The Chaconne is treated not as an expansion of a violin solo but as a reduction of an imaginary orchestral score. Among the organ transcriptions are the C major Toccata, the Prelude and Fugue in D, the Toccata and Fugue in D minor, the Prelude and Fugue in E flat (*St. Anne's Fugue*), and nine of the lovely Choral Preludes. A delightful *Duettino Concertante after Mozart* for two pianos proves that he could on occasion command a lighter touch.

Busoni's editions of Bach's Inventions and *Well-Tempered Clavier* show profound love and understanding of the great master, though they are over-analytical and somewhat peremptory in directions for performance. He also undertook an edition of the complete works of Liszt for Breitkopf & Härtel. His keenness of mind may be observed in his short *Sketch for a New Esthetic of Music*. In this tiny volume he suggests a notation abolishing the use of accidentals and makes a logical inquiry into the possibility of dividing the whole tone into three parts as well as into half- and quarter-tones.

In Busoni's playing intellectuality often overcame emotion, so that with all his fame abroad as a pianist he had no great success in America. Our audiences, I think, were made uncomfortably aware of their inferiority to his mental level.

OTTORINO RESPIGHI (1879–1936) is better known for his revival of old Italian pieces in the collection of *Antique Dances and Airs for Lute* and transcriptions of Frescobaldi and other clavecinists than for his *Concerto in the Mixolydian Mode* and *Preludes on Gregorian Melodies*. He is also better known for his orchestral works than for any of his piano pieces.

ALFREDO CASELLA (1883–1947), founder of the Italian Society of Modern Music, pianist, conductor, and composer, wrote with great versatility. In the *Pezzi Infantili*, playable only by sophisticated youngsters, we find such strange contrasts as a *Valse diatonique* on white keys only, a Canon on black keys only, a *Carillon* with the left hand on black and the right hand on white keys, and a British jig (*Giga*) diabolically harmonized. One of Casella's best large pieces for piano is the difficult *Sinfonia Arioso Toccata*, Opus 59, prevailingly dissonant but ending modally. A *Notte alta* (*Poema musicale*) is exclusively atonal and would be excessively difficult to read but for the judicious omission of all unnecessary and "precautionary" accidentals. These works show great strength of invention and workmanship, and deserve the attention of virtuosi able to cope with their difficulties. Casella made a consistent and noteworthy effort to found a modern Italian school of composition. [Casella wrote two excellent works for piano and orchestra, a *Partita* in three movements (*Sinfonia, Passacaglia,* and *Burlesca*), a most worthy vehicle for an accomplished performer avoiding the usual, and one built upon Scarlatti themes and known as *Scarlattiana.*

AMILCARE ZANELLA (1873–1949) composed a *Fantasia e Fugato* (four subjects) for piano and orchestra, a piano trio, and many smaller pieces. His *Tempo di Menuetto* is an example of excellent, delightful keyboard writing.

RICCARDO PICK-MANGIAGALLI (1882–1949). His *Sortilegi,* a symphonic poem for piano and orchestra, is a brilliantly written work. So are all of his many pieces for piano solo, of which the *Dance of Olaf* is still popular.

LUIGI DALLAPICCOLA (1904–   ) has written a *Sonatina Canonica* for solo piano and *Piccolo Concerto* for piano and orchestra.]

Spanish Composers

Spanish music has been influenced in turn by the liturgy of the Byzantine Church, by Moorish invasion, and by gypsy strollers. Like other countries, too, Spain succumbed for a long period to the spell of Italian opera. Yet it has always preserved a peculiarly distinctive character, never borrowing from outside sources without putting its own stamp on them. In early times TOMÁS LUIS DE VICTORIA (1535 or 1540–1611), called by Pedrell "the Spanish Bach," wrote church music of the purest type. His complete works were edited much later by FELIPE PEDRELL (1841–1922). Pedrell, not very successful as a writer of operas, is regarded as the leading archæological authority of his country. He contended steadfastly that folk song should be the foundation of any national school of music, a doctrine accepted in theory and largely put into practice by Albéniz, Granados, and Falla. In modern times the various provinces have cultivated particular forms of song and dance: in Andalusia the beautiful old *cante hondo* is being displaced by the lighter *flamenco;* the boisterous *jota* has its home in Aragon; Castile prefers the gay *bolero* and *seguidilla;* and a more serious tone is favored in Catalonia.

[PADRE ANTONIO SOLER (1729–1783), little-known, though one of the greatest, keyboard composers of the eighteenth century. His music is daring, original, and sensitive, reminding one of the style of Domenico Scarlatti, with whom he may have studied. He wrote a great many sonatas, some minuets, rondos, and polaccas, all of which he performed on the pianoforte in preference to the harpsichord. There is an edition (1957) on the market of some of the best sonatas (Mills Music). It is very well made and is published in three volumes. An informative Preface by the editor, Frederick Marvin, is welcome and of help in the performance.]

The national instrument of Spain is the guitar. Unless one has heard the playing of Segovia and the Aguilar Lute Quartet it is difficult to imagine the beauty and variety inherent in plucked strings. I hope I may say without offense to my friends Carlos Salzedo and Marcel Grandjany that the lute and the guitar, in the hands of masters like themselves, reveal qualities not to be despised by the more lordly harp.

Castanets are an indispensable accompaniment to the Spanish dancer. Their capacities, too, can hardly be appreciated without remembering the delicate nuances of inflection, accent, climax, and personal expression drawn from homely wooden clappers by the art of La Argentina.

The trouble with Spanish music is that it is too exclusively Spanish. The best composers have not yet succeeded in writing universally. This would seem to be a matter of deliberate choice, not of natural limitation, for Albéniz, Granados, and Falla all gave indications of higher powers than they exercised. The tragic death of Granados cut short a career that might have gone very far, and Falla passed away in 1946. The brightest hope for the future probably rests in the Latin-American Carlos Chávez, of whom more later.

However this may be, there is some color to the assertion sometimes made that the best Spanish music has been written by Frenchmen. Bizet's *Carmen* is universal music, and Chabrier's *España,* Debussy's *Soirée dans Grenade,* and Ravel's *Alborado del gracioso* are not narrowly national. If Spanish music could forgo its endless, some-times maddening repetitions of short phrases and catchy rhythms it would move in the direction of a more symphonic development. The way to a significant school of opera lies clear, and what better subjects could be desired than *Don Quixote, The Cid, Gil Blas, Don Juan,* and the plays of Calderón? Some day, no doubt, Spain will produce music comparable with the superb achievements of Cervantes, Velázquez, El Greco, and Goya.

So far Spanish piano music does little more than reflect the lighter aspects of national character. We easily see in it a people devoted to love-making, dancing, and the arena of the bullfight, but as a rule it fails to do justice to the dignity and honor of the Spanish gentleman or the deeper romance and passion of common life.

Isaac Albéniz (1860–1909), began life as a child prodigy. He studied intermittently with Gevaert and Brassin in Brussels, with Jadassohn and Reinecke in Leipzig, and with d'Indy and Paul Dukas in Paris. He enjoyed the friendship of Liszt, Debussy, and Rubinstein, accompanying the last-named on his tour in America. After teaching without much enthusiasm in Barcelona and Madrid, he spent the rest of his days in London and Paris. His restless disposition evinces it-self in his music. The early works were rightly judged by himself of small value; he once sold the popular *Pavana* for the price of admission to a bullfight. Albert Lockwood speaks of "the welter of tangos, habaneras, and seguidillas which dripped too easily from his pen." In Paris he met Debussy, and the acquaintance led him to adopt a more modern style, culminating in a fine set of piano pieces published under the collective title of *Iberia*. But he never completely fulfilled his natural gift or attained a definitive musical personality. J. B. Trend says in *Grove's Dictionary,* fourth edition, that "at the back of his mind there is generally a guitar-player who ends with the 'Phrygian cadence,' a dancer whose castanets are always syncopating against each other, and sometimes (as in *Triana*) the shake and bang of a tambourine."

Iberia is Albéniz's masterwork. Its idealized pictures of Spanish scenes and moods and its superior technical workmanship raise it far above the normal salon level of his compositions. The titles of the twelve pieces are *Evocación, El Puerto, Fête-Dieu à Seville, Rondeña, Almería, Triana, El Albaicín, El Polo, Lavapiés, Málaga, Jérez,* and *Eritaña. Triana,* a difficult concert piece, is the most popular of the set; the name refers to the gypsy quarter of Seville. *Evocación* combines a Navarrese *jota* with an Andalusian *cante hondo*, and there is a similar instance in *Almería. El Puerto, El Albaicín,* and *Eritaña* possess strong individuality.

Parts of *Iberia* have been orchestrated by E. Fernandez Arbós, distinguished violinist and conductor. *Catalonia, La Vega, Navarra,* and *Azulejos* form a sequel to *Iberia;* the last of these, left unfinished, was completed by Granados.

In all, Albéniz wrote about 250 piano pieces, mostly in small form, characterized by strongly conflicting rhythms and the use of harmonies based on intervals of fourths. Many of them enjoyed an ephemeral popularity. The *Suite espagnole* and the *Canti d'Espagne* contain easy numbers for the amateur, and the graceful Tango in D, the *Zortzico* in E (8 time) and the brilliant, not difficult Seguidilla in F sharp, may be selected for special recommendation. Five early sonatas and a concerto have little of interest to offer. Albéniz was a fine pianist and always wrote well for his instrument.

ENRIQUE GRANADOS (1867–1916), like Albéniz, was a gifted pianist and wrote extensively for his instrument. He studied composition with Pedrell and piano with Bériot in Paris. Settling in Barcelona, he produced an opera, founded a Society for Classical Concerts, played in Spain and Rome, and established his reputation as a composer by the publication of his *Goyescas,* a set of pieces named after paintings and tapestries of Goya. The *Goyescas* were later elaborated into a less successful opera of the same name and performed at the Metropolitan Opera of New York during his tour of America in 1916. He met a tragic death on his way home to Spain when the *Sussex* was torpedoed by a German submarine.

The style of Granados is simpler but more original than that of Albéniz. No seeker after modernism, he was satisfied to employ known harmonies, escaping the influence of Debussy and other contemporaries. Only in piano technique did he explore new effects; the *Goyescas* are formidably difficult and the arrangements of Scarlatti's sonatas modern and complicated. On the other hand the four volumes of *Spanish Dances* are easy, natural, and at the same time more genuinely Spanish than any others that I know. In his best works Granados frees himself from the usual limitations of national idiom and addresses himself to a larger world. J. B. Trend observes in them "stateliness, elegance, finish, and an extraordinary sense of poetry," and Lockwood praises their "elemental breadth and sweep."

Goyescas: Los Majos Enamorados (Pieces after Goya). *Los Majos Enamorados* consists of six pieces with the following titles:

1. *Los Requiebros* (Flattery)
2. *Coloquios en la reja* (Love Duet)
3. *El Fandango del candíl.*
4. *Quejas ó la maya y el ruiseñor* (Laments or the Maiden and the Nightingale)
5. *El Amor y la muerte* (Ballad)
6. *Epílogo. Serenata del espectro.*

The suite has a program, telling a story of love and death, epitomized in the fifth number. *The Maiden and the Nightingale* is the gem of the collection.

[The *Goyescas* suite of seven pieces has a program, telling a story of love and death epitomized in the number "*The Maiden and the Nightingale.*" This gem of lyrical and passionate expression can be bracketed with No. 3, the rousing, brilliantly rhythmical *Fandango,* the two in sequence forming an unusually fine program number.]

Besides the *Spanish Dances* the amateur should look at *A la Cubana,* Opus 36, the *Impromptu,* Opus 39, and the *Valse de concert,* Opus 35. Some of the best dances are contained in the third volume.

Those of us who had the good fortune to meet Granados during his stay in America were charmed by his courtesy and polished conversation no less than by the inimitable though entirely unpretentious manner of his playing. The news of his untimely death, coming while his personality was so fresh in our hearts, shocked musicians profoundly and added a curse to the horrors of submarine warfare.

MANUEL DE FALLA (1876–1946) stands head and shoulders above all other recent Spanish composers. His opera *La Vida breve,* his ballets *El Amor brujo (Wedded by Witchcraft)* and *El Sombrero de tres picos (Three-Cornered Hat),* and the marionette opera *El Retablo de Maese Pedro (Master Peter's Puppet-Show)* place him in the front rank of modern writers. The extraordinarily interesting *Retablo de Maese Pedro,* based on an episode in *Don Quixote,* was produced in New York by the League of Composers in 1926 and calls urgently for revival.

Falla's works for piano are few, the best being the *Fantasía Baetica*[3] and the four *Pièces espagnoles (Aragonese, Cubana, Montañesa,* and *Andaluza).* He also wrote a *Homenaje (Homage)* to the memory of Debussy for guitar, playable on the piano, and (for

---

[3] Baetica is the Latin name for Andalusia.

Wanda Landowska) a Concerto for harpsichord and small orchestra. All these are surpassed by the *Noches en los jardines de España (Nights in the Gardens of Spain)*, a truly symphonic work in which the piano, as in d'Indy's *Mountain* Symphony, is treated as more than an obbligato and less than a solo part. It is unfortunate that the majority of piano students know Falla only by his *Ritual Fire Dance*, a very poor arrangement of an excerpt from *El Amor brujo*.

[JOAQUÍN TURINA (1882–1949) wrote tasteful salon music: *Contes d'Espagne, Femmes d'Espagne*, and two suites—*Miniatures* and *Circus*. Both of these latter are delightful and are much used.]

No worthy successor to Albéniz, Granados, and Falla is yet in sight.

Latin-American Music

Long before English colonists set foot in America the Spaniards had introduced music, founded schools where it was taught, and encouraged the Indians to take part in the services of the Church, to develop their primitive instruments, and to compose. The Spaniards were in turn affected by Indian folk song, based on a pentatonic scale and chiefly monodic, though signs are not lacking that some form of harmony was known. They made scholarly studies and collections of Indian tunes and dances and used them freely for local color. When Negroes were brought into South America their idiom was added to the mixture, especially in Cuba and the West Indies. Italian opera at first dominated the stage and the early emigrant composers wrote their operas to Italian texts. Toward the end of the nineteenth century, however, they had thrown off the Italian yoke and asserted their independence. In course of time each country has adopted native features of its own, so that an expert can now distinguish Argentinian music from that of Cuba, Chile, Mexico, or Portuguese Brazil. Happily the Spanish character always prevails, even in dances like the tango (closely allied to the habanera), rumba, and conga, and songs like the *corrido, modinka, saudado,* and *triste*.

The "good neighbor" policy inaugurated after the first World War is encouraged by the United States government chiefly for political reasons. It is no less beneficial and necessary in the world of art, and the duty of observing it rests chiefly on us. For it was inevitable that the Hispano-American republics should turn to Europe for their tradition, study, and inspiration, whereas it was hardly excusable of North America so long to ignore a deep-rooted culture older than its own. We had perforce welcomed such artists as Teresa Carreño, Guiomar Novaës, Carlos Chávez, and Antonia Mercé (La Argentina). But not until quite recently have our composers openly admitted an obligation to their southern neighbors. George Gershwin's *Cuban* Overture, Aaron Copland's *El Salón Mexico*, Harl McDonald's *Rumba* Symphony, and Paul Bowles's *Huepangos* may be cited as graceful gestures of recognition and partial acknowledgment of the welcome extended in early days to the American pianist Gottschalk and later to singers of the Metropolitan Opera Company of New York. "Goodwill" trips to South America have been made by Copland and others, not forgetting an ensemble of woodwind players who toured in 1942 under the auspices of the League of Composers. Arthur Rubinstein has played much of the piano music of Villa-Lobos. Morton Gould and Henry Cowell have incorporated Mexican rhythms and Latin-American folk tunes in their work, and Stravinsky and Prokofiev have made occasional use of the primitive Indian instruments in their scores.

Most of the Latin-American music for piano does not rise beyond the salon type, so that a list of composers for the instrument represents the talent of the continent very imperfectly. The reader should remember that this apparently light output is weighted by important orchestral and choral works and operas.

[The musical situation has changed tremendously during the last ten to fifteen years. Latin America has come to the fore musically. Some of the best American symphony orchestras have invited prominent Latin-American orchestral leaders and composers to be guest conductors, and many of the most successful Latin-American instrumental artists have come to play for our audiences and our press. Important works from the pens of Latin Americans have been heard by us and found great favor. Carlos Chávez of Mexico has been a professional visitor to the United States for many years as a much appreciated conductor and eminent composer. Francesco Mignone, the Brazilian, the Argentine Alberto Ginastera, and the Chilean Domingo Santa Cruz have come north on several occasions, and the foremost Brazilian musician, Heitor Villa-Lobos, was a constant guest in New York. On the other hand, many of our finest Symphony orchestras have toured South and Central America, and our conductors, as well as scores of other American and European artists, have helped to make the concert world of our southern neighbors a richer one. The music life of Rio de Janeiro, Buenos Aires, and other Latin American cities is vying with the New York standards of activity. Opera is flourishing in many Latin-American cities.

HEITOR VILLA-LOBOS (1894–1959), the great music educator of Brazil and the curator and propagandist of Brazilian folk music. Very prolific, very spontaneous, he composed for most solo intruments as well as for orchestra. His two series of solo-piano pieces, *Prole do Bébé* I (The Baby's Dolls) and *Prole do Bébé* II (The Little Animals) are well known for their charm and intimate understanding of the piano. There are five concertos, a piano quartet, a trio, and a quintet. The suites *The Three Maries*, the three pieces of the *Suite Floral*, the *Ciclo Brasileiro*, and the collection of Children's Pieces contain beautifully harmonized and artistically exploited folk songs and folk dances. A *must* for any pianist who can look South is the *Alma Brasileira*, No. 5 of the *Bachianas Brasileiras*. It is a remarkable piece of noble chanting mixed with violent dance ideas. The masterpiece of piano writing from Villa-Lobos's pen is the extensive and very difficult *Rudepoêma*, which he dedicated to Artur Rubinstein.

OCTAVIA PINTO (1890–1950) (Brazil), best known for his delightful suites, *Scenas Infantis* and *Children's Festival*. The little march, "Tom Thumb," is effective. Pinto was the husband of Guiomar Novaës.

ENRIQUE SORO (1884–1954) (Chile). He wrote three piano sonatas, a trio, a piano quintet, and many pieces based on Chilean melodies and dances.

JOAQUÍN NIN (Y CASTELLANOS) (1879–1949) (Cuba), composer and pianist, wrote a Suite of Lyric Waltzes, a *Danza Ibérica*, and Variations on a Frivolous Theme, and was well known for his excellent essays on his art. He also published two very fine collections of early Spanish keyboard music, one of sixteen sonatas, the other of seventeen.

MANUEL PONCE (1882–1948) (Mexico), wrote a piano concerto, a piano trio, and numerous piano pieces, many of which are based on Mexican rhythms. His stay in Paris for additional study made a radical change in his writing: his music became more polyphonic and impressionistic. For piano: Four Pieces for Piano, *Momento Doloroso*, and *Preludio Trágico*. Ponce still stands high in Mexican music history.

SILVESTRE REVUELTAS (1899–1940) (Mexico). Depite a certain lack of academic study, his extraordinary natural talent permitted him to write some fine music for ballet and symphony. There are two string quartets and two piano pieces which became well known—*Canción* and *Allegro*.

ALEJANDRO GARCÍA CATURLA (1906–1949) (Cuba), wrote two sonatas and a *Primera Suite Cubana* for piano and eight wind instruments, also other pieces for piano solo featuring primitive Afro-Cuban rhythms and themes treated with modern techniques and free use of dissonance.

AMADEO ROLDÁN (1900–1939) (Cuba), violinist and eminent conductor, wrote a few pieces for piano.

ESTEBAN EITLER (1913–1960) (Austria-Chile). Among his works for piano are a Sonatina, a Prelude and Capriccio, and Variations on a theme by Debussy, but especially a Concertino for Piano and Eleven Instruments, all of them in twelve-tone style.

BARROZO NETTO (1881–1941) (Brazil). Prolific composer of lyrical pieces in the native manner.

TEODORO VALCÁRCEL (1900–1942) (Peru). He was of pure Indian origin and produced many collections for piano of Indian songs, unpolluted by urban influences. The *Fiestas Andinas* won for him the National Prize for Piano.

JESÚS CASTILLO (1877–1946) (Guatemala). In addition to some orchestral works (in the Fleischer Collection in Philadelphia) his piano pieces from the suite *Popol Buj* (Indian sacred book) are interesting as native music.

ALBERTO GINASTERA (1916–   ) (Argentina). Warmly recommended: *12 American Preludes* and the very impressive Sonata for piano.]

British Composers

After the death of Purcell in 1695 English music fell silent, at least for any note of genius, until the rise of a notable group of modern composers toward the end of the nineteenth century. One minor composer, John Field, has already been mentioned. Others who did credit to Ireland were William Balfe, author of the light opera *The Bohemian Girl*, and William Wallace, composer of *Maritana*. The brightest spot relieving the gloom of two centuries is found in the inimitable operettas of Arthur Sullivan (1842-1900). It is almost a fortunate circumstance that Sullivan's talent, conspicuous as it was, failed to win him a lasting place in serious music. *The Golden Legend*, a cantata, was very popular in England; so was the song *The Lost Chord;* and I suppose that millions have sung the hymn *Onward, Christian Soldiers*, without knowing who wrote it. But Sullivan's name will not be remembered for these works, nor for his one attempt at grand opera, *Ivanhoe*. On the other hand we can spare a whole library of second-grade classics better than we can do without the unique grace, wit, and musicianship of *The Mikado, H.M.S. Pinafore, Patience*, and the *Pirates of Penzance*.

In general, English music through the nineteenth century may be described as academic, scholarly, and uninspired. SIR WILLIAM STERNDALE BENNETT (1816–75), highly honored in his own country, never fulfilled the extravagant predictions of Schumann. Much of his work is for piano. The best pieces I know are the Toccata in C minor and the *Rondo piacevole* in E. The well-known Barcarolle from the Fourth Piano Concerto was often played as a solo. Bennett might have been a greater composer had he not resisted all progressive ideas later than those of Mendelssohn. It is typical of him that he refused an invitation from Leipzig in 1853 to become conductor of the Gewandhaus concerts. He did a good service by founding the London Bach Society in 1849.

SIR HUBERT PARRY (1848–1918) is much better known for his admirable book *The Evolution of the Art of Music* than for his compositions. His work on Bach is also noteworthy.

SIR CHARLES VILLIERS STANFORD (1852–1924), of Irish birth, was completely out of sympathy with modern tendencies, and time has taken its revenge by consigning most of his works to oblivion. The piano pieces have shared this fate, but the *Four Irish Dances* for orchestra, Opus 89, have been transcribed with skill and humor by Percy Grainger; the *Leprechaun's Dance* is especially attractive.

Sir Alexander Mackenzie (1847–1935), a Scottish composer, wrote a *Scotch* Concerto and another Concerto for piano and orchestra, neither of great merit.

Thus the Victorian era, rich in literary and scientific achievement, not undistinguished in painting, was musically barren. Royalty did its best, by liberal bestowal of knighthoods, to encourage what talent there was, but creative ability remained at a low ebb.

A small group of older composers, less rigid in outlook but neither important nor modern in their work, are named briefly because of their interest in the piano.

Sir Granville Bantock (1868–1946), nationalist composer of symphonic and choral works, has also a few sets of piano pieces, *Scotch Scenes, English Scenes, Russian Scenes,* etc. Marion Bauer and Ethel Peyser in their useful book *Music through the Ages* tell us that he wrote twenty-four symphonic poems on Southey's *Curse of Kehama.* One wonders why!

Arthur Hinton (1869–1941) has written a Piano Concerto, Opus 24, and agreeable solo pieces, among others a *Romance* in A flat.

Balfour Gardiner (1877–1950) is a prolific composer of short piano pieces. The prelude *De Profundis* is as favorable a specimen of his work as any.

Joseph Holbrooke (1878–1958) has been rather more venturesome in his *Four Futurist Dances.* No. 1 of his Ten Pieces, Opus 4, is a Valse-caprice on *Three Blind Mice.*

England was finally restored to the family of musical nations by Sir Edward Elgar (1857–1934), Gustav Holst (1874–1934), Ralph Vaughan Williams (1872–1958), and Frederick Delius (1863–1934). Elgar was a classicist, Holst and Vaughan Williams drew on folk lore for their inspiration, and Delius, though swayed for a time by Continental training and the impressionism of Debussy, developed an extremely individual, artistocratic style. By a curious coincidence, Elgar, Holst, and Delius died within a few months of each other in 1934. Most unfortunately none of these illustrious composers gave much attention to the piano. It is only a disservice to Elgar to mention his *Salut d'amour,* a trifle unworthy of him. Delius is ill represented by his Concerto in C minor, though he took the trouble to recast it from the first edition. Holst wrote a humorous Toccata on a Northumberland tune and a lively modernistic setting of *Chrissemas Day in the Morning.* Vaughan Williams has composed a concerto and Piano Quintet in C minor and some smaller pieces.

The piano has been cultivated to a far greater extent by some of the minor composers.

[FRANK BRIDGE (1879–1941), a violist and composer, best known for his chamber music: two piano trios, a quartet, and a quintet. His output for piano solo underwent considerable changes of style, culminating in his dissonant three-movement Sonáta, which makes large musical and technical demands upon the performer.]

CYRIL SCOTT (1879–1960) is much more pianistic, and many of his pieces in small form have been very popular. Almost every amateur knows *Chimes, Lotus Land,* the *Danse nègre,* and the *Passacaglia. Impressions from the Jungle Book* are favorites in England. A sonata, an essay in larger form, was introduced in America by Percy Grainger. Scott is known also as a poet and mystic.

JOHN IRELAND (1879–1962) wrote *Decorations* (containing *The Island Spell*), *London Pieces* (*Ragamuffin,* etc.), and *The Holy Boy,* from a set of Preludes; these are liked for their fancifulness and playability, while the Concerto in E flat, the Sonata, and the Sonatina are comparatively neglected. One of his best works is the Second Sonata for piano and violin, in A minor.

[SIR ARNOLD BAX (1883–1953), of Irish descent, injected a genuine Celtic flavor into British music. Among his larger works are Symphonic Variations for piano and orchestra, a concerto for the left hand alone, and a piano quintet. He composed a great deal for two pianos: a forceful and energetic Sonata, *The Poisoned Fountain, Hardanger, The Devil that Tempted St. Anthony,* and, especially recommended, the *Moy Mell* (The Happy Plain), a real Irish tone poem. Besides four solo sonatas, he composed many other pieces, among them, *Mediterranean, What the Minstrel Told Us,* and *The Slave Girl.* His *Burlesque* and *Whirligig* are full of fun. His style of writing is always significant and at times is very original.

LORD BERNERS (GERALD TYRWHITT) (1883–1950), is well known for his daring *Trois Petites Marches funèbres,* of which the last, *Pour une tante à héritage,* is a masterpiece of irony, decorous attempts at a show of grief overwhelmed by irrepressible exultation for the legacy. He also wrote *Fragments psychologiques* (Hatred, Laughter, A Sigh) and some *Valses bourgeoises.*]

SIR EUGENE GOOSSENS (1893–1962) wrote so fascinatingly in his *Kaleidoscope* and *Four Conceits* that one wishes for more from his pen. There are larger works than these, but not for piano.

[BENJAMIN DALE (1885–1943). Best known for his very fine piano sonata in D minor, performed by Dame Myra Hess. There are also shorter piano pieces.

WILLIAM BAINES (1889–1922) wrote some promising early pieces: *Paradise Gardens, Milestones,* and *Coloured Leaves* before his premature death at the age of twenty-three.

CONSTANT LAMBERT (1905–1951) has to his credit a piano sonata and a concerto for piano and small orchestra but his best and very successful and jazzy *Rio Grande* for solo piano, chorus, and orchestra remains his masterwork.]

ARTHUR BLISS (1891–   ) does not fear to be experimental in his concertos and *Masks*.

HERBERT HOWELLS (1892–   ) offers a concerto, *Snapshots,* and *The Procession,* Opus 14, No. 5.

Australian Composers

ARTHUR BENJAMIN (1894–1960) wrote a Piano Suite, a Concertino for piano and orchestra, a *Concerto quasi Fantasia* for the same combination, and numerous smaller works. His *Jamaican Rumba* and two pieces in his *From San Domingo* are great favorites with audiences.

ROY AGNEW (1893–1944). This gifted writer for the piano has many important works to his credit, including *Fantasia Sonata, Sonata Poem, Sonata Ballade,* and *Sonata Legend-Capricornia*. There are also a *Dance of the Wild Man* and a *Poema Tragica*.]

CHAPTER FOURTEEN

American Composers

Louis Moreau Gottschalk (1829–69)

THE history of American piano music begins[1] with the spectacular career of Gottschalk, born of an English father and a Creole mother at New Orleans. When he made an early debut in Paris, Chopin predicted that he would become a king of pianists and Berlioz credited him with all the possibilities of a great artist. After travels in Europe he appeared in New York, creating such a furor that P. T. Barnum sought to engage him at twenty thousand dollars a year with all expenses paid. Declining this offer, he placed himself under the concert management of Strakosch. In 1855–56 he played no fewer than eighty times in New York alone. Then came six years in the West Indies, more tours in America, and finally a long trip to Latin America, where his popularity was extraordinary. Thus he became the first ambassador of musical good will to Latin America. His death at Rio de Janeiro was caused by overwork. In his short life he had composed operas, symphonies, and innumerable piano pieces.

Gottschalk's programs were always largely made up from his own works, for which he justified himself by the demand of the "dear public" and his duty to himself. Others, he declared, could play the classics as well or better than he, but none could play his own music half so well as himself.

---

[1] This is not strictly fair to Alexander Reinagle (1756–1809), an English musician who migrated to America, settled in Philadelphia, and made his mark there as pianist and composer. Reinagle was a friend of Carl Philipp Emanuel Bach, in whose manner he composed. Some of his piano sonatas are preserved in the Library of Congress.

Today we have only smiles, often tinged with light ridicule, for Gottschalk. But there must have been reason, deeper than the popular taste of the time, for the universal acclaim bestowed on him. It could hardly have been the merit of his compositions, for this was small and ephemeral; they were forgotten almost as soon as he no longer lived to conduct or perform them. Chopin must have been right, and the world must have recognized the force of an impressive personality.

"For ten years," Gottschalk wrote in his diary, "a whole generation of young girls have played my pieces," and he cites *The Last Hope, Marche de nuit, Murmures éoliens, Pastorale et cavalier,* and *Cradle Song* as special favorites. The "young girls" flocked to his concerts like bobbysocksers to Sinatra and distracted his attention by their good looks, causing him, as he often complained, to strike wrong notes. To their sentimental selection we should add *The Banjo* and *Bamboula,* hardier pieces in which we detect the first foreshadowings of ragtime.

Folk Music

It is not easy for music to grow in any country lacking a subsoil of folk lore. The early settlers of America brought songs of many lands with them—Spanish, French, English, German—but had, at least at first, none of their own. Most of these foreign influences were confined to particular localities, Spanish to California and the Mexican border, French to Louisiana and the neighborhood of Canada, English to South Carolina and the Appalachian and Kentucky mountains, German to Pennsylvania and the Middle West. The Dutch troubled themselves little with music, and in New England the Puritans for a long time forbade it entirely except for the unaccompanied singing of psalms and hymns. The Negroes brought with them a lyrical talent that they were quick to develop under the conditions of American experience into the spirituals and plantation songs that are their glory, besides a genius for rhythm (more truly African) that eventually gave us ragtime and jazz. The white man took Negro music to his heart, but for all Dvořák's advice could not build a national art of his own on it, any more than on the slimmer foundation of native Indian music. Stephen Foster, that ill-starred, untaught, inspired lyricist, was the only white American who ever equaled the spontaneous beauty of Negro melody. *Old Folks at Home, Old Back Joe,* and *My Old Kentucky Home* are among our national treasures.[2]

Jazz, on the other hand, was easy to copy. It spread over the world like a wild flower, and few modern composers have altogether escaped the influence of its contrapuntal rhythm and novel orchestration. Jazz was at its best when it was a symbol of zest, the "pep" of its performers sometimes contrasting favorably with the bored routine of overworked symphony orchestras. The life went out of it when it became syndicalized. Since then the crave for ever greater titillation has led through "hot" jazz to "swing" music and "boogie-woogie."

Old English songs from the Appalachian Mountains have been collected and published by Cecil Sharp, the *Lonesome Tunes* of the Kentucky mountains by Howard Brockway. Charles F. Lummis and Arthur Farwell together collected *Spanish Songs of Old California,* H. E. Krehbiel wrote about *Afro-American Folk Songs,* and James Weldon Johnson compiled *The Book of African Negro Spirituals.* Many Negro songs and spirituals have been beautifully arranged by the Negro composers Henry Burleigh, Robert Nathaniel Dett, and Clarence C. White. The material of Negro melodies has been extensively used by many modern writers, including Dvořák, Henry Gilbert, Arthur Nevin, John Powell, and Ernest Kroeger.

The music of the American Indian was also explored, sometimes simultaneously with Negro lore, by many composers. The most active in this field have been Harvey W. Loomis, Charles Skilton, Arthur Nevin, Arthur Farwell, and Charles W. Cadman.

A broader view of American life is presented by the song collections of Carl Sandburg, John Lomax, and John T. Niles. Sandburg's *The American Songbag* is an especially valuable book. Besides selections from Mexican border songs, English and Irish importations, and spirituals, Mr. Sandburg offers a wealth of authentic tunes under such headings as *Pioneer Memories, The Great Open Spaces, Lumberjacks, Loggers, Shanty Boys; Hobo Songs; Railroad and Work Gangs; Picnic and Hayrack Follies, Close Harmony,* and *Darn Fool Ditties.* Cowboy, hillbilly, sailor, tramp, and jailbird all have their place in this remarkable anthology. Aaron Copland, in his orchestral suite *Billy the Kid,* first composed for two pianos, makes striking use of original cowboy tunes and their idiom.

---

[2] Paul Nordoff has arranged a few of Foster's songs for piano.

General History

Many of the most interesting developments of American music had nothing to do with the piano or its literature, but must be briefly mentioned as part of the national picture. The musical capital shifted from Richmond to Philadelphia, then to Boston, then to New York, with a period when Chicago seemed likely to win supremacy. Choral music reigned supreme in New England for a long time, greatly encouraged by the foundation of the Handel and Haydn Society after the War of 1812. German male choruses flourished in the Middle West. Ballad opera was introduced in Philadelphia, Baltimore, and Charleston, and some early operas were written by Americans. From 1801 French opera was given regularly in New Orleans. In 1825 Manuel García and his talented family, including the famous María Malibran, came to America and performed Italian opera. The systematic cultivation of symphony music began with the formation of the New York Philharmonic Society in 1842. The Boston Symphony Orchestra was not founded until 1881, followed by the Chicago Orchestra under Theodore Thomas in 1889. But Theodore Thomas had formed his own orchestra much earlier, in 1864, competing strongly with the New York Philharmonic and taking his men on tour; for a time, too, in 1877 and 1879, he conducted the New York Philharmonic. The Peabody Conservatory of Baltimore was founded as part of the Peabody Institute in 1857 and opened in 1868. The New England Conservatory of Music and the Chicago Musical College, two of our leading educational establishments, both came into existence in 1867. There were schools of music in New York also, but none of first rank until Frank Damrosch organized the Institute of Musical Art in 1905. Chamber music was popularized by the Mendelssohn Quintette Club of Boston and later by the internationally famous Kneisel Quartet. When we still had few eminent pianists we were already building first-class pianos; the firm of Chickering & Sons (at first Stewart & Chickering) began making them in 1823 in Boston, and in 1853 Heinrich Engelhard Steinway (originally Steinweg) founded the pre-eminent house of Steinway & Sons in New York. With the opening of the New York Metropolitan Opera House in 1883 opera secured a firm foothold in America; only a year later Leopold Damrosch came to it as conductor of German opera. Leopold Damrosch had been active in New York since 1871, but he did not live to complete his first season at the Metropolitan. On his death his work was courageously taken up and carried on by his son Walter, then only twenty-three years old. From this point on I may fairly assume that the outline of our progress is familiar or easily accessible to my readers.

I must digress to say that until recently our musical development has been hampered by a weak distrust of our own culture and a somewhat servile acceptance of European importations as necessarily superior to home talent. Let us be just: we had to go through a formative process during which our own genius was undeveloped and imitative; when the visits to our shores of Jenny Lind, Rubinstein, Wieniawski, the engagement of foreign conductors, the examples of European orchestras and opera houses, the benefits of Continental education were vital to our incitement and growth. This was more true, too, in music than in literature, painting, and architecture. But we carried modesty too far, and long after we were well able to think for ourselves in cultural affairs we remained unduly subservient to the glamour of European reputations, much as our fashionable women thought it obligatory to buy their gowns in Paris. This excessively deprecatory attitude ended definitely when the two World Wars exposed the fallibility of European ideals and made us fully conscious of our own powers. Today, with better appreciation of comparative values, we have only to guard against a possible trend to chauvinism. The music of the next hundred years will be produced by the world at large, as in the past, with the accent of importance shifting from one country to another. At the present moment America and Russia have a magnificent opportunity to take the lead both in creative genius and in quality of performance.

New England

To return to the orderly course of history: While New England enjoyed its palmy days an honorable line of musicians worked there disinterestedly and unselfishly for a common cause. Special mention is deserved by the Mason family: LOWELL MASON, organist and composer, who wrote *Nearer, My God, to Thee;* WILLIAM MASON, pianist and teacher; HENRY MASON, founder of the piano firm of Mason & Hamlin, and DANIEL GREGORY MASON (1873–1953), composer and author. Then there were Dudley Buck (1839–1900), John Knowles Paine (1839–1906), Benjamin Johnson Lang (1839–1909), Arthur Foote (1853–1937), George W. Chadwick (1854–1931), Ethelbert Nevin (1862–1901), Horatio Parker (1863–1919), Walter Spalding (1865–1962), Mrs. H. H. A. Beach (1867–1944), Frederick Converse (1871–1940), and Edward Burlingame Hill (1872–1960). None of these were Bachs or Beethovens, but they were talented gentlemen and scholars (I include Mrs. Beach advisedly) in life and art, and did yeoman service in fostering the effort and taste of the country. Charlatanism was incompatible with the spirit of Boston and never dared seek admittance to the St. Botolph Club, that cozy, lettered, hospitable meeting-place of artists.

The contribution to piano literature was small. Arthur Foote's *Five Poems after Omar Khayyám,* Ethelbert Nevin's *Narcissus,* which sold in the millions, Mrs. Beach's Sonata for piano and violin (she also wrote two concertos and solo pieces), and Edward B. Hill's clever *Jazz Study* for two pianos stand out in the general dearth.

At this time Boston's musical life was further enriched by the long residence of Charles Martin Loeffler, distinguished Alsatian-born composer and violinist (1861–1935). After early migrations in Russia, Hungary, Berlin, and Paris, Loeffler came to America in 1881 and soon became attached to the Boston Symphony Orchestra, sitting at the second violinist's desk for twenty-two years. In 1905 he retired to the quietest of lives on a farm at Medfield, Massachusetts, devoting himself for thirty years to composition. Among his most famous works are *The Death of Tintagiles* and the *Pagan Poem,* both for orchestra, though the latter has an important piano part.

We must not forget, too, that Edward MacDowell, of whom we shall next speak, was a New Englander by birth.

Edward MacDowell (1861–1908)

Until he settled in Boston in 1887, Edward MacDowell led the life of a musical cosmopolite. His Irish-Scotch ancestry imbued him with a love of Celtic and Norse legend and stimulated the poetic gift that showed later in the texts of many songs and verses prefixed to some of the piano works. After some boyhood training from Latin-American teachers (Juan Buitrago, Pablo Desvernine, and Teresa Carreño) he entered the Paris Conservatoire at the age of fifteen, studying composition with Savard and piano with Marmontel. One of his fellow students at the Conservatoire was Debussy. Unlike many Americans abroad, MacDowell seized the opportunity to learn French. One day during a class lesson he made a sketch of his teacher and was caught in the act. The amiable professor, far from being annoyed, saw talent in the sketch and showed it to a friend at the École des Beaux-Arts, who in turn offered the youngster a scholarship in painting. It is not on record or evident in his music that MacDowell gained much from his stay in Paris. He decided to go to Germany and after very short periods of work with Ehlert in Wiesbaden found his way to Frankfurt, where he enrolled under Raff for composition and Carl Heymann for piano. Here at last he found able and sympathetic instruction; masters and pupil became fast friends. Raff introduced him to Liszt, who arranged for him to play his First Piano Suite at a meeting of the Allgemeiner Deutsche Musikverein in Zürich. After this event he spent a few years playing, composing, and teaching. His marriage to his pupil Marian Nevins took place in 1884, and their first home was at Wiesbaden.

Up to this time MacDowell could hardly be classed as an American composer. He had won an enviable reputation and written important works in large and small form, chiefly for piano, including the two *Modern Suites,* the two Piano Concertos, the *Witches' Dance, Six Idyls after Goethe,* and *Six Poems after Heine,* and in these he had shown marked individuality while observing classic form. He was yet to become the poet-musician of his native country.

Once he had decided that there was a place at home for a serious composer, MacDowell threw himself whole-heartedly into American life and experience. Having the wisdom to resist the lure of the Negro idiom, and experimenting only casually with Indian folk lore, he found endless inspiration in the varied aspects of our fields and forests, hills and lakes, and was the first to interpret them in music. The *Wild Rose, Water-lily,* and *White Pine* are perhaps over-familiar today just because the objects that inspired them are such common sights of our hedges, ponds, and woods. It has always seemed to me that MacDowell was eminently right in basing a white man's music on the beauty and majesty of American nature. That he did so without deliberate intent was all the better. He wrote as he felt, without much thought whether his work was classical, romantic, impressionist, modern, or nationalistic.

With a European reputation to introduce him, MacDowell had little difficulty in establishing himself successfully in Boston. Later he found peace of mind and leisure to compose at Peterborough, New Hampshire. His tenure of the newly created chair of music at Columbia University (1896–1904) was less fortunate. Probably a conflict was inevitable between pure idealism and the exigencies of the American educational system, which he was ill fitted by his training to understand or direct. His resignation of the post was unhappy for all concerned. Only a year later ill health put an end to his activity; an incurable brain malady developed and led to his death at the age of forty-seven.

Few of the lectures delivered at Columbia were written out in full. They have been edited from what finished material and scattered notes he left by W. T. Baltzell and published as *Critical and Historical Essays.*

MacDowell is essentially a composer for the piano, though he wrote many lovely songs and some choruses for male and mixed voices. His best-known orchestral work is the *Indian Suite,* which makes free use of native themes. [While this important and very attractive work continued to be neglected by orchestras in the United States, the American Negro conductor Dean Dixon put it on the programs at many of his European concerts—with such pronounced success that Breitkopf & Härtel issued it in a new score and parts.]

The First Piano Concerto is an immature effort, but the Second, in D minor, is beautiful and effective. It begins with a slow movement, *Larghetto calmato;* this is followed by two rapid movements with a short slow introduction to the Finale intervening. The brilliant Scherzo, Mrs. MacDowell told me, was inspired by Ellen Terry's performance of Beatrice in *Much Ado about Nothing.* After seeing the play in London, MacDowell went home and immediately sketched the piece for two pianos.[3] No one who ever heard Carreño (to whom the concerto is dedicated) play this Scherzo will easily forget the superb aplomb of her performance.

The Prelude from the *First Modern Suite,* the *Witches' Dance,* and the *Scotch Poem* (No. 2. of the *Six Poems after Heine*) are among the most popular of the smaller early works. If you play the *Scotch Poem* be sure to use the later edition revised by the composer. The *Étude de Concert* in F sharp is also effective, though it has been played too much.

The four imposing sonatas stand in a class by themselves. The *Sonata tragica,* No. 1, written in 1893, still shows European influence.

---

[3] The sketch was originally entitled "Benedick."

It is a noble work, sadly neglected by our concert pianists. Mac-Dowell used a sort of leitmotiv to represent the tragic mood. The first movement begins with it, and it recurs, passingly or importantly, in all the others.

Ex. 304

In the other sonatas MacDowell drew on old myths peculiarly sympathetic to him through his ancestry. The *Eroica,* Opus 50, deals with the Arthurian legend; the four movements might be named: The Coming of Arthur, Merlin, Guinevere, and The Battle with Modred. The last pages hint at the hesitant Sir Bedivere waving Excalibur at the brink of the mystic lake and the coming of the three queens in their dusky barge to bear the stricken king away. [The Guinevere movement contains the most beautiful music that MacDowell composed. It is profoundly felt, and the craftsmanship is superior. No wonder that Lawrence Gilman remarked on how fortunate we are that MacDowell and not the King wrote about the Queen.] The *Norse Sonata,* I confess, seems less inspired. In it a skald of Harald's court is supposed to sing "tales of battles won, of Gudrun's love, and Sigurd, Siegmund's son." The *Keltic,* most concise and mature of the sonatas, is my favorite. MacDowell wrote these prefatory lines to it:

> Who minds now Keltic tales of yore,
> Dark Druid rhymes that thrall,
> Deirdre's song and wizard lore
> Of great Cuchullin's fall.

The most distinctive sets of short pieces are the *Four Little Poems,* the *Woodland Sketches,* the *Sea Pieces,* the *New England Idyls,* and the two sets of twelve studies each, Opus 39, and the Virtuoso Studies, Opus 46. The *Four Little Poems* are taken from Tennyson (*The Eagle*),

Bulwer-Lytton (*The Brook*), Rossetti (*Moonshine*), and Shelley (*Winter*). All are good, not only the favorite *Eagle*. The amateur should give special attention to the *Woodland Sketches,* adding *Will o' the Wisp, In Autumn,* and *From Uncle Remus,* to the *Wild Rose* and *Water-lily.* No. 5, *From an Indian Lodge,* introduces a theme of the Brotherton Indians. *To a Wild Rose* was nearly lost to the world. MacDowell, like Mendelssohn, was in the habit of writing something daily, not necessarily for publication but to keep his hand in. At first he saw no value in this little sketch and accordingly threw it into the wastebasket. There it caught the eye of Mrs. MacDowell as she was tidying the room and she promptly rescued it. *From Uncle Remus* gives us a suggestion of Negro rhythm at

Ex. 305

Of the *Sea Pieces* I like best *To the Sea, A Wandering Iceberg, Song,* and *From the Depths.* The last, not very well known, is exceptionally grave and powerful. The *New England Idyls* contain at least three fine numbers, *In Dark Woods, To an Old White Pine,* and *The Joy of Autumn.* In a similar series of *Fireside Tales* there is another Uncle Remus story, *Of Br'er Rabbit,* and a curious piece, *Of Salamanders.*

A good selection from the Studies would be the *Idyl, Shadow Dance,* and *Hungarian* from Opus 39 and the *Moto perpetuo, March Wind,* and *Polonaise* from Opus 46. The *March Wind* should end softly, as prescribed, so that March, true to tradition, goes out like a lamb.

A charming little piece unfamiliar to most pianists is the *Rigaudon,* Opus 49, No. 2.

It was the cherished dream of MacDowell that his New Hampshire home might become a haven for creative artists of all kinds where they could work undisturbed in the peaceful woodland that he had found so inspiring. The dream was made real by a devoted wife. Shortly after his death Mrs. MacDowell founded the MacDowell Colony at Peterborough, deeding the estate to a Memorial Association and working heroically to raise funds for the maintenance and endowment of the enterprise. The little log cabin where her husband loved to compose has become a Mecca of artists.

Some Middle-Period Composers

To show the rapid spread of creative talent over the country, the following list includes the state of each composer's birth.

EDGAR STILLMAN KELLEY (1857–1944, b. Wisconsin), an honored composer who wrote little music for piano solo, but his piano quintet should not be neglected.

HOWARD BROCKWAY (1870–1951, b. New York) wrote many fine piano pieces. The early *Ballade*, Opus 10, is difficult, but the *Six Pieces*, Opus 26, the *Serenade*, Opus 28, and the *Humoresque*, Opus 36, No. 4, are well worth the attention of student and amateur.

HENRY HADLEY (1871–1937, b. Massachusetts) won an international reputation but is now little played. His compositions for piano include a quintet, two trios, and a suite, *The Enchantment of Pan*.

RUBIN GOLDMARK (1872–1936, b. New York) became most widely known as an eminent teacher of composition. Among his pupils were Frederick Jacobi, Aaron Copland, George Gershwin, Ulric Cole, Nicolai Berezowski, and Vittorio Giannini. He wrote a suite for piano entitled *Prairie Idylls*.

DANIEL GREGORY MASON (1873–1953, b. Massachusetts), versatile and accomplished, wrote for piano a Prelude and Fugue (with orchestra), *Three Silhouettes*, and the charming *Country Pictures*, which include two especially good pieces, the pensive *Whippoorwill* and the brilliant *Chimney Swallows*. Most of the *Country Pictures* are of moderate difficulty.

CHARLES E. IVES (1874–1954, b. Connecticut) is an extraordinary phenomenon in American musical history. Few events have so startled musicians out of complacency as did the publication of the *Concord Sonata*, the *Essays Before a Sonata*, in which the composer expounded his artistic creed, and the *113 Songs*. Here, evidently, was an ultramodern born before his time. The amazement subsided, Ives was almost forgotten, and only quite recently has he been discovered anew by the world.

The full title of the Sonata is *Concord, Mass., 1845.* Its four movements are portrayals of the spirit of Emerson, Thoreau, the Alcotts, and Hawthorne. The quality is variable and difficult to describe; like the songs, the sonata touches pure beauty in places and elsewhere resorts to intended crudity. A superficial feature of debatable merit is the employment of a wood-block of prescribed size to cover "clusters" of notes, white or black, simultaneously.

In a characteristic dedication Ives inscribes the *Essays* to those who can't stand his music, the music to those who can't stand his essays, and the whole to those who can't stand either.

The amateur should be warned that the *Concord Sonata* is extremely difficult.

Nowadays the opportunities for hearing Ives's works and forming a just estimate of them are far more favorable than at the time of their creation.

[I confess belonging among those to whom the music of Ives remains extremely controversial. He was indeed an aggressive pioneer. The disproportion between quality and quantity is in gross evidence in the larger piano works, the First Sonata and the one entitled *Concord.* However, this latter and the Third Symphony no doubt are among the accepted works because of their forcefulness. I feel very sympathetic toward those who look upon this somewhat strange personality as a great composer.]

ERNEST SCHELLING (1876–1939, b. New Jersey), gifted pianist, widely known for his conducting of broadcasts for children by the New York Philharmonic Society, wrote two large works for piano and orchestra, the *Fantastic Suite* and the *Impressions from an Artist's Life;* among his smaller pieces are *Fatalisme* and a Nocturne (*Ragusa*). It was not only children who responded to Schelling's ardent and generous disposition; few musicians have been so universally popular with their colleagues.

JOHN ALDEN CARPENTER (1876–1951, b. Illinois), a versatile composer in modern style, wrote much characteristically American music in which humor is seldom absent. The Concertino for piano and orchestra, the *Polonaise américaine* and *Tango américain* are interesting, effective, and not excessively difficult.

[JOHN POWELL (1882–1963), pianist and composer, wrote two piano concertos and, for piano solo, three sonatas, Variations and Double Fugue, and some suites; a *Dirge* for two pianos; and, for piano and orchestra, a splendid work known on both sides of the Atlantic: the *Rhapsodie Nègre*.]

Charles T. Griffes (1884–1920)

Music suffered a grievous loss in the early death of Charles T. Griffes. It would be hard to name any composer who made so indelible a mark on his time with so few works—they scarcely number forty. If one must classify him at all, he was an impressionist in music, but his style grew to be too distinguished and original to be easily explained. Had he lived longer, he would undoubtedly have been a great composer; as it is, he is the most outstanding talent produced by America since MacDowell.

Griffes studied and for a while taught in Berlin, learning composition with Klatte and Humperdinck and piano with Jedliczka. One day he chanced to hear Rudolph Ganz practising Ravel's *Jeux d'eau* and was at once strongly attracted by a type of music novel to him and at that time to the world. Returning to New York in 1907, he found no fitter employment than that of teacher at the Hackley School in Tarrytown. This drudgery, time-consuming and ill paid, left scant leisure for creative work. Unable to afford the services of a copyist, he sat up nights writing out the parts of his orchestral compositions. He was too proud to let his friends know his straits and died pitifully of overwork and privation. We are still paying him tardy and remorseful honor.

I make no apology for listing the complete piano works of this gifted American. They are:

> *Three Tone Pictures:*
> *The Lake at Evening*
> *The Vale of Dreams*
> *The Night Winds*
>
> *Three Fantasy Pieces:*
> *Barcarolle*
> *Nocturne*
> *Scherzo*
>
> *Four Roman Sketches* (after words of William Sharp):
> *The White Peacock*

> *Nightfall*
> *The Fountain of the Acqua Paola*
> *Clouds*

Sonata

All of these are beautiful and pianistic. Inevitably some, notably the *Scherzo, The White Peacock,* and the Sonata have been played more than others, but I recommend also *The Lake at Evening, The Night Winds, Nightfall, The Fountain of the Acqua Paola,* and *Clouds.* None of these except *Clouds* is very difficult.

[On account of his studies in Berlin, Griffes's early music was very much influenced by what he heard there and in Germany at large. After his return to New York, he became acquainted with the music of Debussy and Ravel and began essaying the impressionistic medium with much success. We became close friends, and I was indeed happy when I read the dedication to me of "The White Peacock." Griffes's untimely death occurred before his Sonata was published by Schirmer. But he knew from some of us, his intimate friends, that the Sonata was to be the monument to his life's work. In this, his largest work for the piano, he finally achieved his own personal style. The Sonata is a major work and will remain so in the literature of American music for many years to come. The craftsmanship is superb and far above anything Griffes had written before.

FREDERICK JACOBI (1891–1952) composed in many forms, having written a concerto and some small pieces for piano: *Moods* and Prelude and Toccata.

ARTHUR SHEPHERD (1880–1958), composer and critic, wrote a *Fantaisie humoresque* for piano and orchestra, two sonatas, a piano quintet, and an *Exotic Dance.*

ALBERT STOESSEL (1894–1943) was a musician of great versatility: composer, conductor, violinist, and teacher. He exerted a wide and beneficial influence on music through his positions at Chautauqua, New York, the Worcester Festival, the Juilliard Graduate School, and the Oratorio Society of New York. He wrote a Concerto Grosso for piano and string orchestra and a *Hispania Suite* of medium difficulty.

BERYL RUBINSTEIN (1898–1952) was a remarkable pianist and a highly gifted composer. In fact, I consider his Concerto for piano and orchestra the finest in that combination written by any American before Barber. It is a great work, and its musical beauty and technical virtuosity should have given it a well deserved place in our concert halls. Other works are the Sonatina (Oxford), the Gavotte, Sarabande and Gigue, and two études, *Ignis fatuus* and *Whirligig* (Oxford). These latter two are gems of pianism and should be revived by good, well-equipped pianists. *Music Fancies,* a set of five pieces for young players, is simple.

ERNEST BLOCH (1880–1959), a remarkable composer, born in Switzerland, and a devoted exponent of Judaism in music, lived in America after 1917 and became an American citizen, but, like Schönberg and Hindemith, had formed his style in Europe. He wrote for piano solo *Five Sketches in Sepia, In the Night, Poems of the Sea* (a cycle of three pieces), and ten sketches entitled *Enfantines.* All of these are good, and the *Poems of the Sea* are recommended to competent amateurs. The Concerto Grosso for string orchestra with piano obbligato is one of his finest works. In the Piano Quintet he makes use of quarter-tones for the strings. His Sonata for viola and piano won the Coolidge prize in 1919. Bloch's style is original, mordant, and effective, shunning technical display and hackneyed figuration.

ERNEST HUTCHESON (1871–1951), born in Australia, pianist, composer, master teacher, executive, and author. He composed some symphonic works, a concerto for two pianos and orchestra, three sets of piano pieces (op. 10, 11, and 12), as well as a number of important transcriptions for two pianos: of Mendelssohn's Scherzo from *A Midsummer Night's Dream,* Wagner's "Ride of the Valkyries," and the "Rakoczy March" by Berlioz. Mr. Hutcheson also published *Elements of Piano Technique* in addition to *The Literature of the Piano.*

GEORGE F. BOYLE (1886–1948), born in Australia. Boyle was a prolific writer of excellent idiomatic piano pieces who gradually modernized his style. Among his larger works are a Concerto in D minor and an imposing Sonata of considerable difficulty. Shorter pieces to be recommended are *Habanera,* Gavotte and Musette, *Pierrot,* Scherzo, *Songs of the Cascade,* and *Curious Procession.* The Scherzo and *Songs of the Cascade* call for dexterous fingers.

PERCY GRAINGER (1882–1961), born in Australia, long active in America. A deservedly popular composer and pianist, universally known for his lighter works such as the *Irish Tune from County Derry, Shepherd's Hey, Country Gardens* and *Sea Chanty (One More Day, My John).* There is more musicianship in these pieces than their light nature indicates. Grainger was one of the few players and writers to make careful investigation of the possibilities of the sostenuto pedal. We must indulge his playful little eccentricities: pieces are "dished up" instead of arranged; "Louden lots" is his Anglo-Saxon for "crescendo molto"; the pianist is obligingly informed that "it doesn't matter exactly what note the glissando ends on"; and miscellaneous information is freely imparted in journalistic "boxes."

BOHUSLAV MARTINU (1890–1959) born in Czechoslovakia, must be regarded as one of the outstanding composers of our era. He composed two concertos and an *Incantation* for one piano and orchestra, also one concerto for two pianos and orchestra, a piano quartet, a quintet, and, for piano solo, *Fantaisie et Toccata, Three Czech Dances, Études et Polkas, "Ritournelles,"* and five *"Esquisses de danse."*

WALLINGFORD RIEGGER (1885–1960), a master craftsman, a prolific composer in many dissimilar styles (non-dissonant, partly dissonant, dissonant, and impressionistic), though all his music is of a highly advanced nature. He wrote a Concerto for piano and woodwinds, Variations for piano and orchestra, a piano quintet, and a number of solo pieces (*Blue Voyage*, twelve piano pieces in various styles, *Four Tone Pictures*).

EMERSON WHITHORNE (1884–1958), in addition to a Poem for piano and orchestra, wrote a piano quintet, *The Royal Road*, and the delightful *New York Days and Nights* for piano solo.

MARION BAUER (1887–1955), pianist and composer. From her pen: *American Youth*, concerto for piano and orchestra, a Dance Sonata, *From New Hampshire Woods, Patterns in Twelve Tone*, and many shorter piano pieces.

THEODORE CHANLER (1902–1961), published a charming Toccata in A-flat major that is a must for piano students interested in running left-hand technique. There are also *Five Short Colloquies.*

GEORGE ANTHEIL (1900–1959), a gifted composer whose early style began where Stravinsky dwelled: *Ragtime, Airplane Sonata, Mechanisms, Sonate Sauvage.* He mellowed considerably later in life and dealt in neo-romanticism and impressionism. There are a concerto for piano and orchestra and four piano sonatas. Mention must be made of his *Ballet méchanique*, which featured eight pianos and all available noise-making instruments. I was present at the New York *première*, which produced an enjoyable scandal of protests from the audience.

JACQUES DE MENASCE (1905–1960) wrote two piano concertos that he performed in the United States and abroad, a Romantic Suite, and *Five Fingerprints.* A Divertimento for piano and strings scored a success at my New York Philharmonic Young People's Concerts in 1946 despite its very contemporary style.

ISADORE FREED (1908–1961), born in Russia, wrote much chamber music and many piano pieces. Co-editor of *Masters of Our Day*, a splendid Presser collection of excellent contemporary educational material for piano.

ROBERT KURKA (1921–1959), a very gifted young composer whose death terminated a very promising career too soon. I recommend his *Sonatina for Young Persons* and the twelve *Notes from Nature* for the younger set. For more advanced players, there is a very attractive Sonata, op. 20, in three movements.]

LOUIS GRUENBERG (1884–1964), born in Poland, was one of the first American composers to incorporate jazz rhythms in symphonic works as well as in pieces for piano, including *Jazzberries, Jazz-Masks, 6 Jazz Epigrams, 3 Jazz Dances,* and *Polychromatics.* There are two piano concertos and several stageworks, but the composer is best known for his opera *The Emperor Jones,* O'Neill's play having served as libretto, and *Creation* for baritone and eight instruments.

Light Music

Something is sadly lacking in a nation if it does not possess a fund of good light music for relaxation and entertainment—music perhaps ignored by frequenters of grand opera and symphony concerts but significant in the life of the people at large. America has an abundance of this music in all its forms. Light opera, musical comedy, and revues[4] have been amply provided by Victor Herbert, Reginald de Koven, Jerome Kern, Irving Berlin, George Gershwin, and Leonard Bernstein. Gershwin's *Porgy and Bess,* Virgil Thomson's *Four Saints in Three Acts,* and Marc Blitzstein's *The Cradle Will Rock,* are hard to classify; they are sincere efforts to find new expression for music in the theater. Douglas Moore's one-act opera *The Devil and Daniel Webster* belongs to serious, not light music, but we return to sheer amusement in the clever stage works of Gian-Carlo Menotti.

The ballet, encouraged by the growth of a native school of dancing, has become extraordinarily popular in recent years and many of our modern composers have met success in this attractive field.

Band music has been brought to a high state of perfection by Patrick S. Gilmore, the "father of American bandmasters," John Philip Sousa, the "March King," and Edwin Franko Goldman, who further

---

[4] An operetta, or light opera, is based on a connected plot, however slight. Musical comedy makes less pretension to plot; the revue makes none. Colloquially all are "shows," like plays, picture exhibitions, and circuses.

developed the concert band. Many excellent jazz and swing bands, too, have arisen since Paul Whiteman showed the way.

The hits from musical comedy and light opera have given us hundreds of really good popular songs. Piano music of the true salon type is not so plentiful, but it would not be difficult to compile a fairly extensive list of pieces humorous in intention.

Jazz, of course, in one way or another, is a main ingredient of modern light music, American and foreign. What is known as "symphonic jazz" came into being with a historic concert organized by Paul Whiteman in 1924 at the long defunct Æolian Hall of New York. The program illustrated the evolution of jazz from its crude beginnings from ragtime to its later finesse of color and orchestration. The event was crowned by the first performance of Gershwin's *Rhapsody in Blue*. This composer, one of the most typically American, richly deserves a few special paragraphs.

George Gershwin (1898–1937)

In the early days of Paul Whiteman, when that genial musician was drawing crowds to hear his band at the Palais Royal Café in New York, there sat at the piano an ingratiating youth whose fingers tingled with melody and rhythm. No amount of daily "plugging" could spoil the natural beauty of his touch or damp his ambition to write a kind of music at once novel and fascinating. He began by composing songs that quickly drew attention to his unique talent. An excellent pianist, with a sure technique and fine sense of tone values, it was not long before he hit on the idea of the *Rhapsody in Blue*, a sort of free concerto for piano and jazz band. At that time he could only indicate some hints for the scoring of the piece; the actual instrumentation was done by Ferde Grofé, whose jazz orchestration has influenced composers like Stravinsky. Gershwin took lessons with Rubin Goldmark and later scored the whole of the Concerto in F and *Porgy and Bess* with his own hand. Meanwhile he was writing a long series of successful "shows," to which his brother Ira contributed delightful lyrics.

The *Rhapsody in Blue* had an immediate and lasting success, easily finding its way to a place on symphonic programs. It is one of Gershwin's best works—better, I think, than the Concerto in F, which betrays an awkwardness in handling larger forms. George always regretted that his intensely busy life never permitted further serious study of composition and piano. He may be said to have had some of the defects of his virtues, but the virtues were always there, honest, unpretentious, and lovable. *Porgy and Bess* may not be an opera, but it is certainly musical entertainment of a very high order. Gershwin was happy in giving pleasure to millions and in enjoying the esteem of serious musicians everywhere.

The songs are probably the perfection of Gershwin's work. His piano writings are limited to the *Rhapsody in Blue,* the Concerto in F, and Three Preludes. The simplified published versions of individual songs give little conception of the ingenious accompaniments he devised or improvised for them. But Beryl Rubinstein's four transcriptions of songs from *Porgy and Bess* are noteworthy, particularly "I got plenty o' nuttin' " and "Bess, you is my woman."

My personal friendship with George Gershwin, which began when he was "plugging" at the Palais Royal, is one of my most happy memories, and not often have I felt deeper grief than that caused by his premature death. It was my good fortune that when he sought a quiet summer retreat to compose the Concerto in F, I was able to provide him with a studio at Chautauqua, New York. It was understood among the piano pupils that his room there was inviolable until four o'clock every afternoon. Promptly at that hour, however, a group of students invaded the room, when George would good-naturedly play and sing to them for a treasured hour. I count it an honor, too, that I was privileged to arrange a private hearing of the *Rhapsody in Blue* shortly before its first public performance, when such musicians as Walter Damrosch and Ernest Schelling were outspoken in their appreciation. George was a wonderful friend and companion, ever reliable, sympathetic, and unshakably well-tempered.

It is a pleasure to observe in our contemporary composers a freedom from dissension and a unity of purpose rare in the history of art. The League of Composers, founded in 1923, and kindred organizations fostered this spirit. The League organized many important concerts, by no means exclusively devoted to American composers, commissioned works by leading writers, and through its organ *Modern Music* (a monthly publication discontinued after 1946) kept the public well informed of the world's latest activities and trends.

CHAPTER FIFTEEN

Recent Composers and the State of Music Since Hutcheson

BY RUDOLPH GANZ

To speak of living composers without discussing and analyzing the recent evolution of the art of music and its present state is hardly possible. The revolution caused by the advent of magnetic tape and of concrete and electronic music created by scientific means has brought about a kind of a friendly universal tug-of-war between "real and reel" expressions of musical values. As there is no progress in music itself, but only in the means of expressing it, the *new* does not eliminate the *old*, but only adds to what has been before. Objection to new expression is as old as the switch from Gregorian monodic chants to two- and three-voiced organum. All the great masters were radicals in their own ways. Some of them succeeded in being understood and accepted during their lifetimes; others received their due recognition only after their deaths. From the past, only those works have lasted which were born out of inspiration and evolved by acquired knowledge, which means supreme craftsmanship. Logically, dissonance defies criticism. Dissonance itself is just a fleeting experience. Yesterday's ugliness may be tomorrow's beauty. Nothing exists on this earth which does not spell beauty for someone, and there is no need to be aroused by something that strikes our ears or eyes as different, new, disagreeable, or even horrifying. Time heals all misunderstandings provided that they represent professional newness. During my privileged long life, I have felt the impact of the post-Wagnerian era, of Impressionism, of neo-Classicism and neo-Romanticism, of Expressionism, of the twelve-tone and linear systems, of interval jumping and dissonant free-for-all counterpoint. Take the case of · Alban Berg's epoch-making opera *Wozzeck*. Hearing the initial American performance by radio from Philadelphia and not seeing the stage pictures pertaining to the lusty story, one easily could have imagined that street riots had broken out in that otherwise quiet and well-behaved city. Today, this unusually aggressive work is conquering the world.

An introduction to the present state of revolutionary tendencies in the history and literature of the piano and its performance has been furnished by the inventor of the "prepared piano," John Cage, a gifted pianist, versatile composer, and highly accomplished author, whose peculiar detours from the usual go in all directions. Hardware stores are friendly to him and his disciples, or vice versa. He himself presents doings that call for hitherto unheard-of publicity, which, to my thinking, is neither enticing nor very sympathetic. He has become the apostle of undistinguished concert behavior that one might endure in not very serious entertainment. He is considered an *enfant terrible* at the European music festivals. His most telling performance, so far, features the unusual piece entitled *Silence*: John Cage enters, sits quietly at the piano, stands up after *Four Minutes and Thirty-Three Seconds*, and retires. It amuses the audiences and embarrasses the serious music-lovers. Kicking over the innocent piano bench, hitting the top of the piano with a lead pipe, extracting some bottles (vintage not given) from the instrument just to throw them to the floor, spreading rosaries among the audience, and hurling eggs at the wall behind him—such extra-artistic activities prevent a healthy evolution. Yet I challenge the curious customers to procure just for perusal the four Cage books of piano music published by Peters. This very progressive publishing organization is also offering *Pieces for Prepared Piano and Strings* by Toshiro Mayuzumi, with a lucid, picturesque "indication" of how to "prepare" your piano. These pieces have been performed by David Tudor with great success in New York, as well as in Berlin and other German cities. The press everywhere speaks enthusiastically of the fascinating sounds produced by this young Japanese (born 1929). He is being called the Japanese Messiaen. Two of Cage's followers and, I believe, disciples, are the two excellent duo-pianists, Art Ferrante and Lou Teicher. The "innards" of their "prepared pianos" are Cage-like, embellished with all kinds of "delicacies" such as tacks, nuts, several sizes of screws and bolts, and pieces of rubber. They make free use of the magic or magnetic tape whereupon passages may be re-recorded and variedly tampered with to the satisfaction of the two performers. But these two artists play upon their pianos with an uncanny virtuosity that is original, exciting, and fascinating. No wonder that they belong to the ranks of the most successful recording personalities. For an appetizer I recommend their *Hi-Fireworks*. If their "preparedness" includes "thwacking of the music rack, beating of the lid of the piano or plucking the strings like a harp," we must accept it as secondary entertainment, for these two young men *can* play upon their keyboards, and they do it in grand style.

More serious attempts and their successful realizations bring us to the authors of *Antiphonal Music*. One of its crafty exponents is Henry Brant (1913–   ), whose Antiphony No. 1 was given its *première* in New York in 1953. The St. Louis Symphony Orchestra under Edouard Van Remoortel performed it some years ago as Leonard Bernstein had for the New York Philharmonic audiences some time before. He and his four younger colleagues conducted the five different groups placed in separate parts of Carnegie Hall. A quote from the program notes: "the effect sometimes approximates several compositions played in the same room at the same time."

The Magnetic Tape and Concrete Music

The now well-known team of Columbia University professors who have successfully "graduated" from excellent musicians to being very effective, experimenting scientists—Otto Luening (1900–   ) and Vladimir Ussachewsky (1911–   )—has made very good use of a well-endowed electronic laboratory and has produced several important works written for tape recorder and symphony orchestra. The Louisville Orchestra commissioned the Rhapsodic Variations in 1954; the St. Louis Orchestra played Concerted Piece in 1960. However, a report of this performance says: "amusing noises of no definite rhythm or pitch which may be likened to the distant clank of plumbing, the howling of the winds in the upper stories of a skyscraper and the laughter of an inebriated chipmunk."

Electronic Music

Its outstanding leader and dominating personality is no doubt the Frenchman, Pierre Boulez (1925-   ). His first piano sonata is still in the usual accepted idiom, but his sonatas II and III demand a new kind of piano technique, different from Schönbergian, Stravinskyan ideas and ignoring Bartók's sensitive experimental sounds and sharply rich rhythms (*Outdoor Pieces*). He firmly advocates the synthesis of the conventional instruments of the symphony orchestra with all possible resources of electronics. He has written impressive works that seem convincing and may survive. His two volumes of *Structures* for two pianos (No. 1, 1956, No. 2, 1961), which the composer performs with immaculate technique and the assistance of the phenomenal (so considered) French pianist, Yvonne Loriod, have been highlights at many occasions abroad. Listen to his recorded *Marteau sans maître* (*Hammer without Master*), not only once, but several times, and you will slowly get accustomed to the unfamiliar sounds and realize a certain commanding force in his new message.

Other Frenchmen, like Pierre Henri and Pierre Schaeffer (the concrete-music opera *Orpheus*), also have recorded some of their daring attempts at eliminating the usual orchestra instruments and depending entirely upon the manifold manipulations of electronic generators. The very distinguished doyen of present French musicians, Olivier Messiaen, is said to be trying his recognized genius on the new "expression" of his disciple, Boulez. In his own works for solo piano, *24 Regards sur l'Enfant Jésus* and many shorter pieces, as well as two books of *Visions de l'Amen*, for two pianos, Messiaen shows an interesting personal style, difficult of execution, but written with masterly craftsmanship. In his four "Bird" concertos for piano and orchestra, he achieves new, unheard-of sounds. Bird-calls from all over the world form a delicate complex of fascinating, rhythmical little themes. Habitual musical bird-watchers should be delighted when hearing these performances.

Among others involved in the creation of unheard-of conceptions of musical values is the young German, Karlheinz Stockhausen, whom voices of the old school have named the "bad boy" of the electronic guild. Stockhausen's piano pieces are the most aggressive in the front rank of the latest pianistic utterances, and create a new approach to opposing dynamics and jumpy virtuosity. I recommend them, against my will, to students and dilettantes who are curious and favored with much leisure time. However, it is necessary to listen to Stockhausen's electronic essays to get a real aural picture of his rather sensational style. Five *Zeitmasse* for five woodwinds, conducted by a champion and sponsor of contemporary music, Robert Craft, have been recorded. Stockhausen's *Contacts,* for electronic tape, piano and percussion, was featured at a Venice Festival. Hank Badings and Dick Raaijmakers represent the new way as originating in the Netherlands. The former is not young, and yet is offering a Capriccio for violin and two sound-tracks. Larger works of his, like *Genese* and *Evolutions,* have had considerable success on account of his unusual skill in producing new sounds. His countryman, Raaijmakers, created a symphonic piece entitled *Contrasts* which, according to one reviewer, harbors "a kind of lethal, insensate fury, and a queer sibilant sound, part shushing, part steam release."

Bo Nilsson, Swedish avant-gardist, has furnished us with a two-page piano piece of twelve bars, with the appropriate title *Quantities,* no doubt with the intention of avoiding qualities. It seems to present one of the latest (maybe one of the last) problems to be solved by living pianists. There are strict indications for the use of "pointed fingers, the palm of the hand, the fist and the forearm." In addition to the prescribed eighty-five time values (*Zeitwerte*) and the ten dynamic indications from pppp to ffff, there is also a diagram for time-stretching (*Zeitdehnung*) among the seven octaves. There is hardly a note without a frequency mark, and the tempo is "as fast as possible." The size of the smallest measure is one inch, of the longest, twelve inches. The first measure (five inches) starts on top of the left side of the first page, the next measures grow in size and move down-ward to the bottom line (twelve inches, plus a five-inch one), and come up again on the second page, the last measure (two inches) being the *Ende* in the upper right corner.

Josef Tal, from Israel, has completed a concerto for piano with electronic accompaniment. The very gifted Italian, Luciano Berio, composes on tape (tapesichord?), as well as with the traditional instruments. His thirty one-minute *Epifanie* and his *Circles,* during the performance of which a woman sings, sighs, laughs, speaks, shrieks, and acts, have been called sensational. However, he is superseded and completely obscured as far as newness is concerned by the more aggressive and entirely different Silvano Bussotti who seems to be the successful inventor of music without notes. These piano pieces (Universal Edition) are dedicated to David Tudor, John Cage's disciple and team-mate, a brilliant performer and composer in his own right.

They look like abstract drawings, purely graphic art, but Stockhausen has succeeded in analyzing these puzzling examples in convincing-looking illustrations.

There can be no question about the fact that a revolutionary era has come upon us. Science has opened the door to a new world of sounds. The door cannot be closed, and it is up to us to learn to listen to a message that is new and will grow logically, as the old ways have grown in the past. An excellent story appeared in the French magazine *Réalité* some years ago, dealing with the extreme changes taking place in the creative art of music. What a title—"Discord within Dissonance"—and the exciting subtitle "Shattering experiments in concrete music, in serial and electronic set off an ear-splitting rivalry among the young avant-garde"! Some real things have come out of the experiments, and it is too late to ask whither is music going. Music is marching, real and reel, all in one. We might ask, what would Beethoven have done had he had a tape recorder at his disposal?

To illuminate and evaluate the most recent evolution in which we are still engaged there has been published a paperback volume with the timely title *Since Debussy: a View of Contemporary Music*, by André Hodeir, French musicologist and also, as it says, a practicing musician. Hodeir's first book, *Jazz: Its Evolution and Essence*, has become a landmark in modern criticism. In this 1961 collection of essays, the author appears as a flag-bearer of a new civilization, of an entirely new art, and his arguments are the fruits of an "original, uncompromising mind that brings passion and conviction back into musical criticism." He calls neo-classicism "the canker of our time," but speaks with mild admiration of early-twentieth-century masters, their rise and downfall. Stravinsky turns out to be a "great dilettante," Schönberg one who, "like Moses, may have shown the way to the Promised Land, but was never allowed to enter it himself." Berg, "less destructive than Schoenberg and less original than Stravinsky, appears to me as the last representative of a great tradition"; Webern had "qualities that equipped him to become the very first explorer of an uncharted world," but "would occasionally stop and retrace his steps as though standing on the threshold of the unknown, he had felt a dizzy spell"; Bartók was "in love with dissonance" and "a great orchestrator," but "despite his modernity, he remains a composer of the past"; Messiaen "stands at the forefront of his generation" and "may be regarded as Western music's great theoretician of rhythm," but "his music is powerless to rise above the level of anecdote and the immediate intoxication of the senses." From among Messiaen's outstanding pupils, Pierre Boulez, Karlheinz Stockhausen, and Jean Barraqué (born but not heard from yet), M. Hodeir picks the last as being perhaps "the greatest composer since Beethoven," despite the fact that "his complete works number only a few hundred pages of manuscript." There seems to be a sonata for the piano (1950–1952) "conceived on a very large scale and lasting over half an hour. Its massiveness is that of a block of marble." Pianists, students, teachers, and even amateurs—watch and be ready for the miracle!

The changes in performance have been evident in all branches of music. The age of accelerated transportation has had its effect upon the piano virtuoso as well as upon the virtuoso conductors and their marvelously functioning organizations. Certain jet tempos have invaded performances in the concert halls, and the struggle between music and technique is only too often in evidence. Radio also has helped to induce performers, especially pianists, to use pedals more carefully or not at all, as I have noticed. Somewhat faster tempos over the air seem understandable because the performer, his hands, and his facial expressions are not seen. TV has, or in some cases, should have, remedied this shortcoming. A timely question arises. Are some recent doings on the concert stage pointing to a new era of vaudeville intrusion? Harpo Marx and Danny Kaye conducting major symphony orchestras, the London Symphony performing Malcolm Arnold's *Seven-course-meal*, set to music as the "first concerto for eater and waiter." The piece is dedicated to a well-known English producer who *did* eat his dinner on the stage, surrounded by the orchestra, in full view of the audience. Is it customary for a justly famous pianist to come upon the stage with a glass of water in his hand, deposit it on the piano, and then start Beethoven's Fourth Concerto with a famous orchestra in Carnegie Hall? And is it necessary for a pianist to double as conductor, waving his left hand at the orchestra when not busy at the keyboard? Misunderstandings between conductor and soloists should be ironed out at rehearsals, it seems. But not long ago an eminent conductor felt the necessity of warning the audience of the impending unorthodox performance of a Brahms piano concerto, the reason being a seeming "incurable" difference of opinion between the pianist and himself regarding the interpretation of that master-work. Is not the experienced conductor the guardian of the score and sole responsible leader of the reading of it? I, at least, have felt and always will that he is. And now we have had the odd by-plays of the originator of the "prepared piano" and the secret glances between the members of improvisation groups, and, finally, Toschi Ichiyanagi's Piano Music No. 6, with ordinary musical notation absent, the pianist being instructed to "play clusters with his hands, fists and arms as fast and as loud as possible until he is exhausted."

A new world of expressive means has been revealed in the use of electro-acoustical processes to create new sonorities. Is it a rise to a new liberty? But liberty cannot exist without order.

Recent American Composers

Our special interest—naturally—concentrates on the men and women living within our borders who create music and thus contribute to the cultural place of our art among the nations of the world. Many of these composers can be listed as successful and recognized; others who have given sufficient proof of their talents will be watched with increasing interest. Though an acknowledged national school of composition may not yet exist, distinct signs have appeared that such a personal expression is in the making. Happily, they are in the direction of serious endeavor, energy, and character. No one can doubt that the influence exercised by some of the foreign composers who left Europe before or during the Second World War was helpful to our younger composers, though I distinctly recall Arnold Schönberg's saying significantly at a luncheon offered in his honor: "Now that I have been able to peruse orchestra scores of young American writers, I wonder if my coming to the United States was superfluous." That is the correct translation of the master's German sentence, which I gave to those present. The evolution of music in our country during the last seventy years has been nothing short of fantastic, astounding, and unheard-of in the annals of music history. No wonder that the German master Paul Hindemith, who became an American citizen, remarked one time that he realized how in our land music was heard by more people and served more individuals of all ages than anywhere else in the world. He may have been thinking of the three purely American musical institutions: the young people's and children's concerts offered in scores of American cities, the grade, high school, college, and university orchestras and bands, and the state and national federations of music clubs, with a membership of over 500,000.

The following list of recent American composers emphasizes particularly their contributions to the literature of the piano.

CARL RUGGLES ·(1876–1971), composer, conductor, wrote a "Polyphonic Composition" for three pianos, also "Evocations" and "4 Chants for Piano," all very dissonant.

RUDOLPH GANZ (1877–1972), born in Switzerland: a "Symphony in E" for orchestra, a piano concerto in E flat, a "Symphonic Overture: Laughter . . . yet Love," and "4 Symphonic Demonstration Pieces" for the four departments of the symphony orchestra; for piano, "Symphonic Variations on a Theme of Brahms" and other pieces, some especially for children, such as the suite "20 Animal Pictures."

IGOR STRAVINSKY (1882–1971), born in Russia, admittedly one of the great music men of the twentieth century, master of rhythm, orchestration, and mixed meters. His early confusing dissonances have settled in the ears of people and he is frequently performed at youth concerts. Of special interest to us are his compositions for the piano: two sonatas, a concerto for piano and wind instruments, a Capriccio for piano and orchestra, a concerto for two pianos alone, eight easy and amusing pieces for duet, four early études, and a Serenade in A. To honor the American youngster he wrote *The 5 Fingers*, eight melodies for beginners (having good teachers). His "Mouvements" for piano and orchestra is extremely contemporary in its Boulezian look. It is difficult, purely and jumpily rhythmical, but—at least—short.

WERNER JOSTEN (1885–1963), born in Germany, wrote much chamber music, especially sonatas and trios in which the piano plays an important part in co-operation with strings and wind instruments.

DEEMS TAYLOR (1885–1966), composer, author, lecturer. The only American who has had two operas presented by the Metropolitan Opera of New York. Two of his books, *Of Men and Music* and *The Well-Tempered Listener*, are widely read. He wrote little for the piano though his "Two Studies in Rhythm" and "The Smuggler" are worthy of being looked into.

EDGAR VARÈSE (1885–1965), born in France. He is not only considered, but also *is* one of the boldest innovators in twentieth-century music. In his early scores, the percussion department became the principle functionary in the orchestra, and in later utterances he introduced sound (noises) from outer space. His writing for the piano is always in connection with wind and string instruments or unusual ones like xylophone, accordion, or balalaika.

ETHEL LEGINSKA (1886–), pianist, conductor and master teacher. From her pen: operas, symphonic pieces, chamber music, a "Fantasy" for piano and orchestra and many shorter piano pieces.

EDWARD ROYCE (1886–), composer of two symphonic Tone Poems, some songs, and a number of piano pieces: Theme and Variations, *Set of Eight*.

ERNEST TOCH (1887–1964), born in Austria, well known for his operas, an oratorio, and many symphonic works, also much chamber

music, especially nine string quartets. He is prolific in his output for
the piano: a piano concerto, a symphony for piano and orchestra, three
sonatas, *Burlesques, 10 Studies for Beginners,* 10 easy studies, 10 of
medium difficulty, 10 recital studies, and 10 studies for concert use, a
real *Gradus ad Parnassum.* Toch writes in a free, strongly contemporary style, always interesting. Good pianists, attention!

PHILIP JAMES (1890–   ), composer, conductor, wrote an opera,
two symphonies, choral works, a piano quartet, and other chamber
music works, a concertino for piano and chamber orchestra.

HAROLD MORRIS (1890–1964), pianist and composer, wrote a successful piano concerto, two piano trios, two piano quintets, four piano
sonatas, and many other piano pieces.

ADOLPH WEISS (1891–   ) is the author of a Fantasy for piano and
orchestra, 12 preludes for piano, a piano sonata, *Protest* for two pianos,
all his later works being in twelve-tone style.

KAREL BOLESLAV JIRAK (1891–   ), born in Czechoslovakia, composer, conductor. In addition to an opera and five symphonies, he wrote
a piano concerto, a piano sonata, two suites, and smaller pieces.

BERNARD WAGENAAR (1891–   ), born in Holland: symphonies and
many chamber music works. For piano, a sonata.

CHARLES HAUBIEL (1892–   ), pianist, composer, and publisher of
music by Americans (Composers' Press), has written many symphonic
works, some with chorus, some chamber music, a Suite for two pianos,
and a large number of piano pieces for all degrees of difficulty.

PAUL AMADEUS PISK (1893–   ), born in Austria, composer and
musicologist, has written a large number of works in practically all
genres: symphonic works, chamber music, music for the stage, and
many piano pieces, including Sonatina in E and Nocturnal Interlude.

DOUGLAS STUART MOORE (1893–1969), composer and educator. In
addition to several successful operas, he has written symphonic works,
some chamber music, and piano pieces.

HERBERT REYNOLDS INCH (1893–   ) has written a symphony and
smaller orchestral works, a piano quintet, and a concerto for piano and
orchestra.

NICOLAS SLONIMSKY (1894–   ), born in Russia, musicologist, conductor. For piano: *Studies in Black and White* and *Silhouettes
Ibériennes.*

WALTER PISTON (1894–   ), eminent composer and master teacher
of many well-known younger American composers. He has written
seven symphonies and many other symphonic works, chamber music, a
delightful Concertino for piano and chamber orchestra. Outstanding
among his piano pieces is the deeply felt Passacaglia.

WESLEY LA VIOLETTE (1894–   ), composer and author, wrote operas, symphonies, chamber music: string quartets, flute quintet, etc. Foremost among these works is the piano quintet.

LEO ORNSTEIN (1895–   ), born in Russia, pianist and composer. In his early years he was considered to belong to the extreme "cubist" left. His style was aggressive, his craftsmanship always excellent. He wrote a piano concerto, four sonatas, a piano quintet, and many characteristic piano pieces, among them *À la Chinoise*, dedicated to me.

MARIO CASTELNUOVO-TEDESCO (1895–1968), born in Italy, prolific composer, wrote for the film, the stage, the symphony orchestra, two Biblical oratorios, six Shakespearean overtures, three violin concertos, much chamber music, two piano concertos, two piano quintets, a piano trio, the *Dances of David*, and a large number of shorter piano pieces.

ERNST LEVY (1895–   ), born in Switzerland, pianist and composer. In addition to thirteen symphonies, choral works, and chamber music, he wrote a Symphonic Fantasy for harpsichord and several sets of piano pieces.

LEO SOWERBY (1895–1968), pianist, organist and composer: four symphonies, an oratorio, and other symphonic works, a ballad for two pianos and orchestra *King Estmere*, a piano concerto, several suites for piano solo.

WILLIAM GRANT STILL (1896–   ), composer of many stage and symphonic works: *Kaintuck* for piano and orchestra, a set of *Traceries*, and other piano pieces.

HOWARD HANSON (1896–   ), composer, conductor, educator, and master teacher. His influence as Director of the Eastman School of Music and as conductor of the American Music Festivals in Rochester, New York, has greatly helped American music and the American composer in general. Besides seven symphonies, one opera, and several choral works he has written a piano concerto, a fantasy for piano and orchestra, two symphonic poems with piano obbligato, a *Fantasy on a Theme of Youth* for piano and strings, Prelude and Double Fugue for two pianos, a quintet, a *Concerto da Camera* for piano and strings, and a number of shorter piano pieces, of which *Reminiscence* is dedicated to me.

ROGER SESSIONS (1896–   ), eminent composer, in the front rank of the aggressively contemporary writers. His two sonatas and his piano concerto are made of considerably new, but always very interesting material, of great technical difficulty. Four pieces *From My Diary* are more accessible.

VIRGIL THOMSON (1896–   ), composer, critic, and author. His works include two operas, two symphonies, chamber music, four piano sonatas, and two sets of Études.

HENRY COWELL (1897–1966), pianist and composer, often called the inventor of "tone clusters," which are produced by striking the piano keys with "bunched fingers," fist, flat hand, forearm, or elbow. A not very well-known embellishment of the French baroque era called *le coup de cannon* (the cannon shot) directs the flat hand to hit both black and white keys in the lowest octave of the keyboard (Paul Brunold: *Traité des Signes et Agréments,* 1925, out of print). You find some of the earliest (and very dissonant) five-finger clusters in the works of the now practically forgotten (because out of print) French Master, Charles-Henri-Valentin Alkan (1813–1888), who, like Chopin, wrote almost exclusively for the piano. Cowell belonged among those performers who love to pluck the strings of the piano and sweep over them. All these mildly revolutionary devices are used in his piano concerto and in many of his other works. He wrote fourteen symphonies, shorter symphonic works, and much chamber music. For piano and orchestra, *Tales of the Countryside* and *Concerto Piccolo,* plus a large number of shorter pieces.

VITTORIO RIETI (1898–   ), born in Egypt of Italian parents, pianist and composer. In addition to several operas, five symphonies, an oratorio, and ballets, he has written a concerto for two pianos and orchestra, several sets of waltzes for two pianos, sonatas, and many shorter pieces.

ERNST BACON (1898–   ), composer, wrote two symphonies, a concerto for piano and orchestra, chamber music, and smaller works for piano solo.

ROY HARRIS (1898–   ), composer who has written prolifically in all styles of music except opera. Seven symphonies, choral works, a concerto for one piano and one for two pianos, a sonata, a piano quintet. For piano solo, the *American Ballads,* a Toccata, a Little Suite, and other pieces.

RANDALL THOMPSON (1899–   ). Of his three symphonies, No. 2 is his best-known, a brilliant strongly American work. Also an opera, choral works, a Jazz Poem for piano and orchestra, and smaller piano pieces, among them *Song after Sundown.*

ALEXANDER TCHEREPNIN (1899–   ), born in Russia, pianist, conductor, and internationally known composer. Has written in all genres: operas, symphonies, ballets, cantatas, some *Russian Dances* (dedicated to me), chamber music and a large number of works for piano. A Fantasy, a Georgian Suite, and three concertos, all for piano and orchestra, several sonatas, two toccatas, the first one also dedicated to me, not to forget the very popular 10 Bagatelles, études, pieces for unusual combinations of instruments: a Sonata for piano and kettle drums and a Concerto for harmonica and orchestra; experiments with the pentatonic, his own nine-tone scale, and some modified Oriental scales, and many shorter works for piano.

AARON COPLAND (1900–), at present one of America's most popular composers, conductor, lecturer, and musical ambassador of good will all over the world. The two-piano suite *Billy the Kid* features cowboy tunes; the early piece for piano solo, *The Cat and the Mouse*, is good fun and strictly student repertoire. There are also 4 Piano Blues and *Sunday Afternoon Music* for children. Copland's two books, *What to Listen for in Music* and *Our New Music*, are penetrating, candid, and discriminatingly warm in appreciation of his contemporaries. He has written three symphonies, an opera, several ballets, a piano concerto and piano sonata, a Passacaglia, the *very* contemporary Variations, and the large-sized Fantasy.

ERNST KŘENEK (1900–), born in Austria, has written some fifteen operas, five symphonies, four piano concertos, a concerto for two pianos and orchestra, much chamber music; for piano alone: six sonatas, five sonatinas, twelve short pieces, a Double Fugue, *Hurricane Variations*, *George Washington Variations*, *Echoes from Austria*, *Basler Massarbeit* for two pianos, and *Sechs Vermessene* for piano solo.

OTTO LUENING (1900–), flutist and composer, wrote one opera, several symphonic works, chamber music, two sonatas for flute and piano, and the Prelude to a Hymn Tune (after William Billings) for piano and small orchestra. In recent years Luening and his colleague Vladimir Ussachevsky have co-operated in writing works for tape-recorder and orchestra.

ANIS FULEIHAN (1900–), born in Cyprus, has written a symphony and other symphonic pieces, two piano concertos (No. 1 with strings, No. 2 with orchestra), also a two-piano concerto with orchestra, four piano sonatas, and a great number of pieces for solo piano.

ABRAM CHASINS (1903–), pianist, composer, author of two piano concertos, twenty-four Preludes with fine teaching values, and *Three Chinese Pieces* that became very popular.

VLADIMIR DUKELSKY (1903–), born in Russia. Besides operas, operettas, ballets, symphonies, he has written ballads for piano and orchestra, a sonata, and several suites for piano alone. Under the pseudonym Vernon Duke, he also has written show tunes and other popular music.

VITTORIO GIANNINI (1903–66), well known for his operas, some of which were written for radio and TV. Two symphonies, a piano concerto, one for two pianos with orchestra, a piano sonata, a brilliant piano quintet, and a trio.

NICOLAS NABOKOV (1903–   ), born in Russia: operas, ballets, symphonies, a piano concerto, two piano sonatas, and smaller piano pieces.

NICOLAI LOPATNIKOV (1903–   ), born in Estonia; two symphonies an opera, a sinfonietta, two piano concertos, a piano sonata, and several groups of smaller piano pieces.

LOUISE TALMA (1906–   ), has written symphonic pieces, choral works, two sonatas, Alleluia in Form of a Toccata, and other pieces for Piano.

PAUL CRESTON (1906–   ), five symphonies, a piano concerto, several concertos for different orchestral instruments, a concertino for marimba, and smaller piano pieces.

ROSS LEE FINNEY (1906–   ), a piano concerto, four piano sonatas, and a piano trio.

BURRILL PHILIPS (1907–   ), a Sinfonia Concertante, some ballets, a concerto, chamber music, the well-known Toccata, 3 Informalities, and three later sonatas still are in photostated manuscript.

ELLIOT CARTER (1908–   ), outstanding composer, has written a concerto, an opera, ballets, choral work, an epoch-making Piano Sonata. His string quartet has scored European successes. Also has written a double concerto for piano, harpsichord, and two chamber orchestras.

HALSEY STEVENS (1908–   ), composer and author (Bartók), a symphony, a Sinfonia Breve, Symphonic Dances, and other symphonic works, much chamber music, Piano Sonata No. 3, seven sonatinas, and smaller piano pieces.

VICTOR BABIN (1908–72), born in Russia, pianist, master teacher, and composer: two concertos for two pianos, Études for two pianos. Internationally known as half of a famous two-piano team, the other artist being his wife, Vitya Vronsky.

PAUL NORDOFF (1909–   ), composer: in addition to an opera and symphonic works, he has written two piano concertos; for solo piano the Bavarian Variations and Preludes and Fugues.

ANTHONY DONATO (1909–   ), composer, teacher, has written two symphonies and other symphonic pieces, three string quartets, a piano and horn sonata, and teaching pieces, among them Five Recreations.

HOWARD SWANSON (1909–   ), composer, well known for his Short

Symphony, an earlier symphony, a piano sonata, and a most charming short piece, *The Cuckoo*.

RAY GREEN (1909–), a symphony, a *Sunday Sing Symphony*, ballets, a Dance Sonata for two pianos, and a large number of shorter piano pieces.

ELIE SIEGMEISTER (1909–): three symphonies and numerous other symphonic works, an *American Sonata* for piano, an *Airplane Suite*.

JOHN HAUSSERMAN (1909–): two symphonies, a harpsichord quintet with woodwinds, a *Suite Rustique* for piano, flute, and cello, and a number of piano pieces.

WILLIAM SCHUMAN (1910–), eminent composer and educator: five symphonies, ballets, a concerto for piano and small orchestra, many symphonic and choral works; for piano solo: the popular *3 Score Set* and the cycle of five pieces entitled *Voyage*.

SOULIMA STRAVINSKY (1919–), born in Switzerland, has written excellent children's pieces and a fine work called *The Art of Scales*.

SAMUEL BARBER (1910–), eminent composer of international fame, wrote one opera, *Vanessa*, which was performed in Salzburg and Spoleto and at the Metropolitan in New York, an oratorio, several much-performed symphonic works; for piano: the challenging great Piano Sonata and the now popular *Excursions*. His piano concerto was heard first in September 1962 at Lincoln Center, New York. The musical profession expected another masterwork, and no one was disappointed.

RICHARD FRANKO GOLDMAN (1910–), bandmaster, composer, and writer. For piano: a Sonatina.

SAM RAPHLING (1910–), composer and teacher, has written some orchestral works and sonatas for different instruments; for the piano: concerto for young students, Concerto No. 3, also arranged for two pianos, and sonatas.

GIAN CARLO MENOTTI (1911–), born in Italy. Successful composer of operas performed on both sides of the Atlantic. For the piano: a Pastorale with string orchestra, *Poemetti* (piano pieces for children), and a Piano Concerto in F.

ALAN HOVHANESS (1911–), composer of many works in different genres; *Lousadzak* for piano and strings, and a large number of pieces for solo piano.

VLADIMIR USSACHEVSKY (1911–), born in Manchuria: some orchestral pieces, a piano sonata and a concerto for piano and orchestra. (See also, above, Otto Luening.)

INGOLF DAHL (1912–), born in Germany, composer, conductor, wrote chamber music; for piano: a *Sonata Seria* and a *Quodlibet on American Folk Tunes* for two pianos, eight hands.

JOHN CAGE (1912–), ultramodern composer, pianist, and author. Has written a piano concerto and many odd piano pieces.

ARTHUR BERGER (1912–), composer and critic; for the piano: a Fantasy, a Partita, and a Capriccio.

KENT KENNAN (1913–), composer; in addition to symphonic and chamber music works, a Suite for two pianos, the very popular Three Preludes, and other pieces for solo piano.

EVERETT HELM (1913–), many works for the stage and for symphony orchestra, Piano Concerto No. 2, and two piano sonatas.

NORMAN DELLO JOIO (1913–), composer of opera and much piano music: three sonatas, a Suite, Preludes, and two Nocturnes.

VIVIAN FINE (1913–), composer and pianist, writes hyper-modern, at times acrid, music: a piano concerto, an oboe-and-piano sonata, a Suite in E-flat major.

GARDNER READ (1913–), prolific composer: four symphonies, a large number of symphonic works, and much chamber music; for piano: *Driftwood Suite, Sonata da Chiesa,* and smaller pieces.

GRANT FLETCHER (1913–), composer and conductor, has written a symphony, an oratorio, a Symphonic Overture; for the piano: two books of nocturnes, four *American Dance* pieces.

MORTON GOULD (1913–), brilliant composer: a great many works for the stage and for symphony orchestra (three symphonies), a piano concerto, Dance Variations for two pianos and orchestra, Invention for four pianos, and three piano sonatas, a Sonatina, and *Boogie-Woogie Étude.*

GAIL KUBIK (1914–): three symphonies and some smaller works for orchestra, *American Caprice* for piano and chamber orchestra; for piano solo: a sonata, a sonatina, and a toccata.

ALEXEI HAIEFF (1914–), born in Siberia: symphonic works and chamber music, piano concerto, piano sonata, sonata for two pianos.

ROBERT GOEB (1914–): three symphonies, chamber music, a piano concerto, and a piano quintet.

DAVID DIAMOND (1915–): five symphonies and many shorter symphonic works, a piano concerto, a piano quartet, a sonatina, children's pieces.

VINCENT PERSICHETTI (1915–), composer and conductor, has written four symphonies, a piano concerto, a concertino for piano and orchestra, several serenades both for piano solo and for four hands, nine sonatas, six piano sonatinas, a concerto for piano four hands, and an interesting *Little Piano Book* for children and progressive teachers.

ROBERT PALMER (1915–): two piano sonatas, a sonata for piano four hands and another for two pianos, symphonic and chamber music, piano quintet, piano quartet, and several shorter piano pieces, among them the popular and somewhat wild *Toccata Ostinato*.

BEN WEBER (1916–): symphony, ballet, chamber music featuring the piano, a piano concerto, and piano pieces.

MILTON BABBITT (1916–), outstanding twelve-tone composer who has entered the electronic field successfully and convincingly: *Vision and Prayer* for soprano with electronic accompaniment. His book *Serial Composition and Atonality* is considered the most enlightening textbook for young composers. In his early (1947) compositions for piano, he still combined the older and the new. In his *Partitions* for piano, the multiple aspects of serial music are worked out in fullest complexity.

ELLIS KOHS (1916–): two symphonies, symphonic pieces, concertos for different instruments, chamber music; for the piano: *Étude In Memory of Bartók*, a Toccata, Ten Inventions, Piano Variations, and a *Fantasy on La, Sol, Fa, Mi, Re*.

ROBERT WARD (1917–), has written three symphonies, much chamber music, and a number of piano pieces, outstanding among them being *Lamentation*.

LOU HARRISON (1917–), composer, conductor, instrument-maker: operas, ballets, a symphony, fourteen sinfonias for percussion, and piano pieces, among them six sonatas and a Suite for piano (1943), serial music.

ULYSSES KAY (1917–): a symphony, ballets, concerto for orchestra, string quartets, a piano sonata, a piano quintet, eight Inventions.

LEONARD BERNSTEIN (1918–), composer, conductor, pianist. Outstanding among his works is *The Age of Anxiety*, scored for piano and orchestra. He also wrote some very successful musical comedies. Among his piano pieces are two sets of *Anniversaries*.

GEORGE ROCHBERG (1918–), composer and editor: a symphony, chamber music, a Capriccio for two pianos, two piano sonatas, and many shorter pieces.

LEON KIRCHNER (1919–), composer of the avant-garde, has written a few works for voice and piano, a string quartet, a piano sonata, a piano concerto, both of which command earnest attention for their vitality, and a Little Suite of five pieces meant for serious young students with accordingly prepared teachers.

HAROLD SHAPERO (1920–) has written some orchestral works, a Four Hand Piano Sonata, and three sonatas for piano alone.

WILLIAM BERGSMA (1921–): a symphony, an opera, other symphonic pieces, two string quartets; for piano: three fantasies, two volumes of *Tangents* with six pieces in each, a most interesting and challenging work.

LEO SMIT (1921–), pianist and composer: one symphony, other orchestral works, chamber music; for the piano: *Five Pieces for Young People*, *Fantasy*, *The Farewell*, and Seven Characteristic Pieces.

ANDREW IMBRIE (1921–): two string quartets, a violin concerto, a piano trio, and a piano sonata.

LUKAS FOSS (1922–), pianist, composer, and conductor; his compositions include an opera, symphonic and choral works, a ballet, two piano concertos, and a Set of Three Pieces for two pianos.

PETER MENNIN (1923–) has written seven symphonies, other symphonic works, a cantata; for the piano: a concerto, a sonata, and some shorter pieces. Mr. Mennin is President of the Juilliard School of Music.

NED ROREM (1923–): two operas, two symphonies, two piano concertos, two piano sonatas, *Sicilienne* for two pianos, and a set of nine piano pieces entitled *A Quiet Afternoon*.

WENG-CHUNG CHOU (1923–), born in China, has written for large and chamber orchestra, chamber music, and piano pieces.

ROBERT STARER (1924–), born in Austria, wrote a short opera, two symphonies, a piano concerto, and a piano sonata.

CARLISLE FLOYD (1926–): besides three operas, he wrote a ballet for two pianos and a piano sonata.

Postscript to the Amateur and Student

I SHOULD like to enlarge a little on some points raised by implications in these pages but perhaps too skimpily treated.

To what extent should the amateur bother with technique? This depends largely on his natural endowment. If he has a good touch, quick fingers, and a feeling for accuracy, a few simple daily exercises, a modicum of scales and arpeggios, and three or four minutes of stretching exercises will suffice. If, on the other hand, his action is heavy and unwieldy, it will assuredly pay him to put himself at a favorable time through something of a grind in order to limber his arms and speed up his fingers, preferably under a teacher's guidance. When satisfactory results are attained the drudgery may be reduced. Generally speaking, technical improvement comes most easily in early years, especially to men. Women usually preserve a more supple physique and often, after neglecting the piano for many years, quickly recover their mechanical ability.

How much theory should the amateur learn? This depends a good deal on his ear, for without a good ear no one ever grasps theory intelligently. So in some way or other every player should always be exercising and improving his hearing. The obvious way to do it is to listen acutely—listen to what others do and (which is much harder) learn to hear oneself objectively. A good course in ear-training is advisable. Then it is not difficult to master the rudiments of harmony, the naming of intervals, scale and chord formations, cadences, the differences between major and minor triads and dominant and diminished seventh-chords. To this the amateur should add a recognition of the nature of dissonance and of modulation from key to key. He can hardly be expected to go very deeply into counterpoint, canon, and fugue; I venture to think that he may find the brief notes given in the chapter on Bach a sufficient help for practical purposes. But I urgently recommend some study of musical forms, using instead of textbooks the definitions in standard dictionaries supplemented by personal examination of various types of composition.

The importance of sight reading can hardly be over-emphasized. I am inclined to say that it is more important to the amateur than to the professional, for the latter, with more working hours at his disposal, can better afford to study laboriously. Reading is principally a matter of practice; if you give ten minutes a day regularly to it you will make quick progress. The rules to follow are simple: before you begin, determine the key, time-signature, and clefs prescribed and scan the new piece to estimate the tempo at which you can play it through without stumbling; then count a preliminary measure and start. *Keep time,* not minding if it is slow. Try to read very accurately, but if you do make a mistake, don't stop—play on to the end and go back afterwards for corrections. And observe phrasing and marks of expression as well as notes. Readiness and accuracy in sight reading heighten the pleasure and benefit of browsing, for you cover a lot of ground without being guilty of mere unprofitable dabbling. You are a useful member of society, too, if you can volunteer an accompaniment or a part in chamber music when occasion offers.

Facility in reading opens the way to familiarity with a far wider literature than the limited amount you can learn to perform. I know players who never cut more pages of a volume than is required by the one number they elect to study. To put it on the lowest level, this shows a lamentable absence of curiosity. Unless you blindly accept outside opinion, how are you to know what is best in a volume without at least a glance at all of it? The solid sphere of our knowledge should be surrounded by a nourishing atmosphere if it is to retain its life and warmth. We should count a hundred acquaintances for every close friend.

Modern custom has made too much of a fetish of playing without notes. The practice has extended to musicians formerly held under no obligation to perform "by heart," conductors, organists, and recently one or two string quartets. The amateur need by no means memorize all his pieces unless memorization comes easily to him. Yet it is a nuisance to be encumbered with a brief-case when visiting friends who may ask one to play and who might possibly omit the request had the brief-case been left at home. In any event, memorization is good discipline for the mind, and preoccupation with the printed notes may detract from naturalness of performance. My advice, therefore, is to cultivate it without letting it become a burden.

The reader may have observed that my attitude toward piano music is one of appreciation and enthusiasm rather than of criticism. It is true that I have a few more or less rooted dislikes. I object to pieces written solely to be taught; I have no use for old music of historical but not æsthetic interest; and I am quite indifferent to modern music of no merit save its newness. Yet I like good pieces written for children; I realize that research is constantly disclosing neglected values of the past; and I know that great care is needed in sifting contemporary production, lest conservatism or prejudice blind us to strange and novel aspects of strength, beauty, and expression. We need not lament the fact that nine tenths of the music composed in any period is mediocre or worthless; it is the other tenth that endures to our delight. Be as selective as we will, the piano literature remains incredibly rich, noble, and varied. May it long engage your mind and content your soul.

APPENDIX A

Technique

BY RUDOLPH GANZ

THERE are two kinds of not entirely successful teachers in the great field of music-education: those who preach technique to the exclusion of musical expression and those to whom musical feeling means everything even though lack of technical equipment in the execution of a piece be disturbing to the listener.

If "m" stands for music, then let us see how many "t's" are needed to bring music to life—tone, touch, tempo, taste, temperament, technique. They lend the real charm to the great fundamentals of the art of performance.

All these elements of expression finally will create a permanent personality in the performer. To have acquired them to a certain degree means to have culture. So we had better begin to teach the most important principles of interpretation to the children at the earliest moment.

Are not *contrasts* the most powerful means of commanding attention during a performance? Is not *contrast* the secret of successful program-making? Why, then, not teach the small child the energetic and vivifying effects of *forte* and the soothing blessings of *piano*? Thus the child begins to live in two worlds, the one around us, the outward one, and the more worthwhile one that dwells within us and which we call our inward one. Every little exercise—scale, broken chord, arpeggio, interval, skip, and so on—should be studied in both *forte* and *piano,* thus eliminating from the start that deadly enemy of personality: *mf,* that compromising go-between, that apostle of indifference, of hesitation and inferiority complexes. Beethoven wrote very few *mf's.* He is the Titan, the creator of contrasts, the uncompromising leader on the paths that lead from the within to the outer world.

Any child who has acquired the ability to portray two distinctly opposite expressions has mastered the principle of contrast and therefore is on the way to interpretation. It is my personal belief that the conquering of the technique of contrast is the first step to worthwhile self-expression: yes and no, black and white, day and night, sun and moon, happiness and sadness, life and death—what riches are contained in these contrasts! They command both nature and humanity by their forcefulness of variety and ever-changing values.

Second in importance as to technical achievement, I consider evenness of tone. By that I mean the playing of any pattern, be it scale- or chord-like with the same quality of tone, first in *forte* and then in *piano.* It takes discipline of the mind and ear to maintain an absolutely correct intensity of tone in any passage, be it legato or staccato. Try for yourself the same exercise with both hands in the same register of the piano, for instance. If you can readily produce the same effect with the left hand and right hand in succession, you have mastered another important principle of self-expression.

Speed is the next goal of the student. Many can play fast. Only a few can control their speed. My advice is to study slowly, and then —with the same distinct quality of tone—double and triple the speed of the exercise. Eighths become sixteenths and sixteenths become thirty-seconds. This is an absolutely sure way of gaining velocity with confidence. Nothing has been accomplished unless this speeding-up has been acquired in both *forte* and *piano.*

The next conquest is again in the direction of expression. Rise and fall are first cousins to loud and soft. They demand a great deal of attention. To be able to play a two- or three-octave scale upward, starting *piano* and gradually increasing the tone to *forte*—or beginning with *forte* and decreasing the volume to a last note played *piano* —is another achievement. Play that scale in three different speeds with these dynamic schemes and you will find yourself on the way to interesting results of interpretation.

If all teachers were conscientious to the point of insisting upon correct first reading of the text as to notes, note values, dynamics and other indications of the composer, life would be easier for all of us, and the creators of the masterworks could rest in peace. No correct interpretation is possible without correct reading. I consider lack of discipline in the approach to first study on the part of the average student a real drawback in the popularization of good music. Indifference and inattention are the foes of clarity of purpose and of good performance.

The secret of dependable memorizing is the absolutely correct first reading of a new work, hands separate, without pedal. The ultimate assurance in performing is photographic memory. Take one or two bars of a not too difficult piece, peruse the meter, the notes and their values, possible rests, dynamics, and phrasings, looking at all of it as if you were a camera. Then close the book and write down on music paper whatever you are able to remember.

As a resumé, may I proffer the following advice to teachers: do not permit the study of anything purely technical without insistence upon contrasting tone qualities. Every difficult passage in any piece should be well analyzed and practiced in different sorts of accentuation and rhythm.

The fundamentals of technical background are, however, scales, solid and broken chords, arpeggios, two- and three-voice exercises for one hand, two-against-three scales, skips, etc. Many excellent books are at the disposal of students of all ages. Contrast and multiplication of speeds make practicing interesting. Bach *Inventions,* *The Well-Tempered Clavier,* and the *Études* of Cramer, Clementi, and Chopin are the pillars of basic applied technical study and are immensely helpful for sight reading. They prepare the student for the greater tasks.

The improvement and constant increase in quality of books of musical instruction for children have been so remarkable during the last thirty years that they make both studying and teaching as interesting and entertaining as one could wish. Teachers have no excuse for lamenting the scarcity or lack of teaching material. Workshops and master classes in scores of institutions of music-education offer the finest opportunities for teachers living far away from the music centers of the land to get acquainted with the latest publications and detailed explanation of their purposes. A good summer's study is the best investment a teacher can make. Special conferences or seminars for piano teachers and students are held in every part of the country. Refresher courses guarantee the enthusiasm for another year of teaching, and knowledge of new material will be welcomed by ambitious students. Even the artists before the public have to renew themselves to remain interesting and ensuingly popular with their audiences. Unless a teacher keeps abreast of the times—that is, with the creative output of contemporary music—he cannot possibly be a growing source of inspiration to students. Think of all the hundreds of attractive American compositions written for young Americans, for beginners and the more advanced children, and look into the voluminous contribution to the literature for the young which foreign composers have made—Casella, Milhaud, Hindemith, Stravinsky (senior and junior), Bartók, Bloch, Gretchaninoff, Tcherepnin, and Prokofiev, to mention just a few of the better-known.

It is rather curious that technical works introducing trends in contemporary music are practically non-existent, though most of the young composers of Europe, South America, and the United States are writing free contrapuntal, polytonal, linear, and even twelve-tone serial pieces for children. The word *dissonance*, its meaning and its sounds, has undergone a great many changes, evolutions, and revolutions during the last five or six hundred years, in particular during the first part of the twentieth century. What was considered unbeautiful yesterday turns out to be acceptable and sympathetic tomorrow. New technical books should be produced to get the young people sanely and safely introduced to contemporary idioms of written music. I trust and hope that some teachers and some bright students will be eager to try out the following examples from my personal teaching material.

Six basic positions for five-finger exercises, to be studied from every key of the chromatic scale, forte and piano, legato and staccato, with dotted notes, one hand even and the other dotted, in double and triple speed, first one hand alone, then with both hands, always two octaves apart.

Ex. 1

Diatonic   *Whole tone*

Diminished Seventh   *Dominant Ninth 1)*

Chordal 2)

1) D flat for smaller hands
2) For larger hands only·

Ex. 2

Ex. 3

Ex. 4

Ex. 5

Ex. 6

Ex. 7

Ex. 8

Ex. 9

Ex. 10

Ex. 11

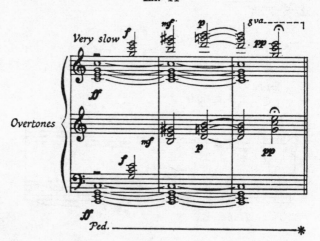

Fingerings

BY RUDOLPH GANZ

ILLOGICAL and thoughtless fingerings in many otherwise good editions are inimical to the music they are supposed to offer, and many teachers and students are misled by adhering to them. For years I have propagandized, together with my associates, some colleagues, and my former students presently in important teaching positions, for a renaissance of intelligent simplicity in the use of fingerings, especially in regard to repeated notes in slow and moderate tempo. The peculiar and unnatural habit of changing fingers on slowly repeated notes, even in easy accompaniments, is bound to detract the player's attention from the more important matters of musical speech. For years I have made the effort to discover who possibly could have been the early delinquents who abandoned some of the simple fingerings used by the classical masters, and when and why. Can it be that Louis Adams (1758–1849), I intentionally do not say *"maître"* Adams, is the one or one of the guilty transformers from natural to fancy fingerings? He advocated the change of fingers on slowly repeated notes. Did he have difficulty in lifting his fingers? Adams was a professor at the Paris Conservatoire, and he is best known for his publication: *Méthode ou Principe général du doigté* [fingering] *pour le Fortepiano* [!], *suivie d'une collection complète de tous les traits possibles avec le doigté*. Strange how many Adamses we have had during the last one hundred years! Some of the guiltiest imitators or unknowing followers of the French "inventor," men whose editions

of the classics and romantics undoubtedly have been of considerable
help to the teaching profession of the last eighty or ninety years,
are men whose names command high esteem or even admiration:
Klindworth (Chopin), Kullack (Beethoven concertos), Mikuli (Chopin), Hans von Bülow, one of the outstanding musicians of the nineteenth century (Bach and Beethoven), and finally Raphael Joseffy
(most of Chopin). Arnold Dolmetsch, in his renowned book *The
Interpretation of the Music of the Seventeenth and Eighteenth Centuries,* has this to say about some of the above-mentioned men of music,
especially Klindworth: "The habit of constantly changing fingers on
the same key in slow or moderate tempo is based on the technical
practice of his day, when the hands were held in a more or less rigid
fashion, practically all energy coming from the wrist. This would
explain the custom of changing fingers which was the only way to
clearness of articulation under such technical circumstances." Brahms
was responsible for much of the revolution in fingerings, and he and
Liszt should be given credit for having initiated a much freer way
of playing the piano. In my view, Bach, Haydn, Mozart, Beethoven,
and Schubert used the natural fingerings, sensible ones. They could
not possibly understand why an editor should puzzle any intelligent
person by offering an enigma like this:

So many of these editions still are in print and sold over the counters.
Will there be a renaissance of thinking that the easy, natural way is
the best?

I know many teachers, and surmise that there are hundreds or
thousands of others, who are in agreement with my complaint. Every-
one knows that the changing of fingers in rapidly repeated notes is
necessary. Scarlatti, in his brilliant D major Sonata (No. 13, Volume I,
in the Kirkpatrick-Schirmer edition) indicates *"mutandi deti"* (changing fingers) in the fast repeated single-note group of six sixteenths.
Bartók's charming and witty *Bear Dance* (which I played first in
Berlin in 1909) is a special study in quickly played groups of four

single notes: both L.H. and R.H. 4321. Regarding the moderately fast triplets in the left hand of the first movement of the "Appassionata," beginning at measure twenty-four, either repeated thumbs or 321 groupings are possible. In measures thirty-three and thirty-four, the repeated second finger of the left hand will enhance the relaxing of the tempo without an unwelcome pulse of finger changes. To state my case explicitly, I present a few examples of strange, if not criminal, fingerings. They are published both as a warning and as helpful advice to the American piano student and teacher and as a friendly invitation to colleagues, old and young, conservative and progressive, to join in this healthful propaganda.

Mozart: from the Adagio movement of the Sonata in C minor (K. 457)

Instead of being able to pay attention to the right-hand melody, the unaware student is supposed to be watching the ruinous changing of fingers in the L.H. accompaniment. And this should appear in an otherwise very fine edition (Tovey-Craxton) as well as in the Bartók edition (Kalmus)! My suggestion permits a quiet repeating of the same fingers as against the encircled set of changing fingers:

Ex. 1

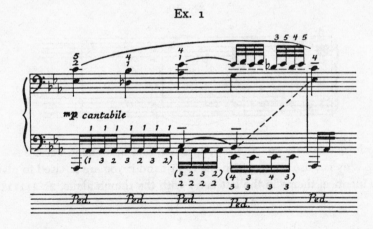

Beethoven: Sonata op. 13, second movement (Schirmer)

Does the slowly and softly repeated E flat in the thumb of the first bar necessitate changing of fingers when in the following bar the same thumb repeats the same E flat, because there is no chance for changing!

Ex. 2

Schubert: Moment Musical in A-flat major, op. 149 (Schirmer, etc.)

Why the disturbing change of fingers in the left hand? Listen to your playing of the lovely melody and use the thumb on all E flats in the bass.

Ex. 3

Beethoven: Sonata op. 26, in A-flat major, first movement, bar 8

Why not use 22 255555 in the right hand if you are advised to play the identical theme in the left hand with the thumb alone, 22 211111?

Ex. 4

Chopin: Étude in F minor, op. 10, no. 8 (most editions)

The dramatic repetition of the fifth finger in the octaves can easily be repeated in the soft single nostalgic echo phrase.

Ex. 5

Chopin: Prelude in D-flat major (most editions)

My suggestion of repeating the continuous c♯ with the second or third finger instead of the cruelly silly 4323 is a logical foreboding of the fifth finger in the following octaves. The use of a single finger permits with ease the coloring of the rise and fall of the melody in the left hand.

Ex. 6

Prokofiev: Music for Children, page 5

Why such awkward fingerings in a slow tempo and a soft quality of tone? Is the simple 332, 113, 221 not more natural, more musical and much easier? During a Master class in a smaller city a very talented seven-year-old girl played some ten pieces from memory. I watched her closely. She never changed fingers on slow or moderately fast repeated notes, not even in melodic lines. What a smart, thoughtful teacher she had!

Ex. 7

Brahms: Paganini Variations, op. 35, first book ed. by Andor Foldes

A brilliant pianist-editor caught in a moment of absent-mindedness. If the left hand can repeat the two middle fingers 33, why not the double 11 for the right hand?

Ex. 8

Beethoven: Sonata in C-sharp minor, op. 27, no. 2 (Schirmer)

The encircled fourth finger represents to me the worst aspect of "pianism on paper." It is a stupid and rhythmically dangerous fingering that makes people (I have heard them) distort the soft flowing rhythm of the mystic idea:

Ex. 9

Chopin: Berceuse, bar 30

The upper fingering is from the admirable Paderewski (Government of Poland) edition and illustrates and completes the lower one as indicated in the Urtext published by Oxford University Press, no doubt Chopin's own:

Ex. 10

Peters (Scholtz) and Schirmer (Joseffy) advocate the following clumsy and painfully difficult fingering distorting the Master's obvious graceful phrasing. They probably wanted to avoid playing two double thirds with the same fingers, and thus created a new and unmusical grouping!

Ex. 11

A few suggestions for the practice of repeated notes without finger change might be welcome:

Ex. 12

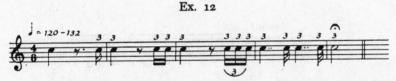

Use every one of the five fingers on the right and left hand, left hand an octave lower, but relax during the short rest. All examples to be practiced both forte and piano with a free shoulder at all times. Study the same rhythmical example with thirds, triads, intervals and chords.

Ex. 12a

Ex. 12b

Ex. 12c

* The editor's added wrong phrasing.

A few additional suggestions for the rapid change of fingers, repeating
each group four times and proceeding upward and downward in all
diatonic, both major and minor, chromatic and whole-tone scales:

Ex. 13

Same fingerings for both hands:

Ex. 14

The following exercises are recommended to ambitious students:

Ex. 15

Same fingerings for both hands, and to be played scale-wise like Ex. 14.

Ex. 16

Suggested Reading
and Reference Books

I. *Dictionaries, Encyclopedias: General Histories and Surveys:*

Apel, Willi; *Harvard Dictionary of Music.* Cambridge, Massachusetts: Harvard University Press, 1955.

Apel, Willi; The Abridged Harvard Dictionary of Music, 1963.

Baker, Theodore; *Baker's Biographical Dictionary of Musicians.* 5th edition, revised by Nicolas Slonimsky. New York: G. Schrimer, 1958.

Blom, Eric; *Everyman's Dictionary of Music.* Philadelphia. McKay, 1946.

Blume, Friedrich, ed.; *Die Musik in Geschichte und Gegenwart.* Bärenreiter Verlag, 35 Kassel-Wilhelmshöhe: 1949-   (The most comprehensive music encyclopedia, not yet complete.)

Grove's Dictionary of Music and Musicians. 5th edition, Eric Blom, ed. New York, London: Macmillan, 1954.

Hull, A. Eaglefield, ed.; *A Dictionary of Modern Music and Musicians.* London: J. M. Dent & Sons, 1924; New York: E. P. Dutton & Co.

Moser, Hans Joachim; *Musik-Lexikon.* Berlin: 1935.

Pratt, Waldo Selden; *The New Encyclopedia of Music and Musicians.* New York: Macmillan, 1945.

Riemann, Hugo; *Musik Lexicon.* New York: Schott Music Corp., 1959.

Scholes, Percy; *The Oxford Companion to Music.* Revised edition. London, New York: Oxford University Press, 1943.

Thompson, Oscar, ed.; *The International Cyclopedia of Music and Musicians.* 3rd edition, New York: Dodd, Mead & Co. 1944.

Bauer, Marion, and Peyser, Ethel E.; *Music Through the Ages.* New York: G. P. Putnam's Sons, 1946.

Bukofzer, Manfred; *Music in the Baroque Era.* New York: W. W. Norton, 1947.

Burney, Dr. Charles; *A General History of Music, from the Earliest Ages to the Present Period.* Originally published 1789; with criticism and historical notes by Frank Mercey. London: G. P. Fowler & Co., 1935; New York: Dover Publications, 1967.

Dannreuther, Edward; *Musical Ornamentation.* London: Novello, Ewer & Co., n.d.

Dart, Thurston; *The Interpretation of Music.* London; New York: 1954. Hutchinson's University Library.

Dolmetsch, Arnold; *The Interpretation of the Music of the 17th and 18th Centuries.* London: Novello and Oxford University Press, 1949.

Elson, Louis Charles; *The History of American Music.* New York: Macmillan, 1915.

Einstein, Alfred; *Music in the Romantic Era.* New York: W. W. Norton, 1947.

Ewen, David; *The Complete Book of 20th Century Music.* New York: Prentice-Hall, 1959.

Fétis, François Joseph; *Biographie universelle des musiciens et bibliographie générale de la musique.* Paris: Firmin Didot, 1860–65.

Howard, John Tasker; *Our American Music.* New York: Thos. Y. Crowell Co., 3rd. edition, 1954.

Lang, Paul Henry; *Music in Western Civilization.* New York: W. W. Norton, 1941.

The New Oxford History of Music. J. A. Westrup, ed. London, New York, Toronto: Oxford University Press, 1957– . (Not yet complete.)

Parry, C. Hubert H., *The Evolution of the Art of Music.* New Edition with additional chapters by H. C. Colles. New York: Pantheon 1946.

II. *Books on the History of the Piano, Its Music and Its Styles.*

Abraham, Gerald; *Chopin's Musical Style.* London: Oxford University Press, 1960.

Apel, Willi; *A Brief Survey of Piano Music.* Cambridge, Massachusetts: Harvard University Press, 1947.

Bach, C. P. E.; *Versuch ueber die wahre Art das Klavier zu spielen.* Originally published 1753–62; Leipzig: C. F. Kahnt Nachfolger, 1906. English translation as *Essay on the True Art of Playing Keyboard Instruments* by W. J. Mitchell. New York: W. W. Norton 1949.

Baines, Anthony (Ed.); *Musical Instruments Through the Ages.* London: Faber, 1966.

Baines, Anthony; *European and American Musical Instruments.* London: Batsford, 1966

Bedbrook, G. S.; *Keyboard Music from the Middle Ages to the Beginnings of Baroque.* London: Macmillan, 1949.

Bie, Oscar; *A History of the Pianoforte and Pianoforte Players.* Translated from the German by E. E. Kellett. New York: E. P. Dutton & Co., 1899.

Bodky, E.; *The Interpretation of Bach's Keyboard Works.* Cambridge, Massachusetts: Harvard University Press, 1960.

Brook, D.; *Masters of the Keyboard.* London: Rockliff, 1946.

Brown, Maurice J. E.: *Chopin: An Index of His Works in Chronological Order.* London: Macmillan. New York! St. Martin's Press, 1960.

Canave, Paz Corazon G.; *A Re-Evaluation of the Role Played by C. P. E. Bach in the Development of the Clavier Sonata.* Washington, D.C.: Catholic University of America Press, 1956.

Carmi, Avner and Hannah; *The Immortal Piano.* New York: Crown Publishers, 1960.

Closson, Ernest; *History of the Piano.* London: Elek, 1947.

Cockshoot, John V.; *The Fugue in Beethoven's Piano Music.* (Studies in the History of Music). Egon Wellesz ed. London: Routledge & Kegan Paul, 1959.

Cortot, Alfred; *French Piano Music.* Translated from French by Hilda Andrews. London: Oxford University Press, 1932. New French edition, 1948.

Cortot, Alfred; *In Search of Chopin.* Translated by Cyril and Reva Clarke. New York: Abelard Press, 1952.

Cortot, Alfred; *The Piano Music of Claude Debussy.* Translated by Violet Edgell. London: J. and W. Chester, 1922.

Dale, Kathleen; *Nineteenth Century Piano Music.* With a Foreword by Dame Myra Hess. London, New York: Oxford University Press 1954.

Demuth Norman; *French Piano Music.* London: Museum Press, 1959.

Dent, Edward J.; *Alessandro Scarlatti; His Life and Works.* New impression with preface and additional notes by Frank Walker. London: Edward Arnold, 1960.

Emery, Walter; *Bach's Ornaments.* London: Novello, 1953.

Evans, Edwin; *Handbook to the Pianoforte Works of Johannes Brahms.* New York: Scribner's Sons; London: W. Reeves, 1936.

Ferguson, D. N.; *Piano Interpretation.* London: Williams, 1950.

Ferguson, Howard; *Style and Interpretation*, vol 1. London: Oxford University Press, 1963

Fischer, Edwin; *Beethoven's Pianoforte Sonatas: a Guide for Students and Amateurs.* Translated by Stanley Godman and Paul Hamburger. London: Faber & Faber, 1959.

Friskin, James, and Freundlich, Irwin; *Music for the Piano.* A handbook of concert and teaching material. New York, Toronto: Rinehart & Co., 1954.

Garvin, Florence Hollister; *The Beginning of the Romantic Piano Concerto.* New York: Vantage Press, 1952.

Geiringer, Karl; *Johann Sebastian Bach.* London: Allen & Unwin, 1967.

Georgii, Walter; *Klaviermusik.* 2nd edition, Zurich, Freiburg iB.: Atlantis-Verlag, 1950.

Girdlestone Cuthbert M.; *Mozart's Piano Concertos.* 2nd edition. London: Cassell, 1958.

Glyn, Margaret H.; *Music in the Days of Shakespeare. About Elizabethan Virginal Music and Its Composers.* London: Wm. Reeves, 1924.

James, Philip; *Early Keyboard Instruments.* New York: F. A. Stokes Co., 1930.

Kirkpatrick, Ralph; *Domenico Scarlatti.* Princeton University Press 1953.

Krehbiel, Henry E.; *The Pianoforte and its Music.* New York: Scribner's Sons, 1911.

Kullak, Franz; *Beethoven's Piano Playing; with an Essay on the Execution of the Trill.* Translated from the German by Theodore Baker. New York: G. Schirmer, 1901.

Loesser, Arthur; *Men, Women and Pianos.* New York: Simon and Schuster, 1954. University of Michigan Press; London: Oxford University Press, 1940.

Lockwood, Albert; *Notes on the Literature of the Piano.* Ann Arbor, Michigan: University of Michigan Press; London: Oxford University Press, 1940.

Michel, N. E.; *Old Pianos.* Rivere, Cal.: by the author, 1954.

Moldenhauer, Hans; *Duo-Pianism.* Chicago: Chicago Musical College Press, 1952.

Murdoch, W.; *Brahms; and an Analytical Study of His Piano Works.* London: Rich & Cowan, 1933.

Newman, William S.; *The Sonata in the Baroque Era.* Chapel Hill, N. Carolina: University of N. Carolina Press, 1959.

Niemann, Walter; *Das Klavierbuch, Geschichte der Klaviermusik und ihre Meister.* Leipzig: C. F. Kahnt Nachfolger, 1922.

Sachs, Curt; *Das Klavier.* Berlin: Julius Bard, 1923:

Sachs, Curt; *The Evolution of Piano Music, 1350-1700.* New York: Marks, 1944.

Terry, Charles Sanford; *The Music of Bach.* London: Oxford University Press, 1933.

Tovey, Donald Francis; *Essays in Musical Analysis.* (Six volumes.) London: Oxford University Press, 1935–39. Volume III, Concertos, is of special interest to pianists.

Tovey, Donald Francis; *A Companion to Beethoven's Pianoforte Sonatas.* London The Associated Board of the R.A.M. and the R.C.M., 1931.

Westerby, H.: *The History of Pianoforte Music.* New York: E. P. Dutton, 1924.

ALSO: Numerous prefaces of *Urtext* or scholarly revised editions of piano works of the standard repertoire, as well as prefaces and introductions to example collections of certain types of piano pieces and to collected editions of individual composers.

III. *Books on Piano Pedagogy.*

Badura-Skoda, Eva and Paul; *Interpreting Mozart on the Keyboard*, trans. by Leo Black. London: Barrie Books, 1965; reprint 1970.

Bodky, Erwin; *The Interpretation of Bach's Keyboard Works.* Cambridge, Massachusetts: Harvard University Press, 1960.

Bolton, Hetty; *On Teaching the Piano.* London: Novello, 1954.

Bonpensiere, Luigi; *New Pathways to Piano Technique; a Study of the Relations Between Mind and Body, with Special Reference to Piano Playing.* New York: Philosophical Library, 1953.

Bowen, York; *Pedalling the Modern Pianoforte.* London: Oxford Univ. Press, 1936.

Broughton, Julia; *Self Analysis of Success in Piano Teaching.* New York: Vantage Press, 1956.

Carré, John F.; *The Psychology of Piano Teaching.* Racine, Wisconsin: published by author. Revised edition 1941. Contains list of graded materials.

Ching, James; *The Amateur Pianist's Companion.* Oxford: Hall, 1950. Several other pedagogic works by the same author exist.

Cohen, Harriet; *Music's Handmaid.* London: Transatlantic Arts Inc., revised edition, 1950.

Cooke, Charles; *Playing the Piano for Pleasure.* New York: Simon & Schuster, 1941.

Coviello, Ambrose; *Foundations of Pianoforte Technique.* London: 1946. Oxford University Press.

Dee, Margaret; *Touch Technique, the Technique of Ten Touches for every Pianist.* Chicago: C. F. Summy Co., 1948.

Deutsch, Leonhard; *Guided Sightreading, a New Approach to Piano Study.* Chicago: Nelson-Hall Co., 1950.

Donington, Robert; *Interpretation of Early Music.* London: Faber, 1963

Everhart, Powell; *The Pianist's Art.* Atlanta, Georgia: published by the author, 1958.

Ferguson, Donald N.; *Piano Interpretation; Studies in the Music of Six Great Composers.* London: Williams & Norgate, revised edition, 1950.

Fielden, Thomas; *The Evolution of the History of Piano Technique.* London: Macmillan & Co., 1933.

Fielden, Thomas; *The Science of Piano Technique.* London: Macmillan & Co., 1927.

Foldes, Andor; *Keys to the Keyboard.* New York: Oxford University Press, 1950. (With a list of contemporary teaching materials.)

Friskin, James; *The Principles of Piano Practice.* New York: H. W. Gray, 1921.

Ganz, Rudolph; *Exercises for Piano, Contemporary and Special.* Evanston, Illinois: Summy-Birchard Co., 1968.

Ganz, Rudolph; *Rudolph Ganz Evaluates Modern Piano Music.* Evanston, Illinois: The Instrumentalist Co., 1968.

Harrison, Sidney; *Piano Technique.* London: I. Pitman, 1953.

Hofheimer, Grace; *Teaching Techniques for the Piano.* Rockville Centre, N.Y.: Belwin, 1954.

Hofmann, Josef; *Piano Playing: A Little Book of Simple Suggestions.* New York: McClure Company, 1920.

Hutcheson, Ernest; *The Elements of Piano Technique.* Baltimore, Maryland: G. Fred Kranz Music Co., 1907.

Leimer, Karl; *Rhythmics, Dynamics, Pedal and Other Problems of Piano Playing.* Philadelphia, Pa.: Theodore Presser Co., 1938.

Leimer, Karl, and Gieseking, Walter; *The Shortest Way to Pianistic Perfection.* Philadelphia, Pa.: Theodore Presser Co., 1932.

Lhevinne, Josef; *Basic Principles in Pianoforte Playing.* Philadelphia, Pa.: Theodore Presser Co., 1924.

Lundin, Robert; *An Objective Psychology of Music.* New York: Ronald Press Co., 1953.

Macklin, Charles B.; *Elementary Piano Pedagogy.* Philadelphia: Theodore Presser, 1925.

Matthay, Tobias; *The Act of Touch in All Its Diversity.* London, New York: Longmans, Green & Co., 1903.

Matthay, Tobias; *First Principles of Pianoforte Playing.* London, New York: Longmans, Green & Co., 1905.

Matthews, Denis (Ed.); *Keyboard Music*. Newton Abbot, Devon: David & Charles, 1972.

Mehegan, John; *Jazz Improvisation*. New York: Watson-Guptill Publishers, 1959.

Newman, William S.; *The Pianist's Problems*. New York: Harper, 1956.

Ortmann, Otto; *The Physiological Mechanics of Piano Technique*. New York: E. P. Dutton & Co.; London: Routledge & Kegan Paul, 1929. Now available in a paperback edition.

Pace, Robert; *Piano for Classroom Music*. Englewood Cliffs, New Jersey: Prentice-Hall, 1956.

Rubinstein, Beryl; *Outline of Piano Pedagogy*. New York: Carl Fischer, 1929.

Russell Raymond; *Harpsichord and Clavichord*. London: Faber, 1959; 2nd impression 1965.

Schnabel Karl Ulrich; *Modern Technique of the Pedal*. New York: Mills Music, Inc., 1950.

Schultz, Arnold; *The Riddle of the Pianist's Finger*. Chicago: University of Chicago Press, 1936.

Shanet, Howard; *Learn to Read Music*. New York: Simon & Schuster, 1956.

Woodhouse, G.; *A Realistic Approach to Piano Playing*. London: Augener, 1953.

Zuckermann, W. J.; *Modern Harpsichord*. London: Peter Owen, 1970.

Index